METHUEN'S
MANUALS OF MODERN PSYCHOLOGY
(Founder Editor C. A. Mace 1946–68)
General Editor H. J. Butcher

*Culture and Cognition:
Readings in Cross-Cultural
Psychology*

Culture and Cognition: Readings in Cross-Cultural Psychology

Edited by
J. W. BERRY and P. R. DASEN

METHUEN & CO LTD
11 New Fetter Lane London EC4

First published 1974
by Methuen & Co Ltd,
11 New Fetter Lane,
London EC4P 4EE
© 1974 J. W. Berry and P. R. Dasen
Printed in Great Britain by
Butler & Tanner Ltd, Frome and London

SBN hardbound 416 75170 9
SBN paperback 416 75180 6

Distributed in the U.S.A. by
HARPER & ROW PUBLISHERS, INC.
BARNES & NOBLE IMPORT DIVISION

Contents

Contents

Acknowledgements

The editors and publishers thank the following for their permission to reprint material from the sources listed below. American Anthropological Association and the author for Chapter 2 by W. C. Sturtevant, from *American Anthropologist*, 66 (1964), 99–113. American Psychological Association and the authors for Chapter 14 by M. Cole and J. S. Bruner, from *American Psychologist*, 26 (1971), 867–76 (© 1971 by the American Psychological Association); and Chapter 21 by D. Price-Williams, W. Gordon and M. Ramirez III, from *Developmental Psychology*, 1 (1969), 769 (© 1969 by the American Psychological Association). Behavioral Science and the author for Chapter 3 by J. A. Fishman, from *Behavioral Science*, 5 (1960), 323–39. Canadian Psychological Association for Chapter 7 by J. W. Berry, from the *Canadian Journal of Behavioural Science*, 3 (1971), 324–36. Center for Cross-Cultural Research, Western Washington State College, and the authors for Chapter 8 by G. Jahoda, from the *Journal of Cross-Cultural Psychology*, 1 (1970), 115–30; Chapter 17 by O. M. Okonji, from the *Journal of Cross-Cultural Psychology*, 2 (1971), 39–49; Chapter 22 by P. R. de Lacey, from the *Journal of Cross-Cultural Psychology*, 1 (1970), 293–304; and Chapter 25 by P. R. Dasen, from the *Journal of Cross-Cultural Psychology*, 3 (1972), 23–39. Ethnology and the author for Chapter 10 by L. W. Doob, from *Ethnology*, 3 (1964), 357–63. The International Union of Psychological Science; Dunod, Publishers, Paris; and the authors for Chapter 5 by H. A. Witkin, from the *International Journal of Psychology*, 2 (1967), 233–50; Chapter 11 by B. M. Ross and C. Millsom, from the *International Journal of Psychology*, 5 (1970), 173–81; Chapter 18 by J. Piaget, from the *International Journal of Psychology*, 1 (1966), 3–13; and Chapter 20 by A. Heron and M. Simonsson, from the *International Journal of Psychology*, 4 (1969), 281–92. Journal of Biosocial Science and the author for Chapter 15 by S. H. Irvine, from the *Journal of Biosocial Science*, Supplement No. 1 (1969), 91–102. The Journal Press and the author for Chapter 6 by M. Wober, from the *Journal of Social Psychology*, 70 (1966), 181–9. McGraw-Hill Book Company for Chapter 1 by T. Gladwin, from *Explorations in Cultural Anthropology: Essays in Honor of George Peter Murdock*, edited by W. H. Goodenough (©

1964 by McGraw-Hill, Inc.). The Psychonomic Society, Inc. and the authors for Chapter 9 by M. Cole, J. Gay and J. Glick, from *Psychonomic Monograph*, 2 (1968), Whole No. 26. South African Psychological Association and the author for Chapter 12 by S. Biesheuvel, from *Psygram*, 1 (1959), 78–80. Southwestern Journal of Anthropology and the author for Chapter 4 by H. Maclay, from *Southwestern Journal of Anthropology*, 14 (1958), 220–9.

Foreword
S. Biesheuvel

Cross-cultural studies are steadily increasing their claim on the attention of psychologists. The current importance of the subject is well illustrated by a number of recent developments. In 1966, the International Journal of Psychology, published by the International Union of Psychological Science, was founded; its contents are focused on 'cross-cultural comparisons of psychological phenomena'. More recently, the *Journal of Cross-Cultural Psychology* was begun to provide a further outlet for comparative studies of culture and behaviour. And most recently, in 1972, the International Association for Cross-Cultural Psychology was established, holding its first international conference in Hong Kong.

The subject crops up in virtually every psychological journal, regardless of its area of specialization, and symposia devoted to some aspect or other of the impact of culture on behaviour abound. A number of needs, both theoretical and applied, account for this interest. There is, for example, the demand for educational and vocational selection tests in developing countries. Pressure for the rapid advancement of the indigenous populations, coupled with limited scholastic and training resources, compelled the sorting out of those who could make the best use of available opportunities. Measuring devices of proved validity in Western contexts generally required substantial modification, or entirely new approaches had to be devised, for effective prediction in different cultures.

The differences in mental structure and function which accounted for culturally-determined behaviour patterns, quite apart from their practical importance and their bearing on measurement, were of interest for their own sake, for the light that could be thrown on factors that influenced mental development and effectiveness. Inevitably this raised questions concerning the nature of group differences and the possibility that other than environmental factors might be involved. The controversy regarding the relative importance of heredity and environment moved to the area of ethnic differences where the problem of cultural equivalence of tests became of crucial importance.

Perhaps the most interesting and important outcome of the debates about concepts, methodology, and interpretation of experimental data in cross-cultural research was a questioning of current assumptions concerning behavioural dimensions and functions. Scientific psychology is the product and reflects the characteristics of the mind of Western man. It has become clear that some restatement of its constructs may be necessary in the light of what has been discovered concerning their cultural relativity.

This applies for example to the concept of intelligence, to the modes of thought, to the motivational aspects of behaviour, to the infusion of perception with noncognitive functions, indeed to the classical distinction between cognitive, affective and conative processes itself.

Cross-cultural research is thus becoming a major influence in the evolution of psychology. The discourse and experimental data that determined the progress of its thinking should be selectively and readily available, to provide perspective for current controversies and guidelines for new hypotheses and future research.

This is the task which Berry and Dasen set themselves and which they have admirably accomplished for published work in the cognitive domain. Their limitation of the subject matter to culture and cognition was inevitable if a representative diversity of source material was to be included in a publication of manageable size. Cognition, moreover, deserves priority because of its major role in the process of adaptation to change and acculturation to Western technological demands with which all developing countries are currently confronted. The editors were wise to exclude major works of historical and methodological importance, as these are sufficiently familiar and readily available.

Professor Berry's introduction capably summarizes the highlights and trends of this body of information and provides the context for the selections that follow, mostly papers likely to be less generally known. Opinions are bound to differ about the significance of their selections, but this is inevitable in readings of this kind. I found the choice of material discriminating, comprehensive and unquestionably useful. I am reasonably confident that both the general psychological reader, as well as the specialist in cross-cultural psychology, will find this book of value as a source of important information and a stimulus to new insights into the many problems which still abound in this branch of psychology.

Johannesburg
September 1972

Preface

This collection of papers is an attempt to bring together, for the first time, a wide variety of psychological research which is explicitly concerned with cognition in its cultural context.

By cultural context is meant that vast pattern of group-shared behaviour which is transmitted by learning from one generation to another; by cognition is meant those aspects of psychological life characterized by the reception, organization and use of information gained through contact with the world outside the individual. The collection will focus on interactions between these two sets of variables in a series of papers which attempts to relate a wide range of cultural contexts to variations in thought, abilities and developmental stages of these human processes.

The primary goal of the book is to provide a handy volume of studies which have not been readily accessible heretofore. The very nature of cross-cultural studies encourages the publication of research findings in a wide variety of journals and in many languages. Thus this collection brings into a single volume articles from both English and French sources which have been either published in specialist journals or are original contributions.

However, we have not been content merely to assemble these various studies in a single volume. We have taken, as a secondary goal, the challenge of placing a 'point of view' on the collection through the choice and organization of the component parts. The three sections, and the individual selections within them, have been structured to raise the questions of qualitative variation, quantitative level and developmental stages in cognition.

The editors believe that the overwhelming influence of Western modes of cognition (including Western science, and specifically Western psychology) should not be permitted to obscure the study of possible qualitative variation; and even more emphatically we believe that where cognitive variation is discovered, we should not automatically interpret this in terms of differential cognitive competence (quantities or levels of cognitive ability). There is no doubt that some cultural groups direct their cognitive potential towards similar goals; however the historical fact that psychology has concentrated its efforts in this relatively homogenous value system should not limit our search for (and readiness to accept) quite a wide variety of cognitive phenomena. Similarly there is no doubt that many parts of the world are becoming more Westernized, and may desire to reorient their cognitive abilities more towards those which are useful in urban or industrial life; however this fact should not nurture our ethnocentrism nor increase our readiness to interpret differences as deficiencies.

To meet our specific aims we have had to limit the scope of the material collected here. Two general collections of cross-cultural work in psychology (Price-Williams, 1969; Al-Issa and Dennis, 1970) have sampled widely from the available literature. We have thus decided to limit our coverage to the central issues of culture and cognition. However the impact of these studies will largely be to open up broad questions, rather than to make definitive or universally acceptable generalizations.

The editing of this volume has been very much a joint effort, with responsibility for the general introduction and Parts 1 and 2 lying primarily with J. W. Berry and for Part 3 with P. R. Dasen. We acknowledge with gratitude the comments and permissions of our colleagues who are represented in this volume. Without them, of course, there could be no collection; however what is more important, without them there would be no advance in the cross-cultural study of cognition.

April 1972   J. W. B., *Kingston*
                                              P. R. D., *Geneva*

Introduction: History and method in the cross-cultural study of cognition

The introduction to this collection will attempt to do two things: to distinguish briefly between 'culture and cognition' and that better-known speciality 'culture and personality', and to trace the historical antecedents and methodological concerns of present-day psychologists working in the field of culture and cognition. The first aim is necessary, not only to limit the focus of our attention, but to show that this field is indeed a somewhat neglected speciality worthy of study. Our second aim is necessitated by the editorial decision not to include any specifically historical or methodological papers; some of this early material is thus excerpted and reviewed in the introductory section. This review will not attempt a complete coverage, but will provide the flavour of early research and thinking in just sufficient detail to raise many of the basic issues still confronting comparative cognitive psychology.

A third aim might have been included: to distinguish between psychological and anthropological approaches to the study of 'culture and cognition'. However, in the interest of minimizing those interdisciplinary barriers, already lowered by Hallowell (1955), Campbell (1961), Kluckhohn (1962), French (1963), Tyler (1969) and most recently by Cole et al. (1971), no resurrection will be nurtured here; on the contrary, psychologists' and anthropologists' writings are mixed freely and no author is included who betrays little competence in the other discipline.

COGNITION AND PERSONALITY IN CULTURAL PERSPECTIVE

Traditionally, psychologists have excluded cognitive measures from their tests of personality, although there is no doubt that most early personality theorists (e.g. Allport, 1937; Murphy, 1947) have been eclectic enough to include cognitive function in their theoretical formulations. This has led to a division in academic psychology, especially in curricula, between the study of socio-emotional and intellectual life.

Bateson (1936), looking at this distinction from the vantage point of an ethnographic field worker, has termed the two aspects *ethos* and *eidos*, defining the first as a 'culturally standardized system of organization of the instincts and emotions of the individual' (p. 118) and the second as 'a standardization of the cognitive aspects of the personality of individuals' (p. 220). As Gladwin (Chapter 1) has pointed out, the former is now well-studied cross-culturally while the latter has been attended to considerably less. Bateson implies in his definition of *eidos* that these cognitive aspects are to be included within the broader term *personality*, thus following early personality theorists. Wallace (1970) too includes individual cognitive organization ('mazeway') within his overview of the culture and personality field as does Honigmann (1967, p. xi).

These recent attempts by anthropologists to view the growth of behaviour in a particular cultural milieu as *integrated*, however, have not produced a corresponding change of view among psychologists. Nevertheless, the two foremost concepts in these discipline sub-areas (*personality* and *intelligence*) are conceptually similar, in that both are inferred from the consistency of peripheral behaviour over time and across situations. Each is a hypothetical state of the organism, attributed on the basis of past behaviour, and found useful by psychologists for the prediction of future behaviour.

There can be little doubt, though, that the distinction between cognition and personality is still a real one for many psychologists and some anthropologists, even though if the question were put, most workers would probably agree that the former is subsumed within the latter. The question of the empirical domination of 'culture and personality' over 'culture and cognition' is an historical fact, but one which need not continue. The comprehensive review by Singer (1961) or text by Honigmann (1967) should be read by those wishing a quick demonstration of this predominance; hopefully the present collection will stimulate further inquiry to balance, and perhaps integrate, our knowledge of total psychological functioning across cultural contexts.

HISTORICAL ANTECEDENTS

Around the turn of the century, as the social science world was feeling the impact of growing specialization, there existed a number of persons who possessed real dual competence; only later were they to be led by the growing disciplinary boundaries to assume a single title as 'psychologist' or 'anthropologist'. Such well-known men as McDougall, Woodworth, Wundt and Bartlett (among those later known solely as psychologists) and Rivers, Boas and Nadel (later known solely as anthropologists) were doing research requiring both psychological and anthropological sophistication. To illustrate this early work, four major monographs will be discussed. The first, by Rivers and McDougall, was primarily concerned with basic sensory and perceptual processes in an exotic cultural setting; the second, by Boas, enquired into the cultural content and context of mental development; the third, by Wundt, examined the mental basis for cultural development; and the fourth, by Lévy-Bruhl, questioned the assumption of identity of mental processes among all groups of mankind.

Rivers

Inevitably the tale must begin with that assemblage of later famous men, who, under the leadership of Professor A. C. Haddon, ventured to the Torres Straits Islands (between Australia and New Guinea) in 1899. Haddon had previously carried out fieldwork in the area and had established valuable contacts and a useful fund of information for the psychologists to build upon; this pattern, of anthropologist preceding psychologist into the field, is a logical one and a practice later to be used when dual competence was no longer possible. Dr W. H. R. Rivers was selected to be in charge of the physiological and psychological studies, and was assisted by Mr Myers, Mr McDougall and Mr Seligmann.

In his introduction, Rivers (1901) discussed a number of problems too often taken for granted in current research: cultural setting, problems of testing in this setting, changes in tests to suit local conditions, and sampling and research strategies in native communities. He also felt obliged to make two apologetic observations on the work about to be reported: 'I am afraid that the introspective aspect of psychological experimentation was almost completely absent in our work' (p. 6); and 'It is perhaps as well to mention that most of our observations on adults were made under the influence of tobacco' (p. 5)!

The Rivers team carried out a large number of observations on memory and perceptual functioning, in visual, auditory, olfactory and cutaneous modes. Their aim was explicitly comparative, to discover whether these basic psychological phenomena were vastly different among such an unusual (to Victorian Britons) people. Many of their observations are placed side by side with data from previous studies in Britain and concurrent studies by Seligmann among people on the

Papua coast just north of the Torres Straits Islands. Subsequently, Rivers (1905) placed these data next to those from his work in southern India among the Toda people, thus gaining an even broader comparative perspective. Viewing all of these data together, what general conclusions were the Rivers team able to come to?

With respect to visual acuity, which many prior writers had speculated to be better among non-Western peoples, Rivers concluded that for these 'savage and half civilized people, [visual acuity] though superior to that of the normal European, is not so in any marked degree' (p. 42). To account for these earlier reports, Rivers drew a distinction between acuity proper, and 'the power of observation depending on the habit of attending to and discriminating any minute indications which are given by the organ of sense' (p. 12) and concluded that

> By long-continued practice, however, in attending to minute details in surroundings with which he becomes extremely familiar, the savage is able to see and recognize distant objects in a way that appears almost miraculous, but it is doubtful whether his visual powers excell those of the European who has trained his vision to any special end. (p. 43)

Observations among the Todas (1905, p. 325) confirmed the previous conclusion that

> There is no great difference in visual acuity between savage or barbarous and civilized races, though the balance of superiority may be slightly on the side of the former.

Thus, although Rivers concluded that there was only a slight superiority in visual acuity for non-Europeans, he accepted the view that by attending frequently to minute details, they became visually more skilled. However, he did not end his analysis there; he went on to argue that this sensory emphasis might explain the frequent characterizations of mental operations among non-Europeans as *concrete* (as opposed to *abstract*):

> Minute distinctions of this sort are only possible if the attention is predominantly devoted to objects of sense, and I think there can be little doubt that such exclusive attention is a distinct hindrance to higher mental development. We know that the growth of intellect depends on material which is furnished by the senses, and it therefore at first sight may appear strange that elaboration of the sensory side of mental life should be a hindrance to intellectual development.

But on further consideration I think there is nothing unnatural in such a fact. If too much energy is expended on the sensory foundations, it is natural that the intellectual superstructure should suffer. It seems possible also that the over-development of the sensory side of mental life may help to account for another characteristic of the savage mind. There is, I think, little doubt that the uncivilized man does not take the same aesthetic interest in nature which is found among civilized peoples . . . experience is strongly in favour of the view that the predominant attention of the savage to concrete things around him may act as an obstacle to higher mental development. (pp. 44–5)

This abstract-concrete argument was to continue for many years (see e.g. Werner, 1940) and was not reliably settled until Price-Williams (1962) demonstrated that little difference existed among cultural groups when test item familiarity was maximized; Chapter 17 further examines this issue.

These great explorations into the comparative study of sensory processes were not without their critics. Titchener (1916) opened for the opposition with the general comment that 'no home-staying experimentalist can read the psychological part of the Report with satisfaction' and opined that the 'tests were inadequate to their purpose' (p. 204).

Despite the severity of this initial comment, the detailed critiques which followed were relatively mild. In fact, Titchener went out of his way to compliment the field workers and to encourage further work, to be carried out cooperatively between laboratory and field worker. This positive orientation was furthered by some suggestions on the requirements of a good 'field-test' which have not always been heeded in subsequent work. These tests should be

. . . capable of performance in a relatively short time and with apparatus that is strong, portable and relatively cheap; it should be laid out so simply that its conduct is easily mastered and so definitely that there can be no variation in its procedure; and it should yield results that are directly relevant to the object of the test, are expressible in numbers and thus are intercomparable. (p. 233)

The overall impression left by Titchener, then, is of a duty to be critical, but also of admiration for persons capable of doing this kind of experimentation. These concerns for mutual support, by the field and laboratory worker, are discussed in the methodological section of this introduction (p. 19).

Following these early papers on basic sensory and perceptual functioning, there appeared a series of monographs on higher level phenomena which were less experimental. The two classics to appear within a year of each other were Boas's *The Mind of Primitive Man* (1911) and Wundt's *Elements of Folk Psychology* (1912 in German; 1916 in English). Both writers stemmed from a rigorous Germanic scientific background, Boas in physics and geography, and Wundt in physiology and experimental psychology, and both brought as much of this rigour as possible to the study of the 'native mind'. Surprisingly, perhaps, to the psychologist who often considers his experimental approach to be more rigorous than the anthropologists' field observational method, it is Boas's volume which is clearest and the least dated of the two.

Boas

The main psychological views of Boas are contained in Chapter 4, 'Mental Traits of Primitive Man and of Civilized Man', and these are extended in Chapter 8, 'Some Traits of Primitive Culture'. He opened his topic by asserting that 'the possession of language, and the use of tools, and the power of reasoning' (pp. 96–7) distinguish man from other animals. By implication then, Boas may be said to consider that man's uniqueness lies in his cognitive capacities rather than in his emotional or motivational life.

Considering the next question, how does 'primitive' man differ from 'civilized' man, Boas argued that

> Apparently the thoughts and actions of civilized man, and those found in more primitive forms of society, prove, that, in various groups of mankind, the mind responds quite differently when exposed to the same conditions. Lack of logical connection in its conclusions, lack of control of will, are apparently two of its fundamental characteristics in primitive society. In the formation of opinions, belief takes the place of logical demonstration. The emotional value of opinions is great, and consequently they quickly lead to action. The will appears unbalanced, there being a readiness to yield to strong emotions and a stubborn resistance in trifling matters. (pp. 98–9)

The latter of these two distinguishing features (the lack of 'control of will') reintroduces emotional/motivational concerns to his framework. Thus, although man differs from lower animals mainly in his cognitive life, 'primitive' man was considered to differ from civilized man in his emotional/motivational as well as in his cognitive life.

However, Boas emphasized that these are differences in *content*, not in *process*.

We recognize that there are two possible explanations of the different manifestations of the mind of man. It may be that the minds of different races show differences of organization; that is to say, the laws of mental activity may not be the same for all minds. But it may also be that the organization of mind is practically identical among all races of man; that mental activity follows the same laws everywhere, but that its manifestations depend upon the character of individual experience that is subjected to the action of these laws. (p. 102)

To support the second alternative Boas paraded details from three areas of mental life of current interest: inhibition of impulses (p. 105), power of attention (p. 110) and power of original thought (p. 110). For all three he concluded that no differences exist in basic processes, but that apparent differences are due to the different cultural content entering into the process:

... the differences between civilized man and primitive man are in many cases more apparent than real; that the social conditions, on account of their peculiar characteristics, easily convey the impression that the mind of primitive man acts in a way quite different from ours, while in reality the fundamental traits of the mind are the same. (p. 114)

The broader conclusion he wished to draw (e.g. p. 124) was that, since 'The principal characteristics of the mind of primitive man occur among primitive tribes of all races ... the inference must not be drawn that these traits of mind are racial characteristics.'

In his later chapter (8), Boas set out 'to formulate more clearly the difference between the forms of thought of primitive man and those of civilized man, regardless of their racial descent'. He firstly examined the question of 'classification of experience' particularly the differences between animate and inanimate objects (p. 198), foreshadowing later psychological interest in 'animism'. Going one step further, he anticipated the development of 'ethnoscience' (see Chapter 2), posing the problem as 'the determination of the fundamental categories under which phenomena are classified by man in various stages of culture' (p. 199).

Secondly, logical processes were examined:

The first impression gained from a study of the beliefs of primitive man is that while the perceptions of his senses are excellent, his power of logical interpretation of perceptions seems to be deficient. I think it can be shown that the reason for this fact is not founded on any fundamental peculiarity of the mind of primitive man, but lies, rather, in the character of the traditional ideas by means of which each new perception is interpreted; in other words, in the character of the traditional ideas with which each new perception associates itself. The difference in the mode of thought of primitive man and that of civilized man seems to consist largely in the difference of character of the traditional material with which the new perception associates itself. When a new experience enters the mind of primitive man, the same process which we observe among civilized man brings about an entirely different series of associations, and therefore results in a different type of explanation. (pp. 202–3)

Thirdly, he examined a topic of long interest to anthropologists:

the occurrence of close associations between mental activities that appear to us as entirely disparate. In primitive life, religion and science; music, poetry, and dance; myth and history; fashion and ethics . . . appear inextricably interwoven. (p. 209)

His discussion of the juxtaposition of rational and irrational thought anticipated current work on the relation of 'tribal' and 'scientific' thought among acculturating peoples (see Chapter 8).

In summary, Boas emphasized the identity of thought process in 'primitive' and 'civilized' man, attributing the difference to a gradual shift from a social and emotional content for thought to a more intellectual one:

When the same concept appears in the mind of primitive man, it associates itself with those concepts related to it by emotional states. This process of association is the same among primitive men as among civilized men, and the difference consists largely in the modification of the traditional material with which our new perceptions amalgamate. Thus an important change from primitive culture to civilization seems to consist in the gradual elimination of what might be called the social associations of sense-impressions and of activities, for which intellectual associations are gradually substituted. (pp. 239–42 *passim*)

Wundt

Within psychology, a major figure was Wundt, who in addition to his great physiological and experimental studies wrote extensively in the field of folk psychology (ten volumes between 1912 and 1921); his translator ventured the opinion that

> One may hazard the prophecy, that the final verdict of history will ascribe to his latest studies, those in folk psychology, a significance not inferior to that which is now generally conceded to the writings of his earlier years. (p. vi)

As defined by Wundt the field originally combined 'into a unified whole the various results concerning the mental development of man as severally viewed by language, religion and custom' (p. 2). However with the development of psychology as a separate discipline, its field narrowed so that at the time of his writing (1911), it 'relates to those mental products which are created by a community of human life and are, therefore, inexplicable in terms merely of individual consciousness, since they presuppose the reciprocal action of many' (p. 3).

For Wundt the question was not as it was for Boas (what is the cultural content and context of mental development?) but what is the mental basis for cultural development? If we consider the

> general cultural conditions of primitive man, and recall the very meagre character of his external cultural possessions as well as his lack of any impulse to perfect these, we may readily be led to suppose that his intellectual capacities also have remained on a very low plane of development.

But Wundt advised his reader to consider two further explanations (as alternatives to low mental capacity). The first was 'the limited nature of the wants':

> the primitive man of the tropics has found plenty of game and plant food in his forests, as well as an abundance of material for the clothing and adornment to which he is accustomed. Hence he lacks the incentive to strive for anything beyond these simple means of satisfying his wants. He seeks for nothing further, since he either finds all that he desires in his environment, or, by methods handed down from the ancient past, knows how he may produce it out of the material available to him. (pp. 110, 111)

The second alternative Wundt considered was the 'fixity of conditions, due to their long isolation. The longer a set of customs and habits has prevailed among a people, the more difficult it is to overturn' (p. 111). However Wundt, like Boas, declined to consider these to be intellectual *deficiencies*:

> It is characteristic of primitive culture that it has failed to advance since immemorial times, and this accounts for the uniformity prevalent in widely separated regions of the earth. This, however, does not at all imply that within the narrow sphere that constitutes his world, the intelligence of primitive man is inferior to that of cultural man. (p. 112)

and concluded that:

> the intellectual endowment of primitive man is in itself approximately equal to that of civilized man. Primitive man merely exercises his ability in a more restricted field; his horizon is essentially narrower because of his contentment under these limitations. (p. 113)

Wundt, approaching the cultural-cognition relationship from the other side, thus echoed Boas that intellectual process and level are comparable between primitive and civilized man, and that the cultural and environmental context and content of the intellect provide sufficient basis for differential individual and group behaviour and attainment.

Lévy-Bruhl

The universality of thought processes claimed by Boas and Wundt soon came under attack from Lucien Lévy-Bruhl who published *How Natives Think* in 1910 and *Primitive Mentality* in 1923. His basic argument was that: 'the mental processes of "primitives" do not coincide with those which we are accustomed to describe in men of our own type . . .' (1926, p. 14).

His particular concerns were for perceptual and logical processes. With respect to perception he held that:

> primitives perceive nothing in the same way as we do. The social milieu which surrounds them differs from ours, and precisely because it is different, the external world they perceive differs from that which we apprehend. Undoubtedly they have the same senses as ours – rather more acute than ours in a general way, in spite of our persuasion to the contrary – and their cerebral structure is like our own. But we have to bear in mind that which their collective representations instill into all their perceptions. Whatever the object

presented to their minds, it implies mystic properties which are inextricably bound up with it, and the primitive, in perceiving it, never separates these from it. (p. 43)

With respect to logical operations, Lévy-Bruhl was concerned to show that 'primitive' thought was 'prelogical'; however he did not consider prelogical thought to be *antilogical* or *alogical*, merely different from our own laws of logical thought. Note that he uses the prefix *pre-* rather than *non-* betraying an evolutionary, if not an ethnocentric, bias. Essentially these different logical connections are 'mystical' (1923, p. 431), with intellectual processes being hopelessly entwined with emotional life (1926, p. 35). In general, he felt his evidence enabled him to conclude that 'the rational unity of the thinking being, which is taken for granted by most philosophers, is a *disideratum*, not a fact' (1926, p. 386).

Challenges were soon forthcoming to Lévy-Bruhl's arguments and assertions. As Hallowell (1955) points out in his review entitled 'The Child, The Savage and Human Experience', the recapitulation theory of the evolutionists (that ontogeny recapitulates phylogeny) was a compelling model for anthropologists; consistent with their belief in evolutionary stages in cultural development was the assumption of concomitant stages in mental development through history, and the findings of psychologists that there were definite stages in ontogenetic development (see Part 3) were taken as support for their assumption. However, in later years Lévy-Bruhl's insistence upon different processes among groups of men was somewhat relaxed and, as psychologists began to explore varieties of intellectual functioning within subgroups of Western man, they discovered reason and logic to be less pervasive than originally thought (Denny and Benjafield, 1969). Thus the clear gulf, which was so strenuously debated for a decade, now appears to have been a matter of bias of observation, just as the abstract-concrete argument receded when ethnocentrism was reduced and culturally appropriate tools of observation were employed.

In summary, the early workers on the problems of culture and cognition passed from primary concern with basic sensory and perceptual processes, to elaborate discussions of 'world view' complete with highly ethnocentric assertions regarding animistic, concrete, and prelogical thought. Despite the dated flavour of many of these passages, the major themes of current research work are contained in them.

Firstly, are there *qualitative* differences in cognitive processes among different cultural groups or are the processes identical (or almost so) throughout the species, with the apparent differences attributable to the different cultural materials entering into the processes? Expressed in other terms, we may ask: Does the nature of cultural experience alter or shape the cognitive processor, so that persons enculturated in different societies possess cognitive processes adapted to their cultural milieu? A further variant of this first question is: What is the relationship between the dominant modes of cognitive operations in an individual and the culturally preferred mode? Although it may be the case that there are *no* differences in cognitive processes *available* for use, certain ones are actually in use (to the exclusion of others), thus giving rise to apparent qualitative differences in cognitive processes.

Secondly, are there *quantitative* differences in cognitive processes among different cultural groups? Are some groups more able, more competent, in their cognitive operations? Crucially important here is the supplementary question: 'Able for what; competent for what; intelligent for what?' The questions of ethnocentrism and cultural value inevitably must be raised; is abstract, logical thought 'better' than concrete, prelogical thought? Or are there other measures of attainment which are free of cultural value such as cognitive capacity, memory span, speed of operation?

Thirdly, are the characteristics of *growth* in cognitive operations (both qualitative and quantitative) similar in all cultural groups? If it is largely a function of the *biological unfolding of capacity* during maturation, then we might expect to find little cross-cultural variation; if it is largely a function of cultural input, then we might expect little similarity across cultures. This third question is worth asking in its own right, but a developmental perspective also provides a useful tool to explore the first two traditional concerns.

These three basic questions still confront psychology today. Of course they are considerably more complex than they have been phrased here, but these elements have spanned seven decades of empirical research. The three sections in this collection are each devoted to one of these questions. The complexity of the problems have been matched by the ingenuity of the research, but there are still no definitive answers, except perhaps that biology, culture and growth interact in ways unimagined by the original formulators of these problems.

METHODOLOGICAL CONCERNS

Given the great importance attached to cognitive functioning by Western psychology, it is essential that our aims, research strategies, and techniques be well defined and beyond reproach when we extend this interest to cognitive functioning in other cultural contexts. Despite this importance, it is safe to say that no culturally-relative or comparative methodology has received general acceptance by psychologists or anthropologists working in this field. What follows is an attempt to display the problems inherent in comparative cognitive research, and to draw together some of the more consensual views regarding their solutions.

Perhaps the most basic question is one of aims or goals: why should psychologists be interested in studying cognitive functioning in a variety of cultural settings? The answer lies in the rejection of one, often ascribed, goal, and in the espousal of two other, rather more legitimate, ones. Comparative cognitive psychological research is *not* aimed at discovering which peoples are clever, smart or intelligent, and which are not; we are often charged with this aim by critics of testing and by supporters of minority group rights. However, there is not a single study published in the conventional academic literature (to our knowledge) which betrays this as a goal. There are, undoubtedly, ethnocentric and race-related uses made of data and results; however the material and authors collected in this volume avoid these ethnocentric assertions, while maintaining a right to ask questions concerning group differences.

The two goals which *are* claimed may be phrased in terms of two contrasting foci:

1. Comparative cognitive psychology attempts to understand the *range*, the *variability*, the *differences* in cognitive processes as a function of cultural (including ecological and social) variables;
2. Comparative cognitive psychology also attempts to understand the *uniformities*, the *pan-human or cross-cultural consistency* in cognitive processes, so that valid generalizations may be made about human cognitive functioning.

Thus, we look intensively *within* cultural systems for the roots of cognitive variation and *across* cultural systems for those characteristics of cognitive functioning which are universal for all mankind. It will be argued in the next section that the latter may be usefully generated from the former; that, paradoxically, *uniformities* may emerge from *differences*.

With regard to hypotheses or 'laws' already established in Western psychology, a third, but prior, aim must be sought. We must avoid the assumption that what is known about a freshman university student processing psycholinguistic materials is applicable to our understanding of a Kalahari hunter processing cues and signals in his ecocultural setting. We must, therefore, test our knowledge about cognitive operations, which has been derived from intensive study of less than 1 per cent of the world's population, to discover its applicability or generalizability to other populations. The most usual set of goals, for a comparative cognitive psychology from the point of view of Western psychology, then, contains three distinct aims:

1. To *transport* our present hypotheses and laws to other cultural settings to *test* their applicability or generalizability;
2. To *explore* new cultural systems to discover cognitive *variations* and differences we have not experienced within our own cultural context;
3. To *compare* our prior understanding with our newer knowledge within diverse cultures to *generate* more universal descriptions, hypotheses and laws of human cognitive functioning.

The basic aims of the comparative method cannot be limited to a mere testing of extant hypotheses; we must be concerned with expanding and integrating our knowledge of human cognitive variation. Thus one of the more recent attempts to define the method for psychologists (Whiting, 1968), which limits the method to hypothesis testing, is too narrow for the needs of cognitive research. Indeed, as Strodbeck (1964) has argued, the *discovery* aspect (aim no. 2) of the method, has more to contribute to our overall aims than the initial *testing* aspect (aim no. 1). Further, Frijda and Jahoda (1966) and Berry (1969a) have argued that perhaps the most important of the three is the last aim, which directs us to an understanding of truly *universal* cognitive processes.

In practice, to meet these aims psychologists must adopt a research strategy and a set of research techniques; let us turn our attention to these tools of implementation. Essentially this implementation involves three kinds of questions: when *may* we compare, *how many* should we compare and *how* must we compare, in order to meet our three goals.

An answer to the first question has been proposed by Duijker and Frijda (1960) and elaborated by Frijda and Jahoda (1966). Very simply, we *may* compare only when we have *dimensional identity*. That is, only when two behaviours fall on a single dimension, is it legitimate to relate one to the other for comparative purposes; otherwise, we descend to the proverbial comparison of apples and oranges. A similar requirement has been advocated by Campbell (1964, p. 325), where he argues that only when perceptual *similarities* are established can perceptual *differences* between groups be meaningfully interpreted; radically different modes of perception cannot validly be compared since a multitude of alternative explanations (e.g. sensory incapacity or communication failure) could not be ruled out. The practical basis for comparing cognitive functioning across cultures, then, is a common baseline inherent in the stimulus, in the organism, and in the interaction between them. The origin of this common baseline or unitary dimension has been sought both in the biologically-based 'psychic unity of mankind' (Kroeber, 1948, p. 527; Wallace, 1961b, p. 129) and in the demonstration of 'cultural universals' (Kluckhohn, 1953). Regardless of its origin or origins, such dimensional identity is essential; we may validly compare only when such continuity exists.

The second question, *how many* elements should be in the comparison, has traditionally been of little concern to psychologists. Typically, comparisons have involved only two elements, very often one Western and one non-Western cultural group. However, Campbell (1961, p. 344) has argued that 'no comparison of a single pair of natural objects is interpretable', insisting that at least three observations are necessary in order to understand or test an hypothesized relationship. Indeed, he has recently argued (Campbell and Levine, 1970, p. 366) that single pair (two entity) comparative studies 'are hopelessly equivocal for hypothesis testing, and can only be viewed as generating hypotheses for future research. . . .' In answer to the question of how many entities should enter the comparison, we are obliged to consider a minimum of three if our first aim (the testing of hypotheses) is to be met. However, if we wish to achieve our second and third goals, it is clear that many more, preferably selected to be representative of all known cultural variation, should be included in the comparative framework.

A framework for the making of behavioural comparisons across cultures (the *how* of our third question) has been advanced by Berry (1969a), and a number of criteria for its successful implementation have been suggested. These criteria are: *functional equivalence, conceptual equivalence* and *metric equivalence*, and each will be elaborated in the context of the comparative framework.

Firstly, Goldschmidt (1966) has argued that aspects of culture are comparable only when they are related to functionally similar problems; that is, two institutions in two sociocultural systems may be validly compared only when both are attempts to solve similar recurrent problems facing each cultural group. For the psychologist interested in comparing behaviours across sociocultural systems, *functional equivalence* of behaviours should be demonstrated before comparisons may be made. This ensures dimensional similarity on the one hand, and goal similarity (see Chapter 13) on the other. Without this initial *functional equivalence*, the psychologist is likely to engage merely in comparisons of unrelated behaviours, which are functionally dissimilar, and which are directed towards unrelated goals.

Once *functional equivalence* is established by examining the role and goal of the behaviour in question, a comparative descriptive framework may be applied (Berry, 1969a, p. 122). This framework parallels the three major goals discussed earlier: transportation and testing of extant hypotheses; exploration to discover new variations; and comparisons to generate newer, more nearly universal, descriptions, hypotheses or laws. A fundamental distinction, first made by Pike (1966) and elaborated by French (1963), is relevant here; following a distinction in linguistics between phonemics and phonetics, Pike has coined the terms *emic* and *etic*. The study of phonemics involves the examination of the sounds used in a particular language, while phonetics attempts to generalize from phonemic studies in individual languages to a universal science covering all languages. By analogy, *emics* apply in only a particular society, while *etics* are culture-free or universal aspects of the world (or if not entirely universal, operate in more than one society). The following table gleaned from Pike's (1966) comments, should exemplify the distinction:

Emic approach	*Etic approach*
studies behaviour from within the system	studies behaviour from a position outside the system
examines only one culture	examines many cultures, comparing them
structure discovered by the analyst	structure created by the analyst
criteria are relative to internal characteristics	criteria are considered absolute or universal

Akin to the *emic* description of culture or behaviour is Sturtevant's (1964) approach (see Chapter 2), which has been termed *ethnoscience*. The main proposition is that 'study of a culture involves the discovery of native principles of classification and conceptualization and that the use of *a priori* definitions and conceptual models of cultural content is to be avoided' (Romney and D'Andrade, 1964, p. 3). This is also a statement of Malinowski's point of view: 'The final goal . . . is, briefly, to grasp the native's point of view . . . to realize his vision of his world'

(Malinowski, 1922, p. 25). Approaches, such as the idiographic, the ethnoscientific and the Malinowskian, are attempts to produce internal descriptions of behaviour, and correspond to the *emic* type of analysis. Our major problem is how to describe behaviour in terms which are meaningful to members of a particular culture (an *emic* approach corresponding to our second goal) while at the same time to validly compare behaviour in that culture with behaviour in another or all other cultures (the *etic* aim, corresponding to our third goal). The proposed solution (Berry, 1969a, p. 124) involves the initial application of extant hypotheses concerning behaviour. We must tackle a research problem from some point of view, and the conventional one has been similar to our first goal; this may be termed an *imposed etic* approach. In doing so, however, we must recognize the culturally specific (perhaps even ethnocentric) origins of our approach, and deliberately remain open to new and even contrary kinds of data variation. If we enter into the behaviour system of another culture, knowing that our point of entry (*imposed etic*) is probably only a poor approximation to an understanding of behaviour in that system, then the first major hurdle is passed. Modification of our external categories must be made in the direction of the behavioural system under study, until we eventually achieve a truly *emic* description of behaviour within that culture. That is, an *emic* description can be made by progressively altering the *imposed etic* until it matches a purely *emic* point of view; if this can be done without entirely destroying or losing all of the *etic* character of the entry categories, then we can proceed to the next step. If some of the *etic* is left, we can now note the categories or concepts which are shared by the behaviour system we knew previously and the one we have just come to understand emically. We can now set up a *derived etic* which is valid for making comparisons between two behaviour settings, and we have essentially resolved the problem of obtaining a descriptive framework valid for comparing behaviour across behaviour settings. This new *derived etic* can then be transported to another behaviour setting (this time as an *imposed etic*), be modified emically, and thence form the basis of a new *derived etic* which is valid in three behaviour settings. When all systems which may be compared (limited by the initial functional equivalence requirement) have been included, then we have achieved a *universal* for that particular behaviour.

In this way it is possible to test hypotheses, examine new variations, and generate more universally valid hypotheses concerning behaviour, thereby meeting our three aims in comparative research. However, two more criteria (in addition to *functional equivalence*) should be met in implementing our comparative strategy. The first of these, *conceptual equivalence*, has been proposed by Sears (1961), and involves assuring that research instruments (concepts, tests, apparatus) possess similar meaning, or lack of meaning, for all groups being compared. Despite a thorough examination of the problem by Tatje (1970, p. 689) for cultural comparisons, there has been no similar analysis for behavioural comparisons across cultures. Perhaps the best that may be achieved is by way of a thorough (*emic*) exploration within each cultural system of the most frequent associative meanings of a particular term or concept (for an example, see Chapter 16); where large communality of meaning is detected between the two cultures, then *conceptual equivalence* may be deemed to exist. It is apparent that this method is simply a further application of the three-step procedure previously advocated.

A major problem element in establishing *conceptual equivalence* is discovering translation equivalence; Frijda and Jahoda (1966), Brislin (1970) and Werner and Campbell (1970) all examine this issue in detail. Essentially, two procedures are suggested whereby equivalent terms may be sought in the two linguistic systems. The first involves *back translation* to the original language by an independent interpreter. If the original and the back-translated versions are identical, or nearly so, then there is strong evidence for equivalence; however, as Brislin (1970) demonstrates, this criterion is not sufficient to establish translation equivalence, since alternative explanations for the similarity might still exist. The second procedure involves the heeding of certain rules in constructing the original version which will be used as the basis for translation (Werner and Campbell, 1970); these are the use of relatively simple sentences, the repetition of nouns (rather than using pronouns), the avoidance of metaphor and colloquial expressions, and the avoidance of passive, hypothetical or subjunctive phrases. The use of these techniques will not guarantee translation equivalence, but should increase the probability of solving this very basic problem in comparative research.

The final criterion which has been suggested may be termed *metric equivalence*. This criterion applies not to the basis of comparison (as does *functional equivalence*), nor to the tools of comparison (as does *conceptual equivalence*) but to the results, the data, of comparisons. The need for this form of equivalence has emerged from the recognition that the comparisons of mean scores is not sufficient for making valid behavioural comparisons across cultures. At least two forms of *metric equivalence* have been employed: subsystem validation (Roberts and Sutton-Smith, 1962), and factorial validation (Irvine, 1966, 1969c). In the former, hypotheses are examined both intraculturally and cross-culturally, so that explanatory variables may be tested at two levels; for example, Berry (1966b) examined the relation between severity of socialization and spatial skill development both within and between Temne and Eskimo samples. In the latter form, similarities in such characteristics as item difficulties, correlation matrices and factorial structure are required between two samples before hypotheses concerning group differences may be validly made. Both of these forms of *metric equivalence* illustrate the necessity of discovering empirical relations within samples which are, at the very least, not inconsistent with those postulated (and perhaps discovered) across samples.

Finally, let us return to the roles of laboratory and field research and to the issue of cooperation and mutual assistance between them which was first raised by Titchener (see page 5 of this introduction). In one sense, the laboratory and the field may be considered to be 'subcultural research settings', and it could be argued that problems of comparisons and translations exist here just as clearly as they do cross-culturally. There are many dimensions on which these two strategies could be contrasted, but only two will be discussed here: control over variables, and the generalization of results.

The degree of manipulation or control of independent variables is generally conceded to be minimal in field research, while it may be high in the laboratory setting. Rather than bemoaning this situation, field-oriented researchers have accepted it and have taken advantage of an associated characteristic of field situations (its inherent variability) to establish a degree of control suitable to their needs. This strategy is simply to sample from the extant variation (often with the help of the Human Relation Area Files: Murdock, 1954) for the levels of variables necessary to test or examine relationships of interest. It is not necessary to create levels of independent variables if one can find them existing naturally; thus, cultures may be considered as *natural laboratory settings* for the comparative study of behaviour (a 'quasi-experimental' design: Campbell and Stanley, 1966). Unfortunately, however, it is rarely possible to determine 'independent' and 'dependent' variables (in the sense of antecedence or cause) in these naturally functioning cultural-behavioural systems; the technique thus more nearly approximates a correlational strategy, while retaining some of the advantages of 'control' over the level of one of the variables.

A second dimension on which laboratory and field research are frequently contrasted is that of *generalizability*. It is clear that observations or measures taken of behaviour which is abstracted from its usual

B

environment (e.g. in the laboratory) is not necessarily generalizable to this usual natural environment. On the other hand, observations or measures taken of behaviour in the field require *no* generalization, since no abstraction of behaviour has taken place. Thus, if our goals are to increase generalizability (our third major aim) then it is not surprising to find that much comparative research takes place in less than rigorous laboratory settings.

These two dimensions have been commented upon extensively in the methodological literature of general psychology. Indeed, Campbell (1957) has argued that they are related (inversely) and that decisions on research strategy require a trade-off, depending upon the specific goals of the study. Essentially, one must usually sacrifice some generalizability to gain control, or sacrifice some control to gain generalizability. At the laboratory end of the dimensions, one may have high control, but low generalizability (high 'internal validity', but low 'external validity' in Campbell's terms), while at the field end of the dimension, one may have the opposite mixture. However, optimal mixtures are not ruled out, and the most likely conditions for maximizing both internal and external validity exist when there is major cooperation between the laboratory and the field, as Titchener (p. 5) has already argued. If we are to establish a science of behaviour, validly based and universally generalizable, then behavioural scientists of all research persuasions must integrate their efforts to gain optimal levels of rigour and relevance. The passing of problems back and forth between the laboratory and the field should thus be a basic strategy in comparative behavioural research.

PART ONE

Quality and variation of cognitive processes

Introduction

This first section attempts to stretch cognitive phenomena as widely as possible, to display them in a variety of cultural contexts. It is intended to help convince the sceptic that qualitative aspects of cognitive behaviours do indeed differ, that styles, processes and skills vary with language and ecology, values and functions.

Deeper than this mapping task, this display of variability, however, there is a more detailed goal; this is to attempt to relate (sometimes causally) this variability in cognitive behaviour to specific cultural variables. Thus, language and socialization in particular are frequently examined for possible relationships with logic, classification, cognitive style, belief, measurement, imagery and memory.

Chapters 1 and 2 introduce the concerns of anthropologists. Gladwin (Chapter 1) argues that different cognitive strategies and logical processes may be employed by people living in cultures with different problems to solve. Relying largely upon observations among Micronesian canoe navigators, he concludes that these differences are indeed real, and that psychologists must take them into consideration if they are not to remain 'culture-bound'. This author has recently elaborated this point of view (Gladwin, 1970) in a more detailed analysis of Micronesian navigation. This emphasis on studying what people do, and how they go about doing it, is emphasized by Sturtevant (Chapter 2) in his advocacy of *ethnoscience*, the study of 'the system of knowledge and cognition typical of a given culture'. Although only a tool or a means for the study of culture for the anthropologists, it may be considered an end or goal for the psychologist, in that it requires the comprehending of the cognitive categories of people living in other cultures. This knowledge of the categorization of experience by individuals permits the anthropologist to move on to study the culture, but since it is cognitive behaviour in itself, it comprises a major focus of study for the psychologist working cross-culturally.

A major tool in the *ethnoscience* approach is the study of language. How a language carves up the physical and social environment is thought to indicate the cognitive categories in use. Chapters 3 and 4 emphasize the importance of language in understanding cognitive behaviour, by outlining and systematizing the basic assertions of Whorf (Fishman,

Chapter 3), and by carrying out experimental work (Maclay, Chapter 4) to evaluate them.

Another major set of cultural and cognitive variables is introduced with Chapter 5 (Witkin), in which a theory relating socialization to *cognitive style* is illustrated with reports of two cross-cultural studies of this perceptual-cognitive dimension. Specifically, the degree of *differentiation* (analytical approach to cognitive or perceptual problems) is shown to vary cross-culturally with child-rearing practices which are themselves related to the ecological setting of the cultural system. A qualification to this general finding is offered by Wober (Chapter 6) who argues that a high level of differentiation may be limited to a specific sense modality (e.g. vision in Western cultures or audition in some African cultures) within which cognitive growth may be largely confined. A further extension by Berry (Chapter 7), arguing from a position of ecological functionalism, demonstrates that across four ecocultural settings, high visual differentiation varies systematically with a cluster of ecological and cultural variables, including the importance of hunting, the severity of socialization, the quality of arts and crafts production, and the assistance from a complex vocabulary of 'geometrical-spatial' terms.

The final chapters deal with a variety of cognitive variables as they are exhibited in a number of African cultural settings. Beginning with *beliefs*, and tying-in with the previous three chapters Jahoda (Chapter 8) explores the notion that there can emerge a change in cognitive structure in the direction of coexistence between African and Western ideas and beliefs. Cole, Gay and Glick (Chapter 9) examine in detail the cognitive behaviour involved in making *quantitative judgements* in Liberia, dealing sensitively with such subjects as geometric concepts, disjunction and conjunction, and volume, time, length and number estimates. This set of studies demonstrates the use of concepts discovered within the culture (*ethnoscientific* use of *emic* units) for designing field experiments in cognitive behaviour. More recent studies, employing this same strategy, are reported in Cole *et al.* (1971).

In cultural systems which function without the benefits of literacy, there have frequently been assumed to exist alternative ways of coding and remembering information. Doob (Chapter 10) explores the possibility that *eidetic images* (persistent and accurate image traces of the original stimulus) may be more used in nonliterate than in literate cultures. Although in the chapter presented here, Doob found a greater incidence of eidetic images among Ibo subjects than among Westerners, Doob (1966) has more recently discovered no consistently greater use of this memory aid among other samples from nonliterate populations. Another possibility, however, is that in cultures where writing is not available to record events, *memory* may be relied upon to a greater extent, and hence may be better under experimental conditions. Ross and Millsom (Chapter 11) test this alternative in Ghana and New York, following up a long tradition of studies on the topic (Bartlett, 1932).

Throughout this first section then, the emphasis is on variability in cognitive behaviour, and on the cultural factors associated with this variability. Clearly these studies are concerned with processes and styles, and not with basic capacity or intellectual competence. Studies which comment on this latter issue will be sampled in the second section. However, while exploring the cross-cultural variability of cognitive performance, the reader may wish to consider the kinds of inferences about competence which might validly be made from these data.

I

T. Gladwin (1964)

Culture and logical process

W. H. Goodenough (ed.) *Explorations in Cultural Anthropology: Essays in Honor of George Peter Murdock* (McGraw-Hill Book Co.), pp. 167–77

In 1936, Gregory Bateson published *Naven* (1958), an admittedly partial ethnography of the Iatmul of New Guinea. The importance of this book lay in his attempt to formulate some theoretical constructs with respect to psychological process and social dynamics, constructs which would embrace his observations of the Iatmul, and would at the same time be of general validity. One of these, *schizmogenesis*, was developed extensively and ultimately led Bateson into cybernetics and the flourishing field of general systems research. The other really new concept in *Naven*, *eidos*, has never enjoyed the equal development it deserves.

Eidos, in Bateson's terms, is 'a standardization (and expression in cultural behaviour) of the cognitive aspects of the personality of individuals' (1958, p. 220). It is complementary to *ethos*, the 'expression of a culturally standardized system of organization of the instincts and emotions of ... individuals' (1958, p. 118). Early in the history of research in culture and personality, Bateson thus made explicit the necessity for giving to the cognitive aspects of personality a weight and attention equal to that devoted to the emotional.

However, earlier exploratory thinking by Edward Sapir and others on the relationship between culture and personality had been rooted in the concepts of psychoanalysis, a system of theory anchored almost exclusively to the biological and emotional determinants of psychological process. Then, the year following the publication of *Naven*, Ralph Linton went to Columbia and soon became the dominant figure in a group of anthropologists collaborating with the distinguished analyst, Abram Kardiner. The impact on anthropology of their work was so great that since that time the main stream of research and theoretical development in culture and personality has virtually taken for granted the assumption that its primary data are to be found in the realm of emotion. It is ironic that of all the fields of inquiry into human behaviour, anthropology, with its primary emphasis on the regularities of behaviour as they are transmitted through culture from one generation to the next, is the one which most consistently ignores the cognitive learning involved in this cultural transmission.

True, the theory of learning formulated by Clark Hull has had considerable vogue in anthropology, but this theory is far more concerned with motivation and reward for learning than it is with the cognitive integrations accomplished in learning. Aside from Hullian theory, attention to the processes of learning and thinking and to the nature of intelligence has been minimal in anthropology. Bateson did carry *eidos* one step further, developing in collaboration with Margaret Mead the concept of *deutero-learning* (Bateson, 1942), referring to learning how to learn or to the content and logical process of learning. This was a useful concept, and although they did not develop it further, both Bateson and Mead are far more careful than most anthropologists to make explicit the nature of the learning process in the cultures they have described. More recently the emerging field of psycholinguistics and contributions to a few symposia have reflected a growing interest in cognitive categories and processes, but this remains a scattered effort.[1] It is in no way comparable to the numerous but sometimes frustrating endeavours of anthropologists to derive a variety of personality types from common emotional experiences ordered within a Freudian framework.

I became acutely aware of this neglect by anthropologists some six years ago when, in collaboration with Seymour B. Sarason, I undertook a review of research in mental subnormality (Masland, Sarason and Gladwin, 1958). The first question of course was 'What is mental normality?' – i.e. 'How do we define intelligence?' This is obviously a difficult question, even disregarding cultural differences. Most psychologists in effect define intelligence operationally as being that which intelligence tests measure. People with high IQs are intelligent, and those with low IQs are variously dull, duller, or idiots. There has been much soul searching by psychologists on this score, but no more adequate definition has yet gained general acceptance.

[1] e.g. Symposium on Cognitive Structures (J. L. Fischer, chairman), American Anthropological Association, Mexico City, December 1959, at which an earlier version of this paper was presented. See also Tanner and Inhelder (1960) and Gladwin and Sturtevant (1962).

I also found that numerous non-European peoples, many of whom do rather bright things, had been given intelligence tests by both psychologists and anthropologists with due attention to linguistic and other handicaps and had consistently come out with low IQs. This could mean either that we are of a master race, or else that we are in effect accepting an assumption that there is only one really good way to use the human brain, and that is our way – whatever that may be. Since the latter explanation seemed more reasonable, I endeavoured to find out what anthropologists had done to rectify the situation.

More particularly, I hoped to find in the work of anthropologists some substantive research which focused on cultural differences in modes of thinking and problem solving, research which could point to other criteria of intelligence than those valued by European-American professionals. Such studies would permit us to define – and ultimately to measure – different *kinds* of intellectual achievement, rather than, as now, to seek ever more ingenious (or ingenuous) ways of measuring *our* kind of achievement. From this in turn might come a more comprehensive and operationally useful definition of intelligence. However, my conclusion from this search was essentially the one set forth above; emphasis by anthropologists has been almost exclusively on the emotional determinants rather than on the cognitive aspects of personality.

I then turned to re-examine an earlier collaboration with Sarason, a personality and culture study of Truk (Gladwin and Sarason, 1953). We had tried a simplified intelligence test and had at least been enlightened enough to see that it was inappropriate to Trukese perceptual patterns rather than to conclude that their poor performance reflected poor brains. We, or particularly Sarason, had discussed at some length the very concrete, non-abstract nature of Trukese thinking. We earned an honourable mention for that bit of insight, but no medal. A medal was unwarranted for several reasons. First, in my fieldwork I had paid little attention to learning, and no attention to how the Trukese learn to think and learn (Bateson's *deutero-learning*), so we could offer only rather weak speculations as to how this style of thinking developed. Second, we had not developed our analysis of Trukese thinking in a frame of reference such as to command the theoretical attention of other psychologists or anthropologists. We did not, in other words, relate it to theories of cognition and intelligence in a meaningful way. Finally, in undertaking the analytic interpretation of Trukese personality development, I sat just as firmly at the feet of Freud as did any of my contemporaries, in spite of the realization that Trukese thinking and learning was significantly different from that employed by the patients or subjects of

Freud or of contemporary psychologists. I did not yet appreciate that if behaviour is learned, as we culturally-oriented anthropologists keep insisting, the nature of the learning process must have something to do with the kinds of behaviour learned.

I cannot in this paper attempt to expiate all my past errors and omissions. I of course still have no data on how Trukese learn to think. Speculation on the relationship between the nature of learning and the kinds of behaviour learned is tempting, but could only be speculation. Instead I shall attempt to place in meaningful perspective the nature of Trukese intellectual achievement, differing as it does from our own in the kinds of thinking employed. Description of a variety of cognitive styles is a necessary first step toward the goal of studying how people learn to think.[1]

In our culture we value (and measure crudely with intelligence tests) relational or abstract thinking, in which bodies of knowledge are integrated and related to each other through unifying symbolic constructs. The Trukese seemingly do not, relying instead on the cumulative product of the adding together of a great number of discrete bits of data, summed together in accordance with predetermined parameters, to arrive at a desired conclusion. Both we and the Trukese operate within a *gestalt*, a conception of the problem as a whole. However, we seek a unifying concept which will comprehend all the relevant facts more or less simultaneously, developing an overall principle or plan from which individual steps toward a solution can be derived deductively. In contrast the Trukese work toward a solution by improvizing each step, but always with the final goal in mind. The Trukese start with a simplified *gestalt*, whether or not they can describe it in words, and fill in the details as they go along. We prefer to look a situation over and design a somewhat special *gestalt* which will at the outset embrace all the essential details.

If we take as an example the work of the navigator of a sailing canoe, I believe this process will not only become clear, but will also be seen to require a substantial feat of intellect. I say this in spite of the fact that I believe that the Trukese would do badly even on a perceptually appropriate intelligence test, and that in my experience they proved themselves generally incapable of mastering even the relatively simple organizing concept of system functions needed to locate a malfunction in

[1] In preparing the material which follows I have benefited substantially from discussions with Dr Ulric Neisser of Brandeis University. However, I can state with assurance that responsibility for the final product rests with me alone since our discussions had the pleasant attribute of consistently leaving some issues unresolved.

an internal-combustion engine – which they could almost tear down and reassemble blindfolded provided it required only cleaning and overhaul.

Voyages spanning over one hundred miles of open ocean are still made in sailing canoes, and longer ones were made in the past. The destination is often a tiny dot of land less than a mile across, and visible from any distance only because of the height of those coconut trees which may grow in its sandy soil. From a canoe, virtually at the level of the ocean's surface, even a forested island is visible only three or four miles away. To assure that the travellers will come close enough to their destination to sight it after covering miles of empty ocean, with shifting winds and currents, the crew usually rely on one of their number who has been trained in a variety of traditional techniques by an older master navigator, usually a relative of his. These techniques do not include even a compass (although some carry them now for emergencies), to say nothing of chronometer, sextant, or star tables.

Essentially the navigator relies on dead reckoning. He sets his course by the rising and setting of stars, having memorized for this purpose the knowledge gleaned from generations of observation of the directions in which stars rise and fall through the seasons. A heading toward a given island, when leaving another island, is set at a particular season a trifle to the left, or perhaps the right, of a certain star at its setting or rising. Through the night a succession of such stars will rise or fall, and each will be noted and the course checked. Between stars, or when the stars are not visible due to daylight or storm, the course is held constant by noting the direction of the wind and the waves. A good navigator can tell by observing wave patterns when the wind is shifting its direction or speed, and by how much. In a dark and starless night the navigator can even tell these things from the sound of the waves as they lap upon the side of the canoe's hull, and the feel of the boat as it travels through the water. All of these complex perceptions – visual, auditory, kinesthetic – are combined with vast amounts of data stored in memory, and the whole is integrated into a slight increase or decrease in pressure on the steering paddle, or a grunted instruction to slack off the sail a trifle.

If the prevailing wind will not permit sailing directly to an island, but requires tacking first in one direction and then in another, the problem becomes even more complex. Tacking involves radical changes in course. While tacking, the canoe is never sailing directly toward its destination, but instead heads considerably to the left and then to the right of a true heading in order to keep the sail filled with wind. Although under conditions of changeable weather (which are common) the navigator may proceed by a series of short tacks which multiply the opportunities for error, the scope of his task can be most readily visualized in terms of a long voyage under a fairly steady but opposing wind. Under these circumstances he may sail for up to a hundred miles on one course, and then make a single turn to a new heading which he will hold, perhaps for a comparable distance, until he sights his destination. The first course, the second course and the point of change are all invisible pathways across the water which have reality only in the mind of the navigator, and for which there are no physical points of reference. Yet when, for example, the change in course is made the navigator must know exactly where he is in the ocean, and where his destination lies, at the time he changes course. This knowledge can only be gained through a cumulative estimate of the rate, time and direction of travel. The course change may have to occur after two or three days of sailing, out of sight of land and with several shifts in wind velocity and direction. Nevertheless the navigator must change to a new tack within only two or three miles of the ideal point if he is to arrive within sight of the island of his destination.[1] In the old days of European navigation this was done with frequent observations of the compass and of a spinning log line and chronometer, with plottings on a chart. Increasingly now it is accomplished by accelerometers and computers combined into an inertial guidance system. The Trukese navigator, however, does it all in his head. This is an astounding intellectual achievement.

Furthermore, the navigator is likely to have received his training because he happened to have a relative who knew the skills and wanted to keep them in the family, rather than being selected entirely because of his intelligence.

What kind of information is the navigator utilizing, how is he selecting it, and how does he have to manipulate and integrate it in order to produce a useful end product – e.g. differential pressure on the steering paddle? His information consists of a large number of discrete observations, a combination of motion, sounds, feel of the wind, wave patterns, star relationships, etc. Each is a concrete, largely unequivocal factual observation. Either the boat is heading toward the correct star or it is not. The wind is from a certain direction and of a certain velocity; although

---

[1] Sharp (1957) contends on *a priori* grounds that tacking upwind in this fashion on long voyages is impossible in a sailing canoe without European navigation aids. Firsthand testimony by Americans, notably the Reverend John K. Fahey, S.J., and the Reverend William E. Rively, S.J., refutes this and some of Sharp's other pessimistic conclusions. A number of other authorities also disagree with Sharp (see Golson, 1963).

it takes practice to observe this accurately, the fact is unambiguous. The significance of each observation is established by a comparison with remembered observations from past experience, a result of training. This training and experience also determines unequivocally what phenomena shall be observed and what ignored. The selection and accumulation of necessary information thus requires a minimum of reasoning or logical choice.

It is as routine and automatic as are the observations of a motorist who, for example, is approaching an intersection or curve and must decide whether to slow down, stop, shift gears, or whatever. The motorist, almost without conscious thought and often while he is carrying on a conversation, observes and relates to previous experience the visibility, the road surface, the bank of a curve, and even the minor cues which suggest that a crossroad is or is not heavily travelled. Furthermore, the highway upon which the motorist is driving may have other traffic. Cars and trucks are travelling in front of and behind him, at different speeds and with different rates of possible acceleration, manœuvrability, etc. Yet if he is an experienced driver he can predict almost exactly where each will be at any given moment. An occasional glance ahead or into the mirror will suffice to keep these position estimates up-to-date. In other words the motorist simultaneously integrates a large number of estimates of rate, time, direction and distance, plus predictive extensions of these variables, into a constantly changing *gestalt* which defines his relative position both in the flow of traffic and with respect to the approaching curve in the highway.

This is the same process that is employed by the Trukese navigator. His progress across the ocean is guided by a constant awareness in his own mind of his location relative to the position of every island and reef in the area through which he is travelling. Each bit of information – whether a perception of changed conditions or an awareness of continuing progress under constant conditions – is integrated into a cumulative but changing knowledge of position and travel thus far. The navigator's mental image is analogous to a radar screen on which a moving spot of light shows his position relative to other objects at any moment. His navigational decisions are then made on an *ad hoc* basis to assure continued progress toward his goal. The operational judgements regarding changes in sailing directions would actually be arrived at in exactly the same way if he were constantly within sight of land; the differences lies not in how the boat is handled but in being able to *know* where the landmarks lie without being able to see them.

Contrast this with the more familiar navigational procedures in the

European tradition. Western navigators plan their entire voyage in advance. A course is plotted on a chart and this in turn provides the criteria for decisions. Progress is assessed at any given moment relative to a position along the plotted line. Unless the navigator is sailing a direct point-to-point course, he does not carry in his mind a physical sense of where he is going. In his mind is an overall plan, and an estimate of the amount of this plan which has thus far been accomplished. He can always draw a line on the chart between his on-course position and his destination, thus determining where he is relative to his goal, but unless someone inquires he need never be aware, as he stands by the helm, just where over the horizon his destination lies.

We have, then, a contrast between two cognitive strategies. One, the European, begins with a single unifying plan which is then implemented piecemeal with minimal further reference to the overall goal synthesized within it (cf. Miller, Galanter and Pribram, 1960). Almost all the thinking is done in advance of its implementation. The other strategy, the Trukese, operates with reference to its beginning and particularly its ending points, and a point between. The point between, the present position of the boat, is constantly being related to the ending point. Each move is successively determined on an *ad hoc* basis. Thinking is continuous, and in our culture we should consider it a series of improvisations. The tools – mechanical aids versus sensory perceptions – are different in the two examples, but either set of tools could within limits serve either strategy.

The contrast is especially clear operationally when external conditions change, forcing a change in sailing directions. The Trukese navigator simply adds the new dimensions to his overall perception of the situation and keeps on sailing appropriately toward his destination. The European navigator, however, is forced to depart from his original plan. Before he can change course he must develop a new plan. He expresses this in a new set of course lines between his present position and his destination. Only after he has linked these points together in a new synthesis can he make the first tactical response to the changed conditions.

The European and Trukese cognitive strategies just outlined differ in at least two essential respects. One is that the European procedure can be described fully in words by the navigator. At any time he is prepared to give a 'logical' explanation of what he is doing. He has a complete and adequate plan from which he can deduce each necessary step, even including a new plan. This ability to conceptualize and verbalize a plan is, often implicitly, assumed to be an essential attribute of 'intelligent' behaviour as we understand it in our culture. In contrast the Trukese navigator can point to his destination over the horizon, something the European generally cannot do, but he cannot possibly put into words all of the myriad perceptions which have led him to be sure at that moment where the island lies. This is not merely because the Trukese are unaccustomed to describing in words what they are doing. The simultaneous integration of several discrete thought processes defies verbalization. The navigator can probably inventory all of the factors to which he must be alert, but the process whereby these are weighed and combined is both complex and fluid.

The other difference lies in the logical processes employed by each. The cognitive strategy of the European navigator can be characterized as essentially deductive, proceeding from principles to details. Before he embarks upon a voyage, or upon a new course, he takes into account a number of factors, both general and specific, which will govern his subsequent actions. These may include the condition of his vessel, policies of his organization, the urgency of his cargo, probable weather conditions, and an appropriate time of day for arrival at his destination. Out of the possibly conflicting mandates flowing from these considerations he will develop a plan which will incorporate compromises but will constitute his organizing principle of operation. In implementing this plan he will again be governed by navigational and other techniques which are concrete applications of basic principles. Some of these, such as the movement of celestial bodies, are highly abstract in nature and are translatable into a navigational fix only through several steps of deductive logic. The navigator may or may not understand all of the theory which lies back of his techniques, but they had originally to be developed through an explicit sequence of logical steps. However, once the European navigator has developed his operating plan and has available the appropriate technical resources, the implementation and monitoring of his navigation can be accomplished with a minimum of thought. He has simply to perform almost mechanically the steps dictated by his training and by his initial planning synthesis.

It would be satisfying to suggest, in contrast to the European deductive strategy, that the Trukese navigator operates inductively, proceeding from details to principles. He does indeed start with details, but he never arrives at any discernible principles. The details are of several kinds. There are categories of phenomena which he has learned, through training, he must observe. In attending to these he applies criteria, based upon both training and experience, which permit him to evaluate their relative importance. Finally, there are the characteristics of his canoe in its present condition and loading which determine the nature and magnitude of the actions necessary to maintain a desired heading or speed. The input of information (observations) and its synthesis (application of weighting criteria) is a continuous process characteristically involving multiple simultaneous operations. The output takes two forms: decisions relative to handling the canoe, and a constantly changing mental perception of where the canoe lies relative to its destination.

This total process goes forward without reference to any explicit principles and without any planning, unless the intention to proceed to a particular island can be considered a plan. It is nonverbal and does not follow a coherent sequence of logical steps. As such it does not represent what we tend to value in our culture as 'intelligent' behaviour. It certainly does not represent the kind of inelligence measured by virtually all intelligence tests. We might refer to this kind of ability as a 'knack', and respect a person for his competence, but we would not on these grounds qualify him as a profound thinker. Yet it is undeniable that the process of navigating from one tiny island to another, when this is accomplished entirely through the mental activity of the navigator, must reflect a high order of intellectual functioning.[1]

I do not wish to raise here the question of whether the Trukese are more or less intelligent in an absolute sense than Europeans. This question will probably always be unanswerable. It certainly will never be answered until we have eliminated the deficit in our knowledge which it is the primary purpose of this paper to underscore. This is an essential lack of clarity, indeed a lack of definition, with respect to the nature of intelligence and of intellectual and cognitive processes. Some psychologists – Bartlett, Bruner, Guilford, Hebb and Piaget, to name a few – are concerned about this lack of clarity and are attempting to develop a basis for a theory of thinking. However, their work immediately strikes an anthropologist as culture-bound. Their starting point is our familiar symbolic logic and relational abstract thinking. They do not have before them a range of other possible basic approaches to thinking, learning and problem solving. In other fields of inquiry into human behaviour anthropology has made rich contributions to theoretical perspective and to the documentation of alternative modes of behaviour.

[1] This lack of preplanning leads to some interesting speculation. The Trukese, in common with probably the majority of non-European peoples, lack a meaningful orientation of the self toward the future. They are not poised to think about the later phases of their life trajectories and are unlikely to consider the long-term consequences of their present behaviour. They do not, in other words, plan ahead in their lives. It is tempting to conclude that the lack of future orientation and planning is somehow functionally related to the lack of planning in cognitive or problem-solving activities. However, this must remain entirely speculative until data from other cultures are available.

But anthropology has permitted the study of intelligence and learning, especially as it is related to education, to develop into a major concern of many nations of the world without giving it more than the most passing attention. Anthropologists stoutly defend the equality of all men, especially with respect to intellectual potential, without any attempt to analyse or document the nature of similarities and differences in thinking. In this vital area we make no cross-cultural comparisons, and indeed have no theoretical framework within which to make them.

My analysis of the work of the Trukese navigator is frankly speculative, and at best is a crude first approximation to what actually goes on in his head. But analyses of this sort, particularly those developed on the basis of fieldwork directed to this end, can have real value in providing just that perspective on cognition which is so sorely needed and which in other contexts is the stock-in-trade of anthropology.

2

W. C. Sturtevant (1964)

Studies in ethnoscience[1]

Extracted from A. K. Romney and R. G. D'Andrade (eds.) Trans-cultural Studies in Cognition, *American Anthropologist* (Special Publication), 66(3), Part 2, pp. 99–113, 123–4

This paper is a survey and explication of a new approach in ethnography – of what one might well call 'the New Ethnography' were it not for that label's pejorative implications for practitioners of other kinds of ethnography. The method has no generally accepted name, although one is clearly required. 'Ethnoscience' perhaps has the widest acceptance, in conversation if not in print, and has the advantage of freshness. However, some of this word's undesirable implications should be disavowed: 'The term "ethnoscience" is unfortunate for two reasons – first, because it suggests that other kinds of ethnography are *not* science, and second because it suggests that folk classifications and folk taxonomies *are* science' (Spaulding, 1963). Although the name may have been chosen partly because of the first of these implications, it would be impolitic if not impolite to insist on it; in any case, the method should stand or fall on its own merits. To dispose adequately of the second implication would require a discourse on the definition and philosophy of science. It is perhaps sufficient to remark that the most appropriate meaning to assign to the element 'science' here (but not necessarily elsewhere) is, essentially, 'classification'. This restricted implication

[1] In revising the original version of this paper I have profited greatly from the papers, discussion, and criticism presented by the other participants in the Conference on Trans-Cultural Studies of Cognitive Systems. I acknowledge also my debt to many discussions over several years with Harold C. Conklin, Charles O. Frake, Dell H. Hymes, and Floyd G. Lounsbury. Helpful written criticisms of the earlier version of this paper were provided by the editor and by Conklin (at first from the field), Hymes, Richard N. Adams, Robbins Burling, Wallace L. Chafe, Paul Friedrich, Ward H. Goodenough, and Duane Metzger. I thank them all, and do not intend to commit any of them to agreement with everything said here.

has been well expressed by G. C. Simpson in a somewhat similar context:

> The necessity for aggregating things (or what is operationally equivalent, the sensations, received from them) into classes is a completely general characteristic of living things. . . . Such generalization, such classification in that sense, is an absolute, minimal requirement of adaptation, which in turn is an absolute and minimal requirement of being or staying alive. . . . We certainly order our perceptions of the external world more fully, more constantly, and more consciously than do any other organisms. . . . Such ordering is most conspicuous in the two exclusively human and in some sense highest of all our activities: the arts and sciences. . . . The whole aim of theoretical science is to carry to the highest possible and conscious degree the perceptual reduction of chaos . . . the most basic postulate of science is that nature itself is orderly. . . . All theoretical science is ordering. (Simpson, 1961, pp. 3–5)

'Ethnoscience' is appropriate as a label because it may be taken to imply one interpretation of such terms as 'ethnobotany', 'ethnogeography', etc. – although it is important to emphasize that the approach is a general ethnographic one, by no means limited to such branches of ethnography as are often called by the names of recognized academic 'arts and sciences' coupled with the prefix 'ethno-'. This prefix is to be understood here in a special sense: it refers to the system of knowledge and cognition typical of a given culture. Ethnoscience differs from Simpson's 'theoretical science' in that it refers to the 'reduction of chaos' achieved by a particular culture, rather than to the 'highest possible and conscious degree' to which such chaos may be reduced. To put it another way, a culture itself amounts to the sum of a given society's folk classifications, all of that society's ethnoscience, its particular ways of classifying its material and social universe. Thus, to take an extreme example, the 'ethnopornography' of the Queensland Aborigines is what *they* consider pornography – if indeed they have such a category – rather than what was considered pornography by the Victorian ethnologist who titled the last chapter of his monograph on Queensland aboriginal culture 'Ethno-pornography', warned that 'the following chapter is not suitable for perusal by the general reader', and described under this heading such topics as marriage, pregnancy and childbirth, menstruation, 'foul language', and especially genital mutilations and their social and ceremonial significance (Roth, 1897, pp. 169–84). Similarly, 'ethnohistory' is here the conception of the past shared by the bearers of a particular culture, rather than (the more usual sense) the history (in our terms) of 'ethnic groups'; 'ethnobotany' is a specific cultural conception of the plant world, rather than (again the more usual sense) a description of plant uses arranged under the binomials of our own taxonomic botany.

It is not a new proposal that an important aspect of culture is made up of the principles by which a people classify their universe. A rather clear statement to this effect was made by Boas (1911a, pp. 24–6); the notion was hinted at by Durkheim and Mauss (1903, pp. 5–6); Malinowski clearly stated that 'the final goal, of which an Ethnographer should never lose sight . . . is, briefly, to grasp the native's point of view, his relation to life, to realise *his* vision of *his* world' (1922, p. 25). Even E. B. Tylor can be understood in the same sense, when he warned that the ethnologist 'must avoid that error which the proverb calls measuring other people's corn by one's own bushel' (1881, p. 410). However, the explicit definition of culture as a whole in these terms, and the proposition that ethnography should be conceived of as the discovery of the 'conceptual models' with which a society operates, was first stated quite recently in an elegant, brief paper by Goodenough:

> A society's culture consists of whatever it is one has to know or believe in order to operate in a manner acceptable to its members, and to do so in any role that they accept for any one of themselves. . . . It is the forms of things that people have in mind, their models for perceiving, relating, and otherwise interpreting them. . . . Ethnographic description, then, requires methods of processing observed phenomena such that we can inductively construct a theory of how our informants have organized the same phenomena. It is the theory, not the phenomena alone, which ethnographic description aims to present. (Goodenough, 1957, pp. 167–8)

It has long been evident that a major weakness in anthropology is the underdeveloped condition of ethnographic method. Typologies and generalizations abound, but their descriptive foundations are insecure. Anthropology is in the natural history stage of development rather than the 'stage of deductively formulated theory' (Northrop, 1947), it is history rather than science (Kroeber, 1952, pp. 52–78), it has not discovered a fundamental unit comparable to the physicists' atom (a common complaint, variously worded: e.g. Kluckhohn, 1953, p. 517; Spuhler, 1963). One may try to make the best of this situation by insisting that one prefers to remain a historian or a humanist, or one may look for improvement in ethnography. Taking the latter choice, the best strategy is not, I think, to seek to modify existing generalizations on the basis of intensive fieldwork of the traditional sort in one or two societies (Leach, 1961a, 1961b), nor to elaborate *a priori* typologies and apply them to more and more old descriptions by means of fancy retrieval procedures, hoping that the errors and incommensurabilities in the descriptive sources will balance out in the statistical manipulations used to yield generalizations. It is on this latter score that Needham (1962) attacks Murdock's methods (e.g. 1953, 1957), justifiably although intemperately. An interesting methodological contrast of this sort is provided by the exchange between Goodenough (1956b) and Fischer (1958) on Trukese residence rules: Goodenough pointed out the discrepancies resulting from his and Fischer's attempts to apply the usual *a priori* typology of residence in their independent censuses of Truk as a basis for urging that ethnographers should drop this method and substitute the search for the rules significant to the bearers of a particular culture in their own choices of residence. Fischer responded by tinkering with the *a priori* typology to take account of the Trukese peculiarities Goodenough had noted – yet there is no guarantee that the next culture examined will fit his new typology any better than Truk fitted the old one.

What is needed is the improvement of ethnographic method, to make cultural descriptions replicable and accurate, so that we know what we are comparing. Ethnoscience shows promise as the New Ethnography required to advance the whole of cultural anthropology.[1]

The ethnoscientific approach is now about ten years old[2] and has a rapidly growing body of practitioners in general agreement on methods and aims, in close communication with each other, and sharing an enthusiasm for the rehabilitation and revivification of ethnography. There are several excellent programmatic general statements about ethnoscience (Conklin, 1962a; Frake, 1962; Wallace, 1962), which include (usually simplified) examples. However, most previous discussions and exemplifications have been couched in such terms that many anthropologists assume that what is being described is not ethnography but some kind of linguistics or 'kinship algebra' or both, so that there

[1] I use the term cultural anthropology to include ethnology (of which social anthropology is one variety) and archaeology. Obviously ethnology/social anthropology generalizes and typologizes on the basis of ethnographies, and it is a commonplace that archaeology depends ultimately on ethnography for its cultural interpretations.

[2] It is significant that Olmsted in a general survey of the relations between linguistics and ethnology made in 1950 envisaged nothing like the present adaptation of linguistic methods to ethnography.

may now be room for a more informal, less technical characterization. The sections which follow attempt to present briefly and in rather general terms the main features of ethnoscience as a method, and to indicate some of the areas in which further work is needed. Usually, examples are either not given, or not described in sufficient detail for adequate comprehension of their relevance. The sources cited should be examined for more complete exemplification.

PRINCIPLES

1. *Etics and emics*

If a folk classification is ever to be fully understood, an ethnoscientific analysis must ultimately reduce to a description in terms approximating culture-free characteristics. Colours may be among the significant features in a folk taxonomy of plants; but colour itself is classified by principles which differ from culture to culture, hence is a domain which must be analysed ethnoscientifically before the botanical folk taxonomy is translatable into our terms (Conklin, 1955). Enough is known about colour, and the classificatory features involved are ordinarily sufficiently concrete, so that the colour classification of a given culture may be relatable to culture-free physical and physiological features. Obviously there are very few aspects of culture where reductionism of this type is even remotely foreseeable. In domains where such reduction is not yet possible, the local perceptual structure may nevertheless be largely discoverable, even though incompletely translatable (see now Frake, 1964, p. 134). In fact, in some domains the very difficulties in observation which prevent the outside observer from analysing the significant features in culture-free terms also force the bearers of the culture to utilize explicit verbalized defining attributes in learning and communicating about their own folk classification – hence make easier the discovery of attributes on this level – in contrast to classifications where the objects and their attributes are so concrete and frequent that the classifications may well be learned by exemplification rather than description (Frake, 1961, pp. 124–5). Nevertheless, full understanding of a culture or an aspect of a culture and particularly its full description in a foreign language require the ultimate reduction of the significant attributes of the local classifications into culture-free terms. Lamb's discussion of the relationship between his semantic and sememic strata, and the parallel relationship between the phonetic and phonemic strata (Lamb, 1964, pp. 75–7), is highly relevant here.

Culture-free features of the real world may be called 'etics' (Pike, 1954). The label may also be applied to features which are not truly culture-free, but which at least have been derived from the examination of more than one culture, or to the sum of all the significant attributes in the folk classifications of all cultures. Most of ethnography has operated with characteristics of this sort; ethnology has devoted much attention to the accumulation and systematization of features which *might* be significant in any folk classification, but it has given little attention to comparison of folk classifications or their principles as such. These results are by no means wasted from the point of view of ethnoscience: the ethnographer's knowledge of etics assists him in discovering the locally-significant features by guiding his initial observations and formulation of hypotheses.

Pike contrasts an etic approach with one which he calls emic, which amounts to an ethnoscientific one: an attempt 'to discover and describe the behavioral system [of a given culture] in its own terms, identifying not only the structural units but also the structural classes to which they belong' (French, 1963, p. 398). An emic description should ultimately indicate which etic characters are locally significant. The more we know of the etics of culture, the easier is the task of ethnoscientific analysis. Thus the great attention to kinship in the past, as well as the great amount of knowledge concerning cultural variability in kinship terminologies (the basic paper on the etics of kinship being a half century old: Kroeber, 1909) is one reason why emic analyses of kinship are easier than those of art, or law, or religion. Better knowledge, at least among anthropologists, of the physiology and physics of colour than of taste or smell more readily permits an ethnoscientific analysis of colour, even though it is clear (Conklin, 1955) that a folk domain including colour need not be congruent with what the physicists understand by colour. It seems probable that the vast accumulation of anthropological (both ethnological and archaeological) knowledge of the etics of material culture will allow the ethnoscientific approach to be quite readily applied in this presently-neglected field. Furthermore, in material culture the objects classified are concrete and easily examined and usually readily observable in many examples during the time available for normal fieldwork – in contrast to diseases, deities, etc. In classifications of concrete but natural, noncultural phenomena such as plants and animals, the range of variation which is classified is both extreme and beyond the direct control of the classifiers, who must select only certain features to which classificatory significance is given (Lévi-Strauss, 1966, pp. 73–4). But with cultural artifacts the corpus is smaller and the significant features are largely produced by the classifiers and hence should be more distinctive and more readily recognizable; also the ethnographer can here subject at least some of the features to controlled variation in order to test informants' reactions to their significance (cf. Berlin and Romney, 1964, for an illustration of some of these advantages).

The nature of learning and of communication implies that a culture consists of shared classifications of phenomena, that not every etic difference is emic. But it should be emphasized that an emic analysis refers to one society, to a set of interacting individuals. Cross-cultural comparison, if we take culture in Goodenough's sense, is another level of analysis which involves the comparison of different emic systems. There is no reason why one should expect to find emic regularities shared by cultures differing in space or time. Thus Dundes's 'emic units in the structural study of folktales' (1962) are not emic units in the sense here intended, in so far as the 'systems' of which they are analytical units is comparative (an etically defined 'motif', 'tale', or 'tale type', whose actual manifestations in different cultures are treated as 'variants'). On the other hand, Lévi-Strauss's brief characterization of some of the defining attributes of the 'gustèmes' of the English, French and Chinese cuisines (1963) is a comparison of the emics of different cultures, although the emic analysis of each of the three cuisines is not presented in sufficient detail to be convincing. Even so, 'slippage back and forth between individual systems, and any and all systems, as context for structural relevances, recurs in his [Lévi-Strauss's] work' also; 'the first step in a resolution of the problem ... is to refer structural contrast exclusively to within the domain of individual systems, where its cognitive basis can be empirically warranted' (Hymes, 1964, pp. 45, 16).

2. *Domains*

One of the most important principles of ethnoscience, and one of those most often overlooked, is the necessity for determining in a non-arbitrary manner the boundaries of the major category or classification system being analysed, i.e. for discovering how a domain is bounded in the culture being described rather than applying some external, cross-cultural definition of the field. If this is not done, the description of the internal structuring of the domain is likely to be incomplete if not entirely erroneous, and the utility of the analysis for predicting the classificatory placement of new instances will suffer. (See now Hymes, 1964, pp. 16–18)

Any two cultures differ in the way they classify experience. Everyone with any familiarity with more than one realizes that this is true for the lower, more specific classificatory categories, and trivial examples are easily found. But we cannot assume that the higher, more general levels of the folk classifications of different cultures will coincide either; there is no reason to suppose that the total range of a set of categories will match that of the 'corresponding' set in another culture even though the ranges of the lower categories in the two sets are different.

Thus every anthropologist recognizes that 'uncle' is not a universal category, but most seem to suppose that 'relative' or 'kinship' is – i.e. that a set of categories defined by consanguinity and affinity is everywhere a 'natural' set, that features such as ritual relationships must somehow be always outside the core system; the term 'fictive kinship' is significant of the analytical bias. In contrast, Conklin (1964) specifically does not assume that 'kinship' is a domain everywhere bounded in the same manner.

It is also customary to assume that everywhere there are just two systems of kinship terms: those used in 'reference' and those used in 'address'. Thus an *a priori* decision is made as to the significant defining features and the number of coexistent systems. Such an analysis of the American kinship system blurs many distinctions: 'mother's brother' and 'father's brother' are required instead of 'uncle' in some referential contexts; different forms of address are often used to differentiate co-resident 'grandmothers' or 'mothers' (Mo vs WiMo/ HuMo); such terms as 'father, dad, daddy, pop, old man' are not synonymous.

> The classic distinction between terms of address and terms of reference is not of much help in dealing with the American system. It tends to obscure certain important processes, partly, at least, because it presumes that there is a single term used in all referential contexts. . . . In the contemporary American system the wide variety of alternate forms allows them to differentiate a variety of different contexts. (Schneider and Homans, 1955, pp. 1195–6)

It seems probable that these 'alternate forms' would turn out to be quite systematically structured, that several domains could be specified, were the contexts to be analysed ethnoscientifically. One would expect a higher degree of agreement between informants in the usage of these terms if the contexts were discovered by the observation of natural situations or the asking of natural questions than is the case when informants are asked (e.g. Lewis, 1963) to sort the 'alternates' into contexts which are supplied ahead of time by the investigator, even though he himself is an American.

Frake (1960, pp. 58–9) has made the same point with regard to the Eastern Subanun. Conklin (1951) described several Tagalog 'co-existing sets of relationship terms', with their defining contexts. Swartz (1960) shows the relevance of situational environments to the choice between two Trukese terms. According to Chao's analysis (1956), there are three major sets of Mandarin Chinese kinship terms, which are not entirely synonymous even in their kinship referents; furthermore, the contexts in which Chinese 'terms of address' (pronouns, kinship terms, proper names and titles) are used can be analysed in terms of the intersection of seven main categories of hearers and ten main categories of person spoken of or addressed (Chao, 1956). Presumably this kind of situation is quite general. Yet Norbeck can still conclude a discussion of the 'errors' in Morgan's schedule of Japanese kinship terms by urging 'the importance of making clear distinctions between terms of address and terms of reference' (1963, pp. 214) when it is clear from his preceding discussion (and from Befu and Norbeck, 1958) that there are many more than two systems here, and that some of Morgan's 'errors' in fact represent accurate reporting of one of these systems.

The arbitrary delimitation of major domain boundaries persists in kinship studies even though the analytical procedures here are the most developed ones in ethnography. It is an even more obvious fault in other areas. Many of the difficulties, for example, in discussions of 'primitive art' are seen in a new light when one ceases to assume that 'art' is a universal category. The assumption that 'cultures . . . have in common . . . a uniform system of classification . . . a single basic plan' (Murdock, 1945, p. 125) is stifling to ethnoscientific analysis.

There may be domains – perhaps kinship is one of them – which are more nearly universal than others, where cross-cultural comparison would show greater sharing of significant features for higher level taxa than for lower level ones. But this is a significant hypothesis to be tested by the comparison of domains from different cultures, each analysed without prejudice, rather than being a postulate determining the delimit-ation of domains to be analysed. Prior assumption of the universality of domains, as in much work on kinship and other domains (e.g. colour), prejudges the case and masks some of the variability the explication of which is a classical task of anthropology.

But procedures for the definition of domains are not yet well worked out – this remains one of the more difficult problem areas of ethno-science (Conklin, 1962a, p. 124, and 1964; Öhman, 1953; Voegelin and

Voegelin, 1957). However, the problems do not differ in kind from those involving the identification of categories on lower levels, or the discovery of significant contexts or environments.

3. *Terminological systems*

Research in ethnoscience so far has concentrated on classifications as reflected by native terminology, on 'discerning how people construe their world of experience from the way they talk about it' (Frake, 1962, p. 74).

The analysis of a culture's terminological systems will not, of course, exhaustively reveal the cognitive world of its members, but it will certainly tap a central portion of it. Culturally significant cognitive features must be communicable between persons in one of the standard symbolic systems of the culture. A major share of these features will undoubtedly be codable in a society's most flexible and productive communication device, its language. (Frake, 1962, p. 75. Cf. Conklin, 1962a; Goodenough, 1957; Lounsbury, 1963.)

The main evidence for the existence of a category is the fact that it is named. As a result, the analyst faces the problem of locating *segregates* (segregate: 'any terminologically-distinguished . . . grouping of objects', Conklin 1962a, pp. 120–1; Frake, 1962, p. 76). Much work on the 'Sapir-Whorf hypothesis' has assumed that any morpheme, word, or grammatical construction labels a category of meaning, that the semantic structure of a language is built up only of these units. But it is clear that contrasting categories within a terminological system, and within a single level of a system, are frequently named with units whose position in the strictly linguistic system vary markedly – morpheme, word, phrase, etc. (Conklin, 1962a; Frake, 1961, 1962; Lounsbury, 1956, pp. 190–2). These labels of classificatory categories, whatever their grammatical status, have been called 'lexemes'. Alternatively, a lexeme is a 'meaningful form whose signification cannot be inferred from a knowledge of anything else in the language' (Conklin, 1962a, p. 121; see also Weinreich, 1963, pp. 145–6; Lamb's use of the term [1964] is nearly equivalent). Thus for example 'stool' is a lexeme in English, and *kwêi chéi* ('stool') is a lexeme in Burmese labelling an approximately equivalent segregate, even though *kwêi* ('dog') and *chéi* ('leg[s]') are also nouns occurring independently as labels for other segregates. The analyst must differentiate between lexemes and other linguistic forms of similar grammatical status which do not serve as segregate labels. The solution of this problem depends partly on knowledge of the language, both comprehension of it and technical knowledge of its structure. Comprehension is required because translation prior to semantic analysis causes insuperable difficulties because of the incommensurability of the semantics of any two languages (Conklin, 1962a, pp. 125–7, gives a nice example). Furthermore, in practice much of the best data comes from observing linguistic behaviour outside the formal eliciting situation with an informant. One task of ethnoscience, in fact, can be viewed as the solution of the old problem of translation.

Knowledge of the linguistic structure is necessary because the category names belong to two systems, one linguistic and one nonlinguistic; or, in Lamb's terms (1964), because lexemes are related by representation to both the morphemic and sememic strata. 'While identity between the two planes is incomplete, it is a useful starting-point from which to describe the lack of isomorphism actually found' (Weinreich, 1963, p. 117). Lamb (1964, pp. 62–6) catalogues the different possible discrepancies between units on different strata.

The many discussions within linguistics of the relevance of meaning to the analysis of phonology and grammar apply here also; even if form and meaning are in principle independent, or at least not isomorphic, and if (as some have maintained) an appeal to meaning is methodologically unsound in linguistic analysis, nevertheless the practice of linguistic fieldwork has established that in order to get the job done within a reasonable time, on the basis of a corpus of practical size, it is essential to appeal to meaning in some manner – by the same or different test, the pair test, or some less explicit test where the linguist is analysing his own native language (see Voorhoeve, 1961, pp. 41–2, on the semantic element in such tests). The converse applies to ethnoscientific analysis: although the two systems are not entirely congruent, the overlap is sufficient so that an 'appeal to linguistic form' is a very useful field technique in working out a terminological system. In fact, the development of ethnoscience will certainly eventually assist strict linguistics in handling the 'problem of meaning'.

Efforts to discover nonterminological systems in such areas as behaviour units (Barker, 1963; Barker and Barker, 1961; Barker and Wright, 1955), folktales (Lévi-Strauss, 1955; Leach, 1961c), and values (Kluckhohn, 1956, 1958) have not employed rigorous, replicable procedures for identifying units without the application of criteria foreign to the cultures analysed; in this regard they differ little from many previous ethnographies. These studies attempt to discover classifications without first establishing the communication systems by which they are transmitted.

Nonlinguistic communication systems are also structured. Birdwhistell's work with kinesics (1952) and Hall's with proxemics (the structuring of space in interpersonal relations: 1963a, 1963b) are concerned with establishing the units of the codes, and to some extent with discovering categories of meanings, but both jump to rather anecdotal cross-cultural comparisons before working out the structure of any one system. The nonisomorphism of sememic and lower strata can be expected to hold here also. Other communication systems are also relevant, including paralanguage (voice qualities and nonlinguistic vocalizations; see Trager, 1958). Material culture resembles language in some important respects: some artifacts – for example, clothing – serve as arbitrary symbols for meanings (i.e. noniconic signs: Goodenough, 1957) and occur in a limited number of discrete units whose combinability is restricted. Possibly complex phenomena of aesthetics would yield to a similar approach. Studies in these areas are potentially of much importance for ethnography, and it seems wise not to restrict the meaning of ethnoscience to the study of *terminological* systems.

4. *Paradigms and componential analysis*

A key concept in ethnoscience is that of the contrast set. This is a class of mutually exclusive segregates which occur in the same culturally relevant environment (setting, context, substitution frame, surroundings, situation, etc.). These segregates 'share exclusively at least one defining feature' – i.e. that which characterizes the environment in which they occur (Conklin, 1962a, p. 124; cf. Frake, 1962, pp. 78–9). The domain of the set is the total range of meanings of its segregates.

The notion of contrast is relative to the environment within which it occurs. Thus the mutual exclusion in English between 'ant' and 'ship' (Conklin, 1962a, p. 127) or between 'hamburger' and 'rainbow' (Frake, 1962, p. 79) is not contrast in this sense, because the environment which they share is not culturally relevant. As Frake (1962, p. 79) puts it, 'In writing rules for classifying hamburgers I must say something about hot dogs, whereas I can ignore rainbows. Two categories contrast only when the difference between them is significant for defining their use. The segregates "hamburger" and "rainbow", even though they have my members in common, do not function as distinctive alternates in any uncontrived classifying context.' Although 'ant', 'ship', 'hamburger' and 'rainbow' are all 'things', the subsets of 'things' to which they belong are so far removed from each other that these four segregates themselves are never distinctive alternates. Any culturally significant partitioning of 'things' would involve contrasts between segregates on a much higher level. Lower level environments are of primary importance – in this case, for example, the environment in which such segregates as 'hamburger', 'hot dog' and 'cheeseburger' contrast, and the environments in which such adjacent segregates as 'sandwich', 'pie' and 'something to eat' occur (Frake, 1962, pp. 78–82).

One may conceive of a contrast set containing only one segregate; if, as seems likely, there are no complete synonyms, then every segregate does occur in an environment which no other segregate shares. But 'contrast' implies that the set contains at least two segregates, and the term is normally understood in this way. Since these minimal two contrast in the same environment, each must have some unique feature of meaning.

A paradigm is a set of segregates which can be partitioned by features of meaning, i.e. a set some members of which share features not shared by other segregates in the same set (Chafe, 1962; Conklin, 1962a, p. 132; Goodenough, 1956a, pp. 197, 202; Lounsbury, 1960, pp. 127–8.) A set of only two segregates can be considered a paradigm, but normally the term is applied to sets of three or more segregates, so that at least some of the subsets consist of two or more segregates sharing some feature of meaning.

It is important to note that while all contrast sets are paradigmatic, not all paradigmatic sets are *complete* contrast sets. A paradigmatic set may not be equivalent to its containing contrast set: it is possible to analyse paradigmatically a collection of items which do not *exclusively* share any feature, which do not exhaust the membership of a class occurring in a single environment (Conklin, 1964). Thus Burling (1963) has made a paradigmatic analysis of a set of 'core kinship terms' which however do not form a complete contrast set – there is no culturally relevant environment which differentiates these terms from the other Garo kinship terms. A parallel example from phonology (where a paradigm involves phonetic rather than semantic features) is Chafe's (1962, pp. 338–9) paradigm of English consonant phonemes, which excludes some phonemes (*l*, *r*, perhaps also *y*, *w*, *h*) which are included in the relevant contrast set.

This difference between a paradigm and a contrast set is not always recognized in ethnoscientific work. Yet if the analysis is required to reflect the cognitive system of the bearers of the culture, before attempting a paradigmatic analysis one should show that one is dealing with a

C

complete contrast set, that there is a culturally relevant environment in which all and only the segregates in the set occur. This is the problem of definition of domains seen from a somewhat different angle.

A componential analysis is an analysis of a paradigm in terms of the defining features, the 'dimensions of contrast' of 'criterial attributes' of the segregates in the set. The aim is to discover the 'rule for distinguishing newly encountered specimens of [a] category from contrasting alternatives' (Frake, 1962, p. 83). The procedure is to search for the minimum features of meaning which differentiate segregates in the set. Each feature has two or more contrasting values, termed 'components'. Each segregate is then defined in terms of the presence or irrelevance of each component; i.e. a bundle of components defines the segregate. It is normally assumed that the number of componential dimensions will be smaller than the number of segregates they define. The paradigm may then be viewed as a multidimensional structure, in which the categories are placed according to the componential dimensions. (Useful references on componential analysis include Conklin, 1962a, 1964; Frake, 1962; Wallace, 1962; Lounsbury, 1956; Goodenough, 1956a; Sebeok, 1946; Chafe, 1962. Lamb's [1964] sememes are similar to, if not identical with, the semantic components of these authors.)

There are two points of view regarding such componential analyses (Burling, 1964). According to one of them, the componential analysis should reflect the classificatory principles utilized by the bearers of the culture, the components should be 'cognitively salient'; such an approach has been labelled an aim for 'psychological reality' (Wallace and Atkins, 1960, p. 64). However, this is a difficult requirement: such features are often not consciously formulated,[1] and furthermore different bearers of the same culture may utilize different features and yet share the same categories and communicate perfectly (Wallace, 1962). The other position is what Wallace and Atkins (1960, p. 64) refer to as an aim for 'structural reality', and what Lounsbury calls a 'formal account'. This position drops at this point the requirement that an ethnoscientific analysis should reflect the cognitive world of the bearers of the culture being analysed. Having discovered the culturally-significant sets and their included units, say these workers, we now try

---

[1] I well remember once asking my father, a specialist on the taxonomy of the Diptera, how he could so readily identify Drosophila to the species in a glance at his collecting bottle. He replied, 'How do you tell a horse from a cow?' The answer may at first seem surprising, coming from one intimately familiar with precisely those characters taxonomically significant for differentiating the species, but the situation is surely quite an ordinary one for biological systematists no less than for others.

to determine the most economical componential analysis which will define (or 'generate') their paradigmatic relationship – we are concerned only with predictability, economy and inclusiveness, not any longer with cognitive saliency. Others take an intermediate position, and allow the use of hints from the culture in deciding between variant componential solutions which are equally or nearly equally economical – for there will often (if not always) be such variants, and furthermore the criterion of economy (simplicity, parsimony) is not an easy one to define and apply (see R. Wells, 1963, p. 42, on this last point). Romney and D'Andrade (1964) discuss this problem, and illustrate some testing procedures for determining the cognitive saliency of alternative componential analyses of the same set of terms. Cancian (1963) has illustrated another method, which may be used to evaluate a componential analysis of a multi-position classification. If it is possible to determine the position in this classification of some items whose exact position is not known to all informants familiar with the classification, the correctness of the components used in setting up the classification can be tested by means of the magnitude of informants' errors in placing items unknown to them. If errors are extreme, the classification is shown to be erroneously understood by the ethnographer. 'When an informant makes an error that results from lack of precise information, he is most likely to approximate the truth in terms that are meaningful to him' (Cancian, 1963, p. 1073).

Weinreich (1963, pp. 148-9) points out that componential analysis is more appropriate in some domains than in others. In a given culture, some domains will be more highly patterned; in these, 'distinguishing components recur in numerous sets of signs, [whereas] the bulk of the vocabulary is of course more loosely structured and is full of components unique to single pairs, or small numbers of pairs' of segregates. While componential analysis is still possible in these latter 'non-terminologized fields', Weinreich suggests that the cognitive saliency of components will be greater in the more structured domains and the validity of the componential analysis can be more readily checked by informants' reactions in these domains.

It is important to note that not every componential analysis is ethnoscientific. Semantic and ethnoscientific studies have adapted the method from its use in another area, phonology (e.g. Harris, 1944). When semantic componential analysis is applied to paradigms which are not complete contrast sets, the results are not strictly ethnoscientific. Furthermore, the method essentially amounts to focusing on the differentiating features of a classification rather than on its categories or pigeonholes. Hence any classification is amenable to analysis resembling a componential one, and the technique is very useful for extending and elaborating purely etic typologies having nothing to do with ethnoscience. Thus, for example, Pike (1943) was able to improve greatly on existing compendia of articulatory phonetics by attending to the distinctive features of previous phonetic typologies, and extending and recombining them to produce new phonetic types and a more logical classification. Similarly, Balfet (1952) produced the best available typology of basketry techniques by abstracting the components of previous classifications and rearranging them to produce logical grids with many new classificatory slots, some of them as yet unknown in actual specimens even though fully possible. Malkiel (1962) describes a typology of dictionaries which explicitly borrows from the method of componential analysis.

5. *Taxonomies*

Different segregates within a folk classification may be related to each other in various ways: as part to whole, as sequential or developmental stage to stage, as different grades of intensity, etc. (Conklin, 1962a, p. 129, and 1962b; Frake, 1964). The kind of relationship between segregates which has so far received the most attention is that of inclusion; segregates related in this way form a taxonomy – a folk taxonomy in the case of folk classifications. In a taxonomy, there is a series of hierarchical levels, with each segregate at one level included in (only) one segregate at the next higher level. It is sometimes possible to analyse componentially a contrast set which forms one level of a folk taxonomy, but it is impossible to analyse in this way the whole taxonomy, even though the boundaries of the whole must define a domain: a single contrast set is limited to one taxonomic level (Conklin, 1962a, p. 128, and 1964; Frake, 1962).

A single folk classification may contain sets of segregates interrelated in different ways. From one point of view, any folk classification is a taxonomy since the domain or environment of the whole classification may be taken to define the most inclusive taxonomic level. But if the segregates within such a classification are not further related by inclusion, the taxonomy has only two levels and is relatively uninteresting as such; what is then more interesting is the kind of nontaxonomic relationship between the lower level segregates. A folk taxonomy of more than two levels, interesting as such, may also contain within it segregates which are interrelated in some nontaxonomic way (e.g. as developmental stages) which together form a domain which itself is placed within a taxonomic series.

Some attention has been devoted to folk taxonomies, particularly in ethnobotany, and the prospects are good for comparisons of folk taxonomic principles intra- and interculturally, but much of the methodology still requires attention. Further discussion will be found in Conklin's recent (1962a) excellent general treatment of folk taxonomies.

6. *Discovery procedures*

Since the ethnoscientific method aims at discovering culturally relevant discriminations and categorizations, it is essential that the discovery procedures themselves be relevant to the culture under investigation. While arbitrary stimuli – i.e. stimuli foreign to the culture – may yield nonrandom responses, the patterning involved derives from the cognitive system of the bearers of the culture, and the principles of this system are not likely to be made clear by answers to the wrong questions. Regularities will appear if one measures continental European manufactured goods with an American or British yardstick, but measuring with a metre stick will much more readily reveal the principles of the system relevant in European culture.

If an ethnography is to reflect the cognitive system of the bearers of a culture, the validity of the description depends on the discovery procedures. Hypotheses must be checked in the field situation, and revised if they turn out not to fit the field data. Thus it is impossible to make a strictly ethnoscientific analysis of data previously collected, by oneself or by someone else, according to different procedures. Any componential or similar analysis made of such old data must be treated as an inadequately checked hypothesis. Structural restatements of even the best old field data may prove impossible. Lévi-Strauss illustrates some difficulties which

> result from our ignorance of the observations (real or imaginary), facts, or principles which inspire the [folk] classifications. The Tlingit Indians say that the wood worm is 'clever and neat', and that the land-otter 'hates the smell of human excretion'. The Hopi believe that owls exert a favorable influence on peach trees. If these attributes were taken into account in placing these animals in a [folk] classification of beings and objects, one could search indefinitely for the key,

were not these minute but precious indications furnished by chance. (Lévi-Strauss, 1966; 1962 ed., p. 81: my translation)

Criterial attributes must be investigated in the field.

The general principle here is widely recognized, but only very recently has attention been devoted to making explicit the discovery procedures involved. Discussion and exemplification so far have concentrated on the use of questions in the native language and *chosen from the customary repertory* of the culture being studied. Frake's explication of interlinked topics and responses of queries in Subanun is an excellent example. His general suggestions on distinguishing questions which are appropriate to particular topics from those which are inappropriate (1964, pp. 143-4) should be particularly noted. Sarles (1963) describes a related procedure, in this case applied to Tzotzil, for identifying questions and their responses in conversational texts, determining acceptable permutations of the questions, and manipulating these to discover classes of appropriate responses. Metzger and Williams, in a series of papers as yet only partly published, have emphasized the discovery, selection, and use of question 'frames' appropriate for eliciting specific folk classifications, particularly among the Tzeltal and Ladinos of Chiapas (Metzger, 1963; and Metzger and Williams, 1962, 1963a, 1963b, 1966, 1967). These papers are important particularly in that the frames utilized are explicitly stated, as a means of ensuring replicability and demonstrating the reliability of the analyses. Conklin (1964) has suggested some improvements in the genealogical method applicable to field studies of kinship systems, including the use of question frames, the recording of conversations in native settings,[1] and the use of 'ethno-models' or native metaphors and diagrams of classifications (including diagrams volunteered by informants to aid in explaining to the ethnographer and influenced by observation of the ethnographer's charting attempts).

The emphasis on the classes of responses elicited by appropriate questions is beginning to show the expectable extreme complexity of the cognitive map of any culture, with multitudinous interlocking and overlapping contrast sets. Even so, these papers concentrate on the discovery of categories and their significant environments; as yet

[1] Definitions of categories in response to an explicit question about classification may differ from the definitions implicit in the actual conversational use of the same categories. Thus I recently heard my sister's husband refer to my wife in speaking to a friend of his who does not know her; he said, 'My sister-in-law is a good cook.' I then asked him, 'Do you call your wife's brother's wife your sister-in-law?' 'No', he immediately replied, and remarked that he had done so 'because it was easier than explaining'.

insufficient attention has been devoted to the development of reliable techniques for elucidating the further underlying complexities in cognitively salient semantic components.

I have already mentioned the relevance of ethnoscientific methods to material culture, where the possibility of pointing to and manipulating concrete objects may partially replace the use of question frames and the reliance on terminological systems in eliciting significant categories and contrasts. Another area where similar comparison of concrete cultural manifestations may be possible is music. Recent published discussions by ethnomusicologists of their problems in developing appropriate notation systems imply, at least to a nonspecialist, that the etics in this field have developed to the point where the application of ethnoscientific methods would resolve many difficulties and lead to a true *ethno*musicology (see Bright, 1963, pp. 28–31).

CONCLUSIONS

It is claimed that ethnoscience is a general ethnographic method. It may be useful to indicate a few of the classical interests of ethnology to which the relevance of the new methods is already quite obvious. The measurement and significance of individual variation among bearers of a culture is touched on in ethnoscientific contexts by Frake (1964), Romney and D'Andrade (1964), and Metzger (1963), among others. Lévi-Strauss (1962, 1966) has devoted much attention recently to symbolism seen as the equating and movement between folk classifications in different domains. It seems likely that there are great differences between cultures in the pervasiveness of symbolic or metaphoric equation between folk classifications; the Dogon (Hopkins, 1963; Griaule and Dieterlen, 1954; Palau Marti, 1957, pp. 53ff.) and the Ancient Chinese (Bodde, 1939) seem to exhibit such symbolism to a higher degree than is indicated by the usual ethnographic literature for most other cultures. Perhaps this is best viewed as one aspect of the interlinking of domains noted by Frake (1964, p. 140); the manner in which these networks may be revealed by Frake's interlinking queries promises to clarify some of the meanings of the concept of function in cultural analysis. Barnett's view of the process of innovation makes particularly obvious the relevance of ethnoscience to the study of culture change. He sees innovation as essentially a process of cognitive reorganization, where innovators substitute an element from one folk classification into another, and this often by a sort of idiosyncratic metaphorical equating of different domains (Barnett, 1961; see Wallace, 1961a, Ch. 4, for a critical expansion of this idea). Adams (1962), in a somewhat similar approach to culture change, is examining changes in the formal definitions and the frequency of occurrence of behavioural segments.

Ethnoscience raises the standards of reliability, validity, and exhaustiveness in ethnography. One result is that the ideal goal of a complete ethnography is farther removed from practical attainment. The full ethnoscientific description of a single culture would require many thousands of pages published after many years of intensive fieldwork based on ethnographic methods more complete and more advanced than are now available. The emphasis in ethnography will therefore continue to be guided by ethnological, comparative, interests. Some domains will receive more attention than others.

In the present state of interest in cross-cultural comparisons, continued ethnoscientific emphasis on domains such as kinship is assured. Existing generalizations require testing, and new theories require development, by the comparison of ethnographic statements which reveal the relevant structural principles. It is the classificatory principles discovered in ethnography which should be compared, not the occurrence of categories defined by arbitrary criteria whose relevance in the cultures described is unknown (cf. Goodenough, 1956b, pp. 36–7).

But fuller development of ethnographic method and theory, and also intracultural comparisons to determine the 'nature of culture' or the nature of cognition, the generality and interrelations of classificatory and other cognitive principles and processes within any one culture, both require that the New Ethnography be applied to a variety of domains, not just to areas of much current interest in ethnological theory.

Cross-cultural comparison of the logic of classification requires a great deal more knowledge of the varying logics of different domains in the same culture, as well as better ethnographies of different cultures.

It is probable that the number, kind and 'quality' of these logical axes [of relations between classificatory categories] are not the same in different cultures, and that the latter could be classed as richer or poorer according to the formal properties of the reference systems they appeal to in erecting their classificatory structures. However even cultures less endowed in this respect operate with logics of several dimensions, of which the inventorying, analysis, and interpretation require a richness of ethnographic and general data which is too often lacking. (Lévi-Strauss, 1966, pp. 85–6: my translation)

Ethnoscientific work so far has concentrated on the sorts of cognitive structure involved in selection classes: the interrelations of categories considered as sets of possible alternatives under varying environmental conditions. Little attention has yet been paid to the methods required for the investigations of the sort of structures involved in rules of combination, the temporal or spatial ordering of co-occurring categories from different selection classes. To understand 'how natives think'[1] we need to know about both kinds of structure.

[1] The phrase is the translator's title of one of Lévy-Bruhl's books. But of course, as Lévi-Strauss stresses (1966), 'la pensee sauvage' is typical of us all.

3

J. A. Fishman (1960)

A systematization of the Whorfian hypothesis

Behavioral Science, 5(4), pp. 323–39

INTRODUCTION

During the late twenties and throughout the thirties two American linguists – Edward Sapir and Benjamin Lee Whorf – strikingly formulated anew the view that the characteristics of language have determining influences on cognitive processes. Since the languages of mankind differ widely with respect to their structural, lexical, and other characteristics, it followed that monolingual individuals speaking widely different languages should, therefore, differ with respect to their symbolically mediated behaviours. This formulation immediately rekindled interest in this topic area among linguists and social anthropologists and, with the passage of time, their interest has been increasingly transmitted to general semanticists, psychologists, social psychologists, and sociologists. Currently, interest in the Whorfian hypothesis (at times also referred to as the Sapir-Whorf hypothesis, the Korzybski-Sapir-Whorf hypothesis, the linguistic Weltanschauung hypothesis, and the linguistic relativity hypothesis) is high – although there is no little difference of opinion as to its proper interpretation, its limits, its verifiability, and its validity. This essay represents an attempt by a social psychologist to systematize some of the work in this problem area.

SOME LANGUAGE-THOUGHT RELATIONSHIPS NOT SUBSUMABLE UNDER THE WHORFIAN HYPOTHESIS

Since psychologists have been crucially interested in the impact of verbal habits on other kinds of behaviour from the very beginning of the emergence of psychology as a scientific discipline (viz. Ebbinghaus's work with nonsense syllables, 1897, and Galton's with word association, 1879), it is probably desirable to begin our deliberations with a clear indication as to why most of these studies are *not* concerned with the phenomena of interest to students of the Whorfian hypothesis. The classical psychological interest in this area is in terms of language as a human capacity. Psychologists have not been noticeably concerned with the unique 'Englishness' of English and how it affects cognition – in the individual and in the culture – differently than the 'Navahoness' of Navaho. For the large number of American psychologists who have in recent years reported on the impact of verbal habits on perception (e.g. Solomon and Howes, 1951; Miller, Bruner and Postman, 1951; Postman and Conger, 1954; Postman and Rosenzweig, 1957), the fact that the language involved was English was of no particular concern. The same is true of those who have earlier and also recently studied the relationship between language and learning (e.g. Lyon, 1914; Gates, 1917; Tsao, 1948), language and memory (e.g. Reed, 1924; Miller and Selfridge, 1950), and language and thinking (e.g. Eidens, 1929; Sells, 1936; Wilkins, 1928). Similarly, the studies of Piaget (*1923*), Vygotski (1939), Luria (1959), and other European psychologists in this tradition have not been interested in the unique or characteristic verbal habits of *French*-speaking or *Russian*-speaking individuals and how such habits uniquely or characteristically affect *French* thinking or *Russian* thinking. Even those studies that have worked with various 'levels of approximation' (in an information theory sense) to the actual word sequences or letter sequences of some language (usually American English) have not been reacting to anything different in this respect than they would have been interested in were they working with some entirely different written or spoken language.

Furthermore, the 'other variable' in all of these studies (whether this other variable be perception, learning, memory, reasoning, etc.) is of interest to the psychologist only as it is manifested through verbal habits. Thus, Woodworth and Sells (1935) are not concerned with the impact of verbal or symbolic habits on nonverbal reasoning. Rather, they are interested in *reasoning with verbal or symbolic materials* to determine how such reasoning is affected by our long ingrained verbal or symbolic habits. Similarly, Postman and his students and colleagues (references cited above) have been concerned not with the impact of *verbal* habits on the perception (visual or auditory) of *nonverbal* stimuli, but, rather, with the extent to which and the ways in which verbal habits control the perception of verbal stimuli. In other words, most classical psychological research in this area is not really concerned with the relationship between verbal habits on the one hand and certain nonverbal or nonlinguistic behaviours on the other.

Although the Whorfian hypothesis has been discussed via data at various levels of linguistic and nonlinguistic behaviour, it differs from most psychological research dealing with the impact of verbal habits on behaviour either in *one* or in *both* of the respects indicated above:

a. Research pertaining to the Whorfian hypothesis is concerned with those verbal habits that derive not from the mere fact of having acquired language but, rather, with those verbal habits that derive from some characteristic or unique aspect of one or more *given* languages. Thus, the Whorfian hypothesis is not so much concerned with verbal determinism in general as it is with relative linguistic determinism based upon contrasts between the characteristics of specific languages.

b. Much, though by no means all, research on the Whorfian hypothesis is concerned with relating these data pertaining to the unique characteristic nature of one or more given languages to some nonlinguistic behaviours of the individual speakers of these languages.

THE WHORFIAN HYPOTHESIS: A BRIEF HISTORICAL
INTRODUCTION

As is the case with many of the most fertile ideas of interest to social scientists today, it is possible to trace back some of the ingredients which go to make up the Whorfian hypothesis at least to the mid-nineteenth century, if not further. That multifaceted genius, Wilhelm von Humboldt, ventured to say in 1848 that 'man lives with the world about him principally, indeed . . . exclusively, as language presents it' (cited by Trager, 1959). Although we may not now agree that von Humboldt demonstrated this proposition, we must admit that he and his followers amassed a wealth of linguistic evidence from language groups all over the globe in the process of their dedication to this proposition. In fact, it is from their early efforts that ethnolinguistics arose as a recognizably separate area of scholarly activity. It was also in reaction to this activity that a particular brand of logical and scientific criticism developed which long steered the major body of American linguistics away from ethnolinguistic concerns. This criticism was derived from the superficiality of the data and the prematureness of the conclusions via which ethnolinguistics arrived at the conclusion that the 'soul of a people' and the 'mind of a people' was not only reflected by its language but, indeed, shaped by it.

Humboldtian ethnolinguistics itself has long and intricate roots in the folklores of many peoples. The association between a people's individuality and its language is certainly an ancient one in the history of Western and Near Eastern civilizations. The ancient Greeks applied the term 'barbarians' (those who say ba-ba, i.e. speak an incomprehensible tongue) to those to whom the gods had denied the gift of Greek, and the ancient Hebrews believed that their language was a uniquely holy vehicle that was created even before the world was brought into being and awarded to them as a particular gift of God. Certainly, linguistic awareness, linguistic pride, a belief in linguistic specialness and in the inherent untranslatability of one's own vernacular or some other superposed language have been frequent components of the ethnocentrism and the world views of many peoples, past and present. The Whorfian hypothesis represents a groping toward the scientific restatement and the objective evaluation of language-and-behaviour phenomena that are related to this ill-defined pre-scientific and value-laden area that has hitherto been shaped primarily by strong beliefs and emotions. The Whorfian hypothesis essentially represents an attempt to study linguistic relativity by the means of modern social science methods.

Among the earliest post-Humboldtian attempts to point out the linguistic relativity of symbolically mediated behaviour were those made by the father of American anthropology, Franz Boas. An accomplished comparative linguist (i.e. a disciplined student of the structures of various languages), even by present-day standards, Boas claimed that a 'purely linguistic inquiry' provided the data for 'a thorough investigation of the psychology of the peoples of the world' (1911b). The linguistic data obtained for this purpose Boas considered as superior even to that derivable from psychology directly, due to the fact that informants are more nearly unconscious of the categories in their thinking which language as such reveals.

With the writings of Edward Sapir, we approach the more direct and immediate antecedents of the Whorfian hypothesis. Sapir was a student of Boas and, like his teacher, firmly convinced that language could be regarded as the raw material of which a people's outlook on the world is fashioned. In 1929 Sapir wrote:

> ... The 'real world' is to a large extent unconsciously built up on the language habits of the group. The worlds in which different societies live are *distinct* worlds, not merely the same world with different labels attached. We [as individuals] see and hear and otherwise experience very largely as we do because the language habits of our community predispose certain choices of interpretation.

Here we find clearly expressed a theme to which Whorf and others have returned time and again, namely that language is not 'merely' a vehicle of communication by which man talks about some objective reality 'out there' that exists previous to and independently of his language, but, rather, that language itself represents an objective reality by means of which man structures and organizes the 'out there' in certain characteristic ways. Thus, when languages differ maximally, the organizing schemata which their speakers impose on the non-linguistic world should also differ maximally. In his own words, Sapir claims that language 'does not as a matter of actual behavior stand apart from or run parallel to direct experience – but completely penetrates with it' (1933).

Although Sapir was certainly interested in linguistic relativity and convinced of its validity, his primary scientific and speculative contributions were made in connection with other topic areas. Benjamin Lee Whorf, on the other hand, devoted himself to the advancement of the hypothesis that now carries his name almost from the very beginning of his systematic work in linguistics up until the time of his premature death. In a series of articles – most of which have at long last been gathered together in one publication (Carroll, 1956) – based primarily on analyses of American Indian languages (but also, at times, based on other non-European languages), Whorf constantly reiterated his conviction that a generally unrecognized 'principle of relativity' was operative. In accord with this principle, 'observers are not led by the same picture of the universe, unless their linguistic backgrounds are similar or can in some way be calibrated' (1940).

Whorf's writings have become a common ground on which the interests of many linguists, anthropologists, social psychologists and sociologists come together. Its attraction lies both in its dimly recognized reference to the classical problems of cultural differences, cultural relativity, and cultural universality as well as in its provocativeness for modern, interdisciplinary, objective research. When Whorf says that 'there is a precarious dependence of all we know upon linguistic tools which themselves are largely unknown or unnoticed', he hits all of us where it hurts most – at the foundations of our certainty in our scientific findings and in our everyday decisions. When he attacks the view that grammars are 'merely norms of conventional and social correctness' and claims that they are, instead, the cement out of which we fashion experience, we feel that he must either be pointing at an unnoticed and potentially dangerous popular fallacy or tilting at non-existent windmills. When he says that 'we cut up nature – organize it into concepts – and ascribe significances as we do ... largely decause of the ... absolutely obligatory ... patterns of our [own] language', he stirs in us both our ethnocentric group-pride as well as our universalistic anti-ethnocentrism. In short, Whorf (like Freud) impugns our objectivity and rationality. It is not surprising then that recent years have seen many logical as well as not a few experimental efforts to evaluate and re-evaluate both the conceptual and the empirical grounds upon which the Whorfian hypothesis rests.

LEVEL I. LINGUISTIC CODIFIABILITY AND CULTURAL REFLECTIONS (THE FIRST LANGUAGE-LANGUAGE LEVEL)

The weakest level of the Whorfian hypothesis (in the sense of being least pretentious or least novel) is that which provides evidence that languages differ 'in the same ways' as the general cultures or surrounding environments of their speakers differ. Evidence along these lines has long been provided by ethnologists and folklorists, and its fragmentary and belated presentation by Whorfians can hardly be considered as either a serious contribution to the social sciences generally or as a substantiation of higher levels of the Whorfian hypothesis specifically.

From the point of view of the language data presented at this first level of argumentation, it is not the grammatical structure as such that is under consideration but, rather, the lexical store or the so-called 'semantic structure'. Actually, that which is dealt with at this level might be referred to in present-day terms as contrasts in *codifiability*. Language X has a single term for phenomenon *x*, whereas language Y either has no term at all (and therefore refers to the phenomenon under consideration – if at all – only via a relative circumlocution) or it has three terms, y_1, y_2, and y_3, all within the same area of reference. As a result, it is much *easier* to refer to certain phenomena or to certain nuances of meaning in certain languages than in others. Thus, codifiability is also related to the question of translatability and to 'what gets lost' in translation from one language to another.

The examples that have been given at this level of analysis are legion and no attempt needs to be made to exhaustively catalogue them here. At times they are not accompanied by any explicit claims as to how the noted codifiability differences are related to implicit or explicit cultural differences. The fact that there is no handy English equivalent for the German *Gemütlichkeit* is rarely explained as an indication that Germans *are* more *gemütlich*. The fact that there may not be an exact semantic ('connotative') equivalence between *horse*, *cheval*, and *pferd* is not seriously attributed to different cultural roles for horses or for man-horse relationships in the three cultures from which these words are derived.

Nevertheless, there have been attempts to relate codifiability differences of the above type to behavioural differences. Usually, the behaviour under scrutiny in this connection is *language behaviour*, and the evidence advanced as to the parallelism between *selective codifiability as an aspect of a given language* and *the language behaviour of the speakers of that language* is, at this level of analysis, of an anecdotal or fragmentary variety. Thus, the fact that the German language docs have the term *Gemütlichkeit* does make it *easier* for Germans to be aware of and to express this phenomenon. Americans can also struggle toward a circumlocutious formulation of this concept, but the very fact that it is a struggle may mean that the concept is less clearly formulated and less aptly as well as less frequently expressed. Gastil's concept of *polysemy* (1959) is also relevant at this level. In some languages, certain words have additional shades or ranges of meaning than their cognates or best equivalents in other languages. Thus, in French, one term is used for both 'conscience' and for 'consciousness'. On the one hand, this means that French speakers do not have as *easily* available to them a distinction that we have. On the other hand, it means that they have more easily available to them a partial identity of these two terms that it is very difficult for us to fully appreciate. Lindeman (1938) has demonstrated from textual analysis how this linguistic identity has led to a greater conceptual fusion between these two usages on the part of French philosophers than is true for English or German thinkers. Gastil gives several other examples of polysemy (1959), particularly as between English and Persian, which convincingly demonstrate that code efficiency is differentially selective in different languages with the result that what is easily expressible in one language is not necessarily easily or accurately expressible in another.[1]

Assuming that the above holds true, the question still remains as to whether these observations are really pertinent to the Whorfian hypothesis. Seemingly so, for Whorf himself frequently presents data of this variety. Admittedly Whorf's examples are largely drawn from American Indian languages (and contrasted with American English), and the implication is therefore strong that we are not only dealing with groups whose languages differ markedly but whose lives and outlooks

---

[1] I have previously pointed to codifiability as a precursor of language behaviour in such diverse areas as social stereotyping (Fishman, 1956) and witness performance (Fishman, 1957). In general, to the degree that we are here dealing with codifiability, in the absence of any consistent cultural context our concern with the impact of language habits on language performance is only a shade different than that of the studies that we have previously characterized as not being subsumable under the Whorfian hypothesis.

also differ greatly. Nevertheless, at *this* level of analysis, Whorf (and others even more frequently than he) does not take pains to relate linguistic factors to nonlinguistic ones, but merely presents an enchanting catalogue of codifiability differences. English has separate words for 'pilot', 'fly' (n.), and 'airplane', but Hopi has only one. Eskimo has many words for different kinds of 'snow' but English has only two. On the other hand, Aztec has only one basic word for our separate words 'cold', 'ice', and 'snow'. We have one word for 'water', whereas Hopi has two, depending on whether the water is stationary or in motion. English has such words as 'speed' and 'rapid', whereas Hopi has no real equivalents for them and normally renders them by 'very' or 'intense' plus a verb of motion. English has separate terms for 'blue' and 'green' but only one term for all intensities of 'black' short of 'grey'. Navaho, on the contrary, does not have separate highly codeable terms for 'blue' and 'green' but does have two terms for different kinds of 'black'. English has the generic term 'horse' but Arabic has only scores of different terms for different breeds or conditions of horses. The kinship terminology in some languages is certainly vastly different (and in certain respects both more refined and more gross) than it is in English. In all of these cases, it is not difficult to relate the codifiability differences to gross cultural differences. Obviously, Eskimos are more interested in snow, and Arabs in horses, than are most English speakers. Obvious, also, is the fact that these codifiability differences help speakers of certain languages to be more easily aware of certain aspects of their environment and to communicate more easily about them. This, essentially, was the lesson we learned from Bartlett's early work on remembering (1932). In this sense, then, their languages structure their verbal behaviour in a nontrivial way and ostensibly also structure their preverbal conceptualizations as well.

Other phenomena

Before proceeding to a summary and evaluation of this particular level of the Whorfian hypothesis, it might be well briefly to point out other phenomena that are subsumable under it. The 'phatic communion' concept which Malinowski introduced so long ago (1923), and which so many have quoted but which few have elaborated, may in large part be seen as a codifiability phenomenon at the language-language level. It is probable that all traditioned groups, particularly those sharing many intimate and heightened experiences, develop differential codifiability in their languages. As a result, it is quite likely that they then find it easier, more meaningful, and more accurate to communicate their unique or characteristic experiences in their own language than in any other. The elliptic, highly abbreviated, seemingly mysterious, and nonverbal aspects of 'phatic communion' (to outsiders) may be no more than a result of the differences between what are readily encodeable messages (verbal and nonverbal) for any group in its own language, and what are readily encodeable (and therefore decodeable) messages for some other group of observers who are 'outsiders'. In a sense, we are dealing once more with the relative translatability of the supposedly untranslatable. Since differential codifiability is so very often a correlate of distinctive cultural patterns, it seems quite understandable why most speakers of a language come to feel that no other language can as adequately cope with the very nuances of meaning and the very experiential patterns which are most significant to them in terms of their cultural distinctiveness. From this awareness it is but a short jump to language loyalty and language glorification. Thus, 'word magic' may not be nearly as primitive, childish, or illogical as Freud suggests. There is magic indeed in a language whose differential codifiability makes it peculiarly suitable for the expression of an individual's most central personal and cultural experiences. In contrast to such a language, all others must seem pale indeed.

In conclusion, it must be said that the evidence for the Whorfian hypothesis at this first level is concerned neither with a truly *structural* analysis of language nor with a full-blooded analysis of the *nonlinguistic concomitants* or resultants of language structure. In dealing with language-language relationships, the data are presented in a seemingly anecdotal and selective manner which fails to convince those who require more disciplined and organized approaches both to data and to demonstration. Nothing as grandiose as a 'world view' is produced by data at this level, although quite frequently we must admit that the reporter gives much evidence of having fully immersed himself in the language and culture under study. Whorf himself is truly amazing in this last respect. Nevertheless, this first level is certainly a comedown from the more advanced levels of argumentation that he pursued. Perhaps this can be explained by his sheer fascination – often quite emotional in tone – with the American Indian languages which he had mastered. Undoubtedly the great structural differences between these languages and those that he almost disdainfully called 'Standard Average European' (1941) provided much of the intellectual stimulation for his linguistic relativity hypothesis. On the other hand, he seems so fond of 'playing' with these languages, fondling and dissecting their units of expression, that he may have been unable to withstand the temptation to do so even when he was not contributing thereby to the ultimate argument that he sought to advance. If we are to be satisfied only with the first level just discussed, then we can conclude no more than has Gastil in his discussion of polysemy, namely that

> Languages differ as to the presence or absence of the field distinctions which they make. A language may be seen as a limited group of words and forms available for the use of a man thinking or expressing himself in the medium of that language. If he does not have the means to do a certain job of thinking or expressing, that job will not be accomplished as well as if he had such means. (1959)

Whorf would probably not have settled for as limited a claim as the foregoing.

LEVEL 2. LINGUISTIC CODIFIABILITY AND BEHAVIOURAL CONCOMITANTS

At the second level of analysis of the Whorfian hypothesis, we leave behind the limitations of *inference* from codifiability in language to ease of formulation or expression via language. That is to say, we leave behind the *language-language behaviour* level for the level in which *language-nonlanguage behaviour* becomes of paramount interest to us. That this is a necessary direction for our inquiry to take has been recognized by Carroll and Casagrande, who write in a recent preview of a forthcoming book:

> In order to find evidence to support the linguistic relativity hypothesis it is not sufficient merely to point to differences between languages and to assume that users of these languages have correspondingly different mental experiences. If we are not to be guilty of circular inference, it is necessary to show some correspondence between the presence or absence of a certain linguistic phenomenon and the presence or absence of a certain kind of non-linguistic response. (1958)

Note that the above quotation merely refers to '*a certain linguistic phenomenon*' rather than restricting the *type* of linguistic phenomenon that requires attention. The hallmark of the second level is that the 'predictor' variables seem once more to be of the lexical or semantic codifiability type (and in this respect similar to Level 1, discussed above), whereas the 'criterion variables' are of the nonlinguistic behaviour type (and in this respect different from, and an advance over, those encountered at Level 1). Thus far, there have been only a very few studies which strike me as operating at this level of analysis. The earliest one by far is that of Lehmann (1889) who demonstrated that identifying a different number with each of nine different shades of grey was of substantial help in behaviourally discriminating between these shades of grey. In essence, then, the numbers functioned as verbal labels. The availability (codifiability) of such labels for some *S*s resulted in much better discrimination-identification of the shades of grey than that which obtained in other *S*s who had to perform the same discrimination-identification task without being provided with such labels.

Some exceptionally interesting and sophisticated work with the codifiability concept in the colour area has more recently been reported by Brown and Lenneberg (1954) and by Lenneberg alone (1953, 1957). These investigators have shown that culturally encoded colours (i.e. colours that can be named with a single word) require a shorter response latency when they need to be named than do colours that are not culturally encoded (i.e. that require a phrase – often an individually formulated phrase – in order to be described). At this point, their evidence pertains to Level 1 that we have previously discussed. In addition, these investigators have gone on to show that the more highly codified colours are more readily recognized or remembered when they must be selected from among many colours after a period of delay subsequent to their original presentation. This finding was replicated among speakers of English and speakers of Zuni, although somewhat different segments of the colour spectrum were highly codeable for the two groups of *S*s. The investigators summarize their findings to this point as follows:

> It is suggested that there may be general laws relating codability to cognitive processes. All cultures could conform to these laws although they differ among themselves in the values the variables assume in particular regions of experience. (Brown and Lenneberg, 1954)

Going on from this original statement, Lenneberg (1957) has further refined its experimental underpinnings by showing that the *learning* of colour-nonsense syllable associations was predictably easier or harder as the learning task involved colour categories that varied in degree from the ones that were most commonly recognized by his English-speaking *S*s. He therefore concluded that 'there is good evidence that the shape of word frequency distributions over stimulus continua regulates the ease with which a person learns to use a word correctly'. This conclusion should be as applicable to original language learning as it is to second and to artificial language learning, for it basically pertains not to language usage *per se* but to concept formation as such. The colour continuum seems to be a particularly fortunate area in which to study codifiability-cognition phenomena precisely because it is a real continuum. As such, no 'objective' breaks occur in it and it is a matter of cultural or subcultural consensus as to just which breaks are recognized, just where on the spectrum they are located, and how much of a range they include. The demonstration that these various codifiability considerations influence recognition, recall and learning has been most fortunately executed. Lenneberg and Brown are also alert to the fact that at this level it is perfectly acceptable to work with intra-linguistic designs rather than to necessarily utilize the interlinguistic designs in terms of which the Whorfian hypothesis is most frequently approached. What is easily codifiable, and the specific range and content of easily codeable categories, does depend on the particular language under consideration. It also depends on the particular experiences of subgroups of speakers. As a result, contrasts in rate, ease or accuracy of various cognitive functions should be (and are) demonstrable both intralinguistically and interlinguistically as a function of codeability norms. Intralinguistic codifiability-cognition differentials in various natural population groupings should be of particular interest to students of social stratification.

Brown and Lenneberg have conducted their work with a conscious awareness of the Whorfian hypothesis and how it must be further specified or delimited. On the other hand, there have been other investigators who have also worked in the language-behaviour domain at this level without any particular awareness of the Whorfian hypothesis as such. If the organizational framework here being advanced has been insightfully developed, it should nevertheless be possible to subsume their findings within it. In fact, it may turn out that within the context of the Whorfian hypothesis these other studies will obtain a new coherence and provocativeness. As a start in this direction (and an exhaustive search of the literature would be necessary in order to seriously go beyond such a start), I would classify the oft-cited work of Carmichael, Hogan and Walter (1932) on memory for visual stimuli to which different verbal labels have been attached, as well as the problem-solving work of Maier (1930), and the transactional studies summarized by Kilpatrick (1955) on perceptual learning and problem-solving with and without verbal set as belonging at this level of analysis. These three last-mentioned studies also utilize intralinguistic designs.

The only study at this level that is directly inspired by the Whorfian hypothesis while utilizing an *interlinguistic* design is the one which Carroll and Casagrande refer to as 'Experiment I' (1958). In this study, fluent Hopi speakers were compared with two different groups of English speakers with respect to sorting or picture classifying behaviour. Utilizing the kind of lexic data that we have discussed in connection with Level 1, Carroll hypothesized that in each set of three stimulus plates Hopi speakers would more usually classify a certain subset of two as belonging together (because in Hopi the seemingly dissimilar activities depicted were nevertheless commonly 'covered' by a single verb) whereas English speakers would more frequently classify another subset of two as belonging together (because in English a single verb was commonly used in referring to them). Although Carroll's data are quite far from revealing a uniform association between 'Hopi categorizing responses' and Hopi speakers, or between 'English categorizing responses' and English speakers, they nevertheless do reveal quite a substantial tendency in that direction. In addition, his graduate student *S*s, whom we might have expected to be more 'verbally minded', give the predicted 'English categorizing responses' much more frequently than do his rural white *S*s.

All in all, this is certainly an experimentally exciting level of analysis and one which will undoubtedly develop further in the years ahead. It will certainly be subject to improved experimental techniques since those now working in it are themselves aware of improvements that they hope to introduce into their future work in this area. This would seem to be the level of the Whorfian hypothesis most likely to attract social psychologists and sociologists with empirical interests in language phenomena.

LEVEL 3. LINGUISTIC STRUCTURE AND ITS CULTURAL CONCOMITANTS

When we turn our attention from the second to the third and fourth levels of the Whorfian hypothesis, we progress from lexical differences and so-called 'semantic structure' to the more 'formal' and systematized grammatical differences to which linguists have most usually pointed when considering the structure of a language or structural differences between languages. There is some evidence that although Whorf and others may, at times, have reverted to lower levels of presentation and documentation they, nevertheless, did associate linguistic relativity in its most pervasive sense with structural (i.e. grammatical) rather than merely with lexical aspects of language. This is suggested by such formulations as Sapir's that meanings are 'not so much discovered in experience as imposed upon it, because of the tyrannical hold that linguistic *form* has upon our orientation to the world' (1912: my italics). Somewhat more forcefully stated is Whorf's claim that 'the world is presented in a kaleidoscopic flux of impressions which has to be organized . . . largely by the linguistic *systems* in our minds' (1940: my italics). More forceful still – and there are a large number of possible quotations of this kind – is Whorf's statement that

> . . . the background linguistic system (in other words, the gram-mar) of each language is not merely a reproducing instrument for voicing ideas, but rather is itself the shaper of ideas, the program and guide for the individual's mental activity, for his analysis of impressions, for his synthesis of his mental stock in trade. Formula-tion of ideas is not an independent process, strictly rational in the old sense, but it is part of a particular grammar and differs, from slightly to greatly, between grammars. (1940)

Finally, we may offer in evidence the paraphrasings of the Whorfian hypothesis by two eminent American linguists who have been both interested in and sympathetic to this hypothesis. The first of these says simply that 'It is in the attempt properly to interpret the *grammatical categories* of Hopi that Whorf best illustrates his principle of linguistic relativity' (Hoijer, 1954: my italics). The other, as part of a more extended and systematic argument, says

> Language as a whole has structure and all of its parts and sub-divisions also have structure . . . [if] the rest of cultural behavior has been conditioned by language, then there must be a relationship between the *structure* of language and the *structure* of behavior. (Trager, 1959)

The emphasis on language *structure* as the critical feature in his lin-guistic relativity hypothesis is actually a later and more mature level of Whorf's own thinking in this area. Sapir, on the other hand, as a pro-fessionally trained and professionally oriented linguist, was quite probably interested in language structure from the very outset. Whorf's intellectual and technical development in this topic area shows a tran-sition from diffuse and unsystematic lexical analyses to more focused and interrelated grammatical analyses, the turning point coming most noticeably after his studies with Sapir. Be this as it may, both levels of argumentation do appear in Whorf's writings and even his later writings reveal many instances of regression to the first level discussed above. Thus, it is not strange that in the deliberations of many other students of this problem, whether in the roles of protagonists or detractors, the distinction between the lexical and the grammatical levels of analysis has not been fully exploited.

At the third level of analysis, we once more find ourselves in a realm of rich though ambiguous anthropological and ethnological data. As was the case with Level 1, above, the direct association or chain of reasoning between grammatical structure on the one hand and 'something else' (be it *Weltanschauung* or even some less embracing segment of culture or values) on the other is not explicitly stated. Often, the 'something else' is not stated at all and yet there is the general implication that grammatical oddities of the type presented cannot help but be paralleled by unique ways of looking at or thinking about or reacting to the surrounding environment. Thus, one encounters such evidence as that Chinese has no singular and plural or that it has no relative clauses (which we English speakers *do* have), whereas other languages have more levels of grammatical number (including singular, dual, tri-al, and plural forms – which we English speakers do *not* have). In this vein, the cataloguing of grammatical differences can continue at great length (languages that do recognize gender of nouns and those that do not, languages that have tenses and those that do not, etc.); for both anthropologists, linguists, and a variety of nonspecialists have contributed to the fund of knowledge of phenomena of this type, always with the implication that it is clearly illogical to seriously suggest that linguistic phenomena such as these would have no relationship to life, to thought, and to values.

On the other hand, there are also several investigators that *have* attempted to indicate what the 'something else' might be. In contrasting Hopi with English, Whorf (1940) has pointed to such odd grammatical features in Hopi as the absence of tenses, the classification of events by duration categories such that 'events of necessarily brief duration (lightning, wave, flame, meteor, puff of smoke, pulsation) cannot be anything but verbs', the presence of grammatical forms for indicating the type of validity the speaker intends to attribute to his utterance (statement of current fact, statement of fact from memory, statement of expectation, and statement of generalization or law), etc. To Whorf all of these grammatical features seemed congruent with an outlook on life that was 'timeless' and ahistorical in the sense that past, present and future are seen as a continuity of duration, experience being cumulative and unchanging for countless generations. As a result of the 'timelessness' of Hopi life, it is of greater importance for Hopi speakers to distinguish between the duration of events and their certainty than to indicate when they occurred (1941). A similarly ingenious and sensitive analysis is followed by Hoijer (1951, 1954) in connection with the Navaho verb system in which there is no clean separation between actors, their actions and the objects of these actions. As Hoijer sees it, the Navaho verb links the actor to actions which are defined as pertaining to classes-of-being. Thus it would appear that people merely 'participate in' or 'get involved in' somehow pre-existing classes of actions rather than serve as the initiators of actions. Hoijer interprets these grammatical characteristics as being consistent with the 'passivity' and 'fatefulness' of Navaho life and mythology in which individuals adjust to a universe that is given. Finally, in Nootka, Whorf finds a connection between the absence of noun-verb distinctions and 'a monistic view of nature' (1940).

An example of work of this kind with modern European languages is provided by Glenn (1959). He points to the fact that the adjective most commonly precedes the noun in English whereas it most commonly follows it in French. The former pattern Glenn considers to be descriptive in a narrow or particularistic sense, more in keeping with inductive thought. The latter pattern he considers to be classificatory in a manner that moves from broader to narrower categories, as is the case with deductive thought. Glenn then proceeds to find 'inductiveness' in English behaviours of various kinds (an inductive legal system in which many minute precedents culminate in the inductive formation of the common law, local governmental jurisdictions, and greater attention to pragmatic detail rather than to all-embracing theoretical unities, etc.) and 'deductiveness' in diverse areas of French behaviour (a broad legal code first and then individual decisions deduced from it, centralized governmental authority, the primacy of broad theoretical and philosophical interests, etc.). Whorf, too, has dealt with the world view of Standard Average European speakers, concluding from grammatical analyses that it emphasizes the concrete or material and the quantifiable (1941).

The efforts by Whorf, Hoijer, Glenn and similar scholars (see e.g. Boas, 1938; Lee, 1944) merit considerable respect. They must be separated in our evaluation from pseudoserious efforts to attribute or relate the musicalness of Italians to the light, melodious nature of the Italian language, or the stodginess of Germans to the heavy, lugubrious quality of the German language, or the warm, folksiness of Eastern European Jews to the intimate emotional quality of Yiddish, etc.[1] Superficially, the two approaches may seem similar, but the latter approach does not even have a serious structural analysis of language to recommend it. Nevertheless, the appeal of the Whorfian hypothesis for some lies precisely in the fact that it attempts to apply modern scientific methods and disciplined thought to such 'old chestnuts' as the presumed 'naturalness' that Hebrew (or Greek, or Latin, or Old Church Slavonic) be the language of the Bible, given its 'classic ring' and its 'other-worldly purity'. However, with all of our admiration for those who have had the temerity as well as the ingenuity to attempt a rigorous analysis at this level, we must also recognize the limitations which are built into this approach. As many critics have pointed out (see e.g. Lenneberg, 1953; Gastil, 1959), the third level of analysis has not normally sought or supplied independent confirmation of the existence of the 'something else' which their grammatical data is taken to indicate. As a result, the very same grammatical designata that are said to have brought about (or merely to reflect) a given *Weltanschauung* are also most frequently the only data advanced to prove that such a *Weltanschauung* does indeed exist. Thus, once more, we are back at a language-language level of analysis (language structure ↔ language-behaviour-as-indication-of-world-view). Perhaps social scientists working together with linguists (or individuals trained in both fields) will ultimately be able to overcome this limitation as other evidence concerning national character and cultural mainsprings is amassed and systematized. As soon as there is sufficient 'other' data (based on analysis of folklore materials, personality data, value-orientation measurements, etc.) and sufficient agreement as to how such data should be interpreted, there might well be a kind of Human Relations Area File from which systematic variations in grammatical structure and systematic variations in value structure or lifestyle might be determined. This may not be too different from what Trager (1959) has had in mind in calling for greater attention to the recognition of structure in nonverbal areas of culture in order to push forward with research on the Whorfian hypothesis.

Pending the availability of such data, we might well consider that it is not the language-language nature of argumentation at this level that

[1] Whorf himself makes a disclaimer along these lines when he states, 'I should be the last to pretend that there is anything so definite as "a correlation" between culture and language, and especially between enthnological rubrics such as "agricultural, hunting", etc. and linguistic ones like "inflected", "synthetic", or "isolating" ' (1941).

is, *per se*, its greatest drawback, but rather its susceptibility to selective presentation and to biased interpretation. Verbal behaviour may long continue as our major avenue of insight into values and motives. What we must be ever more dissatisfied with, however, are the self-selected lists of grammatical examples and the self-selected enumerations of cultures, cultural values or themes, and the evidence pertaining to the existence of such themes. In attempting to avoid these particular pitfalls, students of the Whorfian hypothesis have increasingly come to express a preference for a study design which investigates the relationship between grammatic structure on the one hand and *individual* nonlinguistic behaviour on the other. Although this is both a logical and a very promising solution to many of the above-mentioned problems, there is nevertheless no need to conclude at this point in our knowledge that it is the only one possible.

LEVEL 4. LINGUISTIC STRUCTURE AND ITS BEHAVIOURAL CONCOMITANTS

The conceptual and methodological superiority of the fourth level of the Whorfian hypothesis is one thing. The accessibility of this level for study may well be quite another thing. It does seem that this level is in some ways the most demanding of all, for it requires detailed technical training at both the predictor and the criterion ends of the relationship to be investigated. This may be the reason why there currently appears to be only one study which might possibly be said to be an example of work at this level,[1] although in the future we might expect it to elicit greatly increased interest among sociolinguists and social psychologists with technical linguistic training. This is the study by Carroll and Casagrande which they refer to as Experiment II (1958). The grammatic features of interest to Carroll and Casagrande in this study are the particular verb forms required in Navaho verbs for handling materials in accord with the shape or other physical attribute (flexibility, flatness, etc.) of the object being handled. Note that Carroll and Casagrande are concerned here with distinctions in verb *forms* rather than distinctions between mere lexical absence or presence of verbs as such. Presumably it is this fact which permits us to consider Experiment II as a Level 4 study rather than as a Level 2 study. The

[1] Related to this level of demonstration, but dealing with artistic structure rather than linguistic structure, are the findings summarized by Hallowell (1951) on the impact of culturally defined artistic styles on individual perceptions of reality.

nonlinguistic data utilized by Carroll and Casagrande are the object-classifying behaviours of their *S*s when presented first with a pair of objects which differ from each other in *two* respects (e.g. colour and shape) and then with a third object similar to each member of the original pair in one of the two relevant characteristics. The *S*s were asked to indicate 'which member of the (original) pair went best with the (third) object shown him'. If the *S*'s reaction was governed by the requirements of Navaho verbal form, he would have to select a certain one of the original set of objects.

Carroll and Casagrande's hypotheses are quite explicitly stated: '(a) . . . that this feature of the Navaho language would affect the relative potency or order of emergence of such concepts as color, size, shape or form, and number in the Navaho-speaking child (specifically, that shape or form would develop earlier and increase more regularly with age, since this is the aspect provided for in the verb forms themselves), and (b) that he (i.e. the Navaho child) would be more inclined to perceive formal similarities (i.e. shape or form similarities) between objects than would English-speaking Navaho children of the same age.' Carroll and Casagrande also assure us that the verb stems in question

> compromise what Whorf has called a *covert class* and in the absence of native grammarians the pertinent grammatical rules operate well below the level of conscious awareness. Although most Navaho-speaking children, even at age 3 or 4, used these forms unerringly, they were unable to tell *why* they used a particular form with any particular object. Even when a child could not name an object – or may not have seen one like it before – in most cases he used the right verb form according to the nature of the object.

This last concern points up the importance of using unsophisticated *S*s in this area of research in the same way as this is an important requirement in many attitudinal, motivational, or other dynamic fields of inquiry.

Carroll and Casagrande's original *S*s were two very different groups of Navaho children – one being described as 'Navaho dominant' (i.e. *S*s who were either monolingual speakers of Navaho or else were bilinguals in whom Navaho speaking was dominant over speaking English) and the other as 'English dominant'. Finally, a further control group was obtained consisting of white middle-class children in the Boston area. All subjects were of roughly comparable ages. In many respects Carroll and Casagrande's findings are extremely favourable for the Whorfian hypothesis. The Navaho-dominant Navaho *S*s make the choices predicted by Navaho verb-stem requirements significantly more frequently than do the English-dominant Navaho *S*s. In addition, there is quite a consistent increase in the 'Navaho required responses' with age, although the Navaho-dominant *S*s make such responses more frequently at every age from 3 through 10. Thus, when only these two groups of *S*s are considered, the evidence is quite favourable to the Whorfian hypothesis – even though there is far from a one-to-one relationship between language dominance and object-classifying behaviour. However, when the data from the Bostonian *S*s are considered, some provocative difficulties appear. The white middle-class children from the Boston area are even more Navaho in their object-classifying behaviour than the Navaho-dominant *S*s![1] This superficially embarrassing finding is nevertheless of great provocative value both to Carroll and Casagrande and to all of those with concerns in this area, for it forces a consideration not only of the absence or presence of linguistic relativity in cognitive processes, but of the degree ('strength') of this relativity, as well as of its relative strength in comparison to other factors that may affect the direction of cognitive processes in various human groups. Perhaps, then, this may be the appropriate place to pause to consider this very matter.

THE DEGREE OF LINGUISTIC RELATIVITY

The fascination of the Whorfian hypothesis is in some ways compounded of both delights and horrors. We have already speculated concerning the delights. Let us now mention the horrors. The first is the *horror of helplessness*, since all of us in most walks of life and most of us in all walks of life are helplessly trapped by the language we speak. We cannot escape from it – and, even if we could flee, where would we turn but to some other language with its own blinders and its own vice-like embrace on what we think, what we perceive, and what we say. The second horror is the *horror of hopelessness* – for what hope can there be for mankind? What hope that one group will ever understand the other? What hope that one nation will ever fully communicate with the other? This is not the place for a full-dressed philosophical attack on

---

[1] Note: 'I have just within the past couple of months gotten additional data from an age and sex matched group of Harlem schoolchildren. Though by no means affording a perfect control group, I think it is a closer match to my English dominant Navahos than educationally advanced middle-class youngsters from Boston. . . . On inspection the results show the Harlem group to be very close to the English dominant Navahos and, of course, the same age trend shows up' (Casagrande, 1960, personal communication).

these issues. Let us merely consider them from the point of view of the kinds of evidence supplied by some of the very studies we have mentioned.

The most 'reassuring' facts that derive from Levels 1 and 2, the lexical and semantic codifiability levels of the Whorfian hypothesis, are that the noted nontranslatability and the selective codifiability really pertain not so much to all-or-none differences between languages as to differences in relative ease or felicity of equivalent designation. Whenever we argue that there is no English word (or expression) for —, which means so-and-so (or approximately so-and-so, or a combination of Y and Z) in English, we are partially undercutting our own argument. In the very formulation of our argument that there is 'no English word (or expression) for —' we have gone on to give an English approximation to it. This approximation may not be a very successful one but if that becomes our concern we can go through the contortions (both intellectual and gesticulational) that are required for an inching up on or a zeroing in on the non-English word or expression that we have in mind. The amount of effort involved may, at times, be quite considerable and even the final approximation may leave us dissatisfied. However, after all is said and done, this is not so different, in terms of both process and outcome, as the communication problems that we face with one another even within our *own* speech community. We can do no better than to quote Hockett's conclusions at this point, in support of what has just been said.

Languages differ not so much as to what *can* be said in them, but rather as to what it is *relatively easy* to say in them. The history of Western logic and science constitutes not so much the story of scholars hemmed in and misled by the nature of their specific languages, as the story of a long and fairly successful struggle *against* inherited linguistic limitations. Where everyday language would not serve, special sub-systems (mathematics, e.g.) were devised. However, even Aristotle's development of syllogistic notation carries within itself aspects of Greek language structure.

The impact of inherited linguistic pattern on activities is, in general, *least* important in the most practical contexts and most important in such 'purely verbal' goings-on as story-telling, religion, and philosophizing. As a result, some types of literature are extremely difficult to translate accurately, let alone appealingly. (1954)

Turning now to Levels 3 and 4, where we become concerned with the imbedded structural features of a language, it seems to be important that we realize that Whorf never proposed that *all* aspects of grammatical structure must *inevitably* have direct cognitive effects. Thus, to begin with, we are faced with the task of locating those few grammatical features which might have definable but unconscious functional correlates in our unguarded behaviour. This is what Hoijer has in mind when he points to

> ... Mark Twain's amusing translation of a German folktale into English, where he regularly translates the gender of German nouns by the English forms *he, she,* and *it.* [This] illustrates in caricature the pitfalls of labelling the purely grammatical categories of one language in terms of the active structural-semantic pattern in another. (1954)

Lenneberg too has pointed to this very same principle (1953) when cautioning us that differences in metaphorical development in various languages may not only have no differential conscious correlates, but no differential unconscious ones as well.

If we look to Levels 2 and 4, these being the levels in which the behavioural concomitants of linguistic features are experimentally derived, we once more must reach the conclusion that linguistic relativity, where it does exist, is not necessarily an awesomely powerful factor in cognitive functioning. The relationships that have been encountered, though clear-cut enough, seem to be neither very great nor irreversible in magnitude. The very fact that increased infant and early childhood experience with toys and objects requiring primarily a form reaction can result in a *Navaho-like classifying preference* among monolingual English-speaking children also means that other kinds of environmental experiences might very well produce an *English-like classifying preference* among monolingual Navaho-speaking children. No one has yet directly studied the success with which behaviour predicted on the basis of linguistic relativity can be counteracted by either (a) simply making Ss aware of how their language biases affect their thinking, or (b) actively training Ss to counteract these biases. It may be, after all, that this is an area in which Ss can, with relatively little effort, learn how to 'fake good'. Furthermore, one might suspect that the impact of language *per se* on cognition and expression ought somehow to be greater and more fundamental than the impact of one or another language feature. Thus the impact of language *determinism* upon cognition ought to be more pervasive and more difficult to counteract than that of language *relativity*.

None of the foregoing should be interpreted as implying that linguistic relativity, wherever it exists, is an unimportant factor in human experience or one that deserves no particular attention except from those who are professionally committed to unravelling the unimportant in painful detail. Quite the contrary; just because it is such a seemingly innocuous factor it is very likely to go unnoticed and, therefore, requires our particular attention in order that we may appropriately provide for it.

SUMMARY AND CONCLUSIONS

The four levels of the Whorfian hypothesis that have been presented here are essentially subsumable under a double dichotomy. As Fig. 3.1 reveals, we have essentially been dealing with two factors – one pertaining to characteristics of a given language or languages, and the other

	Data of language characteristics	Data of (cognitive) behaviour
	Language data ('cultural themes')	Nonlinguistic data
Lexical or 'semantic' characteristics	Level 1	Level 2
Grammatical characteristics	Level 3	Level 4

Fig. 3.1 Schematic systematization of the Whorfian hypothesis.

pertaining to behaviour of the speakers of the language or languages under consideration. The first factor has been dichotomized so as to distinguish between lexical or semantic structure on the one hand (both of these being considered as codeability features) and grammatical structure on the other. The second factor has been dichotomized so as to distinguish between verbal behaviour *per se* (frequently interpreted in terms of cultural themes or *Weltanschauungen*) and individual behavioural data which is other than verbal in nature.

In a rough way, we might say that Levels 1 and 3 are concerned with *large group phenomena* whereas Levels 2 and 4 are concerned with *individual behaviour*. Whorf was aware of and interested in both kinds of data, for he held that 'our linguistically determined thought world not only collaborates with our *cultural idols and ideals* but engages even our unconscious *personal reactions* in its patterns and gives them certain typical character(istic)s' (1941: my italics).

D

In general, Whorf is not deeply concerned with 'which was first, the language patterns or the cultural norms ?' He is content to conclude that 'in the main they have grown up together, constantly influencing each other' (1941).[1] Nevertheless, he does state that if these two streams are to be separated from each other for the purposes of analysis he considers language to be by far the more impervious, systematic, and rigid of the two. Thus, after a long association between culture and language, innovations in the former will have but minor impact on the latter, 'whereas to inventors and innovators it (i.e. language) legislates with the decree immediate' (1941). Although Whorf is leary of the term correlation it seems most likely that he considered language structure not only as interactingly reflective of 'cultural thought' but as directly formative of 'individual thought'. With proper cautions, the four levels of the Whorfian hypothesis that have been differentiated in this review may be seen as quite consistent with this conclusion.

Some of the characteristics, difficulties, and potentials of further empirical and theoretical study at each of the four differentiated levels have been considered. All levels can make use of both interlinguistic or intralinguistic designs, although Levels 1 and 3 most commonly employ the former – if only for purposes of contrast.

Although evidence favouring the Whorfian hypothesis exists at each level, it seems likely that linguistic relativity, though affecting some of our cognitive behaviour, is nevertheless only a moderately powerful factor and a counteractable one at that. Certainly much experimental evidence has accumulated that points to a large domain of contra-Whorfian universality in connection with the relationships between *certain* structures of particular languages and *certain* cognitive behaviours of their speakers (see Osgood, 1960, e.g.). The time might, therefore, now be ripe for putting aside attempts at grossly 'proving' or 'disproving' the Whorfian hypothesis and, instead, focusing on attempts to delimit more sharply the types of language structures and the types of nonlinguistic behaviours that do or do not show the Whorfian effect as well as the degree and the modifiability of this involvement when it does obtain.

Because of Whorf's central role in making us aware of this phenomenon so that we may now better come to grips with it, both intellectually and practically, none can deny that he richly deserves

---

[1] Sapir also takes this view in his article on language and environment (1912), in which he concludes that grammatical features once did correspond to environmental circumstances but have subsequently developed at a pace and in directions unrelated to environmental changes.

to be characterized by his own standard for what constitutes a real scientist.

All real scientists have their eyes primarily on background phenomena in our daily lives; and yet their studies have a way of bringing out a close relation between these unsuspected realms . . . and . . . foreground activities. (1940)

4

H. Maclay (1958)

An experimental study of language and nonlinguistic behaviour[1]

Southwestern Journal of Anthropology, 14(2), pp. 220–9

This experiment was designed originally to test the Sapir-Whorf hypothesis that the structure of a language conditions nonlinguistic behaviour and thought (Carroll, 1956; Mandelbaum, 1949; for a recent evaluation of this position see Hoijer, 1954). That it is something less than a clear test of this proposition is related to the fact that neither Sapir nor Whorf stated the hypothesis in a form that could be proved or disproved in a single experiment.

Most previous investigations have consisted of an *ad hoc* demonstration that, in a given situation, some aspects of language could be shown to be congruent with some, usually very general, aspects of nonlinguistic behaviour. The point at issue is whether accurate predictions about relatively concrete and specific behaviour in an experimental situation can be derived from the examination of language structure. The present study thus differs from most earlier work in three major respects: (1) the method of investigation is experimental rather than observational; (2) the predictions are made from present language to future behaviour; (3) the behaviour studied consists of specific instances rather than large-scale patterns.

[1] This paper is revised from a University of New Mexico Ph.D. dissertation in anthropology written under the direction of Stanley Newman, to whom I am indebted for both specific advice and general encouragement. The personnel of the United Pueblos Agency and the Albuquerque Indian School were most cooperative and made a special effort to procure subjects with the proper linguistic background, in addition to providing interpreters and space for the administration of the experiment. Charlie De Jolie acted as the Navaho linguistic informant, and provided the formal subject interview which contributed materially to the experiment. Roger W. Weldon offered many helpful suggestions on the experimental design and the statistical interpretation of the results. This investigation has also benefited substantially from discussions with the author's colleagues on the Southwest Project in Comparative Psycholinguistics sponsored by the Social Science Research Council.

The general proposition that the language of a group is not functionally independent of nonlinguistic factors would certainly meet with
little objection. Disagreements arise at the point where attempts are
made to specify the nature and direction of this relation. Both Sapir
and Whorf usually wrote as if language were the initiating factor. Given
this view, a convenient basis for prediction lies in the well known fact
that languages categorize the universe and, further, that referents united
in one language are separated in another. This being the case it should
follow that referents classified together linguistically are likely to be
classified together nonlinguistically. This can be stated more precisely
as follows:

> If it is highly probable that referents *x* and *y* will elicit the same
> linguistic response, this will increase the probability that they will
> elicit the same nonlinguistic response. Conversely, if they elicit
> different linguistic responses this should lower the probability that
> they will elicit the same nonlinguistic response.

Extending this to a cross-language comparison to develop a testable
hypothesis:

> If Language A unites referents *x* and *y* and Language B separates
> them, then speakers of Language A should be more likely than
> speakers of Language B to exhibit the same nonlinguistic response
> to them.

In this formulation a 'linguistic response' involves the oral production
of speech by an informant while a 'nonlinguistic response' refers to any
other behaviour. It is not obvious that such a rough distinction can
readily classify every instance of human activity but it does serve to
separate the particular behaviours used experimentally. 'Elicit' refers
to a procedure where an informant is shown potential referents and
asked to respond verbally (i.e. 'name them') or nonverbally (i.e.
'divide them into groups'). Referents that elicit the same response are
said to be 'united', either linguistically or nonlinguistically, while those
which elicit different responses are 'separated'. Linguistic responses are
the 'same' if they contain the same phonemes and morphemes in the
same order as previously defined by a linguistic analysis. 'Same' or
'different' for the nonlinguistic responses refers to the alternatives
present in the experimental situation.

The deduction of specific predictions from this general hypothesis
is contained in a later section following a description of the experimental design. It should be stated in advance that the writer was

thoroughly convinced that the hypothesis was sound and expected highly significant results.

EXPERIMENTAL DESIGN

This study focuses on the Athapascan-speaking Navaho of New Mexico and Arizona. The structural statement which provides the basis for predicting experimental behaviour is that of Hoijer who states:

> The Athapascan languages employ verb stems that refer not to a characteristic type of event, such as *stand* or *give* or *fall*, but to the class of object or objects conceived as participating in such an event, whether as actor or goal. . . . (Hoijer, 1945)

Of the formally distinct categories described by Hoijer, three were selected for inclusion in the experiment: 'long', 'rope-like', and 'fabric-like'. These will henceforth be called 'slender-rigid', 'slender-flexible', and 'flat-flexible', terms which make more obvious the physical characteristics of their referents. It should be noted that the English labels attached to these classes are a good, though not a perfect, approximation of their actual content in the case of the classes used experimentally. The practical consequences of this system are that one must use different stems in Navaho for saying 'I pick up a cigarette', 'I pick up a rope', and 'I pick up a blanket'. In his verbal behaviour a Navaho is thus in the position of having made very frequent distinctions among objects on the basis of their form. He should, therefore, make these distinctions more readily in his nonverbal behaviour than will a native speaker of a language not containing such obligatory distinctions.

A brief overview of the experimental design should make the detailed descriptions of procedure which follow more intelligible. Three groups of subjects were used: native speakers of Navaho, of English, and of a number of non-Athapascan American Indian languages. These were asked to divide sets of four objects into two groups of two objects each. Divisions could be made on the basis of the Navaho verb categories described above or on other grounds such as function or colour. The primary expectation was that Navaho subjects would make significantly more divisions on the basis of form than would members of the other two groups. A central methodological requirement was that the procedure be as nonlinguistic as possible: that is, an effort was made to prevent subjects from realizing that the experimental task had any connection with their language.

SUBJECTS

Sixty subjects were divided into three groups of twenty each. Sixteen high school students at the Albuquerque Indian School and four students at the University of New Mexico, all native speakers of Navaho, comprised the Navaho group. This group contained a range of English ability from none to almost perfect command. The group consisted of eleven females and nine males whose ages ranged from 14 to 30 years and whose mean age was 17·9 years.

Sixteen students from the Albuquerque Indian School and four students of the University of New Mexico, all native speakers of non-Athapascan Indian languages, constituted the Pueblo group. This group contained a range of English ability from fairly good to almost perfect command and consisted of twelve females and eight males. Ages ranged from 9 to 28 years with a mean age of 16 years. The members of this group were all from Pueblos in New Mexico and were distributed as follows: Isleta–3, Zuni–3, Laguna–3, Acoma–3, San Felipe–2, Santa Clara–2, San Ildefonso–2, Taos–1, and Sandia–1.

The English group consisted of twenty students at the University of New Mexico. All were native speakers of English and all were monolinguals, with the exception of one subject who had spoken French for a number of years. The group contained six females and fourteen males. Ages ranged from 17 to 34 years with a mean age of 21·75.

The types of subjects were chosen with several ends in mind. It had been demonstrated that the verb categories under consideration were obligatory in Navaho but not in any of the other languages represented. A minimum cross-cultural requirement could have involved a contrast between a Navaho group and a non-Navaho group. The English-Navaho comparisons would have satisfied this condition, but it seemed necessary also to have a non-Athapascan-speaking Indian group in order to ensure that the results would not merely reflect an Anglo versus Indian or majority–minority difference. The Pueblo group also acted as a check against the fact that the experimental materials were probably not equally familiar to Indian and non-Indian subjects.

MATERIALS

The materials consisted largely of objects common to American culture. There were forty-eight objects grouped in twelve items of four objects each. The items were further classified in four types of three items each. Objects are symbolized by small letters, items by Arabic numerals, and types by Roman numerals in this presentation. The Navaho verb categories are represented by SR (slender-rigid), SF (slender-flexible) and FF (flat-flexible); these are the categories reflected in the 'form' classification indicated below. The category contrast present in each item is described within the parentheses following the item number. The '*x*', '*y*' and '*z*' notations refer to the three sorts possible for each item and are defined as follows: '*x*' equals an ab/cd division, '*y*' an ac/bd division, and '*z*' an ad/bc division. The '*y*' division correlates with the Navaho verb categories in Types I, II and III.

Type I: Three bases for classification [(*x*): function or material; (*y*): form; (*z*): colour.]

Item 1 (SR *v*. SF):   a. blue ruler; b. green tape measure; c. green candle; d. blue electric cord.

Item 2 (SF *v*. FF):   a. blue rubber band; b. green rubber coaster; c. green cloth shoelace; d. blue handkerchief.

Item 3 (SR *v*. FF):   a. blue pencil; b. green sheet of paper; c. green shoelace; d. blue washcloth.

Type II: Two bases for classification [(*x*): function or material; (*y*): form; (*z*): none.]

Item 4 (SR *v*. SF):   a. metal bolt; b. flexible metal wire; c. cigar; d. string of artificial pearls.

Item 5 (SF *v*. FF):   a. metal spring; b. aluminium foil; c. strand of yarn; d. irregular piece of cloth.

Item 6 (SR *v*. FF):   a. metal needle; b. handkerchief; c. paper straw; d. sheet of paper.

Type III: One basis for classification [(*y*): form; (*x*) and (*z*): none.]

Item 7 (SR *v*. SF):   a. red ruler; b. gold coloured chain; c. wooden paint brush; d. length of rope.

Item 8 (SF *v*. FF):   a. red rubber mat; b. metal pull-chain; c. sheet of paper; d. length of ribbon.

Item 9 (SF *v*. FF):   a. metal nail; b. sheet of cellophane; c. wooden match; d. irregular piece of cloth.

Type IV: No basis for classification [(*x*), (*y*) and (*z*): none.]

Item 10: a. metal padlock; b. yellow crayon; c. plastic sphere; d. cork.

Item 11: a. leather wallet; b. plastic disc; c. rubber band; d. metal hook.

Item 12: a. sheet of plastic; b. rubber eraser; c. small stone; d. bells tied on a ribbon.

The item types were intended to contrast the Navaho verb categories with other ways of classifying the materials. They varied in the number of alternative possibilities placed in the materials by the experimenter.

PROCEDURE

The basic procedure required the subject to divide the four objects in an item into two groups of two objects each. Subjects were seated at a table facing the experimenter and given the following instructions:

> I'm going to put four objects along this line in the centre of the table. I want you to look them over and as soon as you become familiar with them, place two over here on the right and two over here on the left. You may find that they divide easily in two groups and, if you don't notice a natural pairing, and there may be none, please make a division anyway. There is no right division; I'm interested only in your own personal opinion. Now we'll have a couple of practice trials to give an idea of how this is going to work.

Each subject was given three pre-experimental trials to ensure his understanding of the instructions. The writer instructed all subjects except eight monolinguals in the Navaho group. In these cases the procedure was explained by regular Navaho interpreters employed at the Albuquerque Indian School. Each subject was given all twelve items with the order of items and the placing of objects from top to bottom on the table top being randomly varied. Subjects were not given a speed orientation.

Two scores were taken for each subject on each item: latency of response in seconds, and the division of objects (x, y or z). In addition to the scores describing experimental performance the linguistic background of each subject in the Navaho and Pueblo groups was obtained in an interview immediately following the experiment. The subject was asked to estimate for each period in his life whether he had spoken his native language all of the time, most of the time, half of the time, less than half of the time, or none of the time. This resulted in a five-cell table for each subject which contained the absolute number of years he had spent speaking only his native language, mostly his native language, etc. Weights of 1·00, 0·67, 0·50, 0·33, and 0 were assigned to the cells and the sum of the cells was then divided by the subject's chronological age to obtain his Language Experience Index or LEI.[1] The scores on this index can range from 0·000 (had never spoken language) to 1·000 (had spoken language in question exclusively). Although this is a very rough way of rapidly estimating the linguistic experience of an individual, it should correlate fairly well with degree of bilingualism as measured by other methods. It may also be regarded as a measure of acculturation, as experience with language inevitably implies contact with the culture that uses it. In this context an LEI of 1·000 would describe a relatively, but not necessarily completely, unacculturated person, and degree of acculturation would increase as LEI decreased.

There was a detailed interview with one Navaho subject on his reaction to the experiment and his interpretation of the whole situation.

EXPECTED RESULTS

A number of hypotheses were made in advance of the experiment. These are of three types: design validation, sorting and latency.

Design validation

1. The three groups should not differ significantly among themselves nor should any group depart significantly from randomness in the sorts made on Item Type IV. This type was designed to be a random array of objects and all groups should sort it randomly.

2. All three groups should have longer latencies for Item Type IV than for Types I, II and III. The random items, with no obvious classifications, should require a longer response time.

Sorting

3. The Navaho group should make significantly more *y* sorts than the other groups for Types I and II.

4. The number of *y* sorts made within the Navaho group should correlate positively with the LEI, but this correlation should either not exist or exist to a lesser degree in the Pueblo group. This suggests that the more experience a Navaho subject has had with his language, the more likely he is to sort in terms of its categories. The Pueblo, on the

---

[1] The quantification of this index was suggested by Dr Charles Solley of the Menninger Foundation.

other hand, should not show this correlation, since it is presumed that their native language experience has no systematic connection with the experimental materials.

Latency

5. The Navaho group should not differ in latency among Types I, II and III, while the English and Pueblo groups should have significantly longer latency for Type III than for Types I and II. The Navaho should have an equally available solution for all three types whereas the other groups should find Type III, with only a form solution, more difficult.

6. Navaho latencies for y sorts will be less than x or z sorts for Types I, II and III, and this difference will be greater than similar differences, if such exist, within the English and Pueblo groups. This, and the other hypotheses involving latency, are based on the common psychophysical assumption that a difficult task will be associated with a longer response time.

RESULTS

The results are organized in terms of their bearing on the hypotheses put forth in the previous section. Additional results of interest are also presented. Table 4.1 summarizes the sorting and latency results.

1. Chi-square tests on Type IV revealed no significant differences among the experimental groups and no significant variations from randomness in the sorting of any one group. This hypothesis is confirmed.

2. All groups had longer latencies for the random items of Type IV than for the items with built-in solutions, Types I, II and III. An analysis of variance compared the types with regard to latency for each group.[1] The English and Pueblo groups had F's significant at the 0·01 level of confidence while the Navaho F was significant at the 0·02 level. Thus the trend of a latency increase through the sequence of types is validated. However, the Navaho latency for Type IV does not differ significantly from the latency for Type III, while this difference is significant for the other two groups. This hypothesis is confirmed.

3. Chi-square tests were run on the sorting results for Type I, Type II, and the combined total of Types I and II, and in no case did signifi-

---

[1] The analysis of variance permits one to evaluate the differences among a group of means. The resulting value (F) can be tested for significance and the probability of the differences having arisen by chance can be stated. For a full explanation of this procedure, see Edwards (1950).

cant differences exist among the three groups although the Pueblos consistently made fewer *y* sorts than the other groups. An unexpected result was the almost identical Navaho and English performance on these two types. This hypothesis is not confirmed.

4. Product-moment correlations (*r*) were run between LEI and number of *y* sorts for the Navaho and Pueblo groups. The Navaho

TABLE 4.1. *Sorting*

Type	Group	Sort			Latency (seconds)
		x	*y*	*z*	
I	English	34	16	10	190
	Navaho	33	17	10	340
	Pueblo	41	12	7	337
II	English	38	21	1	251
	Navaho	39	19	2	370
	Pueblo	44	13	3	401
III	English	3	51	6	303
	Navaho	12	46	2	626
	Pueblo	17	34	9	484
Total (I, II, III)	English	74	88	17	744
	Navaho	84	82	14	1336
	Pueblo	99	62	19	1222
IV	English	15	21	24	461
	Navaho	11	29	20	738
	Pueblo	13	26	21	694

correlation (+ 0·48) was significant at the 0·05 level while the Pueblo correlation (+ 0·19) was nonsignificant. The difference between the *r*'s was significant at the 0·05 level using a one-tailed test. This hypothesis is confirmed.

5. The analysis of variance described under Hypothesis 2 showed a Navaho latency increase for Type III as against Types I and II significant at the 0·01 level. The same difference for the other groups is significant at the 0·05 level. This hypothesis is not confirmed.

6. Mean times for *y* sorts as against *x* or *z* sorts were obtained for each group. Both the Navaho and English groups took less time for *y* sorts than for *x* or *z* sorts, but these groups could not be separated by differences in relative latency. The Pueblo groups tended to have longer response times for *y* sorts than for *x* and *z* sorts. The results here are much like those under Hypothesis 3, with the Navaho and English groups falling together and the Pueblo group standing apart.

DISCUSSION

The confirmation of the design validation hypothesis (1, 2) on the presumed random sorting and increased latency for the objects in Type IV indicates that the subjects reacted to the items in terms of the possible solutions placed there by the experimenter. This is further supported by the sorting results for Types I, II and III where the built-in solutions were chosen far more often than the alternate possibilities where no obvious classification existed.

The central hypothesis of the study has been stated earlier:

If Language A unites referents x and y and Language B separates them, then speakers of Language A should be more likely than speakers of Language B to exhibit the same nonlinguistic response to them.

Of the predictions of experimental results only the correlation between LEI and number of y sorts in the Navaho and Pueblo groups occurred as expected, and this single affirmative result is weakened by the absence of the English group in the comparison. The direct comparison among the three groups with respect to both sorting and latency failed in every case to produce the expected differences (3, 5, 6). Clearly, the hypothesis must be rejected. This amounts to saying that, given a known linguistic category, it cannot be reliably predicted that nonlinguistic behaviour will correlate with it. The difficulty lies in specifying what 'united' and 'separated' mean in a concrete case. This arises from the fact that it is almost impossible to produce two objects that can be linguistically classified in only one way. The post-experimental interview with a Navaho informant who was asked to name the objects in the experiment and also to use them in the frame, 'I pick up a —', produced information which indicated that the verb categories were not the only bases for classifying the objects in terms compatible with prior linguistic experience with Navaho. It was sometimes the case that, in addition to the built-in form solution, two of the four objects in an item had the same name in Navaho and could thus be said to be classified together linguistically on a lexical basis.

If every object and event participates in a number of intersecting linguistic categories one can never make the absolute statement, 'Navaho does it this way', as if the language systematically cut the universe up into neat and mutually exclusive segments. It is rather the case that any language has a variety of alternative ways of classifying stimuli. If languages, then, can do anything, how can one possibly make meaningful predictions? A way out of this dilemma may lie in the distinction between language and speech or between language structure and language behaviour. The structure is the abstract statement of the potentialities of the system made by a linguist. Language behaviour is the observed verbal activity which such a statement describes. It is evident that a correlation will exist between the two if the structural statement is inadequate. This will not be a perfect correspondence, since a process of abstraction can never take account of every variation in the data which form its basis. A structural description, furthermore, consciously ignores certain aspects of language behaviour such as frequency of occurrence. Newman has stressed the importance of actual selection from structural alternatives in observational studies of relations between language and nonlinguistic patterns of behaviour (Newman, 1954). In the case of experimental investigations relative frequency will probably be an even more important variable; perhaps the single most significant factor. This suggests that experimentation should be preceded by a thorough investigation of actual usage on the language behaviour level. Several ways of grouping particular stimuli may be present in the structure; the experimenter must know in what proportion these are actually used.

It is probable that different linguistic structures have different potentials for indexing nonlinguistic behaviour. The results of this study indicate that direct predictions from structure, while they may correlate with large-scale cultural patterns, are not likely to predict more concrete behaviours accurately unless supplemented by information on frequency.

5

H. A. Witkin (1967)

Cognitive styles across cultures[1]

Extracted from *International Journal of Psychology*, 2(4), pp.233-50

The findings, concepts and methods that have come from recent extensive research on cognitive style have already been applied with profit to cross-cultural studies of psychological development; and because of its value in coping with some of the problems inherent in cross-cultural work, we may expect applications of the cognitive style approach to be more frequent in the future. Beyond their usefulness to students of culture, cross-cultural studies of cognitive style have great potential value for those interested in cognitive development. The opportunity to examine variations in cognitive functioning in a spectrum of naturally occurring variations in socialization may greatly enrich our understanding of the forces shaping cognitive development. 'Cognitive styles' are the characteristic self-consistent modes of functioning found pervasively throughout an individual's cognitive, that is, perceptual and intellectual, activities. They are now known to be manifestations, in the cognitive sphere, of still broader dimensions of personal functioning, evident in similar form in many areas of the individual's psychological activity. Cognitive styles thus speak on more than cognition. Evidence now exists that individual differences in cognitive style are related to differences in family experiences while growing up. To the extent that cognitive styles are end-products of particular socialization processes, they may be used in the comparative study of these processes. This paper seeks to illustrate the value of a cognitive-style approach to cross-cultural research by considering the work that has been done with one intensively studied cognitive style,

[1] Previously entitled 'A cognitive-style approach to cross-cultural research', and expanded from a paper presented at a symposium on Intercultural Studies of Mental Development, at the XVIIIth International Congress of Psychology, Moscow, August 1966. Portions of the work described in this paper were supported by a grant (M-628) from the US Public Health Service, National Institutes of Health.

the global-articulated dimension of cognitive functioning. Before reviewing these studies, it is necessary to characterize this cognitive style and to describe its connection to forms of functioning in other psychological areas. A sketch of our view of the development of this cognitive style in relation to development in other psychological areas will help suggest the kinds of socialization processes that may be influential in its formation. This view has been set forth in detail elsewhere (Witkin, Dyk, Faterson, Goodenough and Karp, 1962) and may be briefly sketched here.

THE GLOBAL-ARTICULATED DIMENSION OF COGNITIVE FUNCTIONING AND ITS RELATION TO OVERALL LEVEL OF DIFFERENTIATION

Perception may be conceived as articulated, in contrast to global, if the person is able to perceive item as discrete from organized ground when the field is structured (analysis), and to impose structure on a field, and so perceive it as organized, when the field has little inherent organization (structuring). Progress from global to articulated, which comes about with growth, occurs not only in perception, where we are dealing with an immediately present stimulus configuration, but in thinking as well, where symbolic representations are involved. Articulated experience is a sign of developed differentiation in the cognitive sphere. The self is as much a source of experience as the world outside. Development of experience of the self also shows a progression from global to articulated; and here again greater articulation signifies developed differentiation. It is likely that at the very outset of life, self and environment are experienced by the child as a more or less continuous body-field matrix. In time, boundaries between the body and the world are formed and some awareness developed of the parts of the body and their interrelatedness. The child's early global conception of his body is replaced by a more articulated body concept, that is, by an impression of the body as having definite limits or boundaries and its parts as discrete and interrelated in a definite structure. An articulated body concept signifies developed differentiation. Progress toward more articulated experience of the self also shows itself in growing awareness of needs, feelings and attributes which the child identifies as his own and as distinct from those of others, that is, a sense of separate identity which implies experience of the self as segregated and structured, in other words, articulated. A definite sense of separate identity may also be taken to indicate developed differentiation.

Extensive research (Witkin, Lewis, Hertzman, Machover, Meissner and Wapner, 1954; Witkin *et al.*, 1962) has shown that a tendency toward more global or more articulated functioning is a consistent feature of a given individual's manner of dealing with a wide array of perceptual and intellectual tasks. Because it represents the characteristic approach which the person brings to situations with him, we consider more global or more articulated functioning to be an individual's cognitive *style*. Research has shown that persons with an articulated cognitive style are also likely to give evidence of an articulated body concept and a developed sense of separate identity. Another way of casting these findings is to say that the person who experiences the field around him in relatively articulated fashion is also likely to show an articulated quality in experience which has body or self as its source. An articulated cognitive style, an articulated body concept and a sense of separate identity are all taken as indicators of developed differentiation. It has been demonstrated in many studies that persons who show these indicators of developed differentiation also show greater differentiation in their tendency to use structured, specialized defences and controls, as intellectualization and isolation, for channelling of impulse and expenditure of energy. In contrast, persons with a global cognitive style, and with it a global body concept and a limited sense of separate identity, are likely to use such defences as massive repression and primitive denial; because these defences involve a relatively indiscriminate turning away from perception of stimuli and memory for past experiences, they represent relatively nonspecific, and hence relatively less differentiated ways of functioning.

The fact that the various indicators of developed differentiation tend to 'go together' in the same person suggests that they are not discrete achievements of separate channels of growth but rather diverse expressions of an underlying process of development toward greater psychological complexity. To the extent that an articulated cognitive style is an outcome of differentiation of the psychological system as a whole, the effects of socialization upon development of cognitive style must be sought not only in social processes acting directly on the cognitive sphere but also in social processes which influence the overall development of differentiation. Of the social influences likely to affect the development of differentiation, and thereby cognitive style, the studies to be reviewed have focused mainly on the influences which may hamper or foster separate, autonomous functioning. Included have been the extent of opportunity and encouragement the child receives to achieve separation, particularly from the mother, in other words, to move toward self-differentiation. Another social influence that has been considered, closely related to encouragement of separation, and, like it, affecting development of autonomous functioning, is the manner of dealing with the child's expression of impulse. Imparting standards for internalization, which become the child's own, and within limits, allowing expression of impulse so the child may learn to identify his impulses and cope with them, are calculated to help the development of autonomous functioning. Some of the studies have also considered personal characteristics of the parents themselves which may influence their role in the separation process and in the regulation of impulse expression. The closely interrelated factors, handling of separation, regulation of impulse expression, and personal characteristics of parents affecting their part in these processes, constitute a 'socialization cluster' which influences a child's progress toward separate autonomous functioning, and thereby toward development of an articulated cognitive style.

The experiences that help shape a child's cognitive development have an additional source in the nature of the ecology in which he grows up. The factor of ecology seems particularly relevant to the global-articulated dimension. What difference may it make for a child's progress along this dimension whether he grows up in a variegated environment which is inherently highly structured, so that articulation is a 'given' of the field, or in a homogeneous environment which has little inner structure? The role played by ecology in the development of articulation is not to be defined in terms of objective properties of the field alone. What matters more is the kind of relation with the particular environment which life circumstances force upon the developing individual. The contribution of ecology, in this person-environment-interaction sense, to cognitive development is not readily separable from the contribution of socialization. In fact, particularly in geographically stable societies, social arrangements and child-rearing practices evolve in close relation to ecology, and at any point in time these factors are in continuous interaction, so that the question of their independent contributions is probably academic.

ASSESSMENT OF COGNITIVE STYLE

From the extensive research done on the global-articulated cognitive dimension, specific tests are available which evaluate this dimension in both perception and intellectual activity and which consider both the analytical and structuring aspects of articulation. Most widely used are the tests which assess the analytical aspect of the dimension in perception. These are tests of perceptual *field-dependence-in-dependence*, described in detail in Witkin *et al.* (1962). In a field-dependent mode of perception, the organization of the field as a whole dominates perception of its parts; an item within a field is experienced as fused with organized ground. In a field-independent mode of perception, the person is able to perceive items as discrete from the organized field of which they are a part. The field-dependence-in-dependence dimension is a continuous one, most persons falling between these two extremes. One test of field-dependence is the Rod-and-Frame Test. The subject is seated in a completely darkened room and adjusts a luminous rod, contained within a tilted luminous square frame, to a position he perceives as upright, while the frame remains at its initial position of tilt. In a relatively field-dependent performance the rod is adjusted close to the axes of the tilted frame. In a relatively field-independent performance the rod is adjusted independently of the frame, and brought close to the true upright through reference to body position. A second test of field-dependence is the Embedded-Figures Test. Here the subject must locate a previously seen simple geometric figure within a complex figure designed to embed it. Some subjects quickly break up the complex figure in order to find the simple figure within it; this is a field-independent performance. For other subjects, at the opposite extreme, the simple figure seems to remain 'fused' with the complex organized design; they take a good deal of time to 'tease out' the simple figure. Finally, in the Body-Adjustment Test, the subject, seated in a tilted room, must adjust his own body to the upright while the room remains tilted. Some subjects require that the body be more or less aligned with the room, tilted at 35 degrees, in order for the body to be perceived as straight. In this field-dependent way of performing perception of body position is dominated in an extreme degree by the axes of the surrounding field. Other subjects, whose perception is field-independent, seem able to keep body separate from field in experience and to adjust the body close to the upright independently of room position.

Individuals show a high degree of consistency in performance across these three tests (Witkin *et al.*, 1954, 1962). A tendency to perform in a relatively field-dependent or field-independent fashion is also a highly stable feature of an individual's cognitive functioning over time, in one study (Witkin, Goodenough and Karp, 1967) over a fourteen-year span (10 to 24 years of age) covering a period of considerable psychological growth. In pinpointing further the nature of the field-dependence-independence dimension, it is important to comment on its relation to intelligence. Performance in tests of field-dependence has been found to show only a low level of relation to scores on a verbal-comprehension cluster (Vocabulary, Information and Comprehension) and an attention-concentration cluster (Digit Span, Arithmetic and Coding) of Wechsler subtests. Field-dependence measures relate very highly to scores on a triumvirate of Wechsler intelligence scale subtests (Block Design, Object Assembly and Picture Completion) which tap the same kind of analytical ability as do the tests of field-dependence. Thus, the field-dependence dimension is represented by performance on portions of standard intelligence tests. The Block Design in fact provides an excellent measure of field-dependence, and it has been used for this purpose in several of the cross-cultural studies to be considered.

Another technique, the Figure-Drawing Test, which should be mentioned here because of its potential value in cross-cultural work, does not assess perception but articulation of body concept, which, as suggested, is another important indicator of differentiation. Ratings of articulation of figure drawing according to a five-point 'sophistication-of-body-concept scale' (described in Witkin *et al.*, 1962) have repeatedly been shown to relate quite highly to measures of field-dependence. Because it is easy to obtain figure drawings and to score them reliably for articulation, the figure-drawing technique has often been used to evaluate the same broad differentiation dimension which tests of field dependence seek to assess. Drawings rated most articulated on the sophistication-of-body-concept scale show such characteristics as high form level, representation of appendages and details in realistic relation to body outline, representation of role and sex. Drawings rated as least articulated show such characteristics as very low form level (body in form of ovals, rectangles, sticks) and lack of evidence of role or sex identity.

STUDIES OF THE RELATION BETWEEN COGNITIVE STYLE AND FAMILY EXPERIENCES IN WESTERN SETTINGS

The initial investigations of family experiences (Witkin *et al.*, 1962; Dyk and Witkin, 1965) were done with children growing up in a large urban centre (New York City), and focused particularly on mother–child interactions. In the first of a progression of studies we used as subjects a group of 10-year-old boys and their mothers. The boys were assessed for cognitive style and for extent of differentiation in other areas of functioning; and the nature of these boys' relations to their mothers was explored through interviews with the mothers. Overall ratings were made of the mother–child interactions in terms of whether, in toto, they appeared to have fostered the development of differentiation or to have interfered with its development. These ratings were anchored to a number of specific indicators or clues, which fall into three categories, together covering the 'socialization' cluster described earlier:

(1) Indicators concerned with separation from mother. Included here were five indicators which, stated in terms of hampering of separation, were: *a.* mother's physical care is not appropriate to child's age; *b.* mother limits child's activity and his movement into the community because of her own fears and anxieties for the child or ties to him; *c.* mother regards her child as delicate, in need of special attention or protection, or as irresponsible; *d.* mother does not accept a masculine role for her child; *e.* mother limits the child's curiosity and stresses conformity.

(2) Indicator concerned with nature of control over aggressive, assertive behaviour in the child. This indicator was: mother's control is not in the direction of the child's achieving mature goals and becoming responsible, or is consistently directed against the child asserting himself. Specific patterns illustrative of this mode of control are: administration of discipline arbitrarily and impulsively, with the use of irrational threats to control aggression; submissive, indulgent maternal behaviour; wavering by the mother between indulgent and coercive behaviour. The child's development of controls is likely to be hampered when the mother is unable to set limits for her child or to help him identify and internalize a set of values and standards.

(3) Indicators concerned with personal characteristics of the mother which may influence her role in the separation process and in the impulse-regulation process. The two indicators were: *a.* mother does not have assurance in herself in raising her child. Lack of self-assurance hampers a mother's ability to define her role as a mother, and, accordingly, her ability to help her child identify himself as a separate person. It is also likely to make it difficult for the mother to set and maintain limits, thereby interfering with the child's achievement of self-regulation; *b.* mother does not have a feeling of self-realization in her own life. A mother who lacks a sense of self-realization is less able to allow her child to separate from her and to develop as an individual in his own right.

Ratings made of mother–child interactions, guided by these indicators, showed a picture of significant correlations with measures of differentiation for the children. Thus, boys who were field-independent and gave evidence of an articulated body concept, a developed sense of separate identity, and a tendency to use specialized, structured defences, tended to have mothers who were judged to have interacted with them in ways that had fostered differentiation. The impression gained from the interviews that mothers of more differentiated and less differentiated boys differed in particular personal characteristics was in general supported when the mothers themselves were assessed by some of the techniques used to assess differentiation in their children. Less differentiated boys were found likely to have mothers who were also less differentiated. It is plausible that mothers who have some of the personal qualities implied by limited differentiation should be handicapped in helping their children separate from them. The finding that relatively more differentiated boys are likely to have relatively more differentiated mothers has been confirmed by Seder (1957) and by Corah (1965).

CROSS-CULTURAL STUDIES

The initial studies in which patterns of mother–child interactions associated with cognitive style and level of differentiation were first identified were done with families from a large urban setting, predominantly Jewish and middle-class. The relations observed do not seem limited to this particular kind of social group, however. For example, in the study by Seder (1957) the families were from a small suburb of Boston, in the United States, middle-class, and of diversified religious backgrounds. The studies to be considered now suggest that the patterns of parent–child interactions we originally found to be associated with a more global or more articulated cognitive style, and with greater or more limited differentiation, in fact hold under a very wide range of social conditions; and they provide additional validation of our original findings.

A study of Temne and Mende, by Dawson

Dawson (1963, 1967a) carried out a study with adult male subjects in Sierra Leone, Africa. He examined individual cognitive functioning in relation to family experiences and compared cognitive style in tribal groups differing in child-rearing practices. From the American investigations, specific hypotheses were available as guides to the study. To assess field-dependence, Dawson used the Embedded-Figures Test, abbreviated and adapted in its administration to the Sierra Leone group, as well as the Kohs Block Design Test. The first hypothesis tested by Dawson was that relatively field-dependent men would more likely have mothers who exercised strict dominant control in rearing them, as compared to field-independent men. Ratings made by the subjects themselves of degree of maternal strictness to which they had been subject showed a significance relation to measures of field-dependence, confirming the hypothesis. A similar check on paternal role yielded a nonsignificant trend in the same direction. This difference in outcome for maternal role and paternal role may be related to the finding of Corah (1965) that children's level of differentiation tends to be related to level of differentiation of opposite-sex parent but not of same-sex parent.

In another part of his study Dawson made a comparison of cognitive style in two tribal groups in Sierra Leone, the Temne and Mende. These groups differ in socialization emphases in ways which, on the basis of our American studies, led to the expectation of relatively greater field-dependence in the Temne. Information about child-rearing practices was obtained both from the social anthropological literature as well as from responses to questionnaires administered for the sake of this study. As described by Dawson (1963, 1967a), the Temne child, after weaning, is subjected to severe discipline. Great stress is placed on conformity to adult authority, and extreme forms of physical punishment are commonly used to enforce conformity. Children are not encouraged to adopt an adult role. Altogether the mother plays an extremely dominant part in raising the child, whereas the father is a background figure; in fact, children very rarely have close contact with their fathers.[1] Consistent with the nature of their interpersonal relations, among the Temne the chief is powerful, and in their responses to a specially devised questionnaire they showed themselves to be strongly tradition-oriented. The Mende present a contrasting picture in a number of these characteristics. They tend not to punish their children to the same extent as the Temne, and their punishment is likely to take the form of deprivation rather than physical punishment. Great emphasis is placed on giving the child responsibility at a very early age. Further, Mende parents tend to be more consistent than Temne parents in their child-rearing behaviour. Particularly important, the Mende family is less dominated by the mother than the Temne family; and the Mende are less tradition-oriented. Reflecting these differences in

---

[1] It is relevant here that Barclay and Cusumano (1967) found a tendency for boys from fatherless homes to be field-dependent. Seder (1957) observed that among field-independent boys, fathers are more often the mediators of discipline than mothers. In our own studies, mothers judged to have interfered with differentiation in their sons complained that their husbands did not participate in the son's raising.

socialization between the Temne and Mende, overall ratings of parental strictness made by members of the two tribes showed the Temne subjects more prone to perceive themselves as strictly raised. Temne ratings of both maternal and paternal strictness were significantly higher than Mende ratings.

This account of socialization practices among the Temne and Mende indicates a marked contrast between them in quite specific features of the 'socialization cluster' found in our American studies to be related to the development of a relatively more global or more articulated cognitive style. Considering the components of the cluster (handling of separation, regulation of impulse expression, and personal characteristics of parents affecting their part in these processes), it may reasonably be expected, as Dawson hypothesized, that Temne children would be relatively more field-dependent than Mende children. This hypothesis was essentially confirmed when perceptual test performances were compared for Temne and Mende males matched for age, occupation, sex, education and intelligence.

A study of Temne and Eskimo, by Berry

Berry (1966a, 1966b) selected for study two societies presenting a striking contrast in the socialization practices found important in our studies and in Dawson's for development of the field-dependence-independence dimension. These societies differed as well in particular ecological characteristics conceived to play a role in the development of this dimension. The two societies were the Temne of Sierra Leone, studied by Dawson, and the Eskimo of Baffin Island. Child-rearing practices among the Temne were described in detail in the preceding section. The summary given by Berry of the available social anthropological literature reveals that among the Eskimo punishment of children is generally avoided; blows or even scolding or harsh words are rarely used, and extreme freedom is allowed the individual child. There is strong encouragement of personal self-reliance, individualism, skill and ingenuity, and discouragement of dependence and incompetence. The personal qualities emphasized in child-rearing are of importance for the kinds of solitary activities in which the Eskimo engage (hunting, kayaking). It is not surprising that the emphasis on individualism evident in both child-rearing and economic activities should be found in the social system as well. Class distinction and social and political stratification are nonexistent. The impressive differences in child-rearing emphases between the Temne and Eskimo were reflected in differences in perception by members of the two societies of the severity of the discipline to which they had been subjected while growing up. Berry's Temne subjects rated their parents as significantly stricter than his Eskimo subjects. Berry predicted that the Eskimo would be much more field-independent than the Temne, a prediction which is entirely appropriate in light of the socialization cluster found in the American studies to be relevant to development of the field-dependence-independence dimension.

Differences in the ecological requirements of the two groups contributed further to Berry's expectation of greater field-independence among the Eskimo. Whereas the environment of the Temne, with its bush and colourful vegetation, is highly variegated, the environment of the Eskimo with its endless, uniform snowfields is extremely homogeneous. Articulation is thus a built-in feature of the visual field of the Temne world but essentially lacking in the Eskimo world. Against this starting difference in their visual worlds there is a marked difference between the two groups in the kind of engagement with the environment which their economies demand. The hunting life of the Eskimo requires that they travel widely. The necessity of finding their way around in a highly uniform terrain must place a great premium during development upon investment in the articulation of space. The fostering of articulation, we may speculate, is likely to be stronger than in a society where the same need to travel widely is met by an environment which is inherently articulated. The Temne, in contrast, endowed with a highly articulated world, do not need to invest in articulation even to the degree of 'taking over' what is available to them as a 'given', for as farmers they tend to 'stay put'. Berry identified in the complex system of geometrical-spatial terms of the Eskimo language a very useful device for helping the growing child achieve an articulated concept of space.

Berry's subjects were two matched groups of Eskimo and Temne, each containing a subgroup drawn from a traditional and transitional society. To permit comparison with Western society, Berry also tested a matched group of Scottish subjects, similarly divided. Field-dependence was assessed by the Embedded-Figures and Kohs Block Design Tests. In keeping with expectations, the Eskimo traditional and transitional groups were strikingly more field-independent than the corresponding Temne groups. In fact, the Eskimo were not significantly different from the Scots in level of field-independence. Berry's finding that the Eskimo are markedly field-independent is consistent with results reported by Vernon (1965a) and MacArthur (personal communication). Examination of the relation between self-ratings of parental discipline and extent of field-dependence within each sample showed the anticipated tendency for greater parental strictness to be associated with more field-dependent perception. Thus, in within-culture comparisons as well as in cross-cultural comparisons, a relation is evident between extent of field-dependence and particular child-rearing practices. To add to this picture, in all three societies the transitional sample was more ficld-independent than the traditional sample.

There is some evidence that it is not in the cognitive sphere alone that the Eskimo are more differentiated than the Temne. For example, Berry found that in an Asch-type of situation, Eskimo subjects in judging line lengths were significantly less influenced by the standard attributed to an authoritative group than were Temne subjects. This tendency of the Eskimo to establish their own standards independently of the prevailing social context is indicative of what we earlier called a developed sense of separate identity, signifying developed self-differentiation. In fact, in some of the American studies which showed a relation between field-dependence and sense of separate identity, situations of the Asch type were used to assess sense of separate identity. (See, for example, Linton, 1955; Rosner, 1956.) Considering the area of body concept, there is some evidence that the Eskimo tend to be highly differentiated here as well. Harris (1963) found figure drawings made by Eskimo children to be even more articulated than drawings made by a comparison group of American children. The high degree of articulation of the world-renowned Eskimo soapstone carvings of human figures is in line with Harris's observation. It is relevant here that Witkin, Birnbaum, Lomonaco, Lehr and Herman (1968) found extent of field-dependence to be related to degree of articulation of clay representations of the human body.

It thus appears that the Eskimo may show a generally high level of differentiation across psychological areas. In seeking to understand the process involved, one possibility to be considered is that investment in articulation of experience of the outer field, compelled by ecological requirements, may result in a generalization of interest in articulation to other areas where the source of experience is body and self. It is equally possible that the socialization and ecological factors operative in the Eskimo child's world may act directly on development of differentiation in each of the areas considered.[1]

[1] In still another cross-cultural study, Wober (1966a) studied field-dependence among Nigerians with the interesting hypothesis that specialized experience in a

SEX DIFFERENCES IN COGNITIVE STYLE

Sex differences in cognitive style have been observed in a wide variety of groups by now. Their existence raises a number of significant questions about the role of socialization in cognitive development and suggests further lines of cross-cultural inquiry. Boys and men tend to be more field-independent than girls and women. The difference between the sexes is small in magnitude, compared to the range of individual differences within each sex, but it is clear-cut and pervasive. Moreover these sex differences are evident over a large segment of the life span, although they may not exist in children below the age of 8 (Crudden, 1941; Goodenough and Eagle, 1963) or in geriatric groups (Schwartz and Karp, 1967). Greater field-dependence in females has been observed in numerous groups of varied educational and social backgrounds in the United States. It has also been observed in a number of Western European countries, including England, Holland, France and Italy (see Witkin *et al.*, 1962) as well as in Israel (Rothman, personal communication), Japan (Kato, 1965), Hong Kong (Goodnow, personal communication), and in Sierra Leone, Africa (Dawson, 1963, 1967a), although, interestingly enough, not among the Eskimo (Berry, 1966a, 1966b; MacArthur, 1967). Moreover, within each sex, extent of field-dependence has been related to scores on masculinity-feminity inventories, which in effect assess the extent to which an individual does what men or women typically do in our culture, in other words, their social roles; greater masculinity within each sex was associated with greater field-independence (Miller, 1953; Crutchfield, Woodworth and Albrecht, 1958; Fink, 1959). Finally, congruent with their greater field-independence, men have been found to show more articulated functioning in intellectual activities as well. (See, for example, Guetzkow, 1951; Sweeney, 1953; Milton, 1957.) There is some evidence in the literature that sex differences in differentiation may exist in other psychological

---

particular sense modality, without an equal degree of experience in other modalities, will lead to a developed analytic competence in the favoured modality alone, with the result that the individual consistency in extent of field-dependence across modalities repeatedly observed among Western subjects will not be found. The absence of significant correlations in one group of Nigerian subjects between the Rod and Frame Test, on the one hand, and the Embedded Figures and Kohs Blocks tests, on the other, was taken to support the hypothesis. However, in a subsample of Nigerian manual workers (Wober, 1966a) the correlations tended to be higher and one of the two obtained was significant. In view of this, and in the absence of a validation study, it seems appropriate to consider that Wober's hypothesis remains to be confirmed. It is a hypothesis which clearly merits further inquiry.

areas as well as in cognitive functioning. A number of studies have identified sex differences in behaviour suggestive of differences in sense of separate identity. For example, it has been found repeatedly that women as a group are more likely than men to use external standards for definition of their attitudes and judgements (for example, Feinberg, 1951; Crutchfield, 1955; Nakamura, 1955; Patel and Gordon, 1961). (See Witkin *et al.*, 1962, for a review of the evidence on sex differences in behaviour indicative of developed sense of separate identity.) Whether sex differences in differentiation do in fact exist across many areas of psychological functioning remains to be checked in further research.

Sex differences in cognitive style, which have now been clearly established for a wide variety of social groups, have to this point not been specifically studied in relation to the socialization process. Some observations that have been made do, however, provide a basis for speculating about the possible source of these sex differences. In our own studies, which focused on mother–son interactions, we formed the impression in those cases where the mothers had daughters, in addition to the sons taking part in our studies, that the mothers were more encouraging of achievement and accepting of assertiveness for their sons but placed more stress on social training for their daughters. This observation seems consistent with the overall impression that our society places greater value for boys than for girls on characteristics associated with developed differentiation. Thus, in Tyler (1965) we find evidence that in America there is a commonly held view that women are dependent and men are independent. Already among children, boys held in esteem by their peers are likely to be independent, whereas esteemed girls tend to be dependent (Tuddenham, 1951, 1952). There is evidence from studies by Carden (1958) and Iscoe and Carden (1961) connecting these social emphases directly to cognitive style. These studies showed that boys prefer other boys who are field-independent, whereas girls prefer girls who are field-dependent. Our sex-role stereotypes, which even young children learn to value, thus include characteristics subsumed under differentiation. Pressure on growing children to comply with these stereotypes may well contribute to the sex differences in field-dependence observed pervasively in the United States, and perhaps to broader overall differences in differentiation.

It is possible that non-Western societies may show some of these characteristics of American culture. Barry, Bacon and Child (1957) have observed that in a large number of cultures, mainly illiterate, men typically engage in activities, such as work and combat, which stress self-reliance and achievement; women in contrast have the nurturant role of homemaking and child-rearing. These differences, in turn, are consistent with differences in training goals for the two sexes, independence being more often stressed for boys. Thus it seems that the emphases in socialization repeatedly found in association with development of a global cognitive style, are, in a wide array of cultural settings, more evident in the raising of girls than of boys. From the data now available the Eskimo seem to be an exception to the consistent picture of sex differences in field-dependence (Berry, 1966a, 1966b; MacArthur, 1967).[1] The absence of sex differences in this group, if confirmed in further studies, would not contradict the observations made about socialization factors important in the development of cognitive style. As Berry points out, despite different economic and social role assignments women are not treated as dependent among the Eskimo and very loose controls are exercised over them. The Eskimo findings raise the possibility that changes in ways of raising boys and girls from those now commonly practised, even if these common ways are derived from originally compelling biological and economic forces, may reduce or even eliminate sex differences in cognitive style and, perhaps with it, sex differences in at least some of the other related characteristics of personal functioning.

For a deeper understanding of the role of socialization factors in the production of sex differences in cognitive style, studies are needed which specifically direct themselves to this issue. Of particular value would be a comparison of extent of sex differences in field-dependence in a series of cultures varying in the degree to which male and female roles are similar or different.

DISCUSSION

On a variety of grounds the global-articulated cognitive style is of considerable value in cross-cultural studies, particularly in studies of the role of socialization processes in psychological development. Extensive research has shown this style to be a salient dimension of individual differences in cognitive functioning (Smith, 1964; Vernon, 1965a; Witkin *et al.*, 1954, 1962). Vernon (1965a), in fact, came to the following conclusion from a review of the factor-analytic literature

---

[1] Davila, Diaz-Guerrero and Tapia (1966) in a recent study found no sex differences among 8- and 12-year-old Mexican schoolchildren. Since the report of the study does not describe socialization practices in the samples tested, it is not possible to determine whether the absence of sex differences is specifically attributable to the socialization practices followed.

on cognitive functioning: 'After removing the general factor (whether by group-factor technique or by rotation of centroid factors), the positive residual correlations always fall into two main groups: the verbal-educational (v:ed) group and the spatial-practical-mechanical group' (p. 725). The global-articulated dimension is clearly subsumed by the second of these two basic cognitive factors. (See Witkin *et al.*, 1962, for a review of the evidence relating field-dependence to spatial ability.) The global-articulated cognitive style is also basic in the additional sense that the function involved is undoubtedly a universally occurring one in individual human development. Further, past evidence, now added to by the findings reviewed here, indicates that individual differences in the global-articulated dimension reflect differences in socialization experiences, and so may serve to compare groups with regard to their socialization practices. Finally, an individual's standing on this dimension, particularly its perceptual component, field-dependence-independence, may be assessed by controlled laboratory tests which are objective and essentially nonverbal.

Implicit in the cognitive-style approach to cross-cultural studies is the view that the performance of cognitive tasks such as tests of field-dependence mirrors the person's social history. When used in cross-cultural studies, these tests deliberately seek to assess cultural influences rather than to get rid of them. In this sense, the tests are certainly not 'culture-free' – quite the opposite. However, to the extent that the task given may be made meaningful to a variety of cultural groups, and the influence of differences in verbal development and verbal facility may be avoided as a factor in test results, tests of the global-articulated dimension may be made 'culturally appropriate'. The studies cited in the section describing studies done in non-Western settings have successfully applied tests of field-dependence to a variety of indigenous groups.

In transferring tests across cultures it is important to establish that the same process is being tapped, that given scores are arrived at by the same route. One indication that in the different cultures to which they have been applied the tests of field-dependence are tapping the same cognitive style as in the American setting for which they were originally devised, comes from the finding in both the Dawson and Berry studies that the tests show significant intercorrelations as they did in the original American studies, as well as similar patterns of relations to other tests.

The occurrence of a sex difference in field-dependence in the very wide range of social groups in which it has been observed makes it tempting to think of this difference as rooted in constitutional and/or genetic differences between men and women. While this is certainly a possibility, it is equally plausible that the sex difference is so pervasive because the same differences between the socialization practices followed in raising boys and girls, particularly those important for the development of differentiation, exist in a great many cultures. Moreover, even if biological differences between the sexes are a source of sex differences in cognitive style, it is quite likely that these biological differences exert their influence through strongly fostering both different methods of raising the two sexes and different social roles for them, even in widely different cultural contexts, and it is these differences in child-rearing and social role which in turn influence the development of cognitive style and related characteristics of differentiation. Biological differences may also contribute to sex differences in differentiation through the role they play in individual psychological development, but again their influence is complex and indirect. As one example, psychoanalytic writers have commented on the fact that the presence of a vagina rather than a penis (of 'hidden' genitals rather than apparent ones) makes for greater confusion in the growing girl as to the nature of her sexual parts and their functioning. Since the genital area is in a way a 'centre of gravity' of the body, both because of the libidinal investment made in it and the significance attached to it by society, confusion about this area may make achievement of an articulated concept of the body altogether more difficult. In still another way may biological differences between the sexes contribute more or less universally to sex differences in differentiation of the body concept, but again by a very indirect route. The body with which the growing boy has greatest early contact, his mother's, is of course different from his own. Confrontation with differences may be a particularly effective route for sharpening the child's awareness of his own bodily characteristics, thereby aiding development of an articulated body concept. Girls have less of this experience of contrast, since an infant's bodily contact with the father is not as great as with the mother.

Still in the biological domain, the possibility must be raised that group differences in cognitive style may be based, in part at least, on genetic differences. Adaptive selection is particularly apt to play a role in groups that have lived in the same environment over a very long period, and have remained in relative sexual isolation from other groups. The Eskimo have both these characteristics; it is conceivable that the highly adaptive value of analytical competence in coping with the world in which they live may have caused selection for this attribute, leading in time to marked field-independence in this quite

E

homogeneous group. As Berry points out, in arguing against this possibility, his transitional Eskimo group was significantly more field-independent than his traditional group. In rejoinder, it cannot be ruled out that this difference reflects the selective migration of relatively field-independent persons to cities. The problem of adaptive selection for particular cognitive characteristics within human populations is an intriguing one for further research.

The marked field-independence of the Eskimo, and their apparently generally high overall level of psychological differentiation, provide further impressive evidence that so-called 'primitive' groups are not uniformly less developed.[1] Equally impressive is the finding that the Eskimo were no less field-independent than the comparison Scottish group, despite the vastly greater educational and material opportunities available to the Scots. That the traditional Eskimo are also very field-independent and relatively differentiated is particularly attention-getting since they receive so little education (a total of 0·4 years, on the average), and in current usage of the term may be considered 'culturally deprived'. The possibility arises from these findings that cultural stimulation, as commonly provided by schools and other social media, may work most of all on behalf of development of verbal-comprehension and social-communication skills. On the other hand, development of the cluster of characteristics which includes an articulated cognitive style, as well as an articulated body concept and a developed sense of separate identity (together signifying self-differentiation), is more under the influence of the quality of relations with critical persons (as in the family) early in life. Given the necessary interpersonal relations, these important attributes of an autonomous person may apparently develop even under conditions of so-called cultural deprivation. The observation in our own studies and in studies by others (see, for example, Cropley, 1964) that socioeconomic status does not relate to field-dependence, but is significantly related to level

---

[1] Beveridge (1939) found a West African group he studied to be more field-independent than a European group on a test similar to our Body Adjustment Test. Beveridge placed his subjects, standing up, within a tilted room and required them to adjust a rod to the upright. Consistent with our observations, subjects tended to tilt the rod toward the tilted room in order to perceive it as upright, but the Africans tilted it less, i.e. were more field-independent, than the Europeans. Beveridge's findings are inconclusive, however, since his European group was very much older than his African group, and the Europeans included women as well as men in contrast to the African all-male group. Because women are more field-dependent than men, and field-dependence tends to be greatest later in life, Beveridge's African group was biased in a field-independent direction.

of verbal-comprehension abilities, is consistent with these views. In cultures such as the American one great emphasis is placed on verbal skills. As one example, Witkin, Faterson, Goodenough and Birnbaum (1966) have reported evidence which suggests that a heavy premium is placed on verbal skills in the 'routing' of children at critical junctures early in life, to the relative disregard of other cognitive abilities. Such an emphasis on verbal skills may have the consequence that when attempts are undertaken to make up for cultural deprivation, it is again the development of these skills that is fostered, perhaps with insufficient attention to development of an articulated cognitive style and self-differentiation. A medium for checking this possibility exists in the programmes now being developed in a number of cities in the United States to make up for the deficit suffered by culturally deprived children. It is a challenge to future social action research to translate into forms appropriate to the school and other social settings the processes which, in the child's early interpersonal relations in the family, have been found to foster the development of an articulated cognitive style and self-differentiation.

6

M. Wober (1966)

Sensotypes

Journal of Social Psychology, 70, pp. 181-9

A. INTRODUCTION

Witkin has shown that styles of approach to perceived surroundings differ among individuals. He has described a style termed field-independence, a highly analytic approach to perceived material. This style in perception is indicated among individuals who can maintain attention to particular parts of a perceived world, no matter how confusing or 'embedding' are the surroundings. Such people were also termed more 'highly differentiated' because the relations among the parts of their perceived world tended to be highly complex, or elaborated. The opposite of this analytic style was termed field-dependence, or global perception, found among people also described as less differentiated. Tests were devised involving visual materials, on which individuals were categorized as more, or less, field-independent.

Having shown systematic individual differences in perceptual style, Witkin also related these styles to types of behaviour. Analytic, field-independent, types were considered to perceive the self as more distinct, more differentiated from surrounding social relations than did field-dependent types. Such people were more individualist than were field-dependent persons, and this arose from the type of parental socialization practices they experienced. Field-dependent people were more sensitive in behaviour to group norms than were field-independent people, and were shown to have a characteristic pattern of early experience in upbringing.

All this was noted by Dawson (1963), who worked in an African society where an extreme of non-analytic approach resulted partly from the prevailing parental practices. Such findings were supported by scores on tests of the type used by Witkin (1962), although it is noteworthy that these all required an analytic approach to visual material. Visual material is the currency of communication in an American,

Western society where the tests were developed. But the visual world and transactions therein may not be so relatively important in an African culture. Berry (1965) showed that not only mode of parental discipline, but also wider environmental factors, such as the demands of the ecology studied by Barry, Child and Bacon (1959), affect analytic behaviour. One factor studied by Berry was the influence of language and the availability of words, and hence ideas as an apparatus necessary to the elaboration of an analytic style in the visual field in which his tests lay.

This study investigates two types of phenomena observed in some African cultures. One is that performance at visually specialized tasks is often poor – as found by McFie (1961), Dawson (1963), and Berry (1965) – although it tends to improve with Western-type education – as noted by Doob (1960) and Irvine (1966); the second is that some African cultures (including the ones studied) contain considerable emphasis on sensory phenomena apart from the visual world. To begin with, among the peoples studied, babies are early in life strapped to their mothers' backs and spend much of their time upright; they learn to walk and even dance extremely early, and dancing and physical expressiveness remain extremely important elements in the activity of the culture. Many West African languages, including those of all the subjects studied, are tonal, and rhythm and tone direction are subjects of elaborated attention: that is, knowledge of subtleties and vigilance over confusions in this field of perception are likely to be well developed. While these are not proprioceived activities, yet they are not visual, and argue for directions of psychological elaboration apart from the visual world.

Evidence will be shown that the Nigerian subjects tested did not react to a range of tests with the same uniformity as that shown by the American subjects reported by Witkin *et al.* (1962). This is taken to suggest, together with cultural evidence, that men in the Southern Nigerian cultures studied may represent what may be called a 'sensotype' different from 'sensotypes' in Western cultures, which are fast becoming established in Southern Nigeria. By 'sensotype' is meant the pattern of relative importance of the different senses, by which a child learns to perceive the world and in which pattern he develops his abilities. These patterns may be predominantly visual in one culture, while in another culture, auditory or proprioceptive senses may have a much higher relative importance.

B. TESTS AND SUBJECTS

Tests used in the study included Witkin's Rod and Frame Test, RFT (1962); a shortened version of his Embedded Figures Test EFT (1950), using the items A3, A4, C1, C4, D1, D2, G1 and F1 illustrated there; other well-known tests including Kohs Blocks (shortened) and Ravens Matrices; and a new auditory test as yet unevaluated. The subjects were 173 workers of all levels from labourers (mostly illiterate) to trained mechanics, employed in a large Nigerian industry. The men included 64 Ibos from east of the Niger, 39 Ibos born in the Midwest, 29 Edos, 22 Urhobos, and 19 others, all from Southern Nigeria. Significant differences between test scores of different tribes were not found, on tests reported here. Of the 173 men, only 88 completed the RFT, and the tribes were represented (in the same order) by 38, 18, 16, 9 and 7 men, respectively. A tactile version of the EFT was also devised. In this version, the same designs as in the visual version were cut into plastic surfaces, the grooves being about 1·5 mm. deep. The subject could thus look at the designs; he was also given a stylus and shown on the practice item how to draw it along the grooves of the diagram, following all the outlines available. Subjects were to see and trace out a simple figure, and then explore a complex diagram with the stylus until they identified where the simple figure was inset.

In interpreting the results, attention was paid to visual, proprioceptive, and tactile aspects of the tasks used, to intercorrelations among the tests, and to their relations with other criteria of ability.

C. RESULTS

The RFT data were examined first (see Table 6.1). In this test, the subject sat on a chair in a completely dark room. Facing him was an illuminated square, set like a picture frame on the wall. The frame could be tilted left or right, to 28 degrees. Pivoted centrally within the frame, like the hand of a clock (equally long each side of the pivot), was an illuminated rod. This could also be tilted to right or left to 28 degrees. Confronted with a rod tilted from the vertical, the subject, whose chair could also be tilted, gave instructions on how to move the rod until it rested in what seemed to be the vertical direction. As handedness (only two out of eighty-eight subjects were left-handed) is a phenomenon experienced proprioceptively, the data were studied for possible biases distinguishing left from right.

In the Discussion section, the relation of handedness, proprioception,

and errors will be dealt with, but it should be clear that proprioceived data are important in RFT performance. Particular proprioceptive variations introduced were due to the tilt of the chair; this has an
effect different from that of tilting the frame, which is a visual variation
(see Table 6.2).

An analysis of variance showed quite clearly that different conditions
of frame and chair tilt with the same subject are measuring the same
thing, and that differences between subjects are considerable; but this is
only for conditions where the frame is tilted. When the frame is not
tilted, errors are about one-tenth the size of errors occurring when the

TABLE 6.1. *Effects of chair tilt, frame tilt, and starting position of rod
on size of error in RFT responses*

Chair position	Frame position	Errors greater when rod is Right	Left	Errors equal	Chi-square
Straight	Right	57	26	5	11·45[a]
,,	Left	25	56	7	11·73[a]
,,	Centre	50	25	13	8·24[b]
Right	Right	50	33	5	3·45
,,	Left	31	52	5	5·26[a]
,,	Centre	34	34	20	0·00
Left	Right	47	29	12	4·26[a]
,,	Left	27	51	10	7·38[a]
,,	Centre	46	25	17	6·14[b]
All positions	Right	154	88	22	18·00[a]
,,	Left	83	159	22	23·86[a]
,,	Centre	130	84	50	9·88[a]

[a] Cases where error is larger when rod starts from the same side as the tilt of
the frame. Significant at 0·05 or better.
[b] Errors greater when rod starts from right side, significant at 0·01 and un-
affected by tilt of frame.

TABLE 6.2. *Effects of chair tilt and frame tilt on the size of error in
RFT responses*

(mean errors from the vertical, in degrees)

Condition	Chair right	Chair straight	Chair left
Frame straight	1·20	1·18	1·29
Frame tilted right	11·16	11·18	12·06
Frame tilted left	11·08	10·86	11·47

frame is tilted, and are about the same regardless of the tilt of the chair. Thus the subjects show that their proprioceptive skills will compensate for the proprioceptive variations of the tilted chair, but that they are not nearly so capable of dealing with a visually registered displacement. Witkin's theories maintain that analytic style in one sense modality is likely to correlate highly with analytic style in another sense modality. While this may be so in an American setting, there is evidence that such is not the case among the Nigerian subjects tested. This may be seen from the following correlations (see Table 6.3).

The interrelationship of the EFT, Kohs Blocks, Ravens Matrices, and education are striking. All these are indices of demands on analytic ability in a visual field. This ability evidently is strengthened with education, which in all cases here is Western education, in the English language, involving literacy and at higher levels familiarity with

TABLE 6.3. *Correlations between tests of field-independence, and other variates*

Variate	RFT	EFT	Kohs Blocks	Ravens Matrices	Education	Job efficiency	N
RFT	1·0	0·184[a]	0·157[a]	0·192[a]	0·036[a]	0·260	88
EFT		1·0	0·633	0·510	0·466	0·068[a]	173
Kohs			1·0	0·532	0·375	0·062[a]	,,
Ravens				1·0	0·295	−0·126[a]	,,
Education					1·0	−0·049[a]	,,
Efficiency						1·0	,,

Note: For $N = 88$, 0·05 significance arises when $r = 0·217$; for $N = 173$, 0·05 significance arises when $r = 0·159$.
[a] Values of r not significant.

diagrams and figures. The RFT, however, does not correlate significantly with any of the other tests, two of which have been labelled and devised as tests of field-independence, and the third of which (Ravens Matrices) seems on the logic of its construction and on the correlations above to be closely related. The RFT is thus apart from the 'book learning' tests of analytic style, or field-independence. It is particularly independent of the effects of formal education, which answers objections that the test was not properly explained to and understood by all the subjects.

The most striking finding, however, is that whereas none of the other 'book tests' of field-independence correlates with the rating made by the men's managers for job efficiency, RFT results do correlate with efficiency. This finding supports the possibility that ability is elaborated among these Nigerians in a way that is not entirely detectable by visual type tests, but is manifest in the RFT test (a test that is not closely related to the purely visual tests of field-independence). The work of Beveridge (1939) is relevant here; he considered that Africans whom he tested in Ghana had skills more elaborated in a proprioceptive than in a visual realm.   (stimuli arising within the organism)

To inquire further into the nature of visual and proprioceptive skills and how they may be interrelated, a tactile Embedded Figures Test was used. The items were the same as those given in the visual EFT. Following the first testing with the visual EFT, two subgroups were chosen so that the EFT score of each man in one subgroup was matched by an equal score of a man in the other subgroup. Five months after doing the first, visual, EFT, the re-test was given. One subgroup completed the test visually, exactly as before; the other completed the tactile version.

No significant difference was found in favour of the group repeating the test in the tactile manner, although in fact this group improved more than the other (see Table 6.4). No differences were significant on any of the matching checks carried out. It is noteworthy that even after a five-month time lag, EFT performances did improve on average by about 20 per cent.

It had been thought that subjects tracing the designs with a stylus as well as looking at them would be in a better position to improve. Particularly, it was thought that errors where mirror-image shapes are

TABLE 6.4. *The effects of tactile cues as an aid to improvement in EFT scores among Nigerians*

Method	First EFT	Gain in EFT	Age	Kohs Blocks	RFT	N
Normal method	27·40	6·83	32·6	8·73	11·86	30
Tactile method	27·40	8·00	33·0	8·60	10·93	30
t	0·0	1·01	0·02	0·02	0·65	—
Significance	—	NS	NS	NS	NS	—

pointed out, and others where correct shapes (although of wrong size) are shown, might be reduced. That tactile cues were not significantly helpful is considered possibly due to a distraction effect that arises when two types of information are available. Attention, it seemed, was not often paid to the tactile 'feel' of the diagrams (which previously some subjects had indicated they might make good use of, by looking away and apparently trying to memorize figures by outlining shapes in the air with their fingers); sometimes, when subjects seemed to be attending to the tactile 'feel', they appeared to mislead themselves as to the visual nature of the figures they were searching for. Thus, for example, a man might gaze into the distance and try to trace out a square instead of a triangle. The test turned out to be unsuitable for investigating proprioceptive sensibility. It appeared to be much too related, in the imagery it required, to visual material. Finally, the figures being used were geometric ones, often without translatable names in the local languages, and thus subjects possibly lacked a principal aid in retaining either visual or tactile impression of an image: namely, names by which to identify the figures.

D. DISCUSSION AND SUMMARY

Results in Table 6.1 showed that the position of the frame relative to the rod in the RFT, as a visual experience, strongly determines the direction in which errors may occur. Secondly, when the frame is kept straight but the chair tilted, errors are more often greater when the rod starts from a tilted-right than from a tilted-left position. An exception to this is when the rod and chair are both tilted right. In directing the rod to be moved away from their position of chair tilt, subjects made smaller errors compared to instances when they directed the rod to be moved toward their position. The inferences are that rod and frame are clearly part of one world of visual experience, and also that handedness plays a part in determining in what circumstances each subject will make his greatest errors. Clearly, more remains to be understood about the way in which visual and proprioceptive sensibilities play their parts in performance of the RFT task. An experiment including a large number of left-handed subjects might confirm some conclusions about handedness.

Table 6.2 suggests that the RFT does not involve the subject in transactions in a visual field alone, but also with proprioceived information. Possibly the test can distinguish between subjects according to the extent to which ability has proliferated in each person in the sphere of proprioception. Further, such proprioceptive elaboration of ability may not be proportional to the ability developed in the world of visual material. This is the suggestion being made about the structure of abilities among the Nigerian subjects tested.

A principal element in Witkin's theory of field-independence has been confirmed in this data from Nigeria: there are important individual differences in cognitive and analytic approach to perceived material.

A second major point of his theory is that within each individual the degree of analytical functioning will tend to be constant throughout a wide range of activities (or sensory fields). This second element of his theory may well be subject to modification from his own work (1968) with congenitally blind subjects. These people performed worse than sighted subjects of similar intelligence with tactile tests, although they performed better than sighted subjects at an aural test of resistance to camouflaging contexts. It is possible to interpret these results in terms of an elaboration of skills and analytic functioning, not as a generalized phenomenon within each individual, but related to particular fields of sensory experience. That is to say, the blind, lacking a visual world, develop their differentiation and analytic abilities in an auditory world.

In the case of many West African cultures, communication styles have not yet widely elaborated what McLuhan (1962) calls 'the Gutenberg Galaxy'. This is the world of print, where representation on paper forms what Bernstein (1961b) refers to as an elaborated code, one that is in a visual context. In such West African cultures there are often found tonal languages, rich experience and discernment of rhythm and of physical movement in dancing. It can be argued that 'the visual arts' in West Africa are often sculptural, in which the visual elements of veracity are of equal or less importance than the solid tactile and social significance of the works. The sensory realms, within which analytic ability or differentiation may be expected to elaborate and prosper, are not so completely visual, then, as is the case in America and the West; in such African cultures, they are more proprioceptive and auditory than visual. An individual skilled in the media of such a culture may be said to represent a sensotype different from that of individuals skilled in a visual world.

A new line of research has been opened by Berry (1965), who suggested that certain African languages may be without the words (necessary labelling apparatus) for identification and analytic activity with printed (visual) designs and material. He showed that the Temne tongue (Sierra Leone) was without words for several geometric shapes, easily visually differentiated and labelled in Western languages. Interview data suggested that similar difficulties, of not having words other than circumlocutions for 'square', 'hexagon', 'diagonal', etc., existed in Ibo and Edo languages, which were mother tongues of most of the subjects tested here. Research remains to show in what directions such African languages are more highly elaborated, and hence wherein men's abilities have opportunity to become differentiated. Thus while Western languages may be shown to make use of a great number of metaphors referring to the sense of vision, perhaps in excess of other sensory metaphors, it remains to be seen (or heard) with which senses African languages prefer to illustrate (or sing of) their experience.

McLuhan (1962), at least, among Western writers, has realized the possible existence of different styles of communication, involving different technologies (apparatus external to the individual). The parallel idea is that different styles of communication (oral tradition, print, or electric recording) are related to different modes of sensory elaboration (apparatus internal to the individual) adapted to these communication media. These different modes, or types of sensory elaboration, are labelled sensotypes.

The evidence in this paper primarily concerns one test, the RFT, established as reliable among American subjects and closely related to visual tests there. This test argues a generality of style of analytic functioning in a given individual, within the American culture. In Southern Nigerian subjects tested, the RFT is shown to be not nearly so closely related (if at all) to visual tests of analytic functioning, which are shown to be related to (Western) education. The Southern Nigerian performance on RFT, however, is related to work efficiency ratings. This test then may be a better measure of ability, as it may lie in the true milieu of elaboration of analytic functioning among such Nigerians influenced by traditional culture. People who are found to show analytic ability especially in one sensory realm, are held to represent a 'sensotype' different from that of persons who develop analytic ability in another realm. The distinction may be forced upon individuals within a culture, as by the circumstances of congenital blindness, or it may arise through a totally different cultural experience.

7

J. W. Berry (1971)

Ecological and cultural factors in spatial perceptual development[1]

Canadian Journal of Behavioural Science, 3(4), pp. 324–36

It is once again a legitimate enterprise for behavioural scientists to investigate the possible role of ecology in shaping human behaviour. Long gone is the environmental determinism which was so easily discarded; workers in both psychology and anthropology have returned now to an ecological perspective, taking care, however, to detail their inquiry and to avoid facile generalizations. For psychology, Brunswik (Hammond, 1966), Barker (1965, 1968) and Wohlwill (1966, 1970), and for anthropology, Steward (1955), Helm (1962), Rappaport (1967) and Vayda (1969) have all attempted to comprehend the nature of ecological-behavioural interactions.

In its weakest form the approach merely asserts that behavioural and ecological variables interact in some systematic way (cf. Vayda and Rappaport, 1968), and in its strongest (not currently espoused), it would assert some ecological determination of behaviour. In its moderate forms, it asserts the ecological limitation of behavioural development (e.g. Meggars, 1954), the ecological source of the probability of behaviour (e.g. Brunswik, in Hammond, 1966) or the behavioural adaptation to ecological pressures; it is this latter version which will be explored in this paper.

[1] Paper delivered at a Symposium on Cross-Cultural Research held by the Centre for the Study of Human Abilities, Memorial University, St John's, Newfoundland, 29 and 30 October 1970.

The paper is an empirical and theoretical extension of work originally published in 1966, and includes data and ideas stemming from recent fieldwork in Australia and New Guinea. A further extension is being made in the form of a monograph, exploring more fully than is possible here the interaction in the data and their theoretical implications.

The research was made possible by grants from the Canada Council, the Government of Quebec, University Research Committees of the University of Sydney and of Queen's University, and by the Australian Research Grants Committee.

For psychologists the role of ecological factors is basic to our science (e.g. in Stimulus-Response theory); however, we have usually explored these ecological-behavioural interactions from a molecular point of view. The molar approach, which characterizes the present study, examines not only the fleeting ecology (the Stimulus) but also the long-term impact on the development of the organism of the persistent and surrounding ecology, more usually termed the physical environment.

The model in Fig. 7.1 exemplifies this molar approach. The overriding arrow indicates the conventional stimulus impinging on the

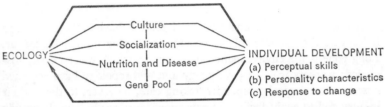

Fig. 7.1 Model relating individual development to ecological and other variables.

individual, as well as the culturally unmediated expectancies based on previous interactions with the environment. The underriding arrow illustrates the potential transformation that the organism can make on his physical surrounds, either through the conventional Response or through group activity such as Technology. The intermediate bonds indicate four of the numerous possible mediating factors present in all mankind:

(i) Culture: within this model, culture is viewed as a group's adaptation to recurrent ecological pressures (cf. Vayda, 1969) and as a contributor to the direction of development of individual human beings. It is also considered to act as a mediator (filter) of the ecology for individuals. In this study particular attention will be paid to language and technology.

(ii) Socialization, although technically a part of culture, is singled out for special attention because of its dominant role in shaping human behaviour, and because of its known adaptive relationship (in subsistence-level societies) to ecological variables (Barry, Child and Bacon, 1959). Both techniques of socialization and its content will be considered in this study.

(iii) and (iv) Nutrition, Disease and Gene Pool are included in the model because of their generally-accepted role in mediating ecology and individual development. Aspects of nutrition and disease considered most important include protein availability and parasites (Cravioto, 1968), while the gene pool is held to be adaptive to the ecological pressures, and in turn a contributor to group and individual differences.

This model is unabashedly *functional*, emphasizing as it must *interactions* rather than *causal sequences*. It of course shares the accepted deficiencies of all functional analyses (Collins, 1965), but gains as a relatively powerful heuristic device for exploring ecological, cultural and behavioural interactions.

It is not possible in a single paper to explore all the possible varieties of individual development; to illustrate the model then, one aspect only has been chosen – visual spatial skill development. Other data are also available on selected value and personality attributes, and on predisposition to acculturative stress, but these will be reported elsewhere.

THE ARGUMENT

Originally (Berry, 1966b) the argument was that the 'ecological demands' placed on a group of people, plus their cultural adaptation to this ecology ('cultural aids') would lead to the development of certain perceptual skills. Specifically, it was argued, persons who inhabit ecologies where hunting was the mode of sustenance should develop perceptual discrimination and spatial skills adapted to the ecological demands of hunting:

1. He must first of all in order to hunt effectively develop the ability to isolate slight variation in visual stimulation from a relatively featureless array; he must learn to be aware of minute detail.

2. Secondly, in order to navigate effectively in this environment he must learn to organize these small details into a spatial awareness, an awareness of his present location in relation to objects around him. (Berry, 1966b, p. 212)

Further it was argued that 'cultural aids' such as language coding, arts and crafts, and socialization would be adapted to these ecological demands, and assist in the development of the requisite skills.

The strategy was to test for differences between two cultural groups (Temne and Eskimo) which were greatly ecologically discrepant, the Eskimo experiencing to a large degree the demands of a hunting ecology while the Temne did so not at all. Visual Discrimination and

Spatial Test results were so divergent (all differences were significant beyond the 0·01 level) that an overall relationship was difficult to comprehend; were the data on the same dimension at all? Further, considerations of 'functional equivalence' (Berry, 1969a) led to the doubting of the usefulness of the original strategy, where ecological divergence was so great. Hence the present strategy is to seek out and rank a number of samples from cultural groups on the ecology dimension, and to examine the nature of the relationship between the ecological and behavioural (perceptual) variables.

The original procedure of analysing the cultural aids as adaptive to the ecology and mediating perceptual skill development has been retained. For language aids, it is argued that the presence of 'geometrical spatial' terms would assist in transmitting spatial and orienting concepts and information, and that their presence in a language would be consistent with the spatial demands placed on that group by their ecology (cf. Whorfian hypothesis). For arts and crafts aids, it is argued that their use would assist the early learning of spatial manipulations and the discrimination of detail, and the development of these techniques would be consistent with the ecological demands.

For socialization, the argument is necessarily more complex, since a somewhat arbitrary distinction is made between *content* and *technique* (although it will be argued later that they are functionally related).

With regard to the *content* of the socialization process, Barry, Child and Bacon (1959) have shown that there is a significant tendency for child-rearing practices to relate to a specific economic variable: the degree to which food is accumulated at the subsistence level. In detail, they were able to demonstrate that in high food accumulation societies (agricultural and pastoral), there was a strong tendency to emphasize responsibility and obedience during socialization, while in low food accumulation societies (hunting and gathering), achievement, self-reliance and independence were emphasized. Their rationale centred on the functional adaptation of child-rearing practices in order to mould adults with personality characteristics best suited to their particular economic pursuits. Despite criticism (Whiting, 1968) of this study, Barry (1969) was able to confirm these relationships while meeting the criticisms.

With regard to the *technique* of socialization, Witkin and his co-workers (1962) have been able to demonstrate consistent relationships between methods of child-rearing and 'cognitive style'. Generally, techniques employed to achieve mother–child separation and to control aggressive behaviour are related to the 'psychological differentiation' attained by a growing child. Specifically, for our perceptual concerns, 'field-independence' has been shown to stem from the encouragement of responsibility and self-assertion and by parental stimulation of the child's curiosity and interests, and is characterized by an 'analytic' approach to a perceptual field. At the opposite pole, 'field-dependence' stems from a stress on conformity, from arbitrary or impulsive discipline, and from the use of irrational threats to control aggression, and is characterized by a 'global' approach to a perceptual field.

Within a functional model, one would expect to find content and technique related to the socialization goals of a particular cultural group. That is to say, one would not expect to discover a society in which independence and self-reliance are conveyed as goals by a harsh, restrictive method of socialization. Nor, conversely, would one expect to discover societies in which conformity is taught by a method characterized by a stimulation of the child's own interests and of his curiosity. This functional expectation is open to empirical check and will be examined for each society in this study.

With respect to the role of genetic factors, no data have been collected in this study. Since it is proposed however that cultural and genetic factors are functionally adapted to ecological demands, no opposition is envisaged between these two variables in their mediation of perceptual development. That is to say, for the purposes of the model, it is not necessary to assess the relative operation of these two variables, although for broader purposes one might wish to do so. The focus upon sociocultural variables (to the exclusion of the genetic) in this study reflects the lack of competence, but not necessarily the bias, of the investigator. Sample characteristics pertaining to the nutrition and disease variables were observed within the communities, although no individual data were taken. Generally data on the adequacy of nutrition (especially of protein) and on the presence of disease (especially of eye problems and parasitic infections) are used to predict performance on tests of perceptual development.

The argument may now be summarized: hunting peoples are expected to possess good visual discrimination and spatial skill, and their cultures are expected to be supportive of the development of these skills through the presence of a high number of 'geometrical spatial' concepts, a highly developed and generally shared arts and crafts production, and socialization practices whose content emphasizes independence, and self-reliance, and whose techniques are supportive and encouraging of separate development. Implicit in this argument is the expectation that as hunting diminishes in importance across samples ranked in terms of this ecology dimension, the discrimination and spatial skills will diminish, as will each of the three cultural aids.

METHOD

To assess this argument, eight samples of subsistence-level peoples were studied; four were termed 'traditional', living as close to traditional ways as could be found, while four were termed 'transitional', comprising samples undergoing Westernization. In general the two kinds of samples were employed to assess the impact of acculturation; in two of the four areas (Sierra Leone and Baffin Island), the traditional and transitional samples were of the same culture, allowing a further assessment – that of persistence of psychological and cultural characteristics beyond the

TABLE 7.1. *Sample locations*

Area and culture	Rural/traditional	n	Urban/transitional	n	Total
Sierra Leone (Temne)	Mayola	90	Port Loko	32	122
New Guinea (Indigene)	Telefomin	40	Hanuabada	30	70
Australia (Aborigine)	Santa Teresa	30	Yarrabah	30	60
Baffin Island (Eskimo)	Pond Inlet	91	Frobisher Bay	31	122
Scotland	Inverkeilor	62	Edinburgh	60	122
Total *n*		313		183	496

subsistence level. Table 7.1 indicates the area, culture and numbers in each of the eight samples. Two groups of Scots were also administered the tests in order that the battery data might be related to scores from better-known Western samples.

The data were collected in communities considered to be representative of their societies, and in each community, samples were drawn so that males and females were approximately equally represented. The age range 10 to 70 years was also sampled, with approximately equal proportions in age ranges: 10–15, 16–20, 21–30, 31–40, and over 40. These two sampling aims were set so that sex and age differences could be adequately examined. In all communities, interpreter/assistants were employed to assist in the sampling, interviewing and testing. This was carried out largely in the traditional language, in an attempt to establish and maintain adequate communication.

In addition to the main dependent variables (tests of discrimination and spatial skills) individual data were collected on severity of socialization, years of education (if any), religion, language, near and far visual acuity and colour blindness; other dependent variables in the same battery have been reported on previously (Berry, 1967, 1968, 1969b). Community data were also gathered to assess degree of Westernization (to ensure correct Traditional v. Transitional placement), ecology (to ensure correct placement on the ecology dimension), typical socialization (as a check on self-reported experiences), arts and crafts, linguistic distinctions made about 'geometrical-spatial' concepts, and typical diet and disease (to assess the other mediating variables). Analyses of these individual and group data are too detailed to report here, and have been prepared as part of a monograph (Berry, n.d.). In general, the contextual (both individual and group gathered) data are internally consistent and are supportive of the proposed model. That is to say community observations support the individual reports with respect to socialization. Further, all mediating variables vary consistently with the ecological setting; rank orderings of these variables for the four samples within the Traditional and Transitional community groups are identical with the rank ordering on the ecological dimension (degree of food accumulation and its concomitant, the presence of hunting).

The major dependent variables were a tachistoscopic test of visual discrimination ability and three tests of spatial skill. The discrimination test consisted of a series of cards with india-ink figures on them, each with increasingly large gaps (from 1 mm to 15 mm) placed randomly in their sides. The smallest gap detected and drawn on paper was taken as the measure of discrimination ability, and the score is expressed in millimetres of gap detected. For all Ss, tests were conducted in a portable tachistoscope (mercury-cadmium battery operated, with a camera shutter set at 20 milliseconds) and the target was 25 cm from the eyes. Since visual acuity (tested by the Landolt Rings) did not differ across samples, ability to detect these random gaps was taken as a measure of discrimination ability, similar to that demanded in a hunting ecology.

The three tests of spatial skills were Kohs Blocks (Original 17 design series), a short form (six items) of the Embedded Figures Test (Witkin, 1950); and the Ravens Matrices (Series A, Ab, B; Raven, 1956). Although all these tests undoubtedly have characteristics other than spatial, it is contended that these are largely spatial in nature. In the case of Kohs Blocks, time limits were extended 30 seconds for each design 1 to 10, while the Matrices were untimed.

RESULTS

Discrimination skill results are presented in Fig. 7.2, while spatial scores are given in Figs. 7.3, 7.4 and 7.5. A low score on the discrimination test indicates that a small gap (expressed in millimetres) could be detected, while a high score indicates that only larger gaps were noticed. For the three spatial tests, a high score indicates high spatial skill. In each table Traditional sample scores are given on the left, while the Transitional scores are on the right. The ranking on the ecology dimension is of course standard throughout the four tables with Mayola and Pond Inlet designating the high and low food accumulating extremes within the Traditional samples, and Port Loko and Frobisher Bay in the same respective positions within the Transitional samples. Telefomin (New Guinea) and Santa Teresa (Arunta Aboriginal) are high-medium and low-medium respectively in the former samples, while Yarrabah (coastal Aborigine) and Hanuabada (coastal New Guinea) are high-medium and low-medium respectively for the latter samples. Note that the Traditional and Transitional Aborigine and New Guinea samples reverse their positions on the ecology dimension, there being little ecological continuity between central and coastal peoples in these two culture areas. In each figure the scores of the comparison (Scottish) samples appear adjacent to the y-axis.

Sex differences, especially in spatial ability, have received previous attention (Berry, 1966b; MacArthur, 1967). Table 7.2 provides mean scores for each sex and level of significance for three tests of spatial skill. It is apparent that, contrary to usual findings stemming from Western or industrialized samples, there is no general superiority of males in tests of spatial ability in these data. The most that may be said is that a pattern of superiority emerges either where male–female role separations are strong (as in urban-industrial society) or where there is no high development in these skills generally, as among the Temne and Telefomin peoples.

Age trends were also previously examined for the Temne and Eskimo data (Berry, 1966, pp. 226–7) and may be further explored here. It was considered that where ecological demands for these skills is low, relatively flat developmental curves (from ages 10 to 70) would appear for the three spatial tests. This expectation (which had previously been expressed by Ferguson, 1954, p. 107) is borne out in both Temne and Telefomin samples; they have relatively little growth of these skills with age, past a basic ability to produce a numerical score on these tests. For the other samples, however, the usual inverted U curve appears across this age range.

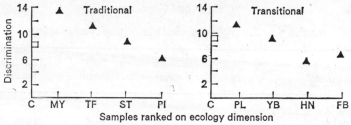

Fig. 7.2 Sample means on Visual Discrimination Test.

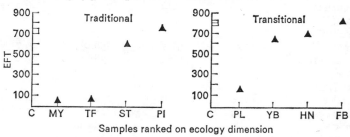

Fig. 7.3 Sample means on Kohs Blocks Test.

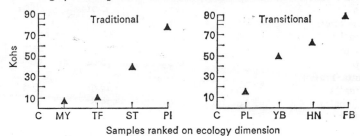

Fig. 7.4 Sample means on Embedded Figures Test.

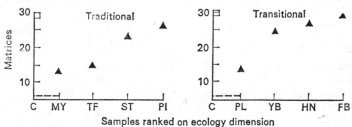

Fig. 7·5 Sample means on Raven Matrices Test.

	Traditional		Transitional
MY	Mayola	PL	Port Loko
TF	Telefomin	YB	Yarrabah
ST	Santa Teresa	HN	Hanuabada
PI	Pond Inlet	FB	Frobisher Bay
C	Comparison (Inverkeilor)	C	Comparison (Edinburgh)

TABLE 7.2. *Sex differences in three tests of spatial ability*

Traditional	N	Kohs mean	EFT mean	Matrices mean
Mayola				
males	45	8·8	55·5	13·7
females	45	3·9	0	11·4
p <		0·01	0·01	0·01
Telefomin				
males	20	11·9	56·4	15·7
females	20	7·1	0	13·7
p <		0·05	0·01	NS
Santa Teresa				
males	20	41·8	595·6	22·3
females	10	35·9	575·8	25·0
p <		NS	NS	NS
Pond Inlet				
males	46	76·8	720·0	27·0
females	45	80·6	754·1	26·6
p <		NS	NS	NS
Inverkeilor				
males	27	91·7	756·0	29·7
females	35	89·1	738·7	29·4
p <		NS	NS	NS
Port Loko				
males	20	17·9	228·8	14·1
females	12	11·8	15·6	13·6
p <		NS	0·01	NS
Yarrabah				
males	15	48·6	718·2	26·4
females	15	53·5	529·7	23·0
p <		NS	NS	NS
Hanuabada				
males	18	62·2	661·9	24·8
females	12	63·3	716·1	28·1
p <		NS	NS	NS
Frobisher Bay				
males	16	92·8	794·0	29·1
females	15	86·9	797·7	28·7
p <		NS	NS	NS
Edinburgh				
males	31	98·4	881·4	31·8
females	29	82·6	745·1	29·9
p <		0·05	0·01	NS

DISCUSSION

The original strategy was to test for the significance of differences between the ecological extremes within the traditional and transitional groups (Temne and Eskimo); in all tests (t tests for discrimination and spatial ability) the Eskimo scored significantly higher at the 0·01 level (Berry, 1966b, pp. 216, 220). The present approach to the data is merely to note firstly that these extremes are significantly different, and secondly that when samples which are ecologically intermediate are included, the pattern of the data displays only a single error in the rank ordering of the dependent variables (Hanuabada and Frobisher Bay on discrimination ability). Such a patterning of data is taken to confirm, without statistical appraisal, the general expectation that across a grading of food accumulation and hunting, peoples will attain the levels of visual discrimination and spatial ability appropriate to the ecological demands.

Comment upon specific characteristics of each graph must await specific analyses of the contextual data; however the single error in ranking should receive some attention now. The major predicted determinant of discrimination ability lies in the hunting demands typically placed on persons; however, transitional groups typically perform slightly better on this test than traditional peoples (even though hunting activity usually is diminished), and this may be attributable to the effects of Western education, especially literacy. Given the much higher average education of the Hanuabadans in relation to the Frobisher Bay Eskimo (7·3 v. 3·0 years), the reversal in the rank ordering is not so surprising.

To what extent do these data support the proposed model? As noted on p. 135, mediating variables of socialization, arts and crafts and language are considered to be related to the ecological dimension in the predicted rank orderings. This conclusion has resulted from field observation and from ethnographic or linguistic reports, and is supported, in the case of socialization, by self-reporting from subjects in the various samples. That is, the Temne and Telefomin respondents report (and are reported in the literature as having) harsh techniques of socialization, emphasizing conformity and reliance upon the group; at the other extreme the Eskimo and Arunta have decidedly lenient and individually supportive socialization, while the other samples are rank ordered as they are on the ecological dimension. Further, within each sample, both individual and group data on socialization content and technique betray no gross inconsistences between these two aspects of the socialization process. In each sample observed and reported content (including aims) of child-rearing are consistent with the techniques employed. For arts and crafts practices, Eskimo and Arunta peoples generally are well-known internationally for exhibiting skill in artistic design and execution, while Temne and Telefomin output is of relatively poor quality and tends to be produced by only a few specialists among these peoples. Finally, the possession of geometrical-spatial terms in the languages of these samples is rank ordered consistently with the ecological dimension. It is therefore considered that these mediating variables are adapted to the ecological demands made upon these groups, and are available to the appropriate extent for the nurturing of the discrimination and spatial skills demanded by the group's ecology.

Although no data have been collected on disease, nutrition or gene pool, the functionally adaptive nature of protein nutrients may be illustrated. We know that a sufficient level of protein is necessary for perceptual/cognitive development (Cravioto, 1968; Dawson, 1966, 1967a), and from our hypothesis, we expect that there is a stronger requirement for perceptual development among some peoples than among others. Specifically, we would expect from the model that to hunt effectively, sufficient proteins should be available, and we note that within the ecological dimension as proposed, it is precisely the hunters who get the protein. In a sense then those who need the protein most to exist in a particular ecology have it available through hunting (Eskimo and Arunta), while those who need it least have lesser amounts available through reliance on rice or cassava farming (Temne and Telefomin).

With respect to the dependent variables, visual discrimination and spatial skills, it is apparent from the data that the visual skills are developed to a degree predictable from an analysis of the ecological demands facing the group, and the cultural aids developed by them. Further it is apparent that there are relationships between the ecological and psychological variables which are more than dichotomized ones; they appear to covary in a systematic way (cf. weak version of ecological-behavioural interaction) and can be demonstrated to be adaptive to the ecological demands placed on the group (cf. moderate version of ecological-behavioural interaction). Finally, the psychological underpinnings of technological development, often isolated as spatial ability, are shown to develop in relation to an ecology, which by way of technological change is open to change itself.

8

G. Jahoda (1970)

Supernatural beliefs and changing cognitive structures among Ghanaian university students[1]

Journal of Cross-Cultural Psychology, 1(2), pp. 115–30

The study of supernatural beliefs in non-Western cultures has hitherto remained almost exclusively within the domain of social anthropologists, whose major contribution has been the analysis of such beliefs within the context of social relations. However, they have usually concentrated on illiterate or semi-literate people and admit that 'very little reliable data exist concerning the status of witchcraft and sorcery beliefs among the modern educated elite' (Middleton and Winter, 1963, p. 20). The lack of knowledge in this sphere is unfortunate because of certain widely held views about supernatural beliefs: (a) it is suggested that their prevalence inhibits the motivation necessary for development (e.g. Hunter, 1962; Gelfand, 1967) and constitutes an obstacle to scientific and technological advance (e.g. Kavadias, 1966; Odhiambo, 1967); (b) it has also long been taken as almost axiomatic by numerous *self-evident* writers that Western education in general and science teaching in particular has, as Nduka (1964, p. 152) dramatically puts it, 'a shattering effect on superstition'. Now if (b) is true then one need not worry unduly about possible inimical effects of such beliefs on development, since the steady growth of education will eliminate them. The psychological assumption underlying such views is that the content of modern Western-type education is either logically contradictory to or dissonant with traditional supernatural beliefs; but as Horton (1967) maintains in a penetrating discussion, such assumptions are ill-founded.

The present study, carried out in Ghana in 1968, was designed to tackle some of these questions empirically. It had three major objec-

[1] The support for this research by the Nuffield Foundation, London, is gratefully acknowledged. The author is also indebted to Dr Cyril Fiscian and Mr Herbert Bulley of the Department of Psychology, University of Ghana, for their valuable assistance.

tives: (1) to establish the prevalence of supernatural beliefs among a student population; (2) to assess the effect of university residence and scientific training; and (3) to explore the correlates of supernatural beliefs and seek to throw some light on the nature of the cognitive structures involved. Findings concerning (2), which showed no discernible influence of university education, have already been reported (Jahoda, 1968); hence only (1) and (3) will be dealt with here. While the design of (1), based on previous work (Jahoda, 1961a, 1962) was a relatively straightforward task, that of (3) presented difficult problems, due to the almost complete lack of systematic psychological research in this sphere. The key question concerned the kinds of variables that could be expected to have relevance to supernatural beliefs; the sometimes rather complex considerations governing their selection must be set out in some detail.

RATIONALE FOR THE CHOICE OF CORRELATES

The mode of arriving at ideas about variables likely to be associated with supernatural beliefs – it would be pretentious to call them 'hypotheses' in this context – was mainly the scanning of anthropological and psychological literature, guided by the writer's experience of the West African situation. Some of them were apparently obvious and common sense, and as will be shown subsequently it was precisely these which often turned out to be false.

First, it was assumed that an individual's beliefs will tend to reflect those prevalent in his social environment; and further, that the frequency of supernatural beliefs in the social environment is likely to be inversely related to exposure to Western influences. From this it would follow that members of coastal tribes, in contact with Europe for several centuries, would hold fewer such beliefs than people from tribes in the northern forest zone and beyond. Regarding family background, the same principle would suggest that parents in Western-type occupations would result in fewer supernatural beliefs; and similarly for depth of literacy, i.e. whether the subject was a first, second or third-generation literate. While the main effect of the family is probably a function of direct transmission of beliefs, a possible indirect effect of parental occupation and literacy via modes of child-rearing has been discussed by Jahoda (1966). Another link between childhood training and adult beliefs is provided by the concept of field-dependence. According to Witkin *et al.* (1962) field-dependent persons tend to be more strongly affected by social influence in their attitudes and judgements. The relevance of this variable in a West African setting has been shown by Dawson (1967a) and Berry (1966b), but one could only hazard the prediction that field-dependent persons are likely to model themselves more closely on the salient features of the social environment. On the assumption that supernatural beliefs remain the norm, it was therefore expected that field-*independent* persons would retain fewer of these. However, it has also been suggested from an entirely different standpoint and without any direct reference to field-dependence that magical beliefs inhibit analytic perception and rational thinking (Vernon, 1969). From this it would follow that people with more magical beliefs should obtain lower (less analytic) scores on measures of field-dependence; presumably they should also do less well on intelligence tests.

A somewhat related issue is implicit in writings by anthropologists and educators working in Africa. They often point out that our Western dichotomy between 'natural' and 'supernatural' is far from being universally shared, the cosmos being conceived as unitary where every event has its meaningful place (e.g. Musgrove, 1952; Beattie, 1964). In other words, as has sometimes been specifically stated (Forde, 1954, p. xi) there is no room for the notion of chance. Piaget and Inhelder (*1951*) concluded that such a notion cannot emerge until an understanding of 'lawfulness' has been firmly established; but since they do not consider the case of the kind of universal lawfulness characteristic of traditional thinking, the bearing of their theory on the problem is unclear. Elsewhere (Jahoda, 1968) the writer has mooted the likelihood of an inverse relationship between the understanding of probability and chance and adherence to traditional supernatural beliefs.

The perusal of anthropological reports is liable to convey an impression of an almost pervasive preoccupation with dangers arising from magic, witchcraft and sorcery. This would be exaggerated, as is evident from discussions dealing explicitly with the saliency of supernatural beliefs (e.g. Crawford, 1967; Marwick, 1965). Nevertheless there is ample evidence, including psychiatric observations (Lambo, 1955) and other relevant studies (Jahoda, 1961c), that variations in one's fortunes in general, and misfortunes in particular, are apt to be attributed to outside agencies. One would therefore expect people in such societies to feel themselves less masters of their own fate than their counterparts in Western industrialized countries; and the extent to which this is the case should be related to the prevalence of supernatural beliefs.

Lastly, it commonly appears to be taken for granted not only that there exists a continuum whose two polar extremes are 'traditional' and

'Western', but that the various constituent elements of such an orientation will cluster together; for instance, this seems to be the assumption underlying Dawson's (1967b) T-W Scale. However, this view is in conflict with the present writer's observations, and it is therefore desirable to examine systematically the relationship between supernatural beliefs on the one hand and social, economic, and political ideas and attitudes on the other.

In addition to the major anticipated sources of variation in supernatural beliefs just discussed, a few others were considered; these will be indicated when the procedures are described.

METHODS

Subjects

These were 280 male full-time students living in halls of residence at Legon University, Ghana. An initial invitation to provide personal details with a view to participating in the research was circulated just prior to the 1967 Christmas vacation; probably in part due to this unavoidably inauspicious timing, only some 40 per cent of the 1,765 eligible students returned that form adequately completed. From these, a sample of 322 stratified by halls and type of course was drawn. The number actually taking part was 297, or 92 per cent of the sample drawn; of these, 17 had to be eliminated because they were non-Ghanaian, or women from a mixed hall included in error. The final sample cannot be claimed to be strictly representative of the whole male student population, and there was probably some volunteer bias. The nature of such a bias among Ghanaian students is unknown; but it seems reasonable to assume that it may not be unlike that in the United States (Rosenthal, 1965). In that case it would be characterized by greater intellectual ability, interest and motivation, which in the present context would mean that the bias acted in a conservative direction.

The main sample took no account of tribal affiliation – in any event practically nothing is known about psychological differences between tribes in Ghana. However, when a subsample was drawn for individual testing, this was confined to members of the Akan group of tribes in order to partly control for this variable. For the 70 students invited the response rate was 94 per cent.

Procedures

For the sample as a whole, instruments were group-administered. Personal background information was obtained, and of this only tribe and parental occupation was treated as nominal. Others were as follows: age, years of residence at university (UYR) and generation of literacy (LIT), with first, second and third-generation literates being assigned scores of 1, 2 and 3 respectively.

The measures of the other major variables, whose rationale has mostly been discussed, will now be briefly described:

(a) Index of Supernatural Beliefs (ISB). This was a measure of the main dependent variable, developed from an earlier one (Jahoda, 1961a, 1962). It consisted of ten 4-choice items dealing with traditional beliefs. The possible range of global scores was from 0 (total disbelief) to 20 (total belief).

(b) Internal versus External Control of Reinforcement (I/E). This was the measure employed to assess the felt degree of mastery over one's own fate. Apart from some minor modifications in wording the scale was applied in the form described by Rotter (1966).

(c) Modernity Scale (MS). The instrument used was the OM Scale devised by Smith and Inkeles (1966). The mode of scoring was modified, but remains equivalent to that of the original version.

(d) Index of Understanding of Probability and Chance (PC). This consisted of four items, the first two adapted from the work of Lambert and Zaleska (1966). Two other items were specially developed Piaget-type tests of the subjects' understanding of the idea of a chance distribution. The total range of scores was from 0 (no understanding) to 8 (complete understanding).

(e) Intelligence was assessed by means of the Perceptual Maze Test (PM). Details of this have been reported by Jahoda (1969a).

(f) Reported Severity of Child Rearing (REA). The form of the question adopted was that used by Berry (1966b); it consisted of asking whether parental treatment was very strict, fairly strict or not so strict, being scored 1, 2 and 3 respectively.

In the actual administration PM came first, followed by the I/E Scale; all subsequent measures, which included some other questions of theoretical interest, were randomized throughout.

In addition to the above, applied to the whole sample, two individual tests were confined to the Akan subsample:

(g) Witkin's Embedded Figures Test (EFT). This is a shortened form of the standard measure of field-dependence.

(h) Kohs Blocks (BD). This is not only a performance test of intelligence, but also serves as an alternative measure of field-dependence. The version used was the Block Design subtest of the Wechsler-Bellevue Scale.

RESULTS

Findings about the prevalence of various types of supernatural beliefs will be presented first, together with some preliminary account of relationships. Then the major variables will be examined, followed by a presentation of the patterns of correlation. In view of the emphasis on age differences, which might seem somewhat odd when one thinks of the rather narrow age range to which most Euramerican students are confined, some explanation is desirable. Ages of Ghanaian students vary from under 20 to over 40, many obtaining the necessary entrance qualifications in their spare time over a long period. Hence the total sample was split into those below 25 ($N = 144$) and those 25 and above ($N = 136$); the corresponding division for the Akan subsample yielded Ns of 32 and 34 respectively.

Supernatural beliefs

The topics of all ISB items together with the degree of assent obtained by each can be seen in Table 8.1. Most of the items were constructed as concrete situations, as it had become clear from previous work that such a form provides more satisfactory measures than abstract questions about beliefs in general.

   The broad picture that emerged was one of a high rate of survival of traditional beliefs among these university students. On over two-thirds of the items a clear majority expressed at least a qualified belief; i.e. they either answered that such an event probably did happen or responded 'probably not', thereby implying at least an acceptance of the possibility that it could have happened. Two of the most striking outcomes were the two-thirds who thought that the future can be foretold (item 8), and the massive consensus that witchcraft may be a real power (item 10).

   The item concerned with the fear of a magical threat against self deserves special comment. More than half the Ss would have taken such a threat seriously to the extent of feeling anxious, and one S in seven declared that they would have resorted to a counter-magical form of protection. Moreover, while age differences on all the other items were consistent but small and statistically insignificant, item 6

TABLE 8.1. *Distribution of responses to individual ISB items*
(percentages based on *N* = 280)

ISB items	Unqualified belief	Qualified belief	Unqualified disbelief
1. Twins different from ordinary children	4·3	54·6	41·1
2. Report of encounter with ghost	2·9	40·0	57·1
3. Day of birth influencing character	2·1	45·7	52·1
4. Adultery makes for difficult childbirth	1·0	49·0	50·0
5. Sudden illness brought on by enemy	0·7	58·3	41·1
6. Fear of magical threat against self	13·6	40·9	45·5
7. Report of dwarfs in the forest	8·9	52·9	38·2
8. Fortune tellers really know the future	0·7	69·4	30·0
9. Report of woman killed by spirit of shrine	6·4	64·3	29·3
10. Existence of witchcraft as a power	35·0	51·0	14·0

was an exception: 19 per cent of the younger students as compared with only 7 per cent of the older ones opted for protection; and the difference between the two sets of responses was significant ($p < 0.02$).

Anthropologists maintain that witchcraft and sorcery are embedded in a context of social tensions; and writers who have discussed the effect of supernatural beliefs on social and economic development have pointed to the vulnerability of the person who moves away from his social group; in particular, success is often believed to give rise to envy on the part of others, and this in turn may lead to a fear of magical attack. On occasions, this may be so acute as to lead to psychiatric breakdown (Prince, 1960; Jahoda, 1961b). In an attempt to collect some data relevant to this problem, respondents were asked whether in their opinion poorer relatives are jealous of the man who has made good; 76 per cent said this happens sometimes, and 15 per cent thought often or always. They were asked further about stories of relatives trying to inflict magical harm on the successful man; and no less than 73 per cent felt that such stories were probably or certainly true. On the assumption

F

TABLE 8.2. *Mean index of supernatural beliefs (ISB) and perceptual maze test (PM) scores in relation to tribe and parental occupation*

Variable	Tribes				
	Ga (N = 54)	Ashanti (N = 143)	Fante (N = 29)	Ewe (N = 12)	Other (N = 12)
ISB	7·11	6·43	6·59	6·93	7·67
PM	7·39	6·49	6·34	6·74	6·08

	Father's occupation[a]						
	Farming, fishing (N=113)	Crafts, other manual (N=27)	Clerical, allied (N=29)	Lower commercial (N=26)	Higher commercial (N=14)	Lower professional (N=40)	Higher professional (N=27)
ISB	6·92	7·00	7·10	6·19	6·93	6·20	5·96
PM	6·16	5·78	7·79	7·27	8·00	6·55	7·41

	Mother's occupation				
	Trader (N = 98)	Farmer (N = 77)	Crafts (N = 25)	Professional (N = 18)	Other (N = 62)
ISB	6·89	6·27	7·24	6·83	6·55
PM	6·86	5·91	6·20	8·39	7·00

[a] In four cases occupation was unclassifiable.

that the formulations of anthropologists and others are valid, one would expect these responses to be related to the degree of anxiety felt in the face of a magical threat; and this was in fact the case. There was a significant association between such anxiety and the view that relatives tend to be jealous ($x^2 = 8·10$; $df = 2$, $p < 0·02$), and between anxiety and the belief that jealous relatives may take magical action ($x^2 = 21·09$, $df = 2$, $p < 0·001$).

Broader social factors that might influence the general level of ISB were considered. Among these, neither tribal origin nor parental occupation appeared to be significant sources of variation. The latter finding was so unexpected as to arouse the suspicion that the mode of classification might be at fault. Hence the same analysis was carried out, as a check, with the Perceptual Maze scores. The outcome, presented in Tables 8.2 and 8.3, gives no reason to think that the classification was defective, and one is forced to the conclusion that neither fathers' nor mothers' occupations are significant determinants of ISB.

TABLE 8.3. *Analysis of variance of ISB and PM scores in relation to tribe and parental occupation*

Source of variance	df	MS	F	p<
ISB				
Between tribes	4	10·65	1·15	NS
Within tribes	275	9·26		
PM				
Between tribes	4	9·99	1·24	NS
Within tribes	275	8·06		
ISB				
Between father's occupation	6	7·44	0·79	NS
Within father's occupation	269	9·36		
PM				
Between father's occupation	6	22·82	2·80	0·01
Within father's occupation	269	8·14		
ISB				
Between mother's occupation	4	6·58	0·70	NS
Within mother's occupation	275	9·36		
PM				
Between mother's occupation	4	28·37	3·51	0·01
Within mother's occupation	275	8·08		

Sample, age and cross-cultural comparisons on major variables

The object of presenting the data in Tables 8.4, 8.5 and 8.6 is, first, to show that the Akan subsample did not diverge in any important way from the total sample; second, the data illustrate the systematic age difference on almost every measure; lastly, where suitable, comparison data from other cultures are available, and these are juxtaposed with the Ghana data.

On ISB the older students scored significantly lower, i.e. they subscribed to fewer supernatural beliefs and/or expressed such beliefs in a more qualified manner. Older students also had a lower score on the Perceptual Maze Test, which is in line with British work by Davies (1965); no comparison data are shown, because Davies had used a

TABLE 8.4. Scores on chief measures by age and sample

Meas-ures	Below 25 years				Age 25 years and above				t values	
	Sample (N = 144)		Subsample (N = 32)		Sample (N = 136)		Subsample (N = 34)			
	M	SD	M	SD	M	SD	M	SD	Sample	Subsample
ISB	7·15	2·84	6·88	3·02	6·17	3·20	5·00	3·33	2·67[b]	2·29[b]
PM	7·26	2·81	6·91	3·27	6·04	2·86	5·82	2·86	3·54[c]	1·41
PC	4·26	1·93	3·91	1·78	4·74	1·98	4·15	1·94	2·03[a]	0·52
MS	63·28	15·73	64·56	16·32	62·52	13·82	65·65	13·34	0·43	0·29
I/E	9·72	4·23	9·00	4·52	7·85	3·93	8·00	3·81	3·71	0·97

[a] $p < 0.05$. [b] $p < 0.01$. [c] $p < 0.001$.

TABLE 8.5. *Measures applied only to Akan subsample*

Measures	Below 25 years (N = 32)		Age 25 years and above (N = 34)		t values
	M	SD	M	SD	
EFT	73·24	36·20	100·62	38·74	2·92[b]
BD	27·59	8·07	22·71	7·95	2·47[a]

[a] $p < 0.05$.   [b] $p < 0.01$.

different version of the test. On the measure of understanding of probability and chance a higher score indicates lower performance, so that older Ss tended to do less well. It is possible to compare results on two of the subtasks with those of French students tested by Lambert and Zaleska (1966); rounded percentages of wrong responses were, respectively, 20 and 38 in Paris as compared with 46 and 56 in Accra. Thus the general level of understanding was clearly much lower, though lack of familiarity with the nature of the task was undoubtedly a contributory factor. The Modernity Scale was the only one that failed to differentiate between the ages. The scale of Internal versus External Reinforcement proved younger students to be more external than

TABLE 8.6. *Comparison data from other cultures*

Measures	Sample	N	M	SD
I/E	Ohio State University male elementary psychology students	575	8·15	3·88
	Kansas State University male elementary psychology students	45	7·71	3·84
	University of Connecticut male elementary psychology students	134	8·72	3·59
EFT	University of Nigeria (Nsukka) male students			
	Urban home background	11	84·48	35·78
	Rural home background	22	103·37	40·33
	New York University male students	34	47·99	23·88
BD	WAIS American standardization sample (age 20–34)		33·0[a]	10·0[a]

[a] Approximate figure.

older ones. The absolute mean values of the I/E score are of great interest when set against American data; it is evident that the mean scores of these Ghanaian students are not significantly different.

The remaining two measures, being individually administered, were confined to the Akan subsample. In relation to EFT it should be noted that a *high* score connotes field-*dependence*; the findings are similar to those obtained by Okonji (1969) in Nigeria. Insofar as Block Design is treated as a measure of field-dependence, the direction of scoring is opposite to that of EFT, so that the results are consistent.

Correlates of supernatural beliefs as a function of age

When the material was first analysed on the basis of the expectations formulated in the introduction, few significant relationships were found and the resulting pattern seemed to make little sense. It was one particular lack of significant correlation, between ISB and EFT, which provided the key to the problem. It led to a questioning of the original hunch that field-dependence would be associated with more supernatural beliefs, through a scrutiny of the assumption that the 'field' had remained constant. With the aim of testing this possibility, the relationship was broken down by age as shown in Tables 8.7 and 8.8. As is evident from the cell values, it turned out that there was a highly significant interaction; the field-dependence variable was relevant for the older, but not the younger subjects. However, contrary to expectation, it was the field-*independent* older students who held more supernatural beliefs.

TABLE 8.7. *Mean ISB by age and EFT*

	ISB scores		
EFT group	*Below age 25*	*Age 25 and above*	*All ages*
Below EFT median (field-independent)	6·21	7·62	6·78
Above EFT median (field-dependent)	7·85	3·38	6·09
All EFT	6·88	5·00	5·90

TABLE 8.8. *Analysis of variance of mean ISB scores by age and EFT*

Source of variance	df	MS	F	$p <$
EFT	I	20·27	2·07	NS
Age	I	39·68	4·06	0·05
Interaction	I	136·10	13·92	0·001
Individuals	62	9·78	—	—

Note: In view of the disproportionate subclass members in this 2 × 2 table the MS are arrived at by correction for disproportion.

When the importance of age became evident, separate correlations for the two age-groups were computed and those between ISB and other variables are given in Table 8.9. Among the top set, which are

TABLE 8.9. *Correlations with ISB*

	Below age 25		Age 25 and above	
Consistent across ages	Sample (N = 144)	Subsample (N = 32)	Sample (N = 136)	Subsample (N = 34)
Internal *v.* external control (I/E)	0·30[b]	0·41[a]	0·30[b]	0·35[a]
Years at university (UYR)	0·11	0·30	0·09	0·32
Probability and chance (PC)	−0·11	−0·23	−0·10	−0·08
Literacy (LIT)	0·03	0·11	0·05	0·20
Perceptual Maze (PM)	—	0·37[a]	0·05	0·06
Differing according to ages				
Rearing permissiveness (REA)	0·17[a]	0·31	−0·05	—
Modernity (MS)	−0·08	−0·03	−0·24[b]	−0·40[a]
Field-dependence (EFT)		0·15		−0·55[b]
Block Design (BD)		−0·09		0·34

Note: Sign of PC reversed, i.e. greater understanding goes with fewer beliefs.
[a] $p < 0.05$.   [b] $p < 0.005$.

broadly consistent across ages, only two were clearly in the expected direction, namely I/E and PC; and the former alone is substantial and significant. Otherwise the modest trend was for subjects who had spent more years at the university and for those from a more literate home background to retain more supernatural beliefs. The single significant correlation with PM is likely to be a mere sampling fluctuation. Within the lower set, reported rearing permissiveness is associated with more supernatural beliefs among the younger subjects. On the other hand it was only the older *S*s who exhibited a significant correlation between *lack* of modernity and adherence to supernatural beliefs. If one adds to this the data on field-dependence, already presented in another form (Table 8.7), it becomes evident that there were some sharp differences in the correlates of ISB according to age.

DISCUSSION

The salient finding is the high overall level of adherence to supernatural beliefs that prevailed among Ghanaian university students in 1968; in particular, belief in the power of witchcraft was rejected by only a small minority. There is evidence supporting the internal consistency of the responses in terms of predictions based on anthropological theory: anxiety about magical threats was significantly related to perceived jealousy on the part of relatives. As had been expected, a high score on external control was associated with high ISB scores. Surprisingly, however, the mean I/E scores corresponded closely to that of American student norms. If one assumes cross-cultural equivalence – and it would be difficult to disprove such an assumption in this case – it implies that the stereotype frequently voiced in the past about superstitious Africans feeling themselves constantly in the grip of malevolent external forces is unfounded. As Crawford (1967, p. 292) remarked about a Rhodesian tribe, 'The Shona no more spends his ordinary waking hours thinking about wizardry than you or I spend our time thinking about the atomic bomb. This, however, does not mean that wizardry is not important in Shona society nor the Atom Bomb in ours.' Some of the coping mechanisms used in this context by Ghanaians have been discussed elsewhere (Jahoda, 1961c).

In view of the extensive penetration of Western influences to all parts of the country, and the greatly increased rate of geographical mobility, the lack of any significant association between tribe and ISB is understandable; what is puzzling is the same lack as regards depth of literacy and type of parental occupation. One can of course speculate *post hoc*: for instance, since children from all kinds of backgrounds spend much of their time in the care of illiterate relations or nursemaids, such beliefs could have been stamped in at an impressionable age. Unfortunately this would fail to account for the fact that some sceptics came from a totally illiterate background; so one has to consider the possibility that subsequent influences may have obliterated childhood ones. The matter is obviously one of considerable complexity. Similarly, it is difficult to see why reported permissiveness of rearing should correlate with high ISB scores in the younger group, especially as the effect does not appear to be mediated through field-independence. There were also indications, not reported in detail, that type of course pursued was differentially related to both age and ISB; but the precise nature of the relationship cannot be properly identified from the present data.

Otherwise the pattern of age differences is clear enough. The younger group holds more supernatural beliefs; both groups subscribe to the same extent to 'modern' as against 'traditional' ideas and values in such spheres as marriage, education, social relationships and power; but whereas in the younger group degree of 'modernity' was unrelated to supernatural beliefs, in the older group there was an inverse relation so that 'traditionalists' had higher ISB scores. Thus only the older group conformed in its cognitive structure to the assumption built into Dawson's (1967b) 'Traditional versus Western Attitude Scale'. Greater understanding of probability and chance goes together with fewer supernatural beliefs in the younger group. Lastly, the field-dependence variable was quite unconnected with ISB among the latter; but in the older group field-*independence* was closely associated with holding more supernatural beliefs.

Before commenting on this finding, it is necessary to raise a fundamental question: are the observed age differences synchronic or diachronic phenomena? In other words, are the characteristics displayed by the older students merely a function of their having entered university at a late stage in their career, or do they reflect mainly a basic secular change in the structure of ideas, beliefs and attitudes? Clearly, a cross-sectional study like the present one cannot itself provide an unambiguous answer. However, as is implicit in the title the writer strongly leans towards the second alternative. The grounds for this, especially as regards cognitive structure, are admittedly little more than impressionistic. Fairly close contact with educated Ghanaians over a period of some fifteen years led to the view that modernity of outlook was gradually becoming dissociated from adherence to supernatural beliefs; and this was one of the observations that provided the impetus for the present study. There are rather more substantial reasons for suggesting that supernatural beliefs are coming to be more widely held by educated Ghanaians. In 1955 a study of various aspects of Westernization was conducted (Jahoda, 1961a) which included some assessment of the prevalence of such beliefs; since the study dealt with all kinds of literates, from those with only primary schooling upwards, the actual content was different and direct comparisons are not possible. What one can do is to take the proportion in 1955 of people with at least secondary schooling who rejected all supernatural beliefs, juxtaposing this with the 1968 students scoring zero on ISB; the respective percentages were 6·8 and 3·2. Considering the high overall level of belief this is of course a rather ineffective measure; but the difference is clearly in the expected direction, though only at the borderline of significance (CR = 1·95). A more striking indication of a rise in supernatural beliefs comes from a study of prophet-healing cults originally undertaken in 1954 (Jahoda, 1961b), followed by a more informal scrutiny in 1968; the doctrine of these cults embodies a mixture of Christian elements and traditional Ghanaian notions of witchcraft and sorcery. Not only does the number of such cults seem to have substantially increased, but their adherents who were in the past largely confined to the illiterate and semi-literate section of the population now include members of the intellectual élite such as doctors, lawyers, university teachers and students. The conclusion is inevitable that there has been something of what Mason (1967) called 'the revolt against Western values'; in this instance it is perhaps better described as a partial return to traditional West African cosmological notions. This is the kind of change exhibited by the younger students, and their declared concern with supernatural threats suggests that it has become an integral part of their cognitive structure, and is not merely a superficial nationalistic gesture.

If this conclusion be granted, it becomes possible to propose an interpretation of the seemingly strange relationship between field-independence and high ISB scores among the older group. At the time when they went to school the prevailing 'field', i.e. the evaluation of traditional supernatural beliefs, still remained strongly negative; holding 'superstitious' beliefs was tantamount to being 'primitive' or 'bush', a very damaging imputation tolerated only by the field-independent people. With the transformation of the intellectual climate the field-dependent ones rejecting many supernatural beliefs found themselves out of step, and one would expect them to adapt themselves to the norms of other university students with increasing exposure; this is in fact what seems to have happened, though numbers in the subsample were too small for significance testing. As far as the younger students are concerned, the change was already well under way by the time they moved through the school system; therefore they largely escaped the cross-pressures which might otherwise have separated them along the field-dependence dimension. All this is of course speculative; it helps to make sense of the data, yet not without raising some awkward problems about possible critical periods when field-dependence might produce maximal acceptance of external influences.

Studies which, like the present one, take as their starting point a dependent variable in an almost completely unexplored field cannot usually yield much systematic and coherent knowledge. Their major function is to clear away some of the undergrowth of unfounded assumption and false stereotypes and help prepare the path for more rigorous research guided by clearly formulated hypotheses. In spite of these limitations it is possible to venture at least the tentative conclusion that the younger generation of Ghanaian students have achieved what Barbichon (1968) called 'a state of cognitive coexistence' between modern ideas and values and some traditional African beliefs.

9

M. Cole, J. Gay and J. Glick (1968)
Some experimental studies of Kpelle quantitative behaviour

Psychonomic Monograph, 2(10), Whole No. 26

Although anthropologists and psychologists have long recognized the mutual relevance of their disciplines, the actual interaction of the disciplines has been largely confined to the broad area of socialization and personality formation (Hsu, 1961; French, 1963; Triandis, 1964). Even those who claim to be concerned with 'cognitive' factors (e.g. Triandis) deal mainly with problems at an interpersonal level.

For many years, data concerning individual cognitive functions (concept formation, memory, perception) came mainly from anthropologists and those philosophers who relied on the reports of anthropologists and missionaries (Boas, 1911b; Cassirer, 1953; Lévy-Bruhl, 1926). Although these accounts proved fruitful of hypotheses (and controversies), these hypotheses in general were not put in a form to be tested by specific experiments.

One possible exception to this generalization comes from the various efforts to gather data on the 'nature-nurture' controversy and the subsequent search for 'culture-free intelligence tests' (Porteus, 1937; Bieshcuvel, 1952b). However, the data of such tests, designed as they are on a pragmatic basis, yielded more information about comparative performances of individuals within different cultures than the cognitive processes at work.

In recent years there has been an increasing trend to seek experimental evidence about the effect of culture on individual cognitive processes through the application of experimental-psychological and linguistic techniques. Much of this work has been motivated by an interest in assessing the generality of Piaget's (1951) theory of cognitive development (Price-Williams, 1961; Bruner, Olver and Greenfield, 1966; and others). Linguistic techniques underlie the effort to develop 'ethnoscientific' descriptions of cultures through an analysis of the classification of the world provided by the indigenous language (Romney and D'Andrade, 1964). Cutting across the entire area is a pervasive interest in the relation between language and cognition usually discussed in terms of the Sapir–Whorf hypothesis.

In the present article we will report on a series of exploratory studies, conducted among the Kpelle tribe of Liberia, which seeks to combine experimental-psychological and anthropological techniques to provide information on a specific area of cognitive behaviour, namely, quantitative and logical thinking.

This research was first undertaken as part of a larger project sponsored by Educational Services, Inc., Cambridge, Massachusetts, to develop mathematics texts for use in African schools.

It is common observation that African children experience difficulties in learning mathematics. In exploring the causes of these difficulties (which are by no means restricted to Africans), various solutions were suggested, among them the development of new, specially written textbooks. One of the present authors (John Gay), who participated in writing these textbooks, was also interested in studying mathematics indigenous to the tribal people for whom the books were to be written. The resulting research has been summarized in a recent book (Gay and Cole, 1967). The series of experiments to be reported here in detail were first described in general form in this book, which also contains a description of the social-cultural context within which the work was done.

Besides influencing the particular problems which we studied, the concern of this initial project with the relation of mathematics education to Kpelle tribal life determined the groups with whom we worked. In addition to tribal adults, the bearers of indigenous mathematical knowledge in its fully developed state, we wanted to study children who were old enough to be attending school, but who had not in fact entered school. We also wanted to study children already in school in order to determine what changes brief exposure to the then-existing academic programme had wrought.

As it turned out, many of the tasks we devised were not those familiar to Western psychology. Consequently, in order to obtain some sort of baseline against which to judge our African results, parallel research had to be conducted in the United States. But this immediately raised the question of what sort of comparison group would be appropriate; certainly no 'control group' in the usual sense of the word could be found. Our strategy was to study a wide range of American groups and to make comparisons where it was deemed useful.

The resulting potpourri of experimental techniques and subject populations makes systematic interpretations in terms of general cultural or developmental factors extremely hazardous. However, it has the virtue of precluding premature overgeneralization and providing a number of useful hints about the direction that future work should take.

A few comments need to be made about the experimental context of these studies, although a thorough discussion is beyond the scope of this paper. (See Gay and Cole, 1967, for more detailed remarks on these matters.)

All of the studies to be reported here were first carried out among the Kpelle tribe in North-Central Liberia. There are approximately 250,000 Kpelle in Liberia, where they are the largest of sixteen major tribes. Approximately the same number live in Guinea, where they are known as the Guerze.

The people live in small towns of between 20 and 300 huts with between 50 and 1500 inhabitants, perhaps ten miles apart. Rice is the basic crop; others merely supplement the diet or the family income. Kpelle-land is dense tropical rain forest.

The Kpelle language is related to Mende in Sierra Leone and Malinke in Mali; Kpelle culture shares many features, in particular, a strong secret-society system, with the neighbouring West African tribes. There is no traditional form of written Kpelle, but a few Kpelle have been taught to read using a phonetic alphabet.

As a rule, our Africa experimentation was done by Kpelle students attending Cuttington College, the base of our operations. These assistants were trained by the authors who were present while many of these data were collected. These experimenter-informants were always consulted as to the proper manner for translating the various instructions from English into Kpelle and were provided with typed versions of the instructions. Experiments were conducted informally in a village house, a local gathering place, or simply on the ground beneath a tree. It was not uncommon for a small crowd to gather nearby to watch the proceedings; participation in the experiments was an amusing diversion for many of the villagers, but where extensive time was required, S was 'dashed' a can of meat or a quarter. Before beginning a series of experiments in a village, the general purpose of our research was explained to the town chief and the villagers, whose cooperation as a group was essential to the success of our work.

GEOMETRIC CONCEPT FORMATION

One of the striking facts about Kpelle geometric terminology is the paucity of terms naming abstract geometric shapes and the imprecision of those terms that are used (see Gay and Cole, 1967). For instance, the term for circle 'kɛrɛ-kɛrɛ' is used to describe the shape of a pot, a frog, a sledge hammer, and a turtle. Some of the figures termed 'kɛrɛ-kɛrɛ' were elliptical, a fact which some informants noted by applying the adjective 'long' to the shape term. In general, however, it appears that this Kpelle term is most closely approximated by the topological-concept of a simple closed path, although some slight measure of circularity is required for the term to be used.

In similar fashion, the term for triangle 'kpɛilaa' is applied to a tortoise shell, arrowhead, bird's nest, and bow. Thus it can be seen that the term is not restricted to figures formed by three straight line segments.

This type of observation led us to hypothesize that part of the Kpelle child's difficulty in working with geometric figures is his prior inexperience with such figures defined in a Euclidean fashion and the consequent paucity of terms for talking about them. In order to determine if the relative absence of geometric terms does influence learning which involves geometric figures, a set of problems was constructed, the solution of which required S to identify a geometrically defined concept.

Method

Subjects. Thirty Ss were drawn from each of the three basic Kpelle groups used throughout this report: Kpelle adults (adults of Kpelle tribal background who do not speak English, have travelled little, and who remain in large measure tied to traditional Kpelle ways; average age, 32 years); Kpelle schoolchildren (children who have attended 1–6 years of school; average age, 14 years); Kpelle illiterate children (children who have not attended school and who know little or no English; average age, 9·5 years). In all cases, ages are estimated to within the nearest year or two because it is rare for a Kpelle to know his exact age. Twenty-five American children drawn from a middle-class kindergarten and first-grade class were run for comparative purposes.

Procedure. Each S was asked to solve ten different geometry identification problems (with exceptions noted below). The problems were: (1) triangle-circle, (2) right angle-non-right angle, (3) circle-ellipse,

(4) straight edge-curved line segment, (5) triangle-rectangle, (6) large area-small area, (7) closed-open curve, (8) wide-narrow figure, (9) larger-smaller angle, (10) quadrilateral-nonquadrilateral. They were presented to S in the order listed.

A problem was considered solved when the S consistently chose the proper classes of figures presented in the experiment. In order to preclude simple recall of specific instances, each concept (class of figures) was represented by sixteen different instances. Each instance was presented twice, so that the entire training session consisted of a maximum of thirty-two trials. The order of presentation ensured that all instances were presented once before any instance was repeated.

The Ss were instructed as follows in the appropriate native language: 'I am going to show you two things. When I show them to you I will have one of these things in my mind. I want you to tell me which thing I am thinking of.' The experimenter then presented the first pair of figures, and the S made a choice. The S was then told 'right' or 'wrong', and the next pair of figures was presented. This procedure was repeated until S had been presented with thirty-two pairs or until he made eight correct responses in a row. After completing each problem S was asked to explain his solution.

The method of stimulus presentation was not held constant during the course of the experiment. For the initial ten Ss in each of the Kpelle groups, the figures were scratched in the sand one at a time and erased with a broom between trials. This procedure, although a traditional means of pictorial representation among the Kpelle, proved so laborious that it was abandoned in favour of a small blackboard on which each pair of figures was drawn at the start of each trial. The more Westernized approach seemed to produce no noticeable difficulties for our Ss.

With the American Ss the blackboard was in turn abandoned for printed cards. Each of the sixteen pairs of figures was drawn on an 8 by 11 inch card; the cards were shown to S one at a time.

Results

The basic datum on which all comparisons are based is the number of trials required to reach a criterion of eight consecutive correct responses. A score of thirty-two was assigned to protocols which did not contain a criterion run.

Table 9.1 contains a summary of the performance of the four groups for each of the ten problems. Taken as a whole, Table 9.1 is difficult to interpret because of the many possible comparisons and varying numbers of data points on which comparisons are based. However, by summing over the appropriate cells of the table and comparing the resulting scores by means of *t* tests, the following generalizations can be made.

TABLE 9.1. *Geometry identification (mean trials to an 8/8 criterion)*

	Kpelle illiterate children (30)[b]	Kpelle illiterate adults (30)	Kpelle school- children (30)	American kindergarten and 1st grade (25)
1. Triangle-circle	8·4	5·2	3·5	5·2
2. Circle-ellipse	12·5	5·5	3·7	1·3
3. Triangle-rectangle	13·0	6·5	2·7	3·5
4. Large area-small area	12·9	7·9	9·6	4·3
5. Large angle-small angle	13·9	7·0	4·6	7·3[a]
6. Wide-narrow	16·3	6·9	6·2	19·4[a]
7. Open-closed figure	15·3	12·5	11·1	8·7[a]
8. Right angle-non-right angle	14·0	14·7	8·0	12·1
9. Straight-curved	17·2	13·6	7·7	6·5
10. Quadrilateral-non-quadrilateral	24·7	19·5	14·4	16·8[a]

[a] These items were run with a group of nine Ss.
[b] The number in parentheses indicates the standard number of Ss in that group.

(1) For less Westernized Kpelle, the speed with which the various concepts are identified increases with age. The overall mean trials to criterion for the Kpelle adults is 10·0, while the mean for the illiterate children is 14·9 ($t = 5·9$, $df = 58$, $p < 0·001$).

(2) The Kpelle schoolchildren ($M = 7·2$) perform better on an overall basis than the Kpelle adults ($M = 10·0$) ($t = 4·5$, $df = 58$, $p < 0·001$).

(3) The overall superiority of the schoolchildren can be accounted for by those problems which have the most relevance to their school-work. We should expect the schoolchildren to excel on those problems where recognizable geometrical figures form the basis for solution. This was the case for problems 1, 2, 3, 5, 8 and 9 in Table 9.1, but not for the remaining problems. When we compare the performance of schoolchildren and adults on the four problems for which the school-children most certainly lacked special training, we find that the two groups do not differ (mean for adults is 11·7; mean for schoolchildren is 10·5; $t < 1$). Thus, the overall superiority of the schoolchildren – see

(2) above – must be based on problems which have received special attention in the schools.

(4) The general performance of the American and Kpelle school-children is quite similar. (The overall means are 7·0 and 7·2, respectively.) The differences which appear on individual problems (for instance, the Americans do better on large area-small area, but worse on wide-narrow) do not easily group themselves into a recognizable pattern, although in some cases, the absolute magnitude of the difference is quite large.

In general, it appears that there are both cultural and developmental differences in the rate with which these geometry problems are solved. The general ease with which the Kpelle schoolchildren solve those problems which involve figures they have encountered in the classroom indicates that the ability to identify geometric figures (or, more precisely, the lack of such ability) is not sufficient to account for the mathematics difficulties these children experience.

LOGIC IDENTIFICATION

The English and Kpelle languages have what appear to be very different ways of expressing logical relations. An example is the disjunctive 'or'. In English, 'or' is an ambiguous word whose meaning must be determined from the context. Thus, one may say, 'I'm coming or I'm staying home'; 'I hear a car or automobile'; 'Billy or Jimmy may come'. The last sentence points up a particularly important ambiguity – is it the case that only one of the boys may come (exclusive disjunction) or that both may come (inclusive disjunction). In Kpelle, as in Latin, the different senses of 'or' are expressed by separate terms.

It is well known in American concept formation studies that disjunctive concepts are more difficult to learn than conjunctive ones (Bruner, Goodnow and Austin, 1956, p. 57; H. Wells, 1963). Will this be true in Kpelle-land, where there is less linguistic ambiguity involving disjunction?

It is possible to design concept identification experiments which embody various logical relations. In this initial report, we will discuss the results for three such conditions, those involving conjunction, disjunction and negation because these are the conditions for which we have the best cross-cultural data. The same general procedure can be used to study implication, equivalence, etc. (cf. Haygood and Bourne, 1965).

Method

Subjects. The Kpelle Ss were the same as those who participated in the geometry experiment. Three groups of Americans participated in this study as well as several of the succeeding ones: two groups of school-children (7–9 years and 10–12 years) from the New Haven school system from working-class backgrounds, and a group of adults from a New Haven working-class neighbourhood whose participation was solicited through a local church. The average age of the adult group was 36 years.

Procedure. For the Kpelle Ss, the stimuli were composed of patches of coloured cloth (red, green, yellow and white) which were placed in front of the S at the start of each trial. The cloth patches were laid out in pairs (for instance, red-green, red-yellow). The S chose one of the two pairs. If the correct pair was chosen, the E said, 'That's right', and the next trial's stimuli were presented. If an incorrect pair was chosen, S was told, 'That is not correct; this one is correct' (pointing), and the next trial was begun. The S was presented stimulus pairs for forty trials, or until a correct choice occurred on ten consecutive trials.

At the start of the experiment, S was shown the first pairs of stimuli and told that the E would have one of the two pairs in mind on every trial. He was urged to try to identify the correct pair as often as possible.

The procedure for the Americans differed only in that the stimuli were presented on 9 by 10 inch white cards, the stimulus pairs being 2 by 2 inch coloured paper patches pasted on to each card.

Results

Table 9.2 shows the mean transformed number of trials to criterion for each of the basic groups.

The most interesting data in Table 9.2 concern the relation between disjunctive and conjunctive concept learning in the two cultures. To evaluate this question, a 2 by 2 by 3 analysis of variance (concept type by culture by age) was conducted on the data in the table. Prior to analysis, the scores were transformed (using $\sqrt{x + 1}$) to reduce the skewness of the raw data. This analysis supports the following conclusions:

(1) The overall difference between concept types is not significant ($F = 2 \cdot 2$, $df = 1/245$, $p > 0 \cdot 10$).

(2) The interaction between culture and concept type is significant

TABLE 9.2. *Identification of logical rules (mean trial of the last error)*

	Kpelle			American		
	Illiterate children	School-children	Adults	7–9 years	10–12 years	Adults
Conjunction	3·67[a]	1·75	4·06	3·80	2·01	3·48
	(20)[b]	(20)	(20)	(22)	(22)	(32)
Disjunction	2·49	1·95	3·98	4·00	3·36	4·98
	(20)	(20)	(20)	(22)	(22)	(17)
Negation	4·33	3·87	4·59	4·60	4·30	4·98
	(20)	(20)	(20)	(37)	(37)	(25)

[a] Means are calculated for the $\sqrt{x + 1}$ transformed raw scores.
[b] Numbers in parentheses represent the number of Ss in the given group.

($F = 9\cdot5$, $df = 1/245$, $p < 0\cdot01$): this reflects the fact that the Kpelle learn the two concept types with about equal ease, while the Americans tend to learn conjunction more easily.

(3) There is a difference among age-groups ($F = 23\cdot9$, $df = 2/245$, $p < 0\cdot01$); the schoolchildren and 10–12 year olds tend to learn more rapidly than the other two groups. Since age and education are essentially confounded, this finding should be interpreted with caution.

(4) There is a significant interaction between age and concept type ($F = 3\cdot4$, $df = 2/245$, $p < 0\cdot05$); referring to the table, one can see that there is a tendency for the older Ss to find conjunction easier in relation to disjunction than the young children.

A separate analysis of the negation data indicated that the apparent tendency for the Kpelle Ss to learn this problem more quickly than the Americans is not significant.

Taken as a whole, these data do give some support to the expectation that the speed at which logical rules can be identified is related to linguistic structure. Since demonstrations of a relation between linguistic factors and cognition are relatively rare (see for instance, Segall, Campbell and Herskovits, 1966) and the variability observed in our experiment was large, we want to be cautious in our interpretations. At present, an experiment is under way which seeks to ask the same question about linguistic-cognitive relationships, but with much more simple stimuli in an effort to distil out the linguistic factors that are at work.

The age differences and age by concept interaction suggest that a serious effort at studying the genesis of the conjunctive-disjunctive difference within American culture would be well worth while. The one study we are aware of (King, 1966) yielded negative results with respect to the interaction between age and the relative difficulty of conjunctive and disjunctive concept learning.

MEASUREMENT

As part of our inquiry into the factors which might contribute to the Kpelle child's difficulties in school mathematics, we were led to ask what kinds of measurements are habitually made in Kpelle tribal life, what measurement systems are used, and the degree of accuracy usually required in making measurements.

Although a detailed description of the anthropological and linguistic aspects of Kpelle measurement behaviour are beyond the scope of this report (see Gay and Cole, 1967), certain of our earlier conclusions are relevant to a description of the data to be presented here.

First, we found Kpelle measurement to be highly situation bound; there are no general metrics to cover measurement along a given dimension. For instance, the American can apply the metric 'foot' to a table, a rug, a floor, the space between two houses, and even a road if he so chooses; he might also use the metrics 'inch', 'yard', or 'mile'. The Kpelle, on the other hand, is likely to use 'handspan' to measure a table, 'armspan' for a rug, 'footlength' for a floor, etc. In other words, he has separate metrics for separate situations requiring measurement. There is no standard relation between the metrics in the sense that the Kpelle does not translate from 'handspan' to 'armspan' in the way that we translate from foot to yard.

A second important initial observation is that the Kpelle speaks in terms of a specific measure only in certain contexts, such as rice farming. In other cases, he is likely to use the qualitative metric, small/large, if asked to describe some quantity. Within any given context, these measurement terms seem to have taken on a generally accepted meaning which imparts a degree of accuracy adequate for most Kpelle purposes. For instance, if one asks a Kpelle man how far it is to the neighbouring town, a typical reply would be, 'It is not far'. Even if asked 'Yes, but how far?' the answer can be, 'Not far'. Only if really pressed for detailed information, is the answer likely to employ the Kpelle metric for long distances, 'It is a walk of (some measure of time)'.

Finally, there are some things to which we might apply measures which the Kpelle does not measure and seems to have a great deal of trouble measuring if asked to do so. This fact was discovered quite accidently when a Kpelle college graduate was asked to say, in Kpelle, how far he was standing from one of the authors. He answered, 'Four feet', in English, but he could not think of a way to say this in Kpelle. Upon questioning, it turned out that there was no proper metric for measuring such a short distance between people and, lacking such a metric, the explicit measurement would not be made except under extraordinary circumstances.

It should be pointed out that these observations made on the Kpelle are not unique. Hallowell (1955) reports very similar findings from his studies of the Saulteaux Indians of North America. Not only are the general sorts of metrics the same as those encountered by Gay and Cole working with the Kpelle, but the conclusions which Hallowell reaches on the basis of the anthropological data are also quite similar; the various units of measurement are independent of one another and adequate for those tasks met daily by the people.

These anthropological observations imply several things about the way in which nontechnological people use measurements. First of all, they are likely to experience difficulties when asked to make a measurement of an object or distance using culturally inappropriate units of measurement. Second, they ought to be most accurate when using traditional units of measurement in traditional situations. Third, there ought to be little relation between the measurements if a given distance (for instance) is estimated in various ways.

In order to evaluate these propositions, we conducted several small experiments each of which involved some sort of measurement or estimation. Both appropriate and inappropriate situations were included, as well as comparison groups from the United States. The inclusion of American Ss provided us with situations in which the measurements appropriate to one group were inappropriate for their counterparts in the other culture. It was hoped that in this way a better evaluation of appropriateness and cultural factors could be obtained.

Volume measurement: the estimation of rice

In the introduction to this section, we stated that only in certain contexts do we find exact quantitative measurements systems among the Kpelle. As we mentioned there, one of these is the case of rice, with a complex set of interrelated measures (see Gay and Cole, 1967, p. 64). To be sure, a small-large metric can also be used, but for some purposes, a very exact metric is brought into play. The existence of this measurement system for rice seems reasonable in view of the critical role that rice plays in the life of the people. At certain times of the year, very small amounts of rice can mean the difference between eating and going hungry.

In order to determine if the relative complexity of the rice-units system and the everyday importance of rice result in accurate estimation of small amounts of rice, the following experiment was conducted.

Subjects. The Kpelle Ss were the illiterate adults and schoolchildren. The American Ss were twenty adults (average estimated age, 36 years) and twenty schoolchildren (5th–6th graders, 10–13 years). The American Ss were all from working-class areas of New Haven.

Procedure. The S stood before a table on which were placed four household canisters containing dry rice. From S's left to right, the canisters contained 3, 6, 4·5, and 1·5 pint cans of rice. The pint can is a standard unit of rice measurement among the Kpelle – it corresponds to the US tall No. 1 can exactly, and contains almost exactly two measuring cups of rice. The canisters, which varied in size for each value, were each approximately half filled.

The S was instructed as follows: 'There is uncooked rice in each of these containers. The idea is to estimate how many cans of rice there are in each container. Here is a standard size can . . .' Instructions were given in the appropriate native language, and there was no feedback between successive guesses.

Results. The performance of the various groups on this task are presented in terms of the relative error of each estimation for each container. The relative error is the ratio of the difference between the S's estimate and the correct amount, divided by the correct amount. Thus, if the S says 'four cans' when three cans are present, the relative error is $(4-3)/3 = +0·333$; if the response is 'two cans' under these conditions, the relative error is $(2-3)/3 = -0·333$. The results are presented in Fig. 9.1.

Two points stand out in these data. First, the Kpelle adults are extremely accurate in their estimates. Second, the American adults are widely inaccurate. The two children's groups perform at an intermediate level of accuracy which is more similar to the Kpelle adult pattern than the American adult pattern. The visual impression of group differences is supported by an analysis of variance comparing the four groups for each amount of rice ($F = 7.5$, $df = 3/76$, $p < 0.01$). However, separate analyses indicate that the two children's groups do not differ significantly from each other or from the Kpelle adult group.

The mixed results leave our initial question in an ambiguous state; the Kpelle are very accurate at this task, as expected, but the relative accuracy of the American children with respect to the American adults remains to be explained.

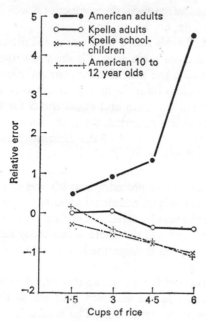

Fig. 9.1 Relative error in estimating the number of cups of rice in bowls containing 1·5 to 6 cups.

Number estimation: piles of stones

Gay and Cole (1967, p. 41 *ff*.) noted that rarely were large numbers used by the Kpelle. When it is obvious that a large number is called for, 100 is likely to be the number used. This would seem to imply that, when a large number of objects is present, Kpelle Ss ought to be poor at judging the quantity involved. Furthermore, they might be expected to use 100 when the number of objects exceeds 30 or 40.

Subjects. The following groups participated in this experiment: Kpelle adults, American adults (in both cases the same Ss who participated in the rice estimation experiment), and Yale undergraduates. There were twenty Ss in each group.

Procedure. The S stood before a row of piles of stones; each pile was covered with a piece of cloth so that the stones were not visible. The sizes of the stones varied, but they averaged about the size to be found in a coarse gravel driveway ($\frac{1}{4}$–$\frac{3}{4}$ inch). They were piled close together so that there was no way to count the stones accurately without moving some of them. From left to right, the number of stones in each pile was: 70, 40, 10, 100, 30, 80, 60, 20, 50, 90.

The S was told, 'In this test, I want you to tell me how many stones you think are in each of these piles. I'll show you the pile for only a short time, after which you should make your estimate.'

The E lifted the cloth from the first pile for a 5–10 second exposure period, then replaced the cloth and asked the S for his estimate. As soon as the response was recorded, the next pile was shown, and this procedure was repeated until all of the estimates had been made. In this phase of the experiment the S was given no information about the number of stones actually present in any pile.

In addition to the above procedure, which was the same for all Ss, the Yale group was given an additional opportunity to make estimates. After completing the regular series, these Ss were shown the pile containing sixty stones and told that there were exactly sixty stones in that pile. They then were run through the series again.

Results. The first question concerning this experiment is whether the various groups differ in the accuracy with which they estimate the number of stones in various piles. The results plotted in terms of relative errors are presented in Fig. 9.2.

It is clear from the overall results in Fig. 9.2 that the experimental groups do differ in their skill at stone estimation. An examination of the specific comparisons of interest yields the following results: the Kpelle adults are significantly more accurate than the American adults ($F = 15.2$, $df = 1/38$, $p < 0.01$), but they are not significantly more accurate than the Yale undergraduates ($F \simeq 1.0$). The Yale undergraduates improve when told the number of stones in the pile containing sixty stones, but with this improvement are not quite significantly more accurate than the Kpelle adults ($F = 4.08$, $df = 1/38$, $p > 0.05$). Judging from Fig. 9.2, it seems that without the information about the sixty-stone pile the Yale undergraduates tend to estimate lower than the Kpelle adults, and with information their estimates tend to run higher than the Kpelle adults.

In addition to information about relative accuracies, the questions posed in the introduction to this section suggest that there may be important differences in the way people in the two cultures use numbers in making their estimates. From the work of Welmers (1948) and Gay and Cole (1967), we know that the Kpelle number system is basically a decimal system, although a subordinate base-five system is buried within the decimal system. Are there differences in the way in which Kpelle and American *S*s use numbers in making their estimates? A

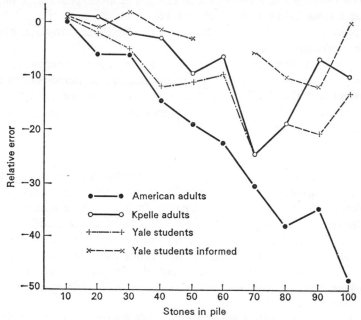

Fig. 9.2 Relative error in estimating the number of stones in a pile.

rough answer to this question can be obtained by determining the percentage of responses that are multiples of either five or ten. The proportion of such responses for the American adult and Kpelle adult groups was 0·815 and 0·880, respectively; this implies that there is a little difference in the use of these units between the two groups. However, when one looks at the distribution of responses in the two categories, multiples of five *v.* multiples of ten, it turns out that for the Kpelle, 0·881 of the responses are multiples of ten and only 0·119 are multiples of five while for the American adults, these proportions are 0·565 and 0·435, respectively. In short, the Kpelle are much more likely to respond in terms of multiples of ten than multiples of five, while the American adults split these responses evenly among the two types of numbers.

At no point in the data was there any indication that the Kpelle Ss were using an inordinate number of 100 responses.

Taken as a whole, these data fail to support expectations based on field observations. With respect to the accuracy data, it is worth noting by way of *post hoc* explanation that, in many situations, the Kpelle use small stones as counting markers (for instance, if it is necessary to count the houses in a village, a man might walk around the village putting a stone in his pocket for each house that he encounters). This practice in estimating stones may give the Kpelle an advantage over the Americans.

The data in terms of number usage run counter to expectations based solely on linguistic evidence, for such considerations would lead us to suspect that the Kpelle, with their partial base-five number system, might use five-base numbers more often than Americans do.

Time estimation

Anthropologists and psychologists have long shown an interest in the concepts of time in nontechnological peoples (cf. Hallowell, 1955; Werner, 1940; Doob, 1960). Generally, 'primitive' time reckoning is characterized as based on the salient events that figure in the life of the people. The movements of the sun, the birth of children, the coming of winter – these are the 'markers' that define the course of time. As Hallowell (1955, p. 217 *ff*) points out, the development of an interlocking logical system for small units of time is a relatively modern occurrence.

When tribal people come in contact with Westerners, conflicts often arise because the Western sense of punctuality is violated (Hall, 1959).

Despite the abundance of both disciplined and casual observations, almost no experimental research has been done on time measurement among non-Western peoples. Doob reports three pilot studies in which it was found that more educated, urbanized people are more conscious of time. His results were equivocal on the question of whether or not his Ss differed with respect to their accuracy in estimating explicitly delineated time intervals (Doob, 1960, p. 298).

The present study investigated the relative accuracy of our Kpelle and American groups in estimating explicit time intervals in two slightly differing situations.

Subjects. The four groups included in this experiment were American adults, Kpelle schoolchildren, and Kpelle adults (all of whom participated in the other measurement tasks), and a group of Kpelle children who had not attended school. Twenty *S*s were included in each group.

Procedure 1. The *S* was shown a stopwatch and asked to observe the second hand's movement. After observing a standard time (which varied between 15 and 120 seconds in 14-second intervals), the *E* started the watch without allowing *S* to observe the movement of the second hand and asked *S* to tell him when the period that he had just been shown had elapsed. No feedback was provided to *S* until the entire experiment was complete.

Procedure 2. Instead of observing the movement of a watch's second hand, *S* was asked to pace off a standard distance (20, 40, 60 or 80 yards) and to pay attention to the time it took him to complete the distance. Then the *E* started a stopwatch and asked *S* to indicate when the interval required to pace off the given distance had elapsed. Again *S* was required to complete the series before any information about his performance was given.

Results. The results for Procedure 1 are shown in Fig. 9.3. The apparent difference among groups is supported by an analysis of variance ($F = 3 \cdot 19$, $df = 3/76$, $p < 0 \cdot 05$). However, generalizations about specific cultural effects are difficult to make. The Americans rather consistently underestimate the time involved, but all groups are relatively accurate. A similar picture emerges from the results of Procedure 2 (Fig. 9.4) except that the trends are somewhat clearer. The Americans consistently underestimate the time involved in pacing the assigned distances ($t = 2 \cdot 4$, $df = 79$, $p < 0 \cdot 01$). The Kpelle groups are very accurate, with the exception of the illiterate children, who grossly overestimate the shorter periods and underestimate the longer ones.

There is certainly no evidence of 'primitivity' of the time sense of our Kpelle *S*s in these data. The variables accounting for the Americans' consistent underestimates and the Kpelle tendency to overestimate must be left to future research.

Measuring the length of objects: handspans

Hallowell (1955) makes a distinction between 'distance away' ('how far is that tree?') and distance involving the length of some manipulable object. This same distinction applies to Kpelle measurement. In a later section, we will make a comparison of three units of measurement

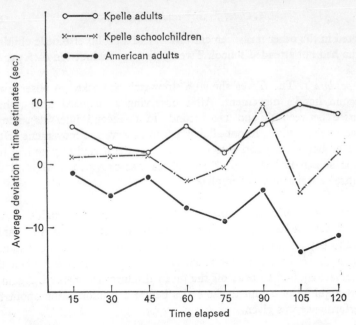

Fig. 9.3 Errors in estimating time elapsed on stopwatch.

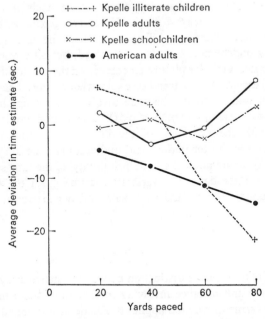

Fig. 9.4 Errors in estimating time to pace specified distances.

applied to distance away. In the present section we intend to look at a common Kpelle technique for measuring relatively small manipulable objects, using the handspans unit.

Subjects. The Ss used in this experiment were the Kpelle adults, American adults, Kpelle schoolchildren, and American 5th–6th graders included in earlier experiments. There were twenty Ss in each group.

Procedure. The S was seated at a table on which were placed sticks varying in length from 4 to 36 inches. He was told, 'I have several sticks here. With each stick, I want you to estimate first how long it is in handspans and then measure it in handspans. Be as accurate as possible.' Instructions were as usual given in the appropriate native language.

The Kpelle Ss all used a standard method of making a handspan, stretching out their middle finger and measuring from the tip of the finger to the tip of the thumb. The American Ss sometimes used this measure spontaneously. Those who did not were shown the 'correct' (i.e. Kpelle) procedure.

The sticks (made of 1 by $\frac{1}{4}$ inch boards) were arrayed on the table in a row. The stick nearest S at the outset of the experiment was 32 inches. The remainder of the sticks in order were 8, 20, 36, 12, 4, 28, 16 and 24 inches long. When a given stick had been measured, it was laid aside and the next stick in the row was considered.

The S began by making a verbal estimate in (handspans) of the length of the stick. He then measured the stick, completing the trial. Thus, his own measurement can be viewed as a kind of information feedback following each estimate.

Results. The results were tabulated in terms of the discrepancy between the S's estimate of the length of the stick and the measurement using his own handspan. Thus, if the estimate is '3 handspans' and the measured stick is $2\frac{1}{2}$ handspans, there is an error of $\frac{1}{2}$ handspan.

Prior to discussing the quantitative results (Fig. 9.5), certain qualitative factors which influenced performance on this task require attention. First of all, the Kpelle Ss were observed to make their measurements with extreme care, meticulously placing thumb to finger and then stretching the hand to its utmost. By contrast, the Americans made handspans in an extremely variable manner. In fact, it appeared that they were apt to tailor the size of the handspan to fit their estimate (an observation which should be kept in mind when evaluating the results of our accuracy analysis). A second observation which does not show up in the accuracy analysis is that the Kpelle Ss rarely used fractional units other than ½. Most Kpelle terms for fractions are borrowed from English (see Gay and Cole, 1967) and the expression of fractions other than ½ is very difficult. For instance, the expression 'a small half' was

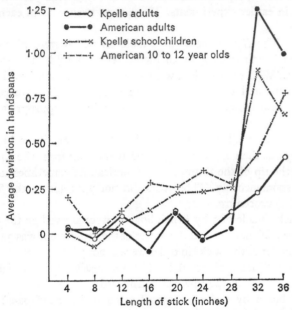

Fig. 9.5 Errors in estimating length of sticks in handspans.

recorded as ¼ since this is the generally accepted meaning of the phrase, but there were very few occasions on which the Kpelle used it. The Americans, on the other hand, used fractions freely in their estimates.

When measured in terms of the relative error of estimation (Fig. 9.5), there seems to be very little difference between the various groups in this experiment, except that the younger Ss seem to do more poorly than the adults. An analysis of variance comparing the performance of all four groups supports the impression of little systematic variation ($F = 2\cdot24$, $df = 3\cdot76$, $0\cdot10 > p > 0\cdot05$).

In view of the 'fudging' observed on the part of the American Ss, it is difficult to know if these findings should be interpreted as indicating the roughly equal abilities of our Ss to estimate the length of sticks in handspans, or the looser criterion of what constitutes a proper handspan among our American Ss.

Distance estimation

In the introduction we mentioned our observation about the specificity of measurement and the seeming lack of interchangeability among various metrics. Here we seek to determine the significance of these observations by asking *S*s to use three different metrics for measuring the same distances. Does the lack of a common metric hinder estimation? Are culturally relevant metrics used more accurately than inappropriate ones?

Subjects. The *S*s participating in this experiment were the Kpelle adults, Kpelle schoolchildren, and American adults who participated in the other measurement studies. There were twenty *S*s to a group.

Procedure. The *S*s were run one at a time in a large room. Markers were placed on the floor 2 to 6 yards from one wall. The *S* stood at the wall and was read the following instructions in the appropriate language: 'You see these markers on the ground. I want you to estimate the distance to each of these markers when I stand on it. I want you to tell me this distance first in terms of footlengths, then handspans, and then armspans.'

Appropriate parts of these instructions were repeated when necessary. Then the *E* stood on the 3·5 yard marker and asked, 'How far is this in footlengths?' After the estimate, the same question was repeated for handspans and armspans. Then the next distance was chosen and the above procedure repeated with each distance in the order 3·5, 6, 5, 2, 4, 3, 2·5, 5·5 and 4·5 yards.

Results. The accuracy of estimates using each procedure is shown in Figs. 9.6 to 9.8 for footlengths, armspans and handspans, respectively.

On the basis of anthropological observations and results such as those in the stick length estimation experiment, we had expected the footlength task to yield the best estimates among the Kpelle because our informants had led us to believe that this was the proper metric in the situation we were using. However, as the results in Figs. 9.6 to 9.8 indicate, no simple explanation in terms of 'cultural relevance' will fit the facts.

Rather than excelling in estimation via footlengths, the Kpelle adults do poorly, grossly overestimating the distances involved (Fig. 9.6). The Kpelle schoolchildren and American adults fare about the same and both are more accurate than the Kpelle adults. An analysis

G

of variance indicates that these apparent group differences are reliable ($F = 15.6$, $df = 2/56$, $p < 0.01$) and that the Kpelle adults perform relatively worse at the longer distance (groups by distance interaction: $F = 3.69$, $df = 16/456$, $p < 0.01$).

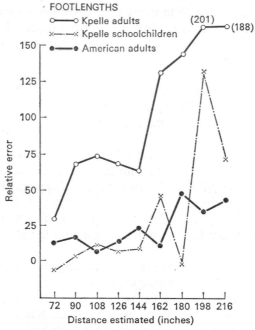

Fig. 9.6 Relative errors in estimating distance in footlengths.

The Kpelle adults' best performance occurs when they estimate in armspans (Fig. 9.7). In this case, their performance is approximately equivalent to the American adults' and both are more inaccurate than the Kpelle schoolchildren ($F = 4.0$, $df = 2/57$, $p < 0.05$). When measuring in handspans (Fig. 9.8), the Kpelle adults again grossly overestimate, performing significantly worse than the other groups ($F = 6.4$, $df = 2/57$, $p < 0.01$).

These data seem to counter our original notion that one could in some way equate cultural appropriateness and accuracy of distance estimation. While trying to rationalize this situation, we were led to reconsider the anthropological evidence that generated our expectations, in particular the idea that nontechnological peoples, lacking an interlocking set of distance measures, ought to employ measures that are independent of each other. This brought us to the realization that

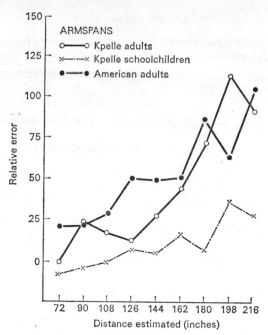

Fig. 9.7 Relative errors in estimating distance in armspans.

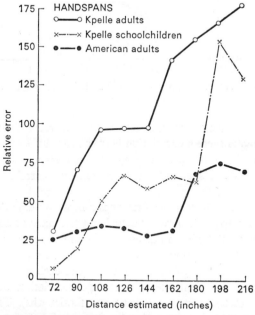

Fig. 9.8 Relative errors in estimating distance in handspans.

by testing accuracy, we were obtaining at best a very indirect measure of the independence hypothesis; it seemed far more appropriate to attempt a direct measure of the independence of various measures using correlational techniques.

Two types of questions seem appropriate when asking about the relation between response measures: (1) When using different measures

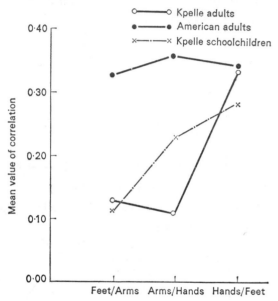

Fig. 9.9a Correlations among errors for different ways of measuring distance.

to measure the same distance, does S use the different measures in the same way; e.g. is there a correlation between the various measures of a given distance? (2) When measuring various distances with the same measurement, do S's successive measurements correlate with each other?

In attempting to answer the first question, we obtained correlations among the discrepancies between actual and estimated scores measured by handspan, footlength, and armspan. A correlation was calculated at each distance. The resulting correlation matrices were then summarized by calculating the average correlation between each pair of measures for each group (for instance, the average correlation between discrepancies obtained using handspans and footlengths). These results are summarized in Fig. 9.9a. As the figure indicates, the American group has a consistently high correlation among the three ways of measuring distance, while a high correlation is observed in the Kpelle groups only in the case of handspans-footlengths. The relationships suggested by the figure are confirmed by an analysis of variance in which the differences between groups (F = 26·23, $df = 2/240$, $p < 0·01$), the pair of measurements being correlated (F = 12·35,

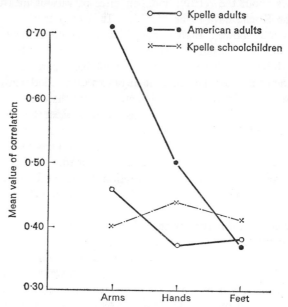

Fig. 9.9b Correlations among errors at different distances for each measure of distance.

$df = 2/160$, $p < 0·01$), and the interaction between groups and the pair of measurements (F = 12·71, $df = 4/320$, $p < 0·01$) were all found to be highly significant. Furthermore, all groups showed significant correlations. The smallest correlation in Fig. 9.9a is 0·11. This was found to differ significantly from a zero correlation ($t = 6·59$, $df = 239$, $p < 0·01$).

In general the same relationships are found when correlations are obtained among the various distances using a given measure (Fig. 9.9b), although the magnitude of the obtained correlation is generally greater. The American Ss exhibit higher correlations than either of the Kpelle groups, except with respect to footlengths in which all the groups are essentially equivalent. Again the analysis of variance on these data indicate that these trends are highly reliable. The F ratios for the differences among groups (F = 7·53, df = 2/105, p < 0·01), measures (F = 15·65, df = 2/210, p < 0·01), and their interaction (F = 11·40, df = 4/210, p < 0·01) are all highly significant. Again it was found that the smallest correlation (0·37) differed significantly from zero (t = 14·68, df = 104, p < 0·01).

On the basis of these data, it appears that our anthropologically based hypotheses about the relative independence of various measurements among the Kpelle have to be modified. It is in general true that the American Ss showed higher correlations between measures and between different distances using the same measure. However, all groups exhibited high correlations between handspan and footlength measurements and for the different distances using footlengths. Moreover, Kpelle correlations are consistently greater than zero.

Perhaps the best strategy at this point is to suggest that this kind of analysis is useful and that future studies be explicitly designed to assess consistency in the use of various measures. One possibility is to have each length represented in one of three media, cloth, sticks, and distance from E, so that the contribution of the task to the various correlations can be separated from the contribution of the measuring unit.

On the basis of this type of analysis we are led to make a distinction between consistency and accuracy. When considering the latter, it is difficult to see how cultural relevance can account for the set of data presented in the various figures. However, when we consider the consistency in the way S uses a given measurement, we find that the culturally sanctioned measure leads to consistent measurements.

TACHISTOSCOPIC IDENTIFICATION

This experiment concerns a different area of Kpelle-American experience, based not so much on specifics such as those of language or measurement system, but rather on observed general contrasts between a slow paced agricultural environment and a modern technological one.

The environments of the American and Kpelle appear to differ in terms of both the variety of information presented to people living in them and the speed at which these informational alternatives are encountered. The present experiment sought to evaluate this gross intuition concerning differential demands for information processing, in terms of the ability to deal with information presented at different levels of complexity and exposure speed.

The form in which this question was asked is based upon a design similar to the American experiments of Hunter and Sigler (1940) and Kaufman, Lord, Reese and Volkman (1949). They investigated the ability to accurately estimate different numbers of dots in a haphazard array presented for a brief time. Their findings suggest that for American *S*s accuracy of recognition is quite good up to a limit of six dots after which there appears to be a sharp decrement in performance.

In summarizing this evidence, Miller (1962) points out that the limit of about six elements characterizes many other types of recognition as well. He suggests that this limit derives from a central process limiting the span of attention. If this central limitation is neurologically given one might expect similar limitations to appear in different cultural groups. If, however, there is a cultural element involved, one might expect that Kpelle and American groups would show differences in the amount of information with which they are able to deal accurately.

This rather simplistic presentation of the problem should not be allowed to obscure the fact that an unambiguous answer concerning cultural differences in 'rate of information transmission' or 'channel capacity' will be difficult, if not impossible to establish. One can readily generate alternative hypotheses if it is found that Kpelle *S*s are less accurate than their American counterparts in judging the number of dots presented for a brief interval in a visual display. Nevertheless, it was felt that the problem was of sufficient interest to justify some effort. At the very least we hoped to determine the sources of difficulty encountered by our Kpelle *S*s with the thought that perhaps our findings would find some application in the classroom. On a somewhat more ambitious level, we believed that the relationship among variables (such as the relative accuracy at a given speed when viewing different numbers of dots) within a culture could yield useful information on cultural differences in information processing.

Subjects. Forty *S*s were drawn from each of the three basic Kpelle groups: illiterate adults, schoolchildren, and illiterate children. Additionally, three American groups, composed of forty *S*s each, were also sampled. These were Yale students, and 10 to 12 year old and 7 to 9 year old schoolchildren. Half of each group was exposed to haphazard stimulus arrays (random condition) and half to patterned arrays (pattern condition). The two conditions will be described separately for ease of exposition.

Random procedure. Each *S* was shown a series of eighteen cards by means of a tachistoscope so that exposure times could be controlled.

This series was composed of three instances each of cards containing 3, 4, 5, 6, 8 or 10 dots in haphazard array. Each instance of any particular number of dots represented a different haphazard array containing that number. All Ss were shown the same series, randomized in blocks of six.

The tachistoscope was made of sheet metal and wood and was divided into two connected parts. The rear part was of rectangular shape (12 × 6·5 inches) and contained a Ray-O-Vac flashlight (powered by eight flashlight batteries). A shutter was placed over the face of the beam so that the duration of light could be controlled. The lack of electric power in rural villages necessitated the use of batteries which have the disadvantage of weakening with time; therefore, a limit of $2h$ was set on battery usage. By using the same type of battery with all Ss and randomizing the order in which groups were run we sought to reduce the interfering effects of the unstable light source. Thus, it can only be claimed that no *systematic* error was introduced by the unorthodox apparatus.

The apparatus was 23 inches long by 13 inches wide at the viewing end, narrowing to $6\frac{1}{2}$ inches at the shutter end. The S viewed the backlighted slides at a distance of $10\frac{1}{2}$ inches by looking through an aperture in which a pair of goggles was mounted. Slides were placed into the apparatus through a slit-like opening in the top.

The slides were transluscent vinyl plastic (0·03 cm thick) and measured $10\frac{1}{2}$ by $8\frac{3}{4}$ inches. Black dots cut out of Artype HR 3017 material were pasted onto the glossy side of the vinyl material. The dots measured 5 mm in diameter.

The procedures for Kpelle and American Ss differed slightly. When a Kpelle S entered the room where the experiment was conducted, he was asked to be seated. He was told that he would be shown spots on a card, but that the spots would appear for only a very short time. The E then held up six of the stimuli, one at a time, and asked S to tell how many spots there were on the slide. In this way, a crude evaluation of S's eyesight and his ability to count the stimuli was obtained. The six cards shown to S were the last six cards from an eighteen card series; the series contained three examples each of stimuli with 3, 4, 5, 6, 8 and 10 dots haphazardly arranged on the slide. Next the S was asked to look into the tachistoscope, where a stimulus containing 5 dots was displayed. When he reported the 5 dots, he was told that the stimuli would appear again for a brief interval. Three such practice trials were given. The last was given with an exposure of 0·01 sec. Then the regular series began and continued until all eighteen stimuli had been presented.

The slides were shown at 0·01, 0·04, and 0·1 sec. exposure intervals in that order, although analyses are presented only for the 0·01 and 0·1 sec. speeds. Consequently, conclusions about the effects of exposure time and practice are confounded. This design defect was permitted in the interest of reliability. Since experimenter-informants were inexperienced, simplification was sought in every possible way. Moreover, at the time the experiment was conducted we were not sure that any useful data could be obtained using the relatively complex apparatus with naïve tribal adults. This confounding of practice and exposure time effects should be kept in mind when interpreting the results.

In the case of the American *S*s the procedure was simplified in the following ways: (1) once *S* was seated he was told that he would be shown a series of slides containing varying numbers of dots; (2) an example of one of the slides was shown to him; (3) the regular training series was begun.

All experimental sessions were run in a darkened room. The trials were spaced at about 10-second intervals, although in some cases *S* was slow to respond and had to be prodded by the *E*. In those cases when *S* was uncertain of the correct response, he was required to guess.

Results. In scoring the results, the number of correct recognitions on the three presentations of a given number of dots was used as the basic datum. Thus, the scores for an *S* on any given number of dots range from 0 (none correct) to 3 (all correct).

In presenting the results, only those comparisons bearing on the main effects of 'culture' will be discussed in detail. As one might expect, older *S*s are more accurate than young children ($F = 15·2$, $df = 2/228, p < 0·01$). Age, however, did not interact in any significant way with culture or any of the other variables in the experiment, and consequently will not be discussed further.

The analysis of variance revealed the following additional interesting results:

(1) Overall, American *S*s recognize dot patterns more accurately than Kpelle *S*s (American mean = 1·65; Kpelle mean = 1·34; $F = 24·6$, $df = 1/228$, $p < 0·01$).

(2) The relationship between accuracy of recognition and the number of dots to be recognized shows a significant cultural difference ($F = 5·6$, $df = 5/1140$, $p < 0·01$). American *S*s (see Fig. 9.10) tend to show a relatively constant accuracy score for dot patterns 3, 4, 5 and 6, and fall off sharply thereafter. Kpelle *S*s, on the other hand, show a

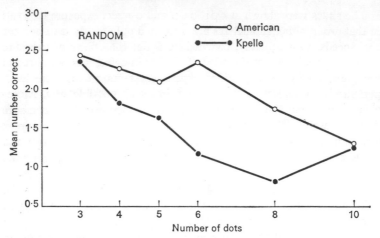

Fig. 9.10 Accuracy as a function of culture and the number of dots in a random visual display.

continuous decrement over these same patterns and remain relatively constant thereafter.

(3) All Ss perform better at the slower exposure speed (F = 123·1, $df = 1/114$, $p < 0.01$), with the greatest effect manifested with the displays containing only a few dots (see Fig. 9.11; F = 12·51, $df = 5/570$, $p < 0.01$).

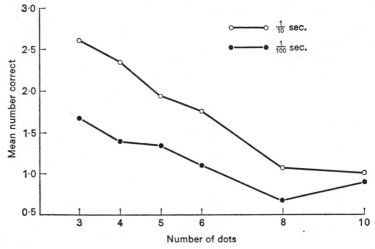

Fig. 9.11 Accuracy as a function of exposure time and the number of dots in a visual display.

These results obtained with random arrays of dots suggested that further consideration might be given to this type of experiment, with closer attention paid to the configuration of dots in order to determine what cultural factors might be at work.

Field observations (Gay and Cole, 1967) suggest that Kpelle Ss have difficulty making use of redundant properties of stimuli as an information processing aid. Thus, to cite an example, in estimating the number of items in a 4 by 4 array, the array properties are not used. The Ss will typically count individual items. Similar observations have been made in classroom situations, where set properties (multiplication operations on redundant patterns) are not used, or are supplanted by dealing with individual items (iteration of single items).

According to this type of reasoning, it might be expected that American Ss, when presented with dot arrays that are arranged into patterns, would be able to make use of the redundant features of stimulation in order to recognize larger numbers more accurately, while Kpelle Ss would not be able to do so. It was in order to test this proposition that the groups with patterned stimuli were run.

Pattern procedure. The procedure used matched that previously described for the random condition with the exception of the arrangement of stimuli presented. Each S was shown a series of eighteen cards which, as in the previous experiment, represented three instances each of 3, 4, 5, 6, 8 and 10 dots. While previously the dots had been arranged in a haphazard manner on the presentation card, in this experiment the dots were arranged in patterns. The major pattern types used were: arrays of parallel rows of dots either vertically or horizontally arranged, and dots arranged in triangular patterns.

Results. Results for the patterned arrangement were scored in the same manner as were those for the random presentation. Since scoring and experimental procedures (with the exception of stimuli) were common, and Ss were roughly matched, this section will compare results between the pattern and random conditions as well as within the pattern condition alone.

Analysis of variance within the pattern condition reveals the following:

(1) Overall, American Ss were more accurate than their Kpelle counterparts (American mean = 2·04; Kpelle mean = 1·51; $F = 37·47$, $df = 1/114$, $p < 0·01$).

(2) As in the random condition, there was a significant interaction

of culture with number of dots. This interaction is presented graphically in Fig. 9.12. Inspection of this figure reveals that, for American *S*s, recognition accuracy is relatively constant between 3 and 6 dots falling off thereafter, while for Kpelle groups the drop begins sooner, with a regular decrease from 3 to 8 dots.

(3) The effect of speed was significant ($F = 150.0$, $df = 1/114$, $p < 0.01$), as was the interaction between speed and number of dots

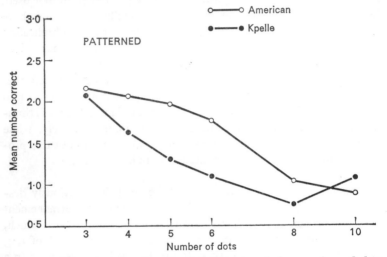

Fig. 9.12 Accuracy as a function of culture and the number of dots in a patterned visual display.

($F = 4.46$, $df = 5/57$, $p < 0.01$). The forms of the functions were very similar to those obtained in Fig. 9.11.

Pattern v. random. Overall recognition was better for the pattern condition (pattern mean = 1.77; random mean = 1.50; $F = 19.85$, $df = 1/228$, $p < 0.01$).

The most important comparison indicating that patterning of stimuli aided recognition differentially for the Kpelle and American *S*s is yielded by the significant interaction found between patterning, cultural group, and number of dots ($F = 3.95$, $df = 5/1140$, $p < 0.01$). This interaction is represented in Fig. 9.13.

Examination of Fig. 9.13 indicates that for American *S*s the influence of the patterning factor is greatest for dots 6 to 10; for the Kpelle, the patterning influence is constant throughout the range tested.

In addition to the analyses dealing with conditions affecting accuracy of information processing, the question concerning use of patterning for recognition purposes may be asked in a different way. It may be the case that the use of redundant information aids accurate recognition of patterns containing such redundancies, but it may also be the case that patterning may influence the type of error made. If it were possible to identify those errors caused by specific pattern usage, one could evaluate the influence of stimulus redundancy independent of absolute accuracy in the use of redundant cues.

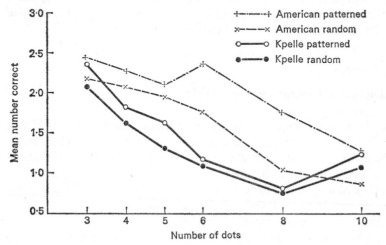

Fig. 9.13 Accuracy as a function of culture, patterning and the number of dots in a visual display.

Several of the patterns used in the pattern condition, particularly for the larger numbers of dots (6, 8 and 10 dots) were constructed in such a way that the dot patterns were arranged in two symmetrical rows. Thus, for example, two of the patterns of 10 dots were arranged in two parallel rows of 5 dots, each of which was aligned either vertically or horizontally. Further, two of the 8-dot patterns and two of the 6-dot patterns were arranged in this manner. If Ss make use of this 2 by n arrangement, one might expect that, even if they make errors, these errors should consist of even number errors (reflecting the use of the redundant information). Accordingly, an analysis was performed contrasting the occurrence of even and odd number errors for these six patterns (two each at 6, 8 and 10 dots). The results were compared with the data for six corresponding random patterns which served in this analysis as control stimuli.

For the random condition, there is little difference in the proportion of even number errors (42·5 per cent for Americans *v.* 44·5 per cent for Kpelle). For the pattern condition, however, there are large differences between these groups (78 per cent for Americans *v.* 54 per cent for Kpelle). These findings indicate that overall, Americans are making pattern determined errors, while Kpelle either do not, or do so minimally. Since the majority of patterns possessing this array property occur in the 6 to 10 dot range, we feel that the error analysis provides a potential explanation for the accuracy analysis reported above, where Americans were shown to profit from patterning largely in the range of stimuli which have the 'array' type of organization.

DISCUSSION

The initial impetus for undertaking the rather heterogeneous set of experiments described in the earlier sections of this paper was the desire to learn enough about the quantitative behaviour of an African tribal group to help design teaching materials and methods which would facilitate their learning of Western mathematics. The educational implications of this research have been discussed elsewhere (Gay and Cole, 1967). More germane to the present article is a discussion of the implications of this type of research for our understanding of the relation between culture and cognitive processes.

The overriding difficulty of cross-cultural research is the problem of knowing whether an experimental comparison is in fact a relevant comparison. Working within a culture, our criteria of relevance are satisfied by the assurance that common experimental conditions exist, if *S*s are to be compared; or that common *S*s are used, if conditions are to be compared (further, that only the variable in question is being varied). In cross-cultural work, however, neither of these criteria are met in the same way as they are met in intracultural comparisons.

In cross-cultural work, we are generally dealing with an inherently confounded experimental design in which many variables we know to be of importance are covarying with culture. An example which may clarify this point is the following bit of data taken from Gay and Cole (1967). Kpelle children were found to learn a single discrimination between wooden blocks varying along two stimulus dimensions faster than a group of American children comparable in age. Does this result indicate that African children have a special aptitude for this kind of task? This conclusion would be justified if we could assume that the task (objects to be dealt with, instructions, etc.) were common. However, the material identity of objects might be called into question on psychological grounds – for example, the particular colours of the blocks used might have been more salient for Africans; or, the task might have been more novel for Africans and therefore more motivating or, had the results been reversed, so novel that the task was incomprehensible to Africans. Dozens of these interpretations might be applied with equal efficacy. It does not seem likely that any finite set of experiments will be able to rule out all of the known (to say nothing of the unknown) factors involved. This leads to an ambiguity of interpretation which seems all but inescapable.

Although many writers have discussed the difficulties of crosscultural research, it appears that few have appreciated their full extent. The excessive claims of the intelligence testers have been adequately criticized by Cryns (1962). However, the more modest approach of a researcher such as Price-Williams (1961) who was attempting to determine the generality of Piaget's developmental stages, is subject to the same logical difficulties. Price-Williams attempted to make the experimental procedures, instructions, materials, and atmosphere 'appropriate' to the cultural setting. The changes he introduced tended to make Western and African performance more similar, although differences remained.

Some writers have recognized this problem and offered solutions. Jones (1966) suggests that one ought to seek conceptual rather than empirical generality; e.g. one ought to seek that set of conditions in the new context which most closely approximates the set of conditions from the original context, rather than carry over the exact experimental procedures. If replication of results is achieved, one infers that the basic dynamics of the situation are under control. The problem arises when replication is not achieved, since the failure might be accounted for either by the change in procedures or the failure to specify correctly the proper set of conditions. Price-Williams (1961) implicitly followed this procedure, but the fact that some differences remain after his modifications had been made leaves us in doubt as to their source.

Campbell (1961) suggests that one way out of the difficulty is to run a series of experiments with converging operations; if the results also converge, we can be fairly confident that the similarities (or differences) we observe are not the result of some trivial or uncontrolled variable. The problem with this approach is that it is not only very expensive to carry out in practice, but also we have no way of specifying the range of relevant variables a priori, so that there is always the opportunity for some important uncontrolled variable to be affecting our results. This is always the case in research, of course, but the depth of our ignorance about the relevant variables in cross-cultural research exacerbates the problem. In considering these problems in the context of our own research, it seems clear that many of our findings are limited by these same difficulties; results are suggestive, but we would want more information about the factors at work before we were convinced 'richness of geometric vocabulary' or 'familiarity with measuring rice' were the critical variables at work in our situations. Perhaps some degree of authority is added by the generally good correspondence between what field observations indicated were 'culturally appropriate' procedures and performance, but the application of Campbell's multiple-method approach would markedly increase our capacity to generalize.

However, not all of our experimental findings are of this type. For instance, in the experiment on learning which involved various types of logical connectives the American groups found the conjunctive problem harder than the disjunctive problem, while the Kpelle groups experienced about equal difficulty with the two types of problems. This finding is like those mentioned in the previous paragraph in that it corresponds to what we know about an aspect of the two cultures (in this case, their languages). However, it has an added virtue in that the importance of the result rests on the relation between performances within each culture. Whereas it is easy to generate hypotheses about the factors causing a difference between two behaviours compared across cultures, the number of hypotheses concerning why, within a single situation within each culture, the relationship between two behaviours should be reversed is considerably smaller. Consequently, we have greater confidence that we are dealing with a reliable cultural (in this case, linguistically determined) difference.

This example suggests a general strategy which is similar in many ways to work of such anthropologists and linguists as Benedict (1934), Lévi-Strauss (1966), Horton (1967), Osgood, Suci and Tannenbaum (1957). These authors take as a starting point the attempt to discover the coherence of ideas and behaviours within cultures as the basic datum for specifying the rules which tie together behaviours between cultures. Thus, for example, one does not compare 'mythic' and 'scientific' thought directly, but one first makes an analysis of the formal structures that characterize myth and science. It is these latter 'coherence' rules that are then compared (Horton, 1967). In our own work, we have, where design and opportunity arise, attempted to use this principle of intracultural comparison as a tool for gaining insight into cross-cultural comparisons.

In addition to the logic identification work, other studies in the present paper illustrate this principle. The tachistoscopic recognition experiment is another example. On the face of it, the fact that Americans are in general more accurate than the Kpelle is difficult to interpret since there are any number of plausible explanations for this difference. However, this study contains a good deal of information about the nature of this overall difference. First, it turns out that intercultural performance is quite similar under certain circumstances (a small number of dots present in a random array), but different under other conditions (a large number of dots present in a random array). Since both of these conditions occur within the same experimental session and within the same *S*, explanations in terms of unfamiliarity, apparatus fear, poor eyesight, etc. are unconvincing; it seems more likely that we are dealing with a nontrivial cultural difference. Similarly, the analysis of errors made to pattern stimuli and the different relative difficulties of patterned and random stimuli within the two cultures argues for an important cultural difference. Although a great deal of research remains to be done in order to pin down the exact causal agents (our speculations in terms of the informational requirements of the two environments remain speculations), trivial alternatives are not likely to account for this pattern of results.

Although other examples could be cited, the point being made should be clear. It might be useful in addition to point out that the problems we have posed, as well as the solution, are applicable outside the area of cross-cultural studies; they apply wherever one is attempting to compare the performances of subject populations which are presumed to differ in a number of ways. The developmental psychologist faces exactly the same problem when attempting to compare the behaviour of toddlers and teenagers, and, as Bitterman (1965) has pointed out, the problem exists when comparing the behaviour of different animal species.

Considering our own area of concern, the cross-cultural study of cognitive processes, we believe that some combination of Campbell's multi-method approach and the within-culture experimental design must be used to preclude overhasty and overextensive generalizations. It is clear that this enterprise will have to be truly interdisciplinary. An adequate experimental design requires an extensive knowledge of the context of the behaviour that we wish to study. To this end, the insights of anthropologists, linguists and psychologists are all necessary.

10

L. W. Doob (1964)

Eidetic images among the Ibo[1]

Ethnology, 3, pp. 357-63

Eidetic images are defined as visual images 'persisting after stimula-tion, relatively accurate in detail, coloured positively, and capable of being scanned' (Haber and Haber, 1964). On the basis of quite casual impressions and of astonishing anecdotes, it has long been opined (e.g. Jaensch, 1923; Husén, 1945, pp. 84-6) that the incidence of such images among nonliterate peoples is likely to be higher than among the literate. The speculation has been based upon the assumption that the images are present among all or most children, perhaps at an early age, but that they tend to disappear in literate societies where emphasis is placed upon verbal memory. The idea behind the speculation is exciting: if validated, it would suggest another way in which people can store essential information in the absence of writing. The present study represents a systematic attempt quickly to explore the problem among the Ibo of Eastern Nigeria in April 1964. So far as can be ascertained, no actual investigation of this kind had previously been carried out in any nonliterate society; interesting but scarcely relevant are findings in the United States that the proportion of eidetikers may be higher among Negro than among white or Mexican children (Peck and Hodges, 1937).

[1] Many years ago, while I was an undergraduate at Dartmouth College, Gordon W. Allport aroused my interest in eidetic images so vividly that ever since I have been aware of eidetikers, especially while carrying on fieldwork in Africa. Ralph N. Haber has encouraged me to undertake this study and most generously has offered sane, thoughtful advice on the basis of his own ongoing research. I am also deeply indebted to Gabriel O. Ede, an Ibo student at the University of Nigeria, who functioned as a conscientious interpreter and friendly guide and who himself is fortunate to be both well-educated and an eidetiker; to Margo T. Johnson, who urged me to return to Eastern Nigeria, who intro-duced me to Mr Ede, and who provided transportation, gracious hospitality, and bubbling ideas; and to the Carnegie Corporation of New York, which is enabling me to investigate attitudes, values, and other forms of behaviour in various African countries.

METHOD

Recently Haber and Haber (1964) have offered a major review of the extensive literature on eidetic images and have reported the results of an extremely careful investigation of schoolchildren in New Haven, Connecticut. Their technique was deliberately adopted in the present study except for a few additions suggested below; more precise details can be found in the cited article. The informant is seated 20 inches away from a screen, which is a blank piece of grey cardboard, 24 by 30 inches, resting on a tilted easel. To accustom him to perceiving images upon that screen, he is first shown a 2-inch red square mounted on cardboard of the same colour and he fixates his eyes upon it for 10 seconds; the square is removed, and he is asked to describe what he sees upon the blank screen, what colour it is, and when it disappears. There follow similarly exposed squares coloured blue, black and yellow. Then four pictures, 8 by 10 inches, are each exposed for 30 seconds, and the subject is told to scan the entire picture. After the removal of the stimulus, he again reports what he sees upon the screen; if he has something to report, he is interrogated at length concerning details, colour and location of the image, and usually is asked to point to the place on the screen where a particular object or person is appearing. Haber and Haber have described their pictures as follows:

> The first picture was of a family scene, black pictures pasted on a grey board to form a silhouette. The second, constructed in the same way, was of an Indian hunting, with deer, other animals, and some birds. The third, in full colour, showed an Indian fishing in a canoe, with many fish in the water. The fourth, also in color, from *Alice in Wonderland*, depicted Alice standing at the base of a large tree staring up at the Cheshire cat.

Obviously these particular pictures were designed to appeal to American children. In the series for the Ibo, three photographs taken in Africa were added: a view of an African town under construction which includes women carrying infants on their backs and metal sheets on their heads; a group of African men carving wooden figures; and a scene at a bus stop in Eastern Nigeria, with two taxis, a large bus, and many Africans clearly visible. The first photograph is black-and-white and was displayed after the two black-and-white silhouettes in the Haber series; the remaining two are in colour and were shown after the two coloured drawings in that series.

This investigator sat directly opposite the informant, whose eyes could thus be easily observed. To the right of the former and the left of the latter was the interpreter, who had been instructed and trained to translate literally. After exposure to the coloured squares, all save five of the forty-five informants reported at least one negative after-image; seven noted one or more positive after-images. Whenever necessary, the few informants not following instructions precisely were reminded to fixate their eyes upon the coloured squares and to scan the pictures. If an informant reported no eidetic image twice in succession, he was asked what he had just seen in the picture, what he could remember; since some details were retained by everyone, it may be concluded that failure to report an eidetic image was not due to inattention to the original picture.

The translations of the interpreter were recorded verbatim; the questions asked by the investigator himself were briefly summarized in his notes. During the exposure of the succeeding picture, the investigator rated the informant's imagery for the preceding picture as follows:

E for an eidetic image, i.e. the informant provided correct, minute details (including colours) concerning the pictures he had just seen; he pointed to a relatively correct place on the screen when asked 'Where is the object (person)?'; he continued to scan the screen and his eyes did not wander off it; as he reported that the image was fading or had faded, he changed tenses from the present to the past.

E – for some evidence of an eidetic image, but the details were less numerous or the duration too short to permit a full report by the informant in the present tense.

O for no trace of an eidetic image (whether or not a negative after-image appeared), or a flat statement to the effect that 'I see nothing'.

Whenever possible – but unfortunately not always, because of the pressure of interviewing – the rating of the interpreter was also simultaneously obtained while the informant was scanning the succeeding picture. The reliability thus informally measured seemed perfect, but regretfully it was not possible in this study to use the far more desirable, objective technique of Haber and Haber, which is to have two judges independently rate the transcribed tape recordings of the subjects' statements.

INFORMANTS

The informants were selected haphazardly, not randomly. For purposes of this analysis, they are divided into two samples, hereinafter called urban and rural. The urban group comes from in and around Enugu, the capital of the Eastern Region of Nigeria, with an estimated population of more than 60,000. Three of the informants in the rural group live in Nsukka, a town of more than 15,000 located 55 miles from Enugu; the remainder are from traditional villages at least 10 miles out of town along trails or unpaved roads. In schools, the headmaster was asked to send children from a specified grade; their ages, according to their own not necessarily reliable accounts, ranged from 8 to 15 with a mean of exactly 11. Adults in Enugu were approached as strangers, and their cooperation was obtained by explaining the nature of the task. The interpreter was known by all informants in Nsukka and in the outlying villages; hence he and the investigator were greeted warmly and enthusiastically by a multitude which immediately assembled.

As soon as the amenities permitted, a small number was haphazardly selected to be tested. These were asked to remain at a distance or inside a house until their turn came; nobody, consequently, saw the pictures in advance while they were being viewed by another person. Without exception, the informants seemed to enjoy the experience of looking at the colours and pictures and of reporting their images; they followed instructions without apparent difficulty. Some of them hesitated at first when asked to state what they saw on the screen after the removal of the first or second colour; they were simply reminded of the black spots which one ordinarily notes after looking at the sun too long. Table 10.1 contains the essential census facts about the two samples.

TABLE 10.1. *Breakdown of total sample*

	Urban			Rural		
	Male	*Female*	*Total*	*Male*	*Female*	*Total*
Children	4	2	6	6	5	11
Adults	8	1	9	11	8	19
Mean age	24·9	22·7	24·4	26·9	25·5	26·3

RESULTS

The data were analysed by assigning each informant to one of four groups:

All E, i.e. scoring E on all 7 pictures;
Mostly E, i.e. scoring no more than 3 E–, the rest E, no O;
Some E, i.e. scoring at least 2 E– or 1 E and 1 E–;
No E, i.e. scoring 6 or 7 O, no more than 1 E or E–.

TABLE 10.2. *Classification of eidetikers*

	Urban	Rural	Total
All E	0	9	9
Mostly E	1	5	6
Some E	3	6	9
No E	11	10	21
Total	15	30	45

The principal findings are presented in Table 10.2. In the total sample, 20 per cent can be classified as pure eidetikers, and an additional 33 per cent satisfy the other less rigorous criteria; hence 53 per cent of the forty-five informants reported a trace or more of eidetic images. The corresponding figures for the rural group as a whole are 30 and 37 per cent, or a total of twenty (67 per cent) out of thirty informants; and for the adults only in that rural group, 21 and 58 per cent, or a total of fifteen (79 per cent) out of nineteen informants.

The incidence of eidetic imagery in the sample as a whole, and especially among the rural adults, is dramatically higher than that normally found in the West. Haber and Haber (1964), for example, indicate that 'all studies' surveyed by them report 'zero or near-zero frequencies among adults' and that no more than 8 per cent of the New Haven sample of children, according to their particular strict and reliable criteria, could be classified as eidetikers.

Even with very small n's, various breakdowns of the data produce significant differences; in all instances p-values are based upon chi square corrected for continuity and with a two-tail test:

1. No matter how the data are grouped, whether by All E *v.* the remainder, All E plus Mostly E *v.* the remainder, etc. a higher proportion of E appears in the rural group ($p < 0.05$).

2. With the criterion of at least Some E, the incidence of E is higher among the children than among the adults in the urban sample ($p < 0.01$) but not in the rural sample.

3. With the same criterion, the incidence among adults is higher in the rural than in the urban sample ($p < 0.02$), but not among the children.

Both samples are combined in Table 10.3, in which the breakdown

TABLE 10.3. *Attributes of eidetikers*

	All or Mostly E	Some E	No E	Total
Number	15	9	21	45
Mean age	24.9	20.1	28.6	25.7
Mean schooling (years)	2.9	3.8	4.3	3.7
Per cent female	47	55	19	36
Per cent children	47	67	19	38
Per cent urban	7	33	52	33

is by type of E response. The differences in age, schooling and sex are not statistically significant. The difference between the percentage of urban informants in the first and third columns, foreshadowed above, is highly significant ($p < 0.01$), as is that between the percentage of children in the second and third columns ($p < 0.05$).

Finally, it can be pointed out that the American and African pictures were indistinguishable with respect to the number or kind of E responses evoked; apparently it made no difference whether culturally irrelevant or relevant pictures served as the stimuli for the imagery. Thus the second black-and-white picture in the Haber or American series evoked 13 E, 10 E–, and 22 O responses; the black-and-white African photograph, which immediately followed, 16 E, 6E–, and 25 O. In fact, informants tended to be very consistent from picture to picture; either they reported eidetic images all or most of the time or they reported none. In Table 10.2, for example, only 33 per cent are classified as Some E.

SIGNIFICANCE

This exploratory study has demonstrated a high incidence of eidetic imagery in a small, haphazard sample of Ibo. The presence of such imagery decreases slightly with schooling and age but not significantly so from a statistical standpoint. It seems most closely related to residence in a rural rather than an urban area. In the latter area but not in the former, the results roughly parallel those from the West: children, not adults, tend to be eidetikers.

Actually this statistics-studded report does not quite convey the truly dramatic nature of the phenomenon of eidetic images being described here. Two instances must suffice, the witnesses to which were also the interpreter and the informants themselves. First, again and again informants who were utterly illiterate could trace correctly the licence numbers on the taxis in the last picture; since they presumably could not read the numbers during the exposure of the photograph, they must have been using the eidetic image as the guide for moving their fingers. Such a feat recalls the ability of eidetic children in England who knew no German and yet, after a 35-second exposure, could spell correctly or nearly correctly the word *Gartenwirtschaft* that had appeared as one of the less interesting details in the original pictorial stimulus (Allport, 1924, p. 109). Second, in the traditional villages, spectators usually stood behind the seated informants and observed the exhibition. In one instance, the informant stated that the Cheshire cat in his projected image was black only, and immediately shouts of disagreement came from the spectators. The investigator looked up from note-taking and saw that the spectators were all concentrating upon the blank screen as if a projector behind them were flashing the picture there. Later these people were asked whether they had been seeing the pictures after each exposure. At least fourteen hands went up, out of roughly eighteen adults and children, a significant number which really ought to be added to the rural sample but which is here simply recorded as another anecdote.

The precise significance of these images within Ibo culture remains unclear. On the one hand, in this study they lasted, the investigator irregularly noted, no longer than four minutes. Such a mechanism is not very efficient for storing information. On the other hand, many of the informants, when directly questioned, indicated that they are accustomed to revive images long after they have perceived aspects of the external world. For example, some stated that before falling asleep and in the dark of their houses they voluntarily recall and 'scan' images of the day's activities. Some university students claim to use images of studied materials in replying to examination questions.

Clearly, additional research is called for. First, the study needs to be repeated among larger numbers of Ibo to verify the findings. The same technique must also be tried in other societies; there appears to be nothing distinctive about Ibo culture which on an *a priori* basis would facilitate eidetic imagery. If a high incidence is verified among the Ibo and duplicated elsewhere, the next step will be to relate the phenomenon to specific cultural or personality factors. In addition, it will then be important to determine exactly how the tendency to be an eidetiker is extinguished, if it really is negatively correlated with age and schooling or the Western character of a community; and to ascertain the social importance of the images in people's memory and in their modes of communicating with one another.

11

B. M. Ross and C. Millsom (*1970*)

Repeated memory of oral prose in Ghana and New York[1]

International Journal of Psychology, 5(3), pp. 173–81

This experiment is concerned with the repeated memory recall of three short prose selections by college students in Ghana and New York City. In contrast to most previous retention studies of connected prose the selections were only heard by the students and not read so that recall of *oral* prose could be tested by written reproductions. It is a common observation that Africans have a strong oral tradition and so might be expected to perform better on this recall task than Europeans or Americans. With the present task a blanket prediction that the Ghanaians would recall better must be tempered by consideration of the nature of the texts and the use of English in reading and reproducing the selections. One prose selection was the well-known North American Indian folktale, 'The War of the Ghosts', extensively studied by Bartlett (1932) and Paul (1959). The second story that was read to the students, also taken from Bartlett (1932), was a short African folktale that was unfamiliar to both subject groups; and the third selection was an anecdote in somewhat archaic seventeenth century English that might presumably give an advantage to the American students.

A second major interest of this study with both subject groups was the extent to which story content and form would stabilize with only three reproductions, the second and third several weeks apart. Bartlett concluded that with repeated reproductions by the same subject 'the general form, or outline, is remarkably persistent, once the first version has been given' (1932, p. 93). Paul (1959, pp. 70–2) contrasted his repeated reproduction results with his serial reproduction results, where a different individual produced each reproduction, and found a 're-markable stability' for the former. His suggestions as to why repeated

[1] This research was supported in part by Social and Rehabilitation Services research grant RD3111.

reproductions are so stable are only weakly spelled out, as he simply states that reminiscence and relearning at each reproduction may be the most important contributing factors. The point seems to have been given only passing mention by both of these earlier investigators that in order for retention of their prose materials to stabilize so quickly after only one or two trials a much greater efficiency is demonstrated than is the case for other types of learning and memory performance.

With the present contrasted subject groups, analyses were designed to determine if and to what degree retention stabilization takes place as well as whether the two culturally distinct groups differed quantitatively in retention. Following Paul, we used both a theme analysis of the original story and a total word count to determine constancy of length of reproductions. Additionally, analyses of individual themes were undertaken to determine if there were cultural predispositions to retain some themes and forget others. The extent to which Paul's hypothesized theme reminiscence, the reinstatement of previously omitted material, occurs was also examined.

METHOD

Subjects

The subjects consisted of three classes in education at the Winneba Training College in Winneba, Ghana, and three classes in child development at New York University (NYU). The NYU students, drawn largely from the New York metropolitan area, were 19 to 21 years old. The Ghanaian students were older, ranging in age from 24 to 35. Both the NYU and Ghanaian students were preparing to be teachers. Although English was not the native language of the Ghanaian students, they had received English language training throughout their years of formal schooling. Instruction at the training college in which they were enrolled was entirely in English. The Ghanaian students were primarily from the coastal and central regions of Ghana and members of the Akan-speaking Ga and Ewe tribes. It might be thought that the Ghanaian students would always be at a handicap in an experiment conducted in a European language. However, Doob (1961, pp. 203–7) has reported that this need not necessarily be the case where formal school education is carried on for a period of years in a European language. He reports a study with Ewe secondary-school children conducted in Ghana in English and in Togo in French where recall of statements was as good or better in the European language as in their own tribal language.

Stories

Exactly the same versions of the two folktales were read that are found in Bartlett (1932). 'The War of the Ghosts', collected by the anthropologist F. Boas, is printed on page 65; 'The Son who tried to Outwit his Father' from the collection by J. H. Weeks, *Congo Life and Folklore* (London, 1911), is printed on page 129. 'The Blind Man who Could See' is reproduced in M. Nicolson, *Science and Imagination* (Ithaca, Cornell University Press, 1956) on pages 141–2. The author attributes the anecdote in its printed form to Robert Boyle with an original publication date of 1664. As no title was given for this anecdote, a title was added by the experimenters. In any case the recall of titles was not required as story titles were always spoken to the subjects to initiate each recall trial. The texts of the three stories to be recalled follows.

The War of the Ghosts. One night two young men from Egulac went down to the river to hunt seals, and while they were there it became foggy and calm. Then they heard war-cries, and they thought: 'Maybe this is a war-party'. They escaped to the shore, and hid behind a log. Now canoes came up, and they heard the noise of paddles, and saw one canoe coming up to them. There were five men in the canoe, and they said: 'What do you think? We wish to take you along. We are going up the river to make war on the people.' One of the young men said: 'I have no arrows.' 'Arrows are in the canoe,' they said. 'I will not go along. I might be killed. My relatives do not know where I have gone. But you', he said, turning to the other, 'may go with them.' So one of the young men went, but the other returned home. And the warriors went on up the river to a town on the other side of Kalama. The people came down to the water, and they began to fight, and many were killed. But presently the young man heard one of the warriors say: 'Quick, let us go home: that Indian has been hit.' Now he thought: 'Oh, they are ghosts.' He did not feel sick, but they said he had been shot. So the canoes went back to Egulac, and the young man went ashore to his house, and made a fire. And he told everybody and said: 'Behold I accompanied the ghosts, and we went to fight. Many of our fellows were killed, and many of those who attacked us were killed. They said I was hit, and I did not feel sick.' He told it all, and then he became quiet. When the sun rose he fell down. Something black came out of his mouth. His face became contorted. The people jumped up and cried. He was dead.

The Son who tried to Outwit his Father. A son said to his father one day: 'I will hide, and you will not be able to find me.' The father replied: 'Hide wherever you like,' and he went into his house to rest. The son saw a three-kernel peanut, and changed himself into one of the kernels; a fowl coming along picked up the peanut and swallowed it; and a wild bush-cat caught and ate the fowl, and a dog met and caught and ate the bush-cat. After a little time the dog was swallowed by a python, that, having eaten its meal, went to the river and was snared in a fish-trap. The father searched for his son and, not seeing him, went to look at the fish-trap. On pulling it to the river-side he found a large python in it. He opened it, and saw a dog inside, in which he found a bush-cat, and on opening that he discovered a fowl, from which he took the peanut, and breaking the shell, he then revealed his son. The son was so dumbfounded that he never again tried to outwit his father.

The Blind Man who Could See. The name of the man was John Vermaasen, at that time about thirty-three years of age, who, when he was two years old, had the smallpox, which render'd him absolutely blind, tho' he is at present an organist in a public choir. The doctor discoursing with him over night, the blind man affirmed that he could distinguish colours by feeling, but not unless he were fasting; for that any quantity of drink deprived him of that exquisite touch which is requisite to so nice a sensation. Upon this, the doctor provided against the next morning seven pieces of ribbon of these seven colours, black, white, red, blue, green, yellow, and grey; but as for mixed colours, this Vermaasen would not undertake to discern them; tho, if offer'd, he could tell that they were mixed. To discern the colour of the ribbon, he places it betwixt his thumb and his forefinger, but his most exquisite perception is in his thumb, and much better in the right than in the left. After the man had four or five times told the doctor the several colours, whilst a napkin was tied over his eyes, the doctor observed he twice mistook, for he called the white black, and the red blue; but still before his error, he would lay them by in pairs, saying, that tho' he could easily distinguish them from all others, yet those two pair were not easily distinguishable from one another. Then the doctor desired to know what kind of difference he found in colours by his touch. To which the blind man reply'd, that all the difference he observed, was a greater or less degree of asperity; for says he, black feels like the points of needles, or some harsh sand, whilst red feels very smooth.

Procedure

Each subject heard only one story. In every case subjects made their first recall about 35 to 40 minutes after the story was read near the close of the same class period. Second and third recalls of the same story occurred at intervals of several weeks at unannounced times in regularly scheduled class periods. The second author read the story to all classes from the front of the classroom. Each story was read aloud twice in succession at a moderate rate of speed. Prior to reading a story, the experimenter told the students to listen carefully but made no mention that recall would subsequently be requested. This was intended to guard against any form of note-taking. When recalls were requested, students were told the story title and wrote with pen or pencil as much of the text as they could recall, signing their names on the sheets they turned in. Exactly the same procedure was used on all three recalls.

With 'The War of the Ghosts' (Ghosts) story the interval between recalls was equivalent for both groups, 16 days between the first and second recalls and 21 days between the second and third. There were temporal variations between groups for the other stories. With 'The Son who tried to Outwit his Father' (Son) story, intervals between recalls were 38 and 32 days for the Ghanaian students and 21 and 42 days for the NYU students. For 'The Blind Man who Could See' (Blind Man) story, intervals were 15 days and 33 days for Ghanaian students and 14 days and 29 days for NYU students. The number of students who were not present for all three recalls proved small and they were dropped from the analysis. The Ns remaining are shown in Table 11.1. All the subjects were female except for the Son story where there were nine female and seven male Ghanaian students and seven female and five male NYU students.

Scoring

The theme analysis for the Ghosts story was the analysis containing 23 themes devised by Paul (1959, pp. 35–6). It was not noticed until the experiment had been carried out and analysed that there was a slight difference in Paul's and Bartlett's original versions of the Ghosts story. Paul's version excludes the two lines – 'One of the young men said: "I have no arrows." "Arrows are in the canoe," they said.' Thus no *arrows* theme is included in the theme analyses. The explicated version sometimes used by Paul, a simplified alternative form of the Ghosts story, was not used at all in the present study.

The authors devised the theme analyses for the Son and the Blind Man stories. Because of the cumulative form of the Son story, the theme analysis was very straightforward. The themes were: (a) son says he will hide, (b) father says he will find son, (c) father goes to rest, (d) son changes himself into kernel of peanut, (e) fowl eats peanut, (f) bush-cat eats fowl, (g) dog eats bush-cat, (h) python eats dog, (i) python snared in fish-trap, (j) father searches but does not find son, (k) father goes to fish-trap, (l) father finds python, (m) father finds dog inside, (n) father finds bush-cat, (o) father finds fowl, (p) father finds peanut, (q) father finds son, (r) moral: son doesn't try to outwit father any more.

The Blind Man story required a greater degree of arbitrariness on the part of the experimenters in constructing a theme analysis. The themes with allowable substitutions were (a) name: John ——, (b) age given (not necessarily correct), (c) smallpox made him blind, (d) John an organist, (e) could distinguish colours only if fasting, (f) several (seven) different coloured ribbons used in testing, (g) knows only that mixed colours are mixed, (h) places ribbon between thumb and forefinger to tell colour, (i) thumb better than fingers in telling colour, (j) right (thumb or hand) better than left, (k) performed blindfolded (napkin tied over eyes), (l) performed correctly some trials (four or five times), (m) made two (some) errors (called white black and red blue), (n) could separate ribbons he made mistakes on from the rest, (o) was asked how he distinguished by touch, (p) only difference degree of sharpness (asperity), (q) black feels like points of needles, (r) black feels like harsh sand, (s) red feels smooth.

The themes were scored as either present or absent. Themes were scored generously in the sense that if an entry for the theme was present it was scored as correct even though literally it was in error. For example, ages, names, lists of colours, etc. did not have to be exact to be scored as correct. It must be emphasized in this regard that the stories were only heard and never seen by the subjects. Some other special allowances were also made. Thus the word 'peanut' is foreign in Ghana being supplanted by the British 'groundnut'; therefore acoustic equivalents such as 'pinnacle' or 'pinnard' and semantic equivalents such as 'casu nut' or 'nut' were scored correct. However, reversals in order such as the claim of the Ghanaian students that the bush-cat would eat the dog and not vice versa was disallowed. Widely varying spelling approximations were scored as correct in both groups. All the recalls of the same story by both subject groups were scored by the same scorer in an attempt to maintain equivalent scoring standards. Total word counts for each recall included all the legible words except the title.

RESULTS

The main results are presented in Table 11.1. Mean percentages of themes retained are shown on the left; with mean percentages of words used in the three recalls as compared to the number of words in the original text on the right. Corresponding standard deviations are shown with each mean. Note that the extent to which words in the recalls are literally the same as those in the text is not tallied. At each recall, tests for significant differences were computed by performing two-tailed t tests between results for Ghanaian and NYU students with theme and word counts. It can be seen in Table 11.1 that for the Ghosts and

TABLE 11.1. *Means and standard deviations for percentages of retained themes and the number of words used in three recalls*

Recall trial	The War of the Ghosts					
	21 themes			330 words		
	Ghana (N = 12)		NYU (N = 18)	Ghana		NYU
1	80 (14)	b	57 (16)	70 (11)	b	48 (12)
2	78 (14)	b	52 (16)	69 (12)	b	42 (13)
3	75 (12)	b	53 (18)	70 (14)	b	45 (14)

	The Son who tried to Outwit his Father					
	18 themes			192 words		
	Ghana (N = 16)		NYU (N = 12)	Ghana		NYU
1	87 (11)	a	65 (23)	84 (27)	a	66 (11)
2	82 (17)		62 (24)	89 (21)	b	62 (14)
3	79 (22)		64 (23)	93 (17)	b	61 (19)

	The Blind Man who Could See					
	19 themes			300 words		
	Ghana (N = 9)		NYU (N = 10)	Ghana		NYU
1	54 (10)		48 (10)	47 (9)		40 (7)
2	30 (16)		38 (9)	29 (5)	a	34 (5)
3	28 (15)		34 (9)	34 (9)		35 (6)

[a] $p < 0.05$.   [b] $p < 0.001$.

H

Son stories, percentages of themes retained and the number of words used at each recall are quite stable with only small percentage decreases. For the more difficult Blind Man story there is more of a fall-off in both measures between the first and second recall with this trend considerably greater for the Ghanaian students. However, there is stabilization between the second and third recalls for both groups.

Although the Blind Man story is clearly the most difficult and the Son story the easiest to retain, the obtained theme percentages should not be viewed as exact quantities since the theme division of the stories and scoring of the themes are both somewhat arbitrary. In the case of the Ghosts story, lower theme recall scores would have been obtained if two themes listed by Paul (1959) in the Bartlett version (these are the same two themes that Paul dropped when he presented the simplified, explicated version) had been included; but they were not counted since no subject mentioned them. Every effort was made to keep scoring consistent between groups and uniform for the three recalls of each story.

When significance tests are considered in Table 11.1, there are highly significant differences at each recall of the Ghosts story favouring Ghanaian over NYU students for both theme recall and word use. For themes in the Son story only the first recall is significantly better for Ghanaian students, although they used significantly more words throughout. Significance was difficult to attain for this story because of the large standard deviations. With the Blind Man story no themes were significant, although the NYU students used significantly more words in the second recall. This was the only case where there was a significant reversal of Ghanaian superiority.

For each story Spearman's rank correlation coefficient was calculated between the Ghanaian and NYU student groups for error rank-ordering of themes summed over the three recalls. Correlation coefficients were 0·69 for the Ghosts story, 0·54 for the Father story, and 0·50 for the Blind Man story. Thus, even though the stories differed in retention ease, there was a considerable degree of commonality in the relative difficulty of specific themes. Comparisons between groups were also made by looking at retention of individual themes. With the Ghosts and Son stories the Ghana students almost uniformly had a higher recall percentage for every theme. For the first test recall of the Ghosts story the Ghana students retained 19 themes better than the NYU students, 1 theme worse, with 1 tie; while for the third recall 17 themes were better retained, 3 worse, with 1 tie. The figures for the Son story were 16 better and 2 worse for the first recall, and 17 better and 1 worse for the third recall. With the Blind Man story a sharp reversal took place between the first and second recall; for the first recall the Ghana students were better on 12 themes and worse on 7, while for the second recall they were better on 7 themes, worse on 11 with 1 tie. This reversal was maintained for the third recall with the Ghana students better on 6 themes and worse on 12 with 1 tie. In line with the rank correlations, it did not appear to be the case that either group had themes that they were particularly partial to.

It was considered that the entries in Table 11.1 can somewhat over-state constancy of retention since some of the deletions which take place from one recall to the next are offset by additions. In fact for the NYU students in the third recall of both the Ghosts and Son stories more additions than deletions occurred. Nevertheless, the number of additions remained small even here as 1·1 was the largest mean number of theme additions per person in any recall trial. Therefore the contribution reminiscence made to retention was relatively small.

DISCUSSION

In general, the Ghanaian students recalled the stories better than the NYU students. This conclusion is qualified by the result that the Ghanaians were not better on the Blind Man story told in seventeenth-century English and that the Son story was of a type familiar in African folklore. Superiority was especially significant for the Ghosts story where, as with the Son story, almost all themes were better retained by the Ghanaians. This general theme superiority and the high error rank-order correlation of 0·69 with NYU performance indicates that it was not just the magical or supernatural aspects of the Ghosts story that were better recalled. It is a considerable achievement that the Ghanaian students could outperform the NYU students when they had to both hear and write stories in English, an acquired second language for all of them. Further, the American accent of the story reader, though personally familiar to the Ghanaian students, was different from what they were accustomed to. Whether a stronger oral tradition accounts for the superior retention of the African students is, of course, not proved, but results are in the expected direction.

Stabilization in terms of number of retained themes and number of words in which they were expressed was reached early, as inferred from subsequent reproductions of the same story where nearly equal amounts of material were recalled. Thus there was little retention decrease after the first recall of the Ghosts and Son stories, and after the second recall of the Blind Man story. Note also that for both subject groups theme retention and word count percentages tended to stay close together. For the total of eighteen recall trials there was only one difference of more than 10 per cent (the Ghanaian students for the third recall of the Son story). This is at least presumptive evidence that any tendency for invented elaborations was weak. These results are in accord with those of Bartlett and Paul for repeated reproductions, though their published results using this memory paradigm were not as extensive as those displayed here.

It is also worth noting that Bartlett stated as a principal conclusion, 'With frequent reproduction the form and items of remembered detail very quickly become stereotyped and thereafter suffer little change' (1932, p. 93). The two- to five-week intervals used here following the original recall appear to fall within Bartlett's category of frequent reproductions. He used a contrasting category of 'long-distance remembering' that had intervals of many months or even years between reproductions. At these intervals he did obtain considerable forgetting; stabilization must after all have its limits.

What explanation can be given for the considerable amount of stabilization that did occur and which both Bartlett and Paul found 'remarkable' in their own results? As concluded above, reminiscence seems to play only a minor role. Paul's other suggestion that relearning takes place at each reproduction does not advance us far, since it leaves unexplained why a fairly immediate reproduction should be so efficient for subsequent retention. The approximate constancy found over several reproductions is also not adequately dealt with by invoking clever encoding strategies. With stabilization achieved after only one or two reproductions, any attempt to 'chunk' themes together into larger aggregates simply does not have sufficient opportunity to be practical.

The present results along with those of Bartlett and Paul are the rule rather than the exception. One memory study (Edwards and English, 1939) for content retention at intervals of sixty and ninety days after an immediate reproduction actually showed a slight reminiscence effect as measured by a recognition test. For other results showing a high degree of retention with repeated reproductions of meaningful prose see English, Welborn and Killian (1934) and Clark (1940). The latter study used a strict criterion of requiring reproduction of ideas in substantially the same words as the original text. Even so, the mean amount retained was quite constant from one recall trial to the next with trials at weekly intervals for four weeks. With the more generous theme scoring criterion of the present study the results would have little interest if both subject groups had initially retained only a small proportion of the heard text, but this was certainly not the case for the Ghosts and Son stories.

Criticism of Paul's suggestions does not, unfortunately, clarify what retention processes can best account for the subject's relatively good performance. A main difficulty is that explanations of forgetting processes have been chiefly based on retention of lists of unrelated items and with the exception of Bartlett there is almost no theory about retention of thematic material. Furthermore, even Bartlett's schema emphasis is too limited in scope to encompass story reproduction when retention is high; thus Paul (1959, Ch. 4) is forced to talk about a wider *schema organization*. Paul (p. 72) also showed that self-produced prose constructions are not always best retained, since the same subjects retained more of a story that they read than somewhat shorter stories that they themselves made up. Therefore the free rein allowed subjects in the method of repeated reproductions cannot be the whole answer. The recent emphasis on generative syntactic transformations that has spread to memory studies from linguistics also can shed only limited light on retention of connected prose in that its application has thus far been restricted to the single sentence or proposition as a functional unit of analysis.

Because of the purposely discrete and simplified material dealt with, retention theories have largely ignored subjects' ability to retain content by verbal paraphrase. Lack of accuracy is almost always judged as a deviation from exact or literal memory. In the cited Edwards and English study (1939) a measure of literal recognition memory was also taken and it showed the usual sharp retention decline at the same time-intervals for which there was a small reminiscence effect for content. It seems unlikely that the two measures were independent of each other even though recognition tests were used. It is probable that for content to be well retained literalness had to be sacrificed as themes became expressed in an individual's personal vocabulary. The point being made is that since an interaction occurs between literal and content retention there cannot be an adequate theory of the forgetting of connected prose by using the single measure of decrement in literal memory; some apparent decrement must result from an effort after content retention. Direct application of rote forgetting theories to material with meaningful content is therefore, in principle, incomplete.

Good serial order retention was particularly striking in our results. Even where omissions occurred, retention order appeared to be well maintained across content gaps with only slight theme order displacements. This finding contrasts sharply with results found for retention of lists of unrelated items but appears to agree with Bartlett's results (1932, p. 80) for repeated reproductions. Both his conclusions and ours are based on qualitative impressions as it is difficult to devise a meaningful quantitative index of order. Familiarity cannot have played much of a role in either our results or Bartlett's in fixing serial order because of the novelty of the material and lack of repetitions. It would instead appear that the actual order is the path of least resistance in recalling themes because the themes tend to imply each other in a unidirectional serial chain. Presumably this is one reason why an older generation sometimes called what we term content memory 'logical memory'.

An example of a strong form of order implication occurs whenever an interrogative structure appears since it usually implies an answer while the inversion answer-before-question is not legitimate. For this reason making up question-and-answer series and fictional anecdotes is often resorted to as a mnemonic device to preserve order relations. Thus people intentionally retain more material than required so that they can recall items with only weak intrinsic connections in a prescribed order. Almost by definition, a folktale that is orally transmitted must include sufficient order indicators to designate clearly which event-sequence has found acceptance through many retellings.

PART TWO

Cognitive level and attainment

Introduction

This second section considers cross-culturally the problem of competence in cognitive behaviour, and largely revolves around our Western notion of *intelligence*. Mental capacity or mental power, to use earlier terms for cognitive competence, may be a unitary and universal characteristic of man as a species; however, this has yet to be established. Indeed, our Western concept of cognitive competence, *intelligence*, may also be an adequate notion to describe this capacity for all men; however, this too should be established before it may be validly used cross-culturally. The answers are certainly not yet available; however, a central theme of this section is that we should at least be open to alternative dimensions of cognitive competence when we engage in cross-cultural studies of cognitive behaviour.

Biesheuvel (Chapter 12) draws a distinction clearly between the power or competence, and the abilities or performance aspects of cognitive behaviour. Indeed so clearly is this distinction made, that it renders unnecessary much of the current argument on cross-cultural studies of intelligence. The next selection, by Berry (Chapter 13), merely serves to emphasize two points which have often been lost in the controversy: one must accept that it is clever to do different things in different cultural systems, and that, if inferences to capacity or competence are to be made, the original observations must be based upon an adequate sample of what people are able to do in their own cultural system. The paper by Cole and Bruner (Chapter 14) further emphasizes these distinctions and applies them to problems of subcultural differences within a single society.

Irvine (Chapter 15) investigates, through the use of factor analysis, the structure of apparent test scores, and argues that current theories do not adequately describe the structures emerging from testing in Africa. In keeping with this new emphasis, two studies of cognitive competence which attempt to grasp the meaning of competence within a culture are presented. The first by Wober (Chapter 16) is a major innovation, in that it applies a Western psychological technique to the problem of defining intelligence from the point of view of the Ganda people. A similarly sensitive study, by Okonji (Chapter 17) from within Ibo culture, demonstrates that ability to deal with abstract categories does not differ between European and African samples. The force of this latter study stems not merely from the conclusion he reached (for he is not the first to make it) but from the fact that it has been reached by a psychologist who has been raised in a non-Western conceptual system.

This survey of cross-cultural studies of cognitive competence, its definition, its measurement and its structure, is intended to demonstrate the great difficulty psychologists have in making any generalizations about competence at all. It is, of course, easy to define our competence as the most competent, and our capacity as the largest; however these studies show that facile ethnocentric generalizations are no longer valid, and that inferences to a single dimension of intelligence may no longer be possible.

12

S. Biesheuvel (1959)

The nature of intelligence : some practical implications of its measurement

Psygram, 1(6), pp. 78–80

Intelligence, a concept within the area of individual differences, reduces itself to two essentials, the power of the mind, and the skills through which this power expresses itself. The former aspect comes nearest to what the man in the street means by intelligence. It can be defined as 'the ability to learn', 'the capacity for understanding', 'the ability to perceive essential relations between things', 'insight into the nature of things'. The 'machines' through which this power expresses itself provide the foundations of abilities – from the highest abilities, such as the solving of mathematical equations, right down to the simplest such as tying one's bootlaces.

Spearman's contribution to the theory of intelligence was to elucidate the nature of the first of these aspects, the power of the mind, by demonstrating the existence of a general mental ability, entering to some extent into any activity whatsoever and for which he formulated the hypothesis of mental energy. What was not attributable to g, he considered to be purely specific to the particular act.

Thurstone clarified the nature of the 'machines' by demonstrating that the wide range of these specific skills could be reduced to a limited number of primary mental abilities, such as verbal comprehension, verbal fluency, spatial relations, number manipulation, memory functions, inductive reasoning and perceptual speed.

Godfrey Thomson and Burt provided a synthesis of the two by insisting that activities were neither g plus specifics, nor a combination of primary mental abilities only, together covering the entire area of g, but that they were generally reducible to one or more broad mental abilities, constituting the elaboration of g into such behavioural entities as 'verbal ability', 'number ability', 'practical ability' and the like, further refinable into more specific skills. Though fully backed by factorial evidence, this point of view was less abstract than that of either Spearman or Thurstone, and produced an analysis of intelligence into basic abilities which were more immediately related to actual behaviour than the mathematical factors which preceded them.

Godfrey Thomson's notion of g being the sum total of bonds that could potentially be established in the brain, whilst the abilities are the actual bonds that do get established as a result of experience and that differentiate themselves out as systems, has much to commend it. Differences in the 'bond potential' would account for differences in intellectual capacity or power, whilst ability differences would reflect not only the different experiences of men, but also different skill endowments, in that it would appear that some people establish one set of bonds, say those involved in visual perception, or in motor skills, or in verbal ability, more easily than others, presumably by virtue of differences in cerebral structure.

For the purposes of scientific analysis, and to demonstrate the differential effects of various environmental influences on the development of intelligence, it is useful to think in terms of factors, each representing a particular degree of abstraction. The growth of 'g' or the power of the mind is not a spontaneous affair, but is dependent on environmental stimulation of diverse kinds. Nutrition, particularly in the earliest years of life, may have a permanently enhancing or depressing effect. Equally important is parental solicitude and care, the material diversity of the environment, the cultural stimulation value of the milieu in which the child grows up, and eventually also the formal education which it receives. The mental skills or 'machines' through which basic mental power expresses itself to give rise to actual abilities are developed on a cultural basis, in accordance with the requirements and values of the society in which the individual grows up, though individual circumstances and opportunities will have much to do with the repertoire each individual acquires. Whereas the growth of g is limited to the period of youth, the proliferation of skills can go on indefinitely.

When we measure intelligence, we may be interested in various things. Generally we want to gauge the power of the mind, and Mental Age or IQ is the best expression of this capacity. But we may be more interested in an assessment of actual mental abilities, in which case we measure verbal, or numerical, or perceptual, or motor skills. Here the 'group factors' rather than the 'general factor' are the objects of our measurement. Their aggregate can also be reflected as an IQ, though it has become customary to distinguish between 'verbal', 'nonverbal', 'practical' IQs, the pattern of which reflects qualitative differences in intelligence.

Whereas achievement can be measured in terms of the specific behaviour concerned, *g* or the power of the mind can only be inferred, and for this inference to be adequate we must sample an individual's abilities widely. Because of the individual differences in respect of the acquisition of skills, and the facility with which they function, *g* does not get an equal chance to express itself through any one of them. Hence tests of the Binet and Wechsler type are the most adequate for the measurement of mental power, because of the diversity of mental skills which they involve. Group tests which utilize verbal, numerical and perceptual skills will give a fair approximation, depending on the diversity of this material.

Differences between cultures and subcultures within a society may exist both in terms of *g* and in terms of the 'machines' or specific abilities through which *g* manifests itself. Cultures are not equally intellectually stimulating; their socioeconomic conditions vary as do their habits of child rearing. They practise different pursuits and value different skills. The contrast between Bantu cultures and Western communities in South Africa is a case in point. A multitude of circumstances, including differences in nutritional levels, complexity of material environment, parental outlook and education, schooling facilities, affect intellectual growth. Some depression of the mental power of Africans below its genetic potential can therefore be expected. The prowess of Africans in the verbal and auditory spheres, as compared with their relative backwardness in handling spatial relations, is well known and referable to their culture circumstances. Even between the English and Afrikaans subcultures in South Africa there are differences in the stimulus value of the environment which translate themselves into significant differences in test performance.

Hence measures of intelligence, as indications of the power of mind, are strictly comparable only within homogeneous cultures. There is no possibility of comparing the ultimate intellectual capacity of different ethnic or cultural groups, except perhaps by means of elaborate experimental designs, involving the training of members of one group within the culture of the other, and even there uncontrolled or sampling factors are likely to invalidate the findings.

If this proposition is accepted, tests should strictly speaking be specially constructed and standardized for every distinct cultural group, which would leave one with a plenitude of IQ scales for White and Black; Afrikaans and English; urban and rural; male and female;

upper, medium and lower socioeconomic group. This would reduce intelligence testing to an absurdity and deprive it of most of its practical value. There is, however, a way out of this difficulty. When behaviour relates to some common norm, such as the ability to pass a particular public examination, to be successful in a vocational training course or in a career open to all, a common test may be used, provided this test is a satisfactory predictor of success for the entire heterogeneous population. It matters little whether the test does not adequately reflect the ultimate potentialities of certain sections of this population, for that which is not there cannot be used in education or on the job either, whatever the reasons for the nondeployment of the mental power may be.

It could happen that, although two cultural subgroups are equally successful in meeting the demands of the common society within which they function, they nevertheless do not perform equally in a test intended to predict this adaptive behaviour. This could result from inappropriate test content for either group, or from diverse attitudes towards being tested. Both these factors would lead to differential test validity, and might necessitate a search for a suitable common instrument, or acceptance of different tests and scales. The conditions to be satisfied before one uses a common test and IQ scale are therefore (a) a common yardstick by which actual behaviour is measured; and (b) consistent validity. The fact that one group might have a lower mean IQ on such a common test would be of no consequence if this also reflected, *all other things being equal*, a lower performance on the behavioural criterion.

13

J. W. Berry

Radical cultural relativism and the concept of intelligence[1]

If psychology is to become a science of all human behaviour, capable of understanding its functioning in all cultures, then concepts which have been developed largely in the West must surely come under close scrutiny. The ethnocentrism inherent in our discipline has become obvious as we have attempted to generalize our concepts and laws to behaviour in other cultural settings.

There have been many schemes advocated for use cross-culturally which may help us to check upon our ethnic-relative assumptions, and to make the necessary modifications in our concepts and descriptive tools. A gradualist approach to making the modifications necessary for behavioural comparisons across cultures has been advanced by the present author (Berry, 1969a). However, the concept of *intelligence* has had such great impact internationally, yet has such firm roots in psychological science, that it may be appropriate to wipe the conceptual slate clean and to adopt a position of *radical cultural relativism* with respect to this concept.

This position in general entails the rejection of assumed psychological universals across cultural systems, and requires the generation from within each cultural system (*emic* approach) of any behavioural concept which is to be applied to it. Specifically for the concept of *intelligence*, this position requires that indigenous notions of cognitive competence be the sole basis for the generation of cross-culturally valid descriptions and assessments of cognitive capacity.

However, for *intelligence* the problem is somewhat more difficult than for the handling of overt behaviours, since it is a capacity or competence inferred from a wide range of peripheral skills and

[1] This article is a revision and condensation of a paper presented to a conference on 'Cultural Factors in Mental Test Development, Application and Interpretation', Istanbul, 22 July 1971.

performances. Thus, in addition to exploring indigenous notions of cognitive competence, we must also ensure that we sample behaviours widely so that cognitive behaviours which are characteristic of the individual are discovered. The balance of this paper is an elaboration of these two basic points. In so doing, we will raise once again the old possibility of inferring qualitatively different 'intelligences' from quantitatively different skills.

DIFFERING NOTIONS OF INTELLIGENT BEHAVIOUR

At least two lines of thought may be explored: firstly the gradual evolution of our own notion of intelligence over the past seven decades, and secondly the valuing of different kinds of cognitive behaviour across cultures.

The history of our own concept of intelligence has been authoritatively traced by the late Sir Cyril Burt (1969), who was, so to speak, present at the birth. Its early definition (by Galton, and accepted by others) as an 'innate general cognitive factor' has now generally been termed 'intelligence A' (Hebb, 1949), and the result of growth of this factor in a particular environmental context has been termed 'intelligence B' (ibid.). An estimate of 'intelligence B', which is some degree of sampling from it, is now generally termed 'intelligence C' (Vernon, 1955). These definitions grew largely in the context of intracultural research, although the two extensions ('B' and 'C') reflect the concerns of the cross-cultural worker. Burt elsewhere (1968) has pointed out that a good deal of our present confusion in employing the term *intelligence*, has resulted from its gradual movement into the popular vocabulary. Thus, many who wish to limit its use to an original and precise meaning are challenged by those who wish to emphasize the cultural patterning of cognitive behaviour. We may discern within our own culture across a short period of history the same problematic issues which arise when the same general notion is transported across cultural boundaries.

The large range of behavioural variation across cultures tends to obscure the continuity of the question. However, it is still essentially in the form, 'Will we always be able to infer the same general cognitive capacity, biologically characteristic of the species, from the great range of culturally patterned cognitive behaviour?' As we saw in the introduction, the bulk of early thought (e.g. Boas, 1911b; Wundt, 1916) concluded that similar cognitive capacity and processes could be assumed since difference in cognitive output could be adequately explained by differences in experiential input. We also saw, however, that Lévy-

Bruhl (1926) found it necessary to conclude that either the process or capacity must differ cross-culturally, if differences in cognitive behaviour are to be explained.

Clearly, Western psychological science is not yet in a position to provide an answer to this basic question. However, just as clearly, psychology never will be until psychologists engage in a thorough exploration of all cognitive behaviour which is valued and exhibited in a wide variety of cultural systems. As a beginning, a number of recent statements have been made asserting the cultural relativity of cognition and the possibility of qualitatively different cognitive competences.

Berry (1969a), following an earlier argument (1966b), claimed that indigenous conceptions of intelligent behaviour often differed widely (cf. the *ethnoscience* approach) and hence differences could not be considered merely as quantitative levels on a single, universal cognitive dimension; further, typical studies to date have considered only 'a scrap of the *emic*' range of these intelligent behaviours. Irvine (1969a) has similarly argued for recognition of the 'value' inherent in our concept, noting that indigenous 'modes of thought' usually escape Western tests. Wober (1969), as well, has distinguished between Western and non-Western cognitive abilities when he asks the two questions 'How well can *they* do *our* tricks?' and 'How well can *they* do *their* tricks?' Vernon (1969) too has acknowledged the usefulness of such an approach:

> We must try to discard the idea that intelligence (i.e. intelligence B) is a kind of universal faculty, a trait which is the same (apart from variations in amount) in all cultural groups. Clearly it develops differently in different physical and cultural environments. It should be regarded as a name for all the various cognitive skills which are developed in, and valued by, the group. In Western civilisation it refers mainly to grasping relations and symbolic thinking, and this permeates to some extent all the abilities we show at school, at work, or in daily life. We naturally tend to evaluate the intelligence of other ethnic groups on the same criteria, though it would surely be more psychologically sound to recognize that such groups require, and stimulate, the growth of different mental as well as physical skills for coping with their particular environments, i.e. that they possess different intelligences. (p. 10)

It is not known whether Vernon would consider this reasoning to be applicable to intelligence A. However, from the point of view of cultural ecology (where cultures and gene pools are viewed as responding to the same environmental pressures: cf. Berry, 1971) it is probable that the acceptance of variation in intelligence B due to eco-cultural factors would lead one to the acceptance of variation in intelligence A due to the same ecological press.

Most importantly, however, indigenous psychologists have begun to examine what it is to be clever or bright in their own culture, and at least one study by a European in an African university has applied Western scientific techniques to the same problem (Wober, 1973). We may conclude, then, that the question of qualitative variation in cognitive competence has been posed once again; with the help of psychologists socialized in a variety of cultural systems, we are in a much better position, this time, to search for an answer.

ADEQUATE SAMPLING OF COGNITIVE VARIATION

Regardless of what answer may emerge to the question of multiple cognitive competences in the human species, it is abundantly clear to most observers that the overt cognitive behaviour – the skills and per-formances – are numerous indeed. It is equally clear that these are closely patterned on the ecological requirements and cultural supports for life in particular parts of the world (see e.g. Berry, 1966b, 1971; Wober, 1966b).

A major problem for psychologists cross-culturally is to adequately describe the skill profile nurtured in any particular eco-cultural setting. As Ferguson (1954, p. 104) has put it, 'The initial problem becomes one of describing the patterns of ability which are characteristic of indivi-duals reared in different cultural environments' since '. . . individuals reared in different cultures will develop different patterns of ability'.

It is only after this descriptive task is relatively complete that the problem of sampling emerges. For Goodenough (1936), who first articulated this concern, the problem was to

be sure that the test-items from which the total trait is to be judged are *representative and valid samples of the ability in question, as it is displayed within the particular culture with which we are concerned.* (p. 5)

Further, she asks:

If we are to look upon intelligence tests as samples of the intellectual requirements of a given culture-group, what basis is there left for applying such a sample of tasks to individuals from another group whose cultural patterns differ widely from those of the original group for whom the test was designed? Very little, I think. About all that can be learned from such a procedure is that the cultures are different; in other words, that the tasks chosen are not representative of the abilities of the subjects. In this way we may be able to find out a little about what these people can not do, but it is not likely that we shall learn much about what they can do. (pp. 8–9)

Without adequate sampling then, it is clear that not only will we be unable to gain an accurate picture of what skills people do possess, but we will also be unable to make valid inferences to any basic cognitive competence or capacity.

If, when these problems of skill description and sampling are honestly begun, we catch a few glimpses of qualitatively different inferred cognitive competences, then we must seriously consider alternative cognitive dimensions to our own notion of *intelligence*.

If, in the end, the argument is supported, then we will know that our concept of intelligence is not a psychological universal; we will know that what we have supposed to be comparisons on a single dimension are in fact comparisons across dimensions; we will know that the notion of a universal intelligence must once and for all be dropped; and we will know that instruments designed to assess it (culture- 'fair, free, or reduced') must be scrapped.

We will also know that much difficult cooperative work remains if behavioural science is to comprehend the nature and variation of human cognitive competence.

14

M. Cole and J. S. Bruner (1971)

Cultural differences and inferences about psychological processes[1]

American Psychologist, 26, pp. 867–76

DEFICIT INTERPRETATION

Perhaps the most prevalent view of the source of ethnic and social class differences in intellectual performance is what might be summed up under the label 'the deficit hypothesis'. It can be stated briefly, without risk of gross exaggeration. It rests on the assumption that a community under conditions of poverty (for it is the poor who are the focus of attention, and a disproportionate number of the poor are members of minority ethnic groups) is a disorganized community, and this disorganization expresses itself in various forms of deficit. One widely agreed-upon source of deficit is mothering; the child of poverty is assumed to lack adequate parental attention. Given the illegitimacy rate in the urban ghetto, the most conspicuous 'deficit' is a missing father and, consequently, a missing father model. The mother is away at work or, in any case, less involved with raising her children than she should be by white middle-class standards. There is said to be less regularity, less mutuality in interaction with her. There are said to be specialized deficits in interaction as well – less guidance in goal seeking from the parents (Schoggen, 1969), less emphasis upon means and ends in maternal instruction (Hess and Shipman, 1965), or less positive and more negative reinforcement (Bee, Van Egeren, Streissguth, Nyman and Leckie, 1969; Smilansky, 1968).

More particularly, the deficit hypothesis has been applied to the symbolic and linguistic environment of the growing child. His linguistic community as portrayed in the early work of Basil Bernstein (1961a), for example, is characterized by a restricted code, dealing more in the

---

[1] A version of this article appeared in the 1972 *National Society for the Study of Education Yearbook on Early Childhood Education*.

stereotype of interaction than in language that explains and elaborates upon social and material events. The games that are played by poor children and to which they are exposed are less strategy bound than those of more advantaged children (Eifermann, 1968): their homes are said to have a more confused noise background, permitting less opportunity for figure-ground formation (Klaus and Gray, 1968), and the certainty of the environment is sufficiently reduced so that children have difficulty in delaying reinforcement (Mischel, 1966) or in accepting verbal reinforcement instead of the real article (Zigler and Butterfield, 1968).

The theory of intervention that grew from this view was the idea of 'early stimulation', modelled on a conception of supplying nutriment for those with a protein deficiency or avitaminosis. The nature of the needed early stimulation was never explained systematically, save in rare cases (Smilansky, 1968), but it variously took the form of practice in using abstractions (Blank and Solomon, 1969), in having dialogue where the referent objects were not present, as through the use of telephones (Deutsch, 1967; John and Goldstein, 1964), or in providing secure mothering by substitution (Caldwell *et al.*, 1970; Klaus and Gray, 1968).

A primary result of these various deficits was believed to express itself in the lowered test scores and academic performance among children from poverty backgrounds. The issue was most often left moot as to whether or not this lowered test performance was easily reversible, but the standard reference was to a monograph by Bloom (1964) indicating that cognitive performance on a battery of tests, given to poor and middle-class children, yielded the result that nearly 80 per cent of the variance in intellectual performance was accounted for by age 3.

DIFFERENCE INTERPRETATION

Such data seem to compel the conclusion that as a consequence of various factors arising from minority group status (factors affecting motivation, linguistic ability, goal orientation, hereditary proclivities to learn in certain ways – the particular mix of factors depends on the writer), minority group children suffer intellectual deficits when compared with their 'more advantaged' peers.

In this section, we review a body of data and theory that controverts this contention, casts doubt on the conclusion that a deficit exists in minority group children, and even raises doubts as to whether any nonsuperficial *differences* exist among different cultural groups.

There are two long-standing precedents for the view that different groups (defined in terms of cultural, linguistic and ethnic criteria) do not differ intellectually from each other in any important way.[1] First, there is the anthropological 'doctrine of psychic unity' (Kroeber, 1948) which, on the basis of the 'run of total experience', is said to warrant the assumption of intellectual equality as a sufficient approximation to the truth. This view is compatible with current linguistic anthropological theorizing, which concentrates on describing the way in which different cultural/linguistic groups categorize familiar areas of experience (Tyler, 1969). By this view, different conclusions about the world are the result of arbitrary and different, but equally logical, ways of cutting up the world of experience. From this perspective, descriptions of the 'disorganization' of minorities would be highly suspect, this suspicion arising in connection with questions like 'Disorganized from whose point of view?'

ah so!

Anthropological critiques of psychological experimentation have never carried much weight with psychologists, nor have anthropologists been very impressed with conclusions from psychological tests. We have hypothesized elsewhere (Cole, Gay, Glick and Sharp, 1971) that their mutual indifference stems in part from a difference in opinion about the inferences that are warranted from testing and experimentation, and in part because the anthropologist relies mainly on data that the psychologist completely fails to consider: the mundane social life of the people he studies. As we shall see, these issues carry over into our criticism of the 'deficit' theory of cultural deprivation.

A second tradition that calls into question culturally determined group difference in intelligence is the linguist's assertion that languages do not differ in their degree of development (Greenberg, 1963), buttressed by the transformationalist's caution that one cannot attribute to people a cognitive capacity that is less than is required to produce the complex rule-governed activity called language (Chomsky, 1966).

Although Chomskian linguistics has had a profound effect on psychological theories of language and cognitive development in recent years, psychological views of language still are considered hopelessly inadequate by working linguists. This criticism applies not only to psycholinguistic theory but to the actual description of linguistic performance

---

[1] It is assumed here that it is permissible to speak of minority group or poverty group 'culture' using as our criterion Lévi-Strauss's (1963) definition: 'What is called "culture" is a fragment of humanity which, from the point of view of the research at hand . . . present significant discontinuities in relation to the rest of humanity' (p. 295). We do not intend to enter into arguments over the existence or nature of a 'culture of poverty', although such an idea seems implicit in the view of most deficit theorists.

on which theory is based. Needless to say, the accusation of misunderstanding at the descriptive level leads to accusations of absurdity at the theoretical level.

A third tradition that leads to rejection of the deficit theory has many sources in recent social sciences. This view holds that even when attempts have been made to provide reasonable anthropological and linguistic foundations, the conclusions about cognitive capacity from psychological experiments are unfounded because the performance produced represents a complex interaction of the formal characteristics of the experiment and the social/environmental context that determines the subject's interpretation of the situation in which it occurs. The need for 'situation-bound' interpretations of experiments is emphasized in such diverse sources as sociology (Goffman, 1964), psychology (Brunswik, 1958), and psycholinguistics (Cazden, 1970). This is an important issue, which we will return to once illustrations of the 'antideficit' view have been explored.

Perhaps the most coherent denial of the deficit position, coupled with compelling illustrations of the resourcefulness of the supposedly deprived and incompetent person, is contained in Labov's attack on the concept of 'linguistic deprivation' and its accompanying assumption of cognitive incapacity (Labov, 1970).

It is not possible here to review all of Labov's evidence. Rather, we have abstracted what we take to be the major points in his attack.

1. *An assertion of the functional equality of all languages.* This assertion is applied specifically to his analysis of nonstandard Negro English, which has been the object of his study for several years. Labov provided a series of examples where young blacks who would be assessed as linguistically retarded and academically hopeless by standard test procedures enter conversations in a way that leaves little doubt that they can speak perfectly adequately and produce very clever arguments in the process.

2. *An assertion of the psychologist's ignorance of language in general and nonstandard dialects in particular.* Labov's particular target is Carl Bereiter (Bereiter and Englemann, 1966), whose remedial teaching technique is partly rationalized in terms of the *inability* of young black children to use language either as an effective tool of communication or thinking. Part of Labov's attack is aimed at misinterpretation of such phrases as '*They mine*', which Labov analysed in terms of rules of contraction, but which Bereiter made the mistake of referring to as a

'series of badly connected words' (Labov, 1970, p. 171). This 'psychologist's deficit' has a clear remedy. It is roughly equivalent to the anthropological caveat that the psychologist has to know more about the people he studies.

3. *The inadequacy of present experimentation.* More serious criticism of the psychologist's interpretation of 'language deprivation' and, by extension, his whole concept of 'cultural deprivation' is contained in the following, rather extensive quote:

> . . . this and the preceding section are designed to convince the reader that the controlled experiments that have been offered in evidence [of Negro lack of competence] are misleading. The only thing that is controlled is the superficial form of the stimulus. All children are asked, 'What do you think of capital punishment?' or 'Tell me everything you can about this.' But the speaker's interpretation of these requests, and the action he believes is appropriate in response is completely uncontrolled. One can view these test stimuli as requests for information, commands for action, or meaningless sequences of words . . . With human subjects it is absurd to believe that identical stimuli are obtained by asking everyone the same question. Since the crucial intervening variables of interpretation and motivation are uncontrolled, most of the literature on verbal deprivation tells us nothing of the capacities of children. (Labov, 1970, p. 171)

Here Labov is attacking the experimental method as usually applied to the problem of subcultural differences in cognitive capacity. We can abstract several assertions from this key passage: (*a*) formal experimental equivalence of operations does not ensure *de facto* equivalence of experimental treatments; (*b*) different subcultural groups are predisposed to interpret the experimental stimuli (situations) differently; (*c*) different subcultural groups are motivated by different concerns relevant to the experimental task; (*d*) in view of the inadequacies of experimentation, inferences about lack of competence among black children are unwarranted.

These criticisms, when combined with linguistic misinterpretation, constitute Labov's attack on the deficit theory of cultural deprivation and represent the rationale underlying his demonstrations of competence where its lack had previously been inferred.

One example of Labov's approach is to conduct a rather standard interview of the type often used for assessment of language competence.

The situation is designed to be minimally threatening; the interviewer is a neighbourhood figure, and black. Yet, the black 8 year old interviewee's behaviour is monosyllabic. He is a candidate for the diagnosis of linguistically and culturally deprived. But this diagnosis is very much situation dependent. For at a later time, this same interviewer goes to the boy's apartment, brings one of the boy's friends with him, lies down on the floor, and produces some potato chips. He then begins talking about clearly taboo subjects in dialect. Under these circumstances, the mute interviewee becomes an excited participant in the general conversation.

In similar examples, Labov demonstrated powerful reasoning and debating skills in a school drop-out and nonlogical verbosity in an acceptable, 'normal' black who has mastered the forms of standard English. Labov's conclusion is that the usual assessment situations, including IQ and reading tests, elicit deliberate, defensive behaviour on the part of the child who has realistic expectations that to talk openly is to expose oneself to insult and harm. As a consequence, such situations *cannot* measure the child's competence. Labov went even further to assert that far from being verbally deprived, the typical ghetto child is

... bathed in verbal stimulation from morning to night. We see many speech events which depend upon the competitive exhibition of verbal skills – sounding, singing, toasts, rifting, louding – a whole range of activities in which the individual gains status through the use of language. ... We see no connection between the verbal skill in the speech events characteristic of the street culture and success in the school room. (Labov, 1970, p. 163)

Labov is not the only linguist to offer such a critique of current theories of cultural deprivation (see e.g. Stewart, 1970). However, Labov's criticism raises larger issues concerning the logic of comparative research designs of which the work in cultural/linguistic deprivation is only a part. It is to this general question that we now turn.

COMPETENCE AND PERFORMANCE IN PSYCHOLOGICAL
RESEARCH

The major thrusts of Labov's argument, that situational factors are important components of psychological experiments and that it is difficult if not impossible to infer competence directly from performance, are not new ideas to psychologists. Indeed, a concern with the relation between *psychological processes* on the one hand and *situational factors* on the other has long been a kind of shadow issue in psychology, surfacing most often in the context of comparative research.

It is this question that underlies the oft-berated question, 'What do IQ tests measure?' and has been prominent in attacks on Jensen's (1969) argument that group differences in IQ test performance are reflective of innate differences in capacity.

Kagan (1969), for example, pointed to the work of Palmer, who regularly delays testing until the child is relaxed and has established rapport with the tester. Jensen (1969, p. 100) himself reported that significant differences in test performance can be caused by differential adaptation to the test situation.

Hertzig, Birch, Thomas and Mendez (1968) made a direct study of social class/ethnic differences in response to the test situation and demonstrated stable differences in situational responses that were correlated with test performance and were present even when measured IQ was equivalent for subgroups chosen from the major comparison groups.

Concern with the particular *content* of tests and experiments as they relate to inferences about cognitive capacity occurs within the same context. The search for a 'culture-free' IQ test has emphasized the use of universally familiar material, and various investigators have found that significant differences in performance can be related to the content of the experimental materials. Price-Williams (1961), for example, demonstrated earlier acquisition of conservation concepts in Nigerian children using traditional instead of imported stimulus materials, and Gay and Cole (1967) made a similar point with respect to Liberian classification behaviour and learning.

Contemporary psychology's awareness of the task and situation-specific determinants of performance is reflected in a recent article by Kagan and Kogan (1970). In a section of their paper titled 'The Significance of Public Performance', they are concerned with the fact that 'differences in quality of style of public performance, although striking, may be misleading indices of competence' (p. 1322).

Although such misgivings abound, they have not yet crystallized into a coherent programme of research and theory, nor have the implications of accepting the need to incorporate an analysis of situations in addition to traditional experimental manipulations been fully appreciated.

EXTENDED IDEA OF COMPETENCE

Labov and others have argued forcefully that we cannot distinguish on the basis of traditional experimental approaches between the underlying competence of those who have had a poor opportunity to participate in a particular culture and those who have had a good opportunity, between those who have not had their share of wealth and respect and those who have. The crux of the argument, when applied to the problem of 'cultural deprivation', is that those groups ordinarily diagnosed as culturally deprived have the same underlying competence as those in the mainstream of the dominant culture, *the differences in performance being accounted for by the situations and contexts in which the competence is expressed.* To put the matter most rigorously, one can find a corresponding situation in which the member of the 'out culture', the victim of poverty, can perform on the basis of a given competence in a fashion equal to or superior to the standard achieved by a member of the dominant culture.

A prosaic example taken from the work of Gay and Cole (1967) concerns the ability to make estimates of volume. The case in question is to estimate the number of cups of rice in each of several bowls. Comparisons of 'rice-estimation accuracy' were made among several groups of subjects, including nonliterate Kpelle rice farmers from North Central Liberia and Yale sophomores. The rice farmers manifested significantly greater accuracy than the Yale students, the difference increasing with the amounts of rice presented for estimation. In many other situations, measurement skills are found to be superior among educated subjects in the Gay and Cole study. Just as Kpelle superiority at making rice estimates is clearly not a universal manifestation of their superior underlying competence, the superiority of Yale students in, for example, distance judgements is no basis for inferring that their competence is superior.

We think the existence of demonstrations such as those presented by Labov has been salutary in forcing closer examination of testing situations used for comparing the children of poverty with their more advantaged peers. And, as the illustration from Gay and Cole suggests, the argument may have quite general implications. Obviously, it is not sufficient to use a simple equivalence-of-test procedure to make inferences about the competence of the two groups being compared. In fact, a 'two-groups' design is almost useless for making any important inferences in cross-cultural research, as Campbell (1961) has suggested. From a logical view, however, the conclusion of equal cognitive competence in those who are not members of the prestige culture and those who are its beneficiaries is often equally unwarranted. While it is very proper to criticize the logic of assuming that poor performance implies lack of competence, the contention that poor performance is of *no* relevance to a theory of cognitive development and to a theory of cultural differences in cognitive development also seems an oversimplification.

Assuming that we can find test situations in which comparably good performance can be elicited from the groups being contrasted, there is plainly an issue having to do with the range and nature of the situations in which performance for any two groups can be found to be equal.

We have noted Labov's conclusion that the usual assessment of linguistic competence in the black child elicits deliberate defensive behaviour and that he can respond effectively in familiar nonthreatening surroundings. It may be, however (this possibility is discussed in Bruner, 1970), that he is unable to utilize language of a decentred type, taken out of the context of social interaction, used in an abstract way to deal with hypothetical possibilities and to spell out hypothetical plans (see also Gladwin, 1970). If such were the case, we could not dismiss the question of different kinds of language usage by saying simply that decontextualized talk is not part of the natural milieu of the black child in the urban ghetto. If it should turn out to be the case that mastery of the culture depends on one's capacity to perform well on the basis of competence one has stored up, and to perform well in particular settings and in particular ways, then plainly the question of differences in the way language enters the problem-solving process cannot be dismissed. It has been argued, for example, by Bernstein (1970) that it is in the nature of the very social life of the urban ghetto that there develops a kind of particularism in which communication usually takes place only along concrete personal lines. The ghetto child, who by training is likely to use an idiosyncratic mode of communication, may become locked into the life of his own cultural group, and his migration into other groups consequently becomes the more difficult. Bernstein made clear in his most recent work that this is not a question of capacity but, rather, a matter of what he calls 'orientation'. Nevertheless, it may very well be that a ghetto dweller's language training unfits him for taking jobs in the power- and prestige-endowing pursuits of middle-class culture. If such is the case, then the issue of representativeness of the situations to which he can apply his competence becomes something more than a matter of test procedure.

A major difficulty with this line of speculation is that at present we have almost no knowledge of the day-to-day representativeness of different situations and the behaviours that are seen as appropriate to them by different cultural groups. For example, the idea that language use must be considered outside of social interactions in order to qualify as abstract, as involving 'cognition', is almost certainly a psychologist's fiction. The work of contemporary sociologists and ethnolinguists (Garfinkle, 1967; Hymes, 1966; Schegloff, 1968) seems conclusively to demonstrate the presence of complex contingent thinking in situations that are all too often characterized by psychologists as consisting of syncretic, affective interactions. Until we have better knowledge of the cognitive components that are part of social interactions (the same applies to many spheres of activity), speculations about the role of language in cognition will have to remain speculations.

In fact, it is extraordinarily difficult to know, save in a most superficial way, on the basis of our present knowledge of society, what is the nature of situations that permit control and utilization of the resources of a culture by one of its members and what the cognitive skills are that are demanded of one who would use these resources. It may very well be that the very definition of a subculture could be put into the spirit of Lévi-Strauss's (1963) definition of a culture:

> What is called a subculture is a fragment of a culture which from the point of view of the research at hand presents significant discontinuities in relation to the rest of that culture with respect to access to its major amplifying tools.

By an amplifying tool is meant a technological feature, be it soft or hard, that permits control by the individual of resources, prestige, and deference within the culture. An example of a middle-class cultural amplifier that operates to increase the thought processes of those who employ it is the discipline loosely referred to as 'mathematics'. To employ mathematical techniques requires the cultivation of certain skills of reasoning, even certain styles of deploying one's thought processes. If one were able to cultivate the strategies and styles relevant to the employment of mathematics, then that range of technology is open to one's use. If one does not cultivate mathematical skills, the result is 'functional incompetence', an inability to use this kind of technology. Whether or not compensatory techniques can then correct 'functional incompetence' is an important, but unexplored, question.

Any particular aspect of the technology requires certain skills for its successful use. These skills, as we have already noted, must also be deployable in the range of situations where they are useful. Even if a child could carry out the planning necessary for the most technically demanding kind of activity, he must not do so if he has been trained with the expectancy that the exercise of such a skill will be punished or will, in any event, lead to some unforeseen difficulty. Consequently, the chances that the individual will work up his capacities for performance in the given domain are diminished. As a result, although the individual can be shown to have competence in some sphere involving the utilization of the skill, he will not be able to express that competence in the relevant kind of context. (In an absolute sense, he is any man's equal, but in everyday encounters, he is not up to the task)

The principle cuts both ways with respect to cultural differences. Verbal skills are important cultural 'amplifiers' among Labov's subjects; as many middle-class school administrators have discovered, the ghetto resident skilled in verbal exchanges is a more than formidable opponent in the battle for control of school curriculum and resources. In like manner, the Harlem youth on the street who cannot cope with the verbal battles described by Labov is failing to express competence in a context relevant to the ghetto.

[These considerations impress us with the need to clarify our notion of what the competencies are that underlie effective performance.] There has been an implicit, but very general, tendency in psychology to speak as if the organism is an information-processing machine with a fixed set of routines. The number and organization of these routines might differ as a function of age, genetic make-up, or environmental factors, but for any given machine the input to the machine is processed uniformly by the routines (structures, skills) of the organism.

Quite recently, psychologists have started to face up to the difficulties of assuming 'all things are equal' for different groups of people (concern has focused on difference in age, but the same logic applies to any group comparisons). The study of situational effects on performance has forced a revaluation of traditional theoretical inferences about competence. This new concern with the interpretation of psychological experiments is quite apparent in recent attempts to cope with data inconsistent with Piaget's theory of cognitive development. For example, Flavell and Wohlwill (1969) sought to distinguish between two kinds of competence: first, there are 'the rules, structures, or "mental operations" embodied in the task and . . . [second, there are] the actual mechanisms required for processing the input and output' (p. 98). The second factor is assumed to be task specific and is the presumed explanation for such facts as the 'horizontal decalages' in which the same principle appears for different materials at different ages. The *performance* progression through various stages is presumably a reflection of increases in both kinds of competence, since both are assumed to increase with age.

The same general concern is voiced by Mehler and Bever (1968). They ask

How can we decide if a developmental change or behavioural difference among adults is really due to a difference in a structural rule, to a difference in the form of the expressive processes or a difference in their quantitative capacity? (p. 278)

Their own work traces the expression of particular rules in behaviour and the way the effect of knowing a rule ('having a competence') inter- acts with dependence on different aspects of the input to produce 'nonlinear trends' in the development of conservation-like performance.

Broadening psychological theory to include rules for applying cog- nitive skills, as well as statements about the skills themselves, seems absolutely necessary.

However, the extensions contemplated may well not be sufficient to meet all of Labov's objections to inferences about 'linguistic deprivation'. In both the position expressed by Flavell and Wohlwill and by Mehler and Bever, 'competence' is seen as dependent on situational factors and seems to be a slowly changing process that might well be governed by the same factors that lead to increases in the power of the structural rules or competence, in the older sense of the word. Yet in Labov's example, the problem is considerably more ephemeral; Labov gives the impression that the subjects were engaged in rational problem solving and that they had complete control over their behaviour. He is claiming, in effect, that they are successfully coping with *their* problem; it simply is not the problem the experimenter had in mind, so the experimenter claims lack of competence as a result of his own ignorance. Acceptance of Labov's criticisms, and we think they should be accepted, requires not only a broadening of our idea of competence, but a vast enrichment of our approach to experimentation.

NECESSITY OF A COMPARATIVE PSYCHOLOGY OF COGNITION

If we accept the idea that situational factors are often important deter- minants of psychological performance, and if we also accept the idea that different cultural groups are likely to respond differently to any given situation, there seems to be no reasonable alternative to psychological experimentation that bases its inferences on data from comparisons of both experimental and situational variations.

In short, we are contending that Brunswik's (1958) call for 'representative design' and an analysis of the 'ecological significance' of stimulation is a prerequisite to research on ethnic and social class differences in particular, and to any research where the groups to be compared are thought to differ with respect to the process under investigation prior to application of the experimental treatments.

Exhortations to the effect that college sophomores with nonsense syllables and white rats in boxes are not sufficient objects for the development of a general psychological theory have produced, thus far, only minor changes in the behaviour of psychologists. The present situations seem to *require* a change.

An illustration from some recent cross-cultural research serves as an illustration of one approach that goes beyond the usual two-group design to explore the situational nature of psychological performance.

Cole *et al.* (1971, p. 4) used the free-recall technique to study cultural differences in memory. The initial studies presented subjects with a list of twenty words divided into four familiar, easily distinguishable categories. Subjects were read the list of words and asked to recall them. The procedure was repeated five times for each subject. A wide variety of subject populations was studied in this way; Liberian rice farmers and schoolchildren were the focus of concern, but comparison with groups in the United States was also made.

Three factors of the Kpelle rice farmer's performance were remarkable in these first studies: (a) the number recalled was relatively small (nine to eleven items per list); (b) there was no evidence of semantic or other organization of the material; (c) there was little or no increase in the number recalled with successive trials.

Better recall, great improvement with trials, and significant organization are all characteristics of performance of the American groups above the fifth grade.

A series of standard experimental manipulations (offering incentives, using lists based on functional rather than semantic classes, showing the objects to be remembered, extending the number of trials) all failed to make much difference in Kpelle performance.

However, when these same to-be-recalled items were incorporated into folk stories, when explicit grouping procedures were introduced, or when seemingly bizarre cuing procedures were used, Kpelle performance manifested organization, showed vast improvements in terms of amount recalled, and gave a very different picture of underlying

I

capacity. Cole *et al.* (1971) concluded that a set of rather specific skills associated with remembering disconnected material out of context underlies the differences observed in the standard versions of the free-recall experiment with which they began. Moreover, they were able to begin the job of pinpointing these skills, their relevance to traditional activities, and the teaching techniques that could be expected to bring existing memory skills to bear in the 'alien' tasks of the school.

CONCLUSION

The arguments set forth in this study can now be brought together and generalized in terms of their bearing on psychological research that is 'comparative' in nature – comparing ages, cultures, subcultures, species, or even groups receiving different experimental treatments. The central thesis derives from a re-examination of the distinction between competence and performance. As a rule, one looks for performance at its best and infers the degree of underlying competence from the observed performance. With respect to linguistic competence, for example, a single given instance of a particular grammatical form could suffice for inferring that the speaker had the competence to generate such instances as needed. By the use of such a methodology, Labov demonstrated that culturally deprived black children, *tested appropriately* for optimum performance, have the same grammatical competence as middle-class whites, though it may be expressed in different settings. Note that negative evidence is mute with respect to the status of underlying capacity – it may require a different situation for its manifestation.

The psychological status of the concept of competence (or capacity) is brought deeply into question when one examines conclusions based on standard experiments. Competence so defined is both situation blind and culture blind. If performance is treated (as it often is by linguists) only as a shallow expression of deeper competence, then one inevitably loses sight of the ecological problem of performance. For one of the most important things about any 'underlying competence' is the nature of the situations in which it expresses itself. Herein lies the crux of the problem. One must inquire, first, whether a competence is expressed in a particular situation and, second, what the significance of that situation is for the person's ability to cope with life in his own milieu. As we have had occasion to comment elsewhere, when we systematically study the situational determinants of performance, we are led to conclude that cultural differences reside more in differences in the situations

to which different cultural groups apply their skills than to differences in the skills possessed by the groups in question⌉(Cole *et al.*,
1971, Ch. 7).

The problem is to identify the range of capacities readily manifested
in different groups and then to inquire whether the range is adequate
to the individual's needs in various cultural settings. From this point of
view, cultural *deprivation* represents a special case of cultural *difference*
that arises when an individual is faced with demands to perform in a
manner inconsistent with his past (cultural) experience. In the present
social context of the United States, the great power of the middle class
has rendered differences into deficits because middle-class behaviour
is the yardstick of success.

Our analysis holds at least two clear implications of relevance to the
classroom teacher charged with the task of educating children from
'disadvantaged' subcultural groups.

First, recognition of the educational difficulties in terms of a *difference*
rather than a special kind of intellectual disease should change the
students' status in the eyes of the teacher. If Pygmalion really can work
in the classroom (Rosenthal and Jacobson, 1968), the effect of this change
in attitude may of itself produce changes in performance. Such difference in teacher attitude seems to be one prime candidate for an explanation of the fine performance obtained by Kohl (1967) and others
with usually recalcitrant students.

Second, the teacher should stop labouring under the impression that
he must create new intellectual structures and start concentrating on
how to get the child to *transfer* skills he already possesses to the task at
hand. It is in this context that 'relevant' study materials become
important, although 'relevant' should mean something more than a
way to motivate students. Rather, relevant materials are those to which
the child already applies skills the teacher seeks to have applied to his
own content. It requires more than a casual acquaintance with one's
students to know what those materials are.

The Soviet psychologist, Lev Vygotski (1962), took as the motto of
his well-known monograph on language and thought an epigraph from
Francis Bacon: Neither hand nor mind alone, left to themselves,
amounts to much; instruments and aids are the means to perfection.[1]
Psychologists concerned with comparative research, and comparisons of
social and ethnic group differences in particular, must take seriously
the study of the way different groups organize the relation between their

---

[1] *Nec manus nisi intellectus sibi permissus multam valent; instrumentibus et
auxilibus res perficitur.*

hands and minds; without assuming the superiority of one system over another, they must take seriously the dictum that man is a cultural animal. When cultures are in competition for resources, as they are today, the psychologist's task is to analyse the source of cultural difference so that those of the minority, the less powerful group, may quickly acquire the intellectual instruments necessary for success of the dominant culture, should they so choose.

15

S. H. Irvine (1969)

Contributions of ability and attainment testing in Africa to a general theory of intellect

Journal of Biosocial Science, Supplement No. 1, pp. 91–102

Sir Cyril Burt has recently pinpointed (Burt, 1968) an area of inquiry for which work in Africa seems peculiarly relevant. This is, in his own words, 'the hidden chain of processes which connect genotype with phenotype'. Stated operationally, this poses questions about what people learn, how they learn and why they learn. In turn, assuming that abilities must represent clusters of related skills, one must ask what relationships these clusters of skills bear to each other, and what influences are most relevant to their underlying relationships.

Hence this paper offers a review of research in Africa on abilities and attainments, particularly where such research has analysed test scores into meaningful patterns. Similarities and differences between results obtained in Africa and results obtained with other, non-Western ethnic groups are noted. One study that analyses wrong responses to a battery of factor marker tests is presented to illustrate what happens in situations of failure to cope with Western-type ability tests. These results in particular are linked with work on African thought systems. All of the empirical evidence leads to an argument for a theory of intellect that is both cognitive and affective in its origins. In other words, the hidden chain of processes that links genotype with phenotype presupposes modes of thinking of different orders. Some modes are considered primary, being the product of group environmental treatments such as language, belief and value systems and individual differences in physiology. These are probably the result of early childhood influences and can be modified formally by learning later in life. Primary modes, however, if they are alien to the material or mode of learning, will reassert themselves in a basic style of behaviour, most evident in perceptual processes and in use of language.

ABILITY 'PATTERNS' AND METHODS

Among recent work on abilities in non-Western cultures have been the factor analytic studies of Vandenberg (1959, 1967) on Chinese-American and Spanish-American students, and Guthrie (1963) on Philippine students. In Africa, a growing body of factor analytic studies has included the pioneering treatment of African recruit data by Macdonald (1944–5), Biesheuvel's (1952a, 1954) work with South African mine-workers, Irvine's (1963, 1964, 1966, 1969c, 1970) work on students in Central and East Africa. Vernon (1967c) has recently reported results from Uganda in context of a much wider cross-cultural study. Dawson (1967a) and Berry (1966b) have successfully concluded work on perceptual and stylistic aspects of behaviour in Sierra Leone among the Temne and Mende people. This in turn has to be regarded as an addition to the large body of work on perceptual illusions collected and discussed at length by Segall, Campbell and Herskovits (1966).

Correlational studies of abilities involving factor analysis, however, may be contrasted with the recent work of Lesser, Fifer and Clark (1965) and Stodolsky and Lesser (1968). The material presented in these two studies of mean profiles of test results from Chinese, Jewish, Negro and Puerto-Rican children in the school systems of New York and Boston are based on analysis of variance that ignores the correlations between tests. If one regards the tests only as operational measures then their claim that the patterns of test scores are unique for each ethnic group is justified. On the other hand, if one takes test scores as the starting point for the development of constructs or underlying abilities, then the correlations between test scores for each separate ethnic group would have to come from the same population of correlations before differences in mean scores could be held to represent different levels of abilities (Irvine, 1966). In other words, the patterns of abilities, as represented in theory by correlations between tests, must be very similar before mean differences in test scores can be said to represent ability differences. At present, the work by Lesser and his colleagues, where correlations between tests used are markedly different between groups, can be said to reinforce what is well-known already, namely, that test scores do not necessarily mean the same thing in different cultures, and that mean differences exist between ethnic groups for reasons that present analyses do not make clear. Hence, the correlational approach, although less than perfect, is still the major probing tool of the psychologist who is mapping ability dimensions in other cultures and offering tentative theoretical discussion which can be reformulated experimentally.

CROSS-CULTURAL CORRELATIONAL STUDIES

Table 15.1 presents in broad summary form the main ability dimensions that have been found in the work of authors who have correlated test scores in non-Western cultures.

While interpretation of Table 15.1 requires caution, because of different levels of education in the samples, different sex ratios and different tests, it is quite possible to advance the basic proposition that tests and people will interact in various cultures in ways that are fairly similar. Second, the constructs derived from test scores fall into the major first-order factor dimensions, reasoning, spatial, manipulative, verbal and numerical. General factors emerge in heterogeneous populations, the differentiation of abilities coming with more homogeneous and progressively more educated groups. Briefly, when Western-based tests purporting to identify abilities are used, they will generally reproduce the same theoretical dimensions in other cultures, although the contributions of individual tests are by no means constant.

Vandenberg (1959) suggests that these correlations are essentially explainable in a basic similarity of neurological structure in all ethnic groups. It is possible to advance, however, the proposition that they are explainable because of basic similarities in educational objectives throughout the world that cause certain skills to be overlearned (Ferguson, 1954, 1956); and because they are in turn highly valued by society (Irvine, 1966, 1969c, 1970).

Vandenberg and Guthrie's own findings that show unique language factors for ethnic groups, a finding partially confirmed by Irvine's 1968 Mashonaland study of memory in the Shona language, indicate that these factors are probably primary mode factors that are overlearned early before formal educational systems take over. They are also distinct from English language skills which are much later acquisitions for a great many non-Western groups. The two language factors then suggest different modes of thinking that could only have emerged as interactive processes which various influences, neurological and environmental, moderate during development.

TABLE 15.1. *Summary of African factor analyses related to other major studies involving non-Western cultures*

| | Cross-cultural factor analyses | | | | | Primary factors | | | | | | |
Author	Year	Group	Years education	Sex	Reasoning	Perceptual	Spatial	Mechanical /spatial	Physical manipulative	Verbal	Numerical	Memory
Macdonald	1944–5	East African recruits	Largely illiterate	M	General practical	—	—	Performance	Sequence dexterity	—	—	—
Biesheuvel	1952–4	South African mineworkers	Largely illiterate	M	General practical	—	—	—	Sorting dexterity	—	—	—
Vandenberg	1959	Chinese-American	13 +	M, F	Figural	Speed	Visualization	—	—	(1) Reasoning (2) Chinese	Ability	Associative
Vandenberg	1967	Spanish-American	13 +	M, F	Figural	Speed	Visualization	—	—	(1) Reasoning (2) Spanish	(1) Facility (2) Series	Associative
Guthrie	1963	Philippines	13 +	F	(1) Inductive (2) Deductive	Speed	Visualization	—	Motor speed	Five factors[a]	(1) Facility (2) Reasoning	(1) Associative (2) Span
Irvine	1962	Mashona	8	M, F	A form of g mainly inductive and closely related to facility in English, the second language	—	—	—	—	(1) Comprehension (2) Information	Facility	—
Irvine	1963	Mashona	9	M, F		—	—	—	—	(1) Comprehension (2) Information	Facility	—
Irvine	1963	Zambia[b]	8	M, F		—	—	—	—	(1) Comprehension (2) Information	Facility	—
Irvine	1963	Zambia mine school[b]	7	M		Closure	—	Figural	—	Comprehension	Facility	—
Irvine	1963	Zambia[b]	10	M, F		—	—	—	—	(1) Comprehension (2) Information	Facility	—
Irvine	1964	Kenya	10–12	M, F	Inductive	Clerical Speed	Visualization	—	—	Fluency	Facility	Associative
Irvine	1968	Mashona	12	M, F	Inductive	(1) Closure (2) Scanning	3D visualization	—	—	Fluency	Facility	(1) Associative (2) Short-term
Irvine	1968	Mashona (wrongs)	12	M, F	(1) Inductive (2) Figural	—	—	—	—	Fluency	Facility	—
Vernon	1967	Buganda 56% Others 44%	All 12 years old Ed. 4–7 years	M	Inductive	—	—	Performance	Drawing	Educational	—	—

[a] Guthrie's five verbal factors were: comprehension, verbal fluency, ideational fluency, English vocabulary and Philippine vocabulary.
[b] The correlation matrices for these analyses were carried out for the *Northern Rhodesia Mental Ability Survey* (MacArthur, Irvine and Brimble, 1964).

ATTRIBUTES AND INFLUENCES CORRELATED WITH CONSTRUCTS

Despite the basic similarity of constructs identified in African testing surveys, there are some unique results that illustrate firmly the relationship of attributes and environmental influences with abilities. These are worth stating briefly in order to complete the present picture before new perspectives are introduced.

1. Maleness is correlated with mechanical-informational and verbal abilities in English at the end of primary and in secondary education. Femaleness was associated with coloured bead-stringing seriation tests in one study where beadwork was a handicraft practised by girls. These results have been largely explained by Irvine (1966) as due to differences in male and female roles in central Africa.

2. Although Dawson (1967a) reports that field-dependence (a cognitive style involving the combination of high verbal, low spatial skills) was associated with African males in Sierra Leone suffering from gynaecomastia, an imbalance of female hormones, this finding has not been repeated in studies involving comparison of males and females in Central Africa because of male superiority in both spatial and verbal tests. Nevertheless, if field-dependence as a style of behaviour is more prevalent in females for neurological, or hormonal, or even role-acquisition reasons, its manifestation in mean differences in verbal and spatial skills need only be relative. That is, the construct of field-dependence/ independence does not need to be identified by mean differences in the same tests in different societies, especially as, we have argued, these test results do not necessarily mean the same thing.

3. Of environmental variables studied in population samples, including socioeconomic status, family size, family position and school quality, only school quality showed significant and consistent relation to ability and attainment tests. Other sources of variation were irrelevant to the skills being learned. This opens up the question of what environmental influences are associated with the formation of 'Western' abilities in any society and, on the other side of the coin, what skills in any society are necessarily open or closed to such environmental influences as exist within that society. There may be skills in African societies that environmental variables influence directly but are simply not tested at present by Western tests of ability.

To conclude this section on environmental influence, mention must be made of Vernon's extensive studies in English, Hebridean, Eskimo, Canadian Indian, Ugandan and Jamaican groups of children aged 11 or 12 years. His preliminary results from all of these groups, circulated in mimeographed form (Vernon, 1967c), show that environmental influences or abilities are by no means constant through these groups. Figural tests of embedded figures, held to be a good measure of field-independence, were positively correlated with measures of female dominance in English and Hebridean samples and male dominance in Jamaica. In the Eskimo sample, noted for its success in spatial and figural tests (a finding confirmed independently by Berry, 1966b), none of the measured environmental variables was related to the factor involving tests of field-dependence. In this group none of male dominance, linguistic background, cultural stimulus, delayed gratification among others was related to individual differences in spatial-perceptual tasks. It seems plausible to suppose that these tasks were all overlearned in an environment demanding acute awareness of minute changes in a relatively featureless landscape, so that variations in home and educational background were irrelevant to such individual differences that existed. Heron (1966) reports no significant median differences in numerical facility between ethnic groups in Zambia at the end of primary school, primarily because the skills were all overlearned, and ethnicity, background, language, and other sources of environmental variation were redundant. Schools are often the source of environmental influence relevant to learning culturally alien skills in a second language. It is hardly surprising that school quality should be related in Central Africa to the acquisition of second-language verbal abilities, which were by no means as overlearned as simple number bonds, where 90 per cent of students came from rural homes and, almost without exception, the parents have only functional literacy in the vernacular language.

Clearly, it is now difficult to ascribe large proportions of variance in test scores to environmental influences as if these influences were static for all societies and as if they acted in the same fashion for all societies. Studies in Africa confirm the need for a close examination of environmental influences free of Western assumptions about what variables should or should not be measured, and on a much greater scale than has been achieved by Vernon, whose work has the virtue of systematic synthesis that enables replication to be carried out, as indeed it must be because of the unrepresentativeness of his samples and their small size, especially as factor analysis has played a major and insightful part in his findings.

The whole of the first part of this paper, concerned with a review of factor analytic studies of abilities and the influences on these of environment and attributes, has raised the issue of whether or not our present theories of abilities, so clearly tied to rather sanguine assumptions of what tests best sample abilities of certain kinds and what environmental influences are liable to affect these test results, can encompass the diversity of results illustrated here. The second and third parts of this paper attempt to answer these questions more fully.

A STUDY OF WRONG ANSWERS

In August 1966 the author administered thirty tests to a group of fifty-nine male and twenty-three female predominantly Shona-speaking African pupils in the twelfth year of education. The tests were given in four sessions a week apart. The tests were drawn from the *Kit of Reference Tests for Cognitive Factors* (French, Ekstrom and Price, 1963) and the original aim was to replicate in Africa Guthrie's (1963) study. Although this aim was only partially realized, tests were chosen to identify the major factors of flexibility and speed of closure, word and ideational fluency, induction, rote memory, number facility, perceptual speed, visualization, verbal comprehension, syllogistic and general reasoning. The results are summarized in Table 15.2.

After analysing the right answers and studying the correlations between right answers and wrong answers among those answers reached, it was decided to factor the wrong answers because the correlations did not warrant the conclusion that the right and wrong answers could be accounted for by the same set of factors. The hypothesis was that cognitive processes in fairly continuous failure would be different from those in fairly constant success in a number of culturally alien tasks. It was also considered possible that the analysis would show the emergence of different levels of cognitive control or direction if higher order factors could be uncovered. Of the tests available, twenty-two were scorable for wrong answers and the data from these were submitted to a principal factor analysis and varimax and promax rotation. Promax rotation was retained and a second-order analysis carried out subsequently. The factor analysis produced eight definable factors: three correlated factors of errors in reasoning and short-term storage; two relatively independent factors of errors in number facility and rote memory; and three other factors showing only slight correlation with reasoning errors but fairly well intercorrelated among themselves, involving errors in scanning perceptual material, inability to separate known patterns from a complex perceptual field, and lack of facility in word usage and verbalizing in complex mental tasks.

These primary factors were analysed once more and this analysis, together with the intercorrelation of the three second-order factors, comprise Table 15.2. The analysis in Table 15.2 shows three main points. First, numerical facility and memory tend to remain at the first order. These seem to be efficiency skills that are specific, overlearned and nontransferable. Next, the first factor relates together three components of mental ability that are of more generalized nature. Finally, factors II and III are related together and would form a single third-order factor of perceptual skills of a stylistic and, probably, determinant nature. Because this last factor emerges at the third level of abstraction it remains a theoretical construct, but it may be closely related to the field-dependence/independence dimensions already discussed. Note that it involves both low perceptual and low verbal scores. It seems that for these students the English language is an analytical tool of some importance, even in perceptual tasks.

TABLE 15.2. *Second-order analysis of wrong scores factors, Mashonaland, 1966 (n = 85)*

	Second-order factors		
Primary factors	I	II	III
Errors figural reasoning	69		
Errors short-term storage	67		
Errors number facility	23		
Errors rote memory			−26
Errors 3D reasoning	72		
Errors perceptual scanning			76
Errors field-independence		47	20
Errors analytical verbal		75	
Intercorrelations	—	−19	14
Second-order factors		—	37
			—

There now remains the problem of knitting together the strands of the material so far presented: and this can be done only with reference to work carried out on African thought systems.

AFRICAN SYSTEMS OF THOUGHT AND THE NOTION OF PRIMARY MODES

Previously, the most telling arguments for a use of knowledge in a causal system that is different from that of Western societies have come from anthropologists such as Evans-Pritchard (1936), Gluckman (1944) and Colson (1962). There has also been a growing awareness that systems of thought in different societies throughout Africa south of the Sahara are in many respects similar (Jahn, 1961). These systems present a unity of assumptions about the world and man's place in it. Briefly, everything that exists contains force. Man and the spirits of his ancestors can activate forces directly and consciously, or inadvertently and by accident. Animals, plants and inanimate objects have forces too, but these can only be released by man and the spirits of men. The reason for man's eminence is mainly his control over words, which themselves have force (*nommo*) and, because they are prime movers of actions, transcend space and time and fuse space and time into a single modality. Words themselves have overtones; and the same word can have different meanings according to the tone of the speaker.

The importance of these concepts lies in their unalterable relation to a system of classification of the world and its objects according to a system of causality that Western minds find difficult to grasp. Some recent work on how the world is classified for individuals of traditional knowledge learned by children has been carried out with African proverbs collected in the Mashonaland regions of Rhodesia.

The author of the Shona dictionary (Hannan, 1959) generously provided over one hundred sayings and beliefs. Although they are not exhaustive by any means, they are believed to be representative of those that are at present in common use and are passed on verbally to children from an early age in the villages, and to some extent in the towns. They regulate behaviour in the social system and it is not putting too great a stress on the word to say that they represent ground rules for intelligent and purposive acts that can be fully understood only within a world view that is African. The Shona word for intelligence, for example, is *ngware* meaning to be cautious and prudent, particularly in social relationships, since the misfortunes of kin always have a spiritual history and a *gestalt* or field of human relationships.

Table 15.3 summarizes the content of the Shona proverbs, omens and beliefs regulating behaviour in villages where all but 10 per cent of the African population live, but three of them are used as examples:

1. A woman must not sit on a hearth stone; her husband might die.
2. Do not express admiration for natural objects (e.g. a tree or its fruits); you might develop an antipathy to marriage.
3. Do not destroy the eggs of a crow; you may cause no rain to fall in your area.

It is possible to classify such statements in terms of the kind of knowledge the learner must have before the statement has meaning;

and second, to classify the statements in terms of the consequence of non-observance of the rule; that is, whether the effects are on kin (statement 1) or on oneself (statement 2), or on natural phenomenon (statement 3, although this is a rare example).

Table 15.3 clearly shows that the most common kind of knowledge is of natural objects and animals, followed by objects with social functions or functions specific to one or other of the sexes, then comes knowledge of one's personal habits or symptoms and knowledge of utensils and utilities.

The consequences of non-observance rebound on self-kin and community, while little or no conscious control seems to be exerted on the environment by contrast. In societies such as these, intelligent acts are then of a conforming kind, having primary reference to the affective climate of one's own relationships with the spiritual force of the living and ancestral spirits of the kin group.

From this evidence there now emerges the basic support for the major hypothesis of the paper. It is that African children develop a primary thought mode that perceives events and uses knowledge in a complex field of personal relationships whose organization is essentially affective. As adults, they continue to use knowledge and to cognize events in this way since their theory of knowledge within a system of spiritual causation demands that they do so. This kind of cognition, which

TABLE 15.3. *Analysis of 113 Mashona observances and omens*

	Knowledge required					
Consequence of action on:	Natural objects, animals	Kin, sex, social	Personal habits, symptoms	Utilities	Seasons, time	Total
Self	22	19	15	7	0	63
Kin and community	14	9	3	7	1	34
Natural phenomenon	5	1	1	1	2	10
Natural objects, animals	1	2	1	2	0	6
Total	42	31	20	17	3	113

imputes purpose and force to inanimate objects, has been compared to Piaget's work on child animism; but to do this is to confuse the processes of children who think animistically because they are not fully developed with those of mature adults who exercise formal logic within the frame of knowledge at their disposal. This primary mode, for Shona subjects at least, seems to be one of permanent, not transitory, involvement in a field of grcat complexity and a relative conformity to its demands and vagaries.

It is further contended that certain Western skills, particularly in scicnce, technical and medical knowledge, vocabulary of a particularly Western nature and spatial orientation would be taught only by inhibiting successfully the primary, causal, social and visual perceptions of African students. Finally, repeated failure would cause learners to regress to the vernacular for solutions (we have evidence of mixed English-vernacular strategies in dealing with Raven's Progressive Matrices: Klingelhofer, 1967; Irvine, 1967) and this would precipitate perception in a field-dependent way. The error analysis of the second part of this paper is the starting point for the argument just developed. We would hope that experimental verification of these corollaries to the main hypothesis could be undertaken.

Elsewhere (Irvine, 1970) a schema was presented for the relationship of (a) tests of cognition that would be made up of traditional ability and attainment tests of the kind that Spearman, Burt, Thomson and Vernon would have advocated for testing intelligent behaviour defined as a highly valid prediction of socially valued academic success (designated R_{11}); (b) tests of the kind that Guilford has used in his structure of intellect model, seeking to find theoretical constructs whether socially valued or not (designated R_{22}); and (c) tests of the skills of intelligence, in the *ngware* sense of the Shona language, that the collection of proverbs indicate (designated R_{33}). Fig. 15.1 represents the model for a factor analysis study involving all these kinds of tests.

Particularly important would be the R_{12} and R_{23} parts of the matrix to determine the relationship of skills peculiar to the African with those imported by educational and other means. It was also suggested in the previous paper (Irvine, 1970) that Guilford's theory of intellect gave more freedom to explore the possibility of certain processes being common in all tests, and here the factor analysis across all cultures suggest that number facility, rote memory and other efficiency tasks, such as clerical and motor speed, would each be characterized by a fairly homogeneous process. There is also strong evidence for the presence, across cultures, of modes of reasoning that result from exposure to educational influences if the treatments are similar enough. Nevertheless it is suggested that primary modes of perceiving the world exert strong cognitive and affective influences on learning. These primary modes may also define subcultures within any single society, and Bernstein's work on restricted and elaborated codes of languages may be only one manifestation of differential modes within societies.

Research, in Africa, then, may call for revaluation of theories of intellect. If we conceive of intelligence as a construct with absolute meaning or meanings across cultures that clearly evaluate intelligent acts differently and reinforce learning by sanctions that are tied to different ideologies and philosophies, then we could seriously mislead

R_{11}	R_{12}	R_{13}
R_{21}	R_{22}	R_{23}
R_{31}	R_{32}	R_{33}

Fig. 15.1 Hypothetical factorial study of Western and African abilities.

further efforts to clarify the roles of language, affect and ecology in the hidden processes that Burt mentions. To understand these processes our theories of intellect cannot afford to inhibit the sampling of behaviours that seem irrelevant to the Western eye but nevertheless must be examined closely. Without investigation, present and past controversies over levels and structures of abilities in different ethnic groups will not be resolved.

SUMMARY

Factor analytic studies in Africa are compared with other cross-cultural investigations into the structure of abilities in different ethnic groups. Similarities and differences are noted; and environmental influences on the acquisition of skills are also summarized. A correlational study of wrong answers to a battery of thirty marker tests given to a group of predominantly Mashona students indicates that efficiency skills of numerical facility and memory remain at the first order of factor extraction, reasoning abilities emerge in second-order analysis, while perceptual styles are present in the third-order level. This study is used to hypothesize, in the context of African systems of thought, the existence of a primary thought mode that asserts itself in conditions involving repeated errors. The controlling aspects of primary-mode thinking are considered to be sociological, in that language and the logic of belief systems are involved, and individual, in that styles of behaviour, both cognitive and affective, that are physiological in origin will effectively moderate learning situations. Postulating primary-mode thinking implies that some of the skills that are essential to the formation of abilities, as they are understood in Western societies, may be learned by different ethnic groups and, indeed, by distinct cultural enclaves within ethnic groups, when primary modes are successfully inhibited. In short, investigations into the structure of abilities within Africa suggest a revision of current theories of intellect in order to encompass results that point to the importance of modes of perceiving and communicating as determiners of ability.

16

M. Wober

Towards an understanding of the Kiganda concept of intelligence

INTRODUCTION

Western psychologists have spent much energy on measuring what we have called intelligence; and it is sometimes acknowledged that the target of this chase has been shifting (though it is more rarely realized that psychologists' procedures have often been, by our own standards, unintelligent). Vernon (1969) writes that 'psychological theories of intelligence have altered very drastically since the 1920s . . .', and distinguishes three separate meanings for intelligence. First, it is 'innate capacity, something which the child inherits . . . and which determines the mental growth of which he is capable'. Secondly, it refers to 'the child or adult who is clever, quick in the uptake, good at comprehending and reasoning, mentally efficient'. Third, it may be 'Mental Age or IQ or score on one of the widely used intelligence tests'.

At least since 1917 (e.g. Loram) psychologists have tried to measure the abilities of Africans. Western tests suitable for indicating Vernon's third kind of intelligence were repeatedly used, and it was even thought that these might measure the first 'type', of general underlying potential among Africans (see Nissen, Machover and Kinder, 1935; Fick, 1939). It was eventually realized, however (Biesheuvel, 1943), that Western tests were unsuited for measuring latent ability in most Africans at that time.

During the last decade it has become widely recognized (e.g. Berry, 1966b) that African cultures are so different from Western ones that not even 'culture-fair' tests are really appropriate for estimating this basic ability in Africans (other than those who are considerably Westernized). Berry writes that 'since people with differing cultures and ecologies tend to develop and maintain different sets of skills, then the concept of intelligence, or its equivalent, is bound to be defined somewhat differently in each society.'

It has been argued (Wober, 1969) that a truly *cross*-cultural approach in research would try to discover the skills which are developed in a culture, and then try to assess how well individuals perform their own skills, rather than exotic ones. In contrast, a *centri*-cultural approach is one which revolves around the culture of the investigator who brings his own tasks and performance criteria to evaluate members of another culture. Similarly, Irvine (1969c) wrote that 'cognitive tests have not begun to tap modes of thought that are the product of African languages and social relationships'. He asks (Irvine, 1969b) 'can our idea of intelligence encompass the *kinds* of skills learned in Africa and recognize the use to which early learned knowledge, which has been passed on orally, is put? . . . What, then, can we mean by the word intelligent?'

Two approaches are possible to the study of how cultural backgrounds affect mental development. One can either give Western tests and try to infer from the results – from which sections are easier or which cause more difficulty – how a particular culture emphasizes some skills and neglects others. Alternatively, one can study the goals of mental development set within a culture and see how these may or may not resemble Western specifications of intelligence.

Vernon (1969) followed the first centri-cultural strategy; he tested fifty boys in two Kampala primary schools in 1966. The boys were good when verbal fluency or careful pencil work was involved, but very low on a vocabulary test, and only on four tests out of twenty-one did performance levels resemble English standards. Vernon thus assessed some Baganda by foreign standards, but he did not attempt to find out what the Kiganda concept of intelligence is, or how this might correspond with or relate to the Western concept.

The second strategy suggested above tries to deal with these questions, and will be used here. Within this strategy, three kinds of steps can be taken. One can review existing literature bearing on the problem; one can collect and analyse cultural materials such as proverbs and folktales; and one can systematically give questionnaires or use other 'psychological' methods to collect peoples' views on the subject. The material will concern one culture in modern Uganda: that of the Ganda people. Their usage of prefixes to distinguish various facets of their identity will be followed here. Thus Baganda refers to the people in the plural; Muganda refers to an individual; Buganda is the country, Luganda the language, and Kiganda the adjective for the culture.

AVAILABLE LITERATURE ON THE KIGANDA CONCEPT OF
INTELLIGENCE

Though it is not easy to find material dealing directly with the local
meaning of a concept of intelligence, there are studies from which one
can infer something of its nature. Paul Kibuuka (1966), himself a
Muganda, has described the traditional educational system and its
goals. The aim of a girl's education was marriage; 'the good qualities
which the Baganda looked for in a girl were diligence in her work,
obedience to her superiors and parents, a good idea of cultivation
(agriculture), and ability to cook.' Talented girls could 'be sent to the
households of chiefs where higher and better education was given' and
a girl might even reach the palace, which was a great honour, particularly in that a girl might become the mother of a future Kabaka or
King.

'Boys were trained to become good leaders in the country. . . .' They
learned language, history ('the different wars and the lives of brave
men . . . the names of different Kings, different heads of his children's
clan were all taught'); they also had stories, songs and visits to ceremonies and journeys to places of interest. Boys' fathers 'introduced
them to different people of their clan. It was a time of intense study . . .
the father would always ask . . . testing the child's knowledge of its
relatives.' Boys learned obedience and politeness: 'since obedience
would raise somebody to a high standard, it had to be taught from the
beginning.' Promotion to chiefs' households was given to 'élite, well
chosen clever boys . . . who would sooner or later become responsible
for keeping laws, beliefs, customs and manners'.

This shows the society was concerned with individual achievement;
and achievement is explicitly defined as successful service to existing
norms and values. Kibuuka says that riddles were taught 'which helped
to train thinking'; however, it seems that many of these riddles were
standard and well-known. Thus their training effect towards producing
a Western type of intelligence, one suited to setting and attacking novel
problems, would only apply at the first time of posing each riddle. Also,
riddles were taught together with proverbs and stories, most of which
encouraged children to respect existing values. The system Kibuuka
describes is one with an emphasis on stability; mental abilities can be
ranked and the higher ranked abilities valued correspondingly. These
higher abilities are those which tend to maintain the essential structure
of the system, rather than to question or challenge it. This analysis
suggests that intelligence may appropriately be thought of as a vector

rather than as a scalar property, which latter conception has persisted because most of the research on intelligence, in Africa and elsewhere, has been essentially centri-cultural to Western societies.

QUESTIONNAIRE INVESTIGATION

A version of Osgood's Semantic Differential (1952) was used to map out something of the network of connotations for a concept which may be the Kiganda equivalent to 'intelligence'. The concept was named, and the whole procedure conducted in Luganda. Luganda dictionaries give *amagezi* as intelligence, a word related to the verb *okugera* meaning 'to measure, evaluate', and the root *-ger* is that which appears as *-gez-* in *amagezi*. A related word is *kutegeera*, 'to understand'. Luganda also has the words *obukalabakalaba* and *obukujukuju*, but these apparently refer more to 'cunning' or 'cleverness', of less scope than *amagezi*. The form of the word actually used was *obugezi*, replacing the prefix *ama* with *obu* – thus in the opinion of the translator indicating the abstract concept, rather than the property actually existing in a person.

A sample of village adults was interviewed, since it was considered that they would most likely harbour traditional Kiganda concepts and attitudes, less influenced by Western ideas. A second sample, of village primary teachers, was also interviewed. These people would presumably show a mixture of Kiganda and Western ideas, the latter gained during their travels and their academic schooling. Both village samples were obtained in places ten or more miles outside Kampala. Two further samples in Kampala were obtained, one a mixture of adult 'élite', being mainly school teachers but including one university professor; and the other consisted of second-year medical students. The first three groups were all Baganda, interviewed in, or given the questionnaire for self-completion in Luganda, by a young female Muganda. The final Kampala area group of medical students included Asians and other non-Baganda Ugandans; they were given the questionnaire in English by the author.

Apart from interviews around and in Kampala, a group of people were interviewed near Fort Portal, 250 miles distant in Western Uganda. The people there are Batoro and speak Lutoro, and were interviewed by a Mutoro assistant who had been trained in the procedure by preliminary interviews with Batoro living in Kampala.

The task used, a nine-point semantic differential scale, was strange to most people interviewed. It had to be explained in detail every time by the interviewer, and it is not possible to say how much the full scope of the scale was understood. However, the whole fieldwork phase was supervised by an experienced Muganda research assistant, and this assured that the operation was as valid as possible, given the constraints of using an unfamiliar technique.

There were twenty-five scales each consisting of pairs of adjectives with opposite meanings in Luganda. These were roughly translated into English so that they can be described here; but they were translated as exactly as possible into Lutoro. The Lutoro words were translated back into English, from which it was clear that the meanings had not strayed too far. Finally, the Luganda–Lutoro translation was again checked by two adults with university training, and only one of the members of one word-pair was found to be 'very similar' instead of 'identical' in Luganda and Lutoro.

RESULTS

It can be seen from Table 16.1 that, including the instance where translation equivalence was not fully achieved, only four adjective scales out of twenty-two significantly distinguish Batoro results from those of the Baganda. The Baganda group tend, with a few dissenters, to associate intelligence with mental order, while the Batoro group include more who are open to the idea that intelligence occurs sometimes with mental turmoil; here we are reminded of the Western notion of mental hyperactivity in genius.

The Batoro group also feel less clearly than the Baganda group that intelligence is rare. But on one adjective scale the views of the two village groups are entirely different. The Baganda likened *obugezi* to *aba mukakanyavu* (persistent, hard, obdurate) while the Batoro took it to resemble *aba mugonvu* (soft, obedient, yielding – in human rather than inanimate terms). One translator has suggested that the Baganda group may have mistaken the term *aba mukakanyavu* for the word *mukkakanya*, which means an arbiter, one who has to be intelligent and firm; had they not been allowed this possible misunderstanding, they would possibly have answered more like the Batoro.

Apart from two intergroup differences which may be due to misunderstandings, two firm differences are left out of twenty-two; by chance, one would expect one difference at a level of $p < 0.05$ among twenty-two comparisons. Therefore the impression remains of a considerable similarity between the two sets of results. As the groups interviewed are at a similar educational level (for the most part with only limited primary education), this similarity of associations with *obugezi*

TABLE 16.1. *Associations made by Baganda and Batoro villagers with 'Obugezi'*

Adjective (score: 1)	Baganda	Chi-square[a]	Batoro	Adjective (score: 9)
Brought by medicine (*buyinza okufunibwa olw' eddagala*)	8·37	0·31	8·67	Comes on its own (*buja bwokka*)
Dangerous (*bwakabi*)	8·42	0·05	7·92	Safe (*sibwakabi*)
Strong (*bwamanyi*)	1·71	0·05	2·00	Weak (*sibwamanyi*)
Dishonourable (*sibwakitibwa*)	8·50	0·04	8·43	Honourable (*bwakitibwa*)
Infectious (*bukwata*)	7·17	1·44	5·75	Not infectious (*tebukwata*)
Happy (*bwasanyu*)	1·83	6·60[b]	1·00	Sad (*bwannaku*)
Modern (*bwamulembe guno*)	8·79	0·76	7·92	Traditional (*bwaffe bwadda*)
Unnecessary (*sibwetagibwa*)	8·87	1·54	9·00	Necessary (*bwetagibwa*)
Spiritual (*guba mwoyo*)	1·21	0·04	1·46	Physical (*guba mubiri*)
Inherited (*buba bwalulyo*)	6·66	2·81	4·94	Acquired (*bukwata bukwasi*)
Private (*buba bwakyama*)	7·58	2·14	8·62	Public (*buba bwalwattu*)
Sane (*aba muterevu wamutwe*)	3·17	4·25	4·25	Crazy (*aba mutabufu wamutwe*)
Rare (*bwabbula*)	2·37	8·81	4·92	Common (*bwajenjero*)
Steady (*aba mwetegefu*)	1·96	3·32	1·54	Unsteady (*tabeera mwetegefu*)
Yielding (*aba mugonvu*)	7·12	26·80	1·94	Obdurate (*aba mukakanyavu*)
Cold (*munyogovu*)	7·83	0·70	7·13	Hot (*wabbugumu*)
Hurried (*bwanguwa*)	7·79	3·41	5·57	Delayed (*bulwawo*)
Active (*akola nnyo*)	2·00	1·32	0·18	Relaxed (*aba waddembe*)
Careful (*aba mwegendereza*)	1·13	3·16	1·00	Hasty (*aba mumagufu*)
Unstable (*aba mutabufu tabufu*)	8·58	0·56	8·46	Straightforward (*aba muterevu*)
Friendly (*baba bamukwano*)	1·21	0·95	1·11	Unfriendly (*tebaba bamukwano*)
Sick (*bulwadde*)	8·33	3·77	8·89	Healthy (*bulaamu*)
N (male/female)	24(10/14)	2·97	37(18/19)	
Mean age	35·9	3·20	45·1	

[a] A single underline refers to a value of chi-square where $p < 0.05$; a double underline denotes $p < 0.01$.

[b] The Lutoro word for sad (*tibulibwokusemererwa*) was judged by two independent university-educated bilinguals as not exactly equivalent to the Luganda *bwannaku*. In that the two sets of villagers were considering different questions then, it is not surprising that their responses were significantly different.

can be taken as evidence of some validity in the questionnaire procedure. The interviewers were different in Buganda and in Fort Portal, so the similarity in results cannot be due to some systematic interviewer influence.

In summary, then, the respondents are obviously offering associations with a traditional concept of intelligence (seventh scale); they think of intelligence as slow, careful, active (this is not necessarily a contradiction, cf. 'still waters run deep'), straightforward, and sane; they do not think intelligence can be inculcated magically, or by 'medicine' (*eddagala*), although they think of it as pertaining to the soul rather than the body ('mind, rather than matter'). The word *myoyo* (soul) is indeed metaphorically used to mean intelligence, as in '*Yenna ng'olaba a weddemu omwoyo*' ('in a blank gaze robbed of his intelligence').

These villagers think of intelligence as necessary, happy, healthy, strong, steady and safe. They also see it as associated with 'friendly', 'hot', and 'public' (as against 'unfriendly', 'cold', and 'secretive' or 'private'). Thus the impression emerges that intelligence is not seen as an inward-looking or introverted characteristic, but as an extroverted one, though without any connotation that 'extrovert' may carry in Western minds with lability or unsteadiness. One may look perhaps for similarities here to the Mediterranean-generated ideas of 'civility' and '*gravitas*', of public-spirited orientation of the mind. The Mediterranean converse of the concept linking the public with the fruitful use of the mind is found in the word 'idiot' – derived from the Greek original meaning a 'private man'.

Next, we may compare Baganda villagers' concepts with those of village teachers, with 'élite' Baganda, and with medical students; the latter group was given the questions in English. The village teachers have at the very least (represented by one case only) completed P8 (primary education); but most have attended a teacher training college, or have School Certificate (equals O level) qualifications. The first point that emerges quite clearly from Table 16.2 is that there are nine scales on which rural Baganda differ significantly from the teachers. This means that the concept of intelligence differs more clearly between groups of different education within the same culture, than between groups of similar education in different (though related) cultures.

Secondly, on the nine scales in which there are significant teacher-villager differences, the élite are much closer in scores to the teachers than to the villagers; further, in six of these nine instances the élite

TABLE 16.2. *Associations among four separate groups with the concept 'Obugezi'*

Adjective scale[b]	Baganda élite	Baganda teachers	Chi-square[a]	Baganda villagers	Chi-square[a]	Mixed origin medical students
Brought by medicine	8·80	7·91	0·29	8·37	—	—
Dangerous	7·85	8·04	0·75	8·42	—	—
Strong	2·30	2·14	0·75	1·71	—	2·05
Dishonourable	7·65	8·27	0·34	8·50	—	8·09
Infectious	5·50	6·14	2·09	7·17	—	—
Happy	2·70	2·54	1·36	1·83	3·74	2·67
Modern	8·55	8·82	—	8·79	34·70	4·83
Unnecessary	8·55	8·82	—	8·87	9·50	7·91
Spiritual	3·60	1·95	1·91	1·21	—	—
Inherited	5·35	4·81	3·13	6·66	—	—
Private	7·30	7·50	0·26	7·58	—	—
Sane	3·50	2·59	0·87	3·17	—	3·38
Rare	3·60	2·68	1·36	2·37	7·25	5·67
Steady	3·15	3·18	4·18	1·96	—	—
Yielding	5·00	5·27	13·82	7·12	17·58	5·47
Cold	6·40	6·45	6·97	7·83	4·47	6·41
Hurried	5·45	4·91	12·82	7·79	29·06	2·84
Active	4·55	3·91	10·45	2·00	4·65	3·24
Careful	3·75	3·00	11·57	1·13	11·11	2·72
Unstable	6·70	6·91	8·88	8·58	—	—
Friendly	4·05	3·63	15·47	1·21	4·05	2·65
Sick	6·10	5·82	16·99	8·33	5·07	7·71
N (male/female)	20(12/8)	22 (14/8)		24 (10/14)		25 (42/13)
Mean age	36·6	35·3 ($t = 0.21$)		35·9		22

[a] A single underline indicates that the value of $p < 0.05$; a double underline indicates that the value of $p < 0.01$; a triple underline indicates that the value of $p < 0.001$.

[b] Complete identification with any of the undermentioned adjectives is shown by a score of 1·00; complete identification with the opposite is the meaning of a score of 9·00.

position is 'on the other side of' the teachers from the villagers. For example, on the careful-careless scale, villagers almost unanimously associate intelligence strongly with careful; teachers are less emphatic in their choice; the élite are still less emphatic, indeed one might interpret their average position as one of 'uncommitted' with just a slight leaning towards 'careful'. Clearly, in none of these groups is intelligence seen as having much connection with any idea of haste or mental impulsiveness or speed.

We must now consider whether the pattern of group differences is merely one of 'response bias'. Do the villagers associate the concept intelligence with the same pattern of ideas that teachers do, while merely expressing these associations in more clear-cut terms? Or is there something more structurally different in the patterns of associations found between the two groups? The answer to this is that this style of questionnaire takes it that a preference for extremities in judgement is in itself an aspect of meaning; if villagers choose more extreme positions than teachers, then this is one way in which we will define their meaning as being structured in a distinctive way. It is tempting to see the situation in the light of Witkin's (1967) concept of 'psychological differentiation'. According to this, increased education can increasingly differentiate cognitive structures. And differentiation means an ability and preference for distinction-making. It is less complex to say 'X is like a' than to say 'X is like a, but not too much so, though more than just a little'. Regardless of the 'quality' of the associations displayed, then, this finding of quantitative differences in patterns of associations characterizing a concept between different groups of people is possibly one of the major outcomes of the study.

The different ways in which various groups use emphatic or more provisional responses is shown in Table 16.3. We need to take note here of the proportion of choices for the central score (5), as this may either mean an association balanced neatly between two opposite alternatives – or even a bored rejection of the task of deciding.

Table 16.3 shows clearly that the élite group, who are the most educationally qualified, have the most moderate (and more complex on account of being less clear-cut) approach to their markings. The teachers are much more inclined than the villagers to use the central, noncommittal score 5; it would be hard to argue that the teachers have done this because they understand the procedure less than villagers do; the villagers have answered distinctly and with a considerable measure of agreement between individuals (this is not evident from Table 16.2, but it is the case that the villagers' scores were bunched closely together

TABLE 16.3. *Differential use of the response scale by various groups*[a]

	Villagers	Teachers	Élite	Medical students
Scores at extremes of scale (9 : 1)	453 (18·9)	288 (13·1)	295 (14·7)	497 (9·0)
Intermediate scores other than at mid-point (5)	30 (1·2)	42 (1·9)	82 (4·1)	212 (3·8)
Scores at mid-point (5)	45 (1·7)	154 (7·0)	63 (3·2)	61 (1·2)
N people	24	22	20	55
N scales	22	22	22	14

[a] Number of scores of particular value, per person, shown in brackets.

for most scales, which is one reason why chi-square statistic and not the *t* test has been used to examine differences between groups). We must conclude that the teachers' use of '5' so often must be due to a measure of genuine indecision in the face of realizing more possibilities and approaches to the task of association-making; and there may also be an amount of boredom with the procedure. However, even taking this preference for '5' into account, teachers have used more intermediate scores per person than have villagers. The medical students, who are *going* to be much more qualified as a group than the élite group here as a whole, are again more complex and less clear-cut than the other groups.

We can now look at the particular ways in which images of intelligence diverge in comparing the villagers with the teachers. We see that all are agreed that the intelligence they are referring to is a traditional entity. Teachers are less clear about intelligence being steady, or associated with a quality of obduracy. Teachers no longer think of intelligence as so slow, or stable, healthy, careful, active, or hot, as do the villagers; nor do teachers so strongly associate intelligence with the idea 'friendly'. Teachers are still inclined to associate intelligence with all these things (except 'slow'), but the differences are all matters of degree rather than of quality. The differences are yet more marked when comparing the villagers' ideas with those of the medical students.

In three scales out of the fourteen they dealt with, medical students have associations for intelligence with adjectives opposite in meaning to those chosen by villagers. Whereas villagers are thinking of intelligence as a traditional entity, students tend marginally to consider it as modern. (This may very well be because villagers were reacting to *obugezi* while students were working in English, with *intelligence*.) While villagers consider their construct of intelligence to be rare, students (not surprisingly in their highly select environment) respond that their version is common. And most conspicuously, while villagers see intelligence as a matter of pause, of delay, students find it to be hurried, or quick. This last difference is not a matter of degree, but of opposite quality.

DISCUSSION

We have now seen something of how Baganda at different educational levels think about intelligence. How does this compare with what may be known about corresponding concepts in other African cultures? The available literature suggests that ideas about intelligence or human ability do indeed differ in East and South Central Africa from Western models. Barbara Levine (1963) writing of the Gusii in Kenya says 'the good child is the obedient child . . . smartness or brightness by itself is not a highly valued characteristic and the Nyansongo concept of intelligence includes respect for elders and filial piety as vital ingredients.'

Margaret Read (1959) provided a similar picture among the Ngoni of Malawi. She writes 'Ngoni adults . . . summed up the aims of upbringing of children in one word, "respect".' They also wished to inculcate wisdom, which was contrasted with 'cleverness', and wisdom included knowledge, good judgement, ability to control people and to keep at peace, and skill in using speech. Not far away, Audrey Richards had earlier written (1956) 'Bemba women . . . say with great emphasis and characteristic repetition "we teach and teach and teach the girls" and they sometimes add "we make them clever" using the causative form of the verb "to be intelligent and socially competent and to have knowledge of etiquette" (*ukubacenjela*).' Irvine (1969b) similarly notes that 'that the Shona word *ngware*, which means caution, prudence and wisdom, should be translated as *intelligence* is not without significance'.

Recently Klingelhofer (1971) has presented evidence gathered in 1966 (i.e. before a major national effort to change peoples' thinking about the aims of education) suggesting that ideas similar to those of the Ngoni, Bemba and Shona are to be found in Tanzania. Over three thousand secondary school students (without specifying tribal or geographical distribution) were asked 'what two things will you try to teach your children?'; 9 per cent of African boys (i.e. not Asians) first mentioned academic skills ('reading', 'study hard at school', etc.), but 59 per cent thought first of obedience ('behaviour', *'heshima'* – respect, discipline, to obey older people, etc.).

More relevant to the present work, Orley (personal communication, 1971) has results of interviews with Baganda villagers. His questions concerned mental health concepts, but wisdom-foolishness was included as one response scale, whose correlation with other scales can therefore be noted. His results suggest that wisdom is related to the ideas 'happy', 'safe', 'healthy' 'honest', 'industrious', 'kind', and 'warm'. Orley also found small (and not statistically significant) correlations between 'wisdom' and 'soft' and 'fast'. It is tempting to liken the link with soft, here, with the idea of obedience reported in the other researches above. This counters the present finding of villagers' direct association of *obugezi* with obduracy or firmness, rather than obedience. The paradox may perhaps be resolved if it were true that the present respondents were thinking of *obugezi* in the older person, who should be firm and command the respect, obedience and pliability of others; while the focus in Orley's and other researches may have rested more on the younger person, required to be soft, yielding, obedient. The issue needs to be resolved with further investigation.

If it is true that traditional African cultures evolved an intelligence model differing from the current Western conception, how did this fit into their scheme of things? Irvine (1969a) speculates that 'given, in many African societies, a view of the universe based on the influence of ancestral spirits and strong beliefs in theories of causation that are non-Western, the probability of enhancement of skills and reinforcement of learning to preserve these aspects of the network of traditional value systems is high'. In other words, a 'conservative' model of intelligence will be fostered in such cultures.

Such models of intelligence can very appropriately be called radical, as they seek to respect and conserve the root structures of a culture. However Western cultures currently label as radical phenomena which reach the roots of a structure to change it. So we are led to distinguish between change-radical and conservation-radical models of intelligence. Paradoxically, Western cultural norms include an undermining component of innovation, of a change-radical ideal of intelligence. This change-radical intelligence has treated ecology as a variable in man's interaction with the environment, in what is increasingly often being identified as a destructive way. A greater respect for man's ecology may run parallel with a conservation-radical intelligence model. If such ideas are to be found in African cultures, they should command our close attention.

Vernon (1969) supports Irvine's argument, and quotes Jomo Kenyatta's words: 'To the Europeans, individuality is the ideal of life; to the Africans, the ideal is right relations with, and behaviour to, other people.' Vernon continues: 'the Western mind fragments and analyses the world in which it lives, the African mind tries to achieve harmony with the visible and invisible worlds.' Also 'the major differences between African and Western intelligence probably arise more from the emphasis on conformity and social integration as against individual responsibility and internal controls; and from the acceptance of magical beliefs which inhibit analytic perception and rational thinking.'

This last assertion is unfortunately itself probably irrational, and stems from a stereotype long held by Westerners that Africans are superstitious (and so are Westerners); but recent work by Jahoda (1970b) refutes the 'stereotype frequently voiced in the past about superstitious Africans feeling themselves constantly in the grip of malevolent external forces'. Jahoda found a modest trend that undergraduates who had spent more years at university and who had more literate home backgrounds had more supernatural beliefs. The issue here is whether, as Vernon seems to imply, African intelligence models are superficial, in the sense that they are responsive to social pressures, irrational and hence not grounded in a personal penetrating understanding of their cultures; or whether they are radical, in the sense that Africans understand the roots and functioning of their own cultures. The answer lies open to empirical study, which should take note of the cultural context of intelligence in trying to define and measure it.

Current Kiganda conceptions of intelligence have probably been influenced from three directions. First, their own traditional ideas on the matter, now largely inaccessible except through oral lore; second, the Baganda have been influenced by Islam and its concepts; and thirdly, there are Western ideas on intelligence (themselves at one stage influenced by Islamic scholars). Let us briefly consider Islamic concepts first.

Arabic has a word *al'aql*, of which the *Encyclopaedia of Islam* (1913) says it is 'the intellectual turn or capacity in man either for understanding, by way of thinking . . . or for receiving this understanding from above'. Nasr (1966) says *al'aql* 'means both reason and intellect – one of the meanings of the root *'aql* is to tie or to bind. The Quran calls those who have gone astray from religion as those who cannot intellect, *la ya'qilun*, those who cannot use their intelligence correctly. It is very significant that the loss of faith is equated in Quranic language . . . with the improper functioning of intelligence.' Nasr's further remarks about intelligence are instructive in showing vividly how a non-Western culture has developed its 'equivalent' concept. He writes: 'Islam poses the ultimate question "What is intelligence and what does it really mean to be intelligent?" Intelligence is not what it has become so often in modern time, a mental acumen and diabolical cleverness which goes on playing with ideas endlessly without ever penetrating or realising them. This is not real intelligence . . . which differs as much from mental virtuosity as the soaring flight of an eagle differs from the play of a monkey.'

Nasr appears to distinguish between 'mental virtuosity', which one might hazard to identify with Vernon's second 'type' of intelligence, and 'real intelligence' (of a sort which is not found in Vernon's models). The latter he calls 'contemplative', and it seems to connote a mental activity with a definite sense of direction, reminding us of the possibility raised in the introduction that intelligence is a *vector* rather than a *scalar* quantity. Successful travel in this direction brings one into the community of Islam, the root of which word 'has two meanings, one peace and the other surrender'; since 'man . . . is always in the state of neglecting this possibility . . . that is why the cardinal sin in Islam is forgetfulness'. Perhaps this more refined view of Islamic ideas may connect with what so many observers report of methods in Koranic schools, where diligent repetition of texts aims to combat forgetfulness of revelation.

The influence of Islam in Africa has reached from Zanzibar off the east coast right over to the far west coast in Senegal; and the concept of *al'aql* has been worked into African cultures all along this range. The Baganda have not evidently borrowed this word, though they may have been influenced by some Islamic ideas at least; however, we can examine one culture in which the word itself has taken root and see how its meaning has developed.

A Francophone group of scholars, Bisilliat, Laya, Pierre and Pidoux (1967), of whom Laya at least was a member of the local culture, examined the concept of '*lakkal*' in the Djerma-Songhai culture in West Africa. Islam is the dominant religion there and '*lakkal*' is the etymological relation of *al'aql*. Of *lakkal* Bisilliat *et al.* say that it 'overlaps, and yet does not embody exactly the following concepts: aptitude for learning, insight and intellectual ability, capability of

social integration and, more generally speaking, capability to integrate
to one's own environment. . . .' The ideal integration of self with
Islamic revelation, in Nasr's exposition, is here apparently transmuted
to an integration of self with existing cultural forms.

The Islamic idea has thus apparently been assimilated into at least
one West African culture. Its effects must be suspected to be manifest
also in the Hausa culture of Northern Nigeria, as they have the word
hankali for intelligence, another relative of *al'aql*. It is worth noting
that in Yoruba, although a substantial proportion of the people have
adopted Islam for well over a century, the words for intelligence do not
include any derivatives of *al'aql*. Coming to East Africa, Swahili has
the word *akili* for intelligence, clearly part of the same family, although
its connotations will not be examined here.

The second model or set of models which may bear upon intrin-
sically Baganda ways of thinking about intelligence comes from Western
cultures. It is instructive to examine the part played here by the family
of ideas related to the Latin word *cernere*, to separate, distinguish, or
understand. To be *discerning* is a well-thought-of condition in English
culture; it is a compliment to be called distinguished (the implication
is that one is distinct from, perhaps 'head and shoulders above' one's
fellows). Intelligent brainwork proceeds by making *discriminations*,
and proper social behaviour is that which is *discreet*, where the individual's needs or ways do not encroach upon those of others. Western
ideas of intelligence did not arise in a vacuum, as these Romance roots
show, and were composed of various (including Islamic) influences.
But the Islamic idea of *al'aql* is presumably inapplicable to Western
thinking because it was overtly opposed by Christianity, which acted
as a hostile rather than as an eclectic ideology.

One important facet of the Western concept of intelligence is that
it has tended to become separated from the area of emotion, or attitudes. This operation is evident in the treatment in most psychological
textbooks of attitudes and abilities as separate entities. For example,
the *Dictionary of Philosophy and Psychology* (1960) prefers to discuss
intellect (rather than intelligence), and says 'there is a tendency to
restrict the term to conceptual thinking'. The dictionary approves one
authority for making intellect 'cover all forms of cognitive process',
which later are described as linked to 'conation and affection'. But
these are not integrated with the concept of attitude, which is taken
to be a 'state of attention primarily and secondarily an expression for
habitual tendencies and interests'.

A glance at a few textbooks will suffice to show the separation between
K

intelligence and attitudes in operation. Cronbach (1961) in his book on testing, a work of over 600 pages, provides 18 references in his subject index to intelligence and general mental ability; but attitude does not appear at all. Vernon (1969) has 7 subject index entries on intelligence, and others on abilities and aptitudes; but none on attitudes. On the other hand, Secord and Backman (1964) in their 600-page textbook have 87 items of reference to various aspects of attitudes; but not a single index entry on abilities, aptitude or intelligence. Again, Proshansky and Seidenberg's (1965) collection of readings with over 700 pages of text has over 70 index items on attitudes, but no items on abilities, aptitudes or intelligence. This conceptual separation is certainly the result of scientific analysis with its 'Western' habit of discrimination and need to proceed by making distinctions; for C. T. Onions's revised _Shorter Oxford Dictionary_ (1936) states that the term _aptitude_ ('natural capacity for any pursuit' and therefore a concept of which intelligence is a special case) is cognate with the term _attitude_, which is hardly surprising, both referring to kinds of 'disposition'.

The Western concept of intelligence has been taken for granted as defined for so long that it is not easy to find in the literature much exploration of what intelligence means normatively. However, there is one investigation at least which gives some information on the connotative meaning of 'intelligence' to a Western group. Bruner, Shapiro and Tagiuri (1958) showed 120 college students in the Boston area the phrase 'people who are intelligent . . .' together with a list of 59 adjectives. People were asked to show how much they associated each adjective with the phrase above, on a five-point scale.

Some of the strong associations found with intelligence were individualistic: those included 'energetic', 'clever', 'imaginative', 'independent'. But several other adjectives link intelligence with ideas on social behaviour; these included 'conscientious', 'honest', 'reliable' and 'responsible'. It is difficult, however, to know to what extent these associations with intelligence imply a model of that concept which involves pressures toward social integration. One notes though that 'submissive' is certainly firmly dissociated from the concept 'intelligent'. The items 'cheerful', 'even-tempered', 'friendly', 'sympathetic', 'sociable', 'sincere' and 'warm' were all associated with the idea 'intelligent', but more weakly than the members of the first list. Certain contradictions seem also to be implicit in this 'normative' American model of intelligence. First, regarding strongly associated characteristics, 'deliberate' and 'imaginative' are in the same list; while not unquestionably opposed, these nevertheless seem to be difficult to fit together.

The issue is of some importance as it concerns the question of the 'speed' element in an intelligence model. It may seem that with 'deliberate', Bruner's normative model resembles the Kiganda and other African models which reportedly emphasize cautionary slowness; however the strong associations of 'energetic' and 'imaginative' suggest that a 'quick' element is more prominent in the American concept.

These and other apparent anomalies detract from the clarity of the image apparent in Bruner's results. However, the impression received from this map of the idea 'intelligent' is that it resembles the ideal implied in the Protestant ethic of individual development and personal efficacy; while not defying social obligations, this image does not particularly suggest a search for or dependence on social integration as a source of satisfaction. As regards speed, there is little to suggest that intelligence is conceived of as being something slow, but there are a few pointers to liveliness ('activity', 'energy', 'imagination') if not to naked speed itself.

SUMMARY

We can now summarize the Baganda's views on intelligence. Kibuuka's account of the traditional means and goals of education has been referred to in the introduction; from this, from the present results from villagers, as well as from the dictionary and most informants, it is clear that the word *obugezi* has a meaning that includes the English referents of wisdom, as well as of intelligence; and where there are any differences between the two English concepts, for example concerning speed, or social conformity, *obugezi* is more like wisdom than intelligence.

As it would seem from Kibuuka's account, intelligence is thought of as acquired rather than as simply an inherited entity – thus differing from the views of the Plateau Tonga (Colson, 1962) and of Jensen (1969). A Luganda proverb is: *Amagezi muliro, bwe guzikira oguggya ewa munno* ('Intelligence is like fire, when it goes out you can get it from your fellow-man'). Another proverb has it that: *Amagezi ntakke, ekula y'ebuuka* ('Intelligence grows in people as they use it'). To emphasize this point, *Ndi mugezi Nga mubuulire* ('The wise one is the one who has been told'). With these thoughts in the folklore, it is not surprising that none of the groups questioned really thought that intelligence was inherited (nor did they answer strongly for that matter that it was acquired). They did not consider that it could be too easily acquired either, since the view of all three groups was that intelligence could not be 'got by medicine'. There is perhaps a distinction here that the respondents were observing; it is sometimes heard that people in Africa resort to medicines to help pass exams. Indeed, an advertisement for a patent medicine 'Sanatogen', in the November 1971 issue of *Drum*, offers to 'Help your thinking power . . .' arguing that 'some people think easily without effort. But some get distracted and restless. They get tired . . . it's their nerves. . . .' This advertising appeal would accord with what has been found here, that among the Baganda at least people do not think that medicine will affect their intrinsic merit – though this does not mean that they are not open to an appeal suggesting that some medicine may help to improve achievement, under the rationale of making the best of existing attributes.

Perhaps a surprising result was that the Baganda villagers associated intelligence with *aba mukakanyavu* (obdurate). This accords with the finding in Bruner's study that 'independent' was associated with intelligent, while 'submissive' was not. One might expect, then, that the Batoro villagers would agree with the Baganda; or that the Baganda teachers or the élite would align 'intelligence' even more closely with 'obdurate'. Neither of these results was found. As has been mentioned before, there may have been some misunderstanding with the Baganda interviews on this point but what this might have been exactly is not known.

The Baganda villagers associate intelligence with 'hot' rather than 'cold', while the élite and teachers are significantly less clear about this association with 'hot'. The associations in Bruner's list, 'efficient', 'deliberate' and 'intellectual', might conceivably connote coldness rather than warmth (even though he found a weaker association of warmth with intelligence than for these 'cooler' adjectives), and in this respect the more traditional Kiganda concept would seem to be more like the affiliative and social model of intelligence found in other African cultures, and with which the traditional Islamic model would seem to be in accord. In fact the villagers associate intelligence strongly with 'friendly', significantly more so than the teachers or the élite. The adjective is also in Bruner's list, where it has been found to have a weak though positive relation to intelligence. In this respect the more Westernized groups appear to regard 'intelligent' in the same way as Bruner's American subjects do. Baganda also resemble Americans in that the former associate intelligence with 'stable', while the latter link it with 'reliable' and 'deliberate'. Both nationalities also find intelligence reminds them of 'active'; however, the big difference arises between the cultures in the speed associated with the operation of intelligence.

The Baganda villagers strongly link 'intelligence' with an idea of delay, or gradualness. The teachers and the élite are very different in their ideas on this point; their positions are noncommittal regarding hurry or delay and their relation to intelligence. The question of speed does not arise clearly in the list of words used by Bruner; this is curious, since the context which seems to be emerging here suggests that speed is a major differentiating characteristic of Western models of intelligence. However, for the Americans 'energetic' was strongly associated with intelligent and 'indolent' strongly dissociated. One can reasonably infer then that an image of gravity in the traditional Kiganda concept may find itself being displaced by one of alacrity. The word *bwanguwa* used for 'hurried' or 'fast' does not apparently carry the negative connotation of carelessness it may have in English; this is clear also since the Baganda groups all link their idea of intelligence with that of 'careful'.

Concerning the possibility that the Luganda concept of *obugezi* might be importantly concerned with correct behaviour, social propriety, or uprightness, there is certainly a clear association with 'honourable', 'happy' and 'public' (i.e. social), and this applies for all the three groups regardless of level of education. The position is similar in some ways to that of Bruner's American group, who link 'responsible' strongly with intelligence, and 'sympathetic' and 'sociable' somewhat mildly therewith; though this American position is somewhat modified by finding 'aggressive' and 'irritable' also mildly linked with intelligence. There is one Luganda proverb which opens the possibility that the benevolent image of *obugezi* is not an exclusive one. This is: *Omugezigezi, akuguza ekibira* ('A clever fellow sells you a forest' – since a forest is a nuisance to basically agricultural people, who have to cut it down to use the land, this is like 'selling refrigerators to Eskimos'). Interpretation of the situation here hinges on whether the proverb refers to a *mugezi* (one who is imbued with *obugezi*); if this is so it would indicate that the concept is much broader than the Islamic model of rectitude implied in the one who possesses *al'aql*; however, it appears that the form *mugezigezi* represents a mutation in meaning from *amagezi*, and it means 'tricky' or 'cunning' rather than 'intelligent'. In this case the proverb refers to a concept of narrower relevance, the cunning man, and the model of *obugezi*, intelligence/wisdom accords with the Islamic and other African models described.

Finally, we may suggest that the existence of two overlapping though different conceptions of intelligence may have important applications in educational situations. In Buganda primary schools, children are subject to traditional ideas and expectations at home, and to more Western ideas on the other hand in school. It has long been known that different sets of attitudes on a wide range of matters distinguish the home from the school environment, and that these may catch children in a conflict; but it has not been so widely realized or suggested that different ways of thinking about intelligence itself might have different, and possibly conflicting, influences on children.

Very much the same structural predicament applies for situations where ideas from a dominant (e.g. white middle-class) subculture are being used in educating children from working-class, immigrant, or other kinds of subcultures. One way to deal with such situations is to expose both the educators and the pupil community concerned to the nature and implication of the educational philosophy – with its embedded conception of intelligence – which it is proposed to use. Progress in such educational enterprises will probably be smoothest if an understanding and acceptance of their basic nature is widely diffused.

In Uganda, as in other developing countries, it is for local educationists to decide if the new concepts are to be favoured and, if so, the best steps to take to attain this goal. If a Western model is to be adopted, more thorough investigation involving larger samples, Ugandan investigators, better-chosen questions and expanded cultural analysis would be needed on which to base better advice to educationists. But, meanwhile, a tentative suggestion in this direction is that specific exercises and methods (e.g. stories praising such qualities, more time-paced activities in school) should be devised and used to foster a taste for speed in response, quickness and urgency, both in action and thinking. If a traditional concept is favoured it must be understood, accepted, and even enjoyed, that life may be dominated more by deliberation than urgency, and by tradition rather than change.

17

O. M. Okonji (1971)

The effects of familiarity on classification[1]

Journal of Cross-Cultural Psychology, 2(1), pp. 39–49

The problem of 'culture-free' and 'culture-fair' tests is largely the problem of the testee's familiarity with test materials. This problem has been particularly acute in psychological testing outside Western countries, especially Africa. In an effort to cope with the problem rather than merely show an awareness of its existence, Price-Williams (1962) used familiar indigenous objects for studying classification among the Tiv of Northern Nigeria. Following this example, Kellaghan (1965) used local materials for the investigation of classificatory behaviour among some Western Nigeria Yoruba children. These studies showed for the first time that when appropriate test materials are used the African children involved were not qualitatively different from their European counterparts in their abstract attitude.

Although the results of these studies are important, they do not throw any light on the nature of the effect of familiarity on test performance in different cultural groups. Some investigators have suggested a type of design that makes easier the investigation of systematic differences across groups. This procedure involves using stimuli to which no differences in response should be expected and those to which differences should be expected. In the study reported here the effect of familiarity with test materials on equivalence grouping was investigated by using two sets of materials that differed in the degree to which they were familiar to two different groups.

[1] I am grateful to Professor Gustav Jahoda of Strathclyde University, Glasgow, for his advice, and to the Commonwealth Scholarship Commission in the UK and the Shell-BP Co. of Nigeria for financial support.

METHOD

Subjects

One hundred and thirty-eight Ibusa and 105 Glasgow male school-children were involved in the study. Their ages ranged from approximately 6 to 12 years. All children of the same age were selected from the same school grade.

Ibusa is a rural town in Midwestern Nigeria. It is located about 12 miles from Onitsha on the river Niger. The main occupation of the people is subsistence farming. Some of the farmers engage in part-time hunting of animals in forests quite far away from the residential areas. Apart from domestic animals, a few wild animals like snakes, squirrels, rats, lizards and some birds are seen in the bushes in the residential areas. As births are not usually registered here ages were estimated by matching stated time of birth with some known historical events that occurred in the same period (in a few cases family written records of births were available).

The Glasgow sample was selected from low-income housing estates to reduce the background disparity between the two sets of children. Table 17.1 shows the distribution of the children according to parental occupation.

TABLE 17.1. *Socioeconomic backgrounds of Ibusa and Glasgow samples*[a]

		Ibusa			Glasgow			
Age	N	Skilled	Partly skilled	Unskilled	N	Skilled	Partly skilled	Unskilled
6	20	—	3	17	15	3	3	9
7	20	4	—	16	15	3	—	12
8	18	2	2	14	15	4	4	7
9	15	3	1	11	15	3	6	6
10	17	—	1	16	15	4	5	6
11	21	8	—	13	15	3	5	7
12	27	5	1	21	15	3	6	6
Total	138	22	8	108	105	23	29	53
%	—	16	6	78	—	22	28	50

[a] The above classification is based on the British system and attempts to show the degree of the similarity between the socioeconomic background of the two groups.

Design and test materials

Two sorting tests were utilized. One test consisted of materials which were more familiar to the Ibusa Ss. The other, consisting of animal models, was considered to be equally familiar in both the Glasgow and the Ibusa Ss. Below are listed the elements in the two sorting tests:

A. Animals (plastic models)

1. A goat (ewu)
2. A sheep (atulu)
3. A snake (agwo)
4. A chicken (okuku)
5. A bird (nnunu)
6. A dog (nketa)
7. A crocodile (aguiyi)
8. A lion (awolo)
9. An elephant (enyi)
10. A springbok (mgbada)

B. Objects

1. A calabash musical instrument (isaka)
2. A gourd flute (akpele)
3. A red plastic flute (oja)
4. A wooden flute (oja osisi)
5. A metal gong (agogo)
6. A drum (egede)
7. A red piece of cloth (akwa ododo)
8. A red leather bag (akpa)
9. A red wooden rod (osisi)
10. A bicycle spoke (spoku anyinya igwe)
11. A transparent packet of Cafenol
12. A packet of Epsom Salts (ogwu nnu)
13. A black metal ring (mgbaka)
14. A bottle of Aboki liniment (aboki)
15. A cooking pot (ite)
16. A mortar (mkpilite)
17. A pestle (aka ngweose)
18. A wooden spoon (ngaji osisi)
19. A clay soup pot (ugbugba)
20. A needle (ntutu)

As can be seen from the list of the objects in B, above, the objects are not all so unfamiliar to the Glasgow group as to make the test incomprehensible.

It was, however, expected that in the sorting of the objects which were more familiar to the Ibusa group, they (Ibusa Ss) would reach higher conceptual levels in their sorting than the Glasgow Ss as indicated by their verbalized bases of sorting, and also be more accurate in their classification where accuracy meant a correspondence between the 'intension' and 'extension' of the classes formed in all age-groups. In the sorting of the animals no difference was expected between the Glasgow and Ibusa samples in terms of the number of 'shifts' made and the conceptual level of the verbalized bases of sorting reached by the subjects in all age-groups, since the animals were equally familiar to both groups. Finally, the overall trend of development was expected to be similar in both samples.

Procedure

Ss were tested individually by E on both tests in one session which lasted for about forty-five minutes. The object sorting task was always done first because being more structured we considered it advantageous to introduce the children to the classification exercise through it. We were aware that some sort of systematic randomization of the order of administering the tests would have been methodologically more acceptable, but since we considered the gains from starting with the structured situation more we opted for the risk involved in not varying the order of giving the tests.

All testing was done in the school premises. Before any real testing was done in the Glasgow schools, the first two to three days were spent going round the classes in the schools, watching the children at work and play and discussing and answering questions about Africa. Through these formal and informal meetings the children got quite used to him. He also had lessons in and practised speaking Glasgow English before the testing was actually begun.

Many of the Ibusa Ss knew the investigator before, and once they got used to the atmosphere of the test situation, which was rather more friendly than the usual classroom atmosphere, they felt perfectly at ease. The instructions here were given in Ibo throughout but Ss were allowed to speak either Ibo or English, as they found each convenient. None answered questions in English, but occasionally an English word was injected into an Ibo sentence. The instructions were cross-translated into English and Ibo by two different people.

Part I: Object sorting

The S sat beside E, was shown the objects and asked to name them. Where S was unsure or hesitated in naming an object he was told just the name. Most of the Ibusa Ss experienced little or no difficulty in naming the objects while many of the Glasgow Ss could not identify *some* of the objects. Names of the objects were supplied in English to the Glasgow Ss whenever they failed to identify them by name correctly. After the identification exercises, a key object (a stimulus object around which sorting was done) was brought out and S was requested to collect all other objects that were like it in some way or that went together with it. The key objects were the gourd flute, the red piece of cloth, the packet of Epsom Salts, the clay pot and the bicycle spoke, which were arbitrarily selected by the investigator. All the actual sorting and verbalization were recorded.

Part II: Animal sorting

(a) Active sorting by *S*s. After identifying the animals, *S* was requested to put together all the animals that went together or were like one another. Having done this he was asked to see if there was any other way he could sort the objects. He was allowed to make new groupings until he indicated he could no longer do so. All the actual sorting and verbalization were also recorded.

(b) Verbalization of *E*'s sorting. *E* made in turn four different groups as follows:

1. Domestic/nondomestic
2. Carnivorous/noncarnivorous
3. Birds/nonbirds
4. Reptiles/nonreptiles

The task of *S*s was merely to verbalize the bases of *E*'s groupings.

RESULTS

As there was no standardized method for the scoring of the sorting tests, aspects of the procedures adopted by Hanfmann and Kasanin (1936), Thompson (1941), Sigel (1953), Vinacke (1954), Wohlwill (1957), Price-Williams (1962), Bruner and Olver (1963), Kellaghan (1965), and Vernon (1965b) were modified and utilized for the analysis of our present data. The results of the tests were analysed mainly on the bases of performance and verbalization.

Performance

The ability to 'shift' one's bases of sorting in a sorting task is considered indicative of the degree to which an individual possesses classificatory ability: 'a change of criterion or "shifting" is simply another expression of operational, and therefore reversible mobility, this being the hall-mark of a complete classificatory structure' (Inhelder and Piaget, 1964). A shift was considered to have been made when a subject broke up the groups he had formed and then formed new groups following some other different basis. Accuracy describes another dimension of performance. By accuracy is meant the degree to which an individual's actual sorting corresponds to the declared basis of sorting. In this respect the sorting made by the subjects were scored as:

   a. Accurate – where his verbalization agrees fully with his sorting.
   b. Overinclusive – where his verbalization is more extensive than his actual sorting.
   c. Underinclusive – where his verbalization is less extensive than his actual classes.
   d. Inaccurate – where the verbalized bases of sorting do not agree with his actual sorting.
   e. Nonverbalization.

Verbalization

The verbalized bases of sorting were assigned to levels of abstraction according to three different levels of abstractness:

Level I. The highest level where verbalization was based on superordinate concepts whether 'itemized' or not, e.g. domestic/nondomestic, carnivorous/noncarnivorous for the animals.

Level II. Groupings formed on the basis of the perceptible attributes and superordinate concepts (e.g. classification of animals on the bases of domesticity and number of legs) at one and the same time.

Level III. Groupings of the following types:

   a. Graphic collections and sorting based on spatial contiguity, e.g. animals lined up horn to horn, or grouped according to those that are together on the desk.
   b. Identity and partial identity of certain attributes of the elements put together, e.g. 'a goat and a springbok are the same only that one lives at home and the other in the forest'.
   c. Affective groupings, e.g. 'the snake makes people fear, so do the elephant and the lion'.
   d. Complexive groupings, e.g. 'a goat has hair on the body, a springbok has hair also but its skin is used for making drums and the skin of the crocodile is also used for making native doctor's drums'.
   e. Groupings based on stories of personal experience with some of

the animals or objects, e.g. 'some time ago I saw a dancing group, enjoyed their dance and they played a drum and a flute like these'.
f. Naming of the objects.

The verbalization of the bases of the experimenter's sorting of the animals were scored as follows:

a. Corresponding – where the subjects' verbalization agrees with the basis *E* had in mind in forming the groups or to others acceptable to *E* as meaningful and at Level I.
b. Noncorresponding – verbalization not agreeing with *E*'s bases of sorting.
c. Nonresponse – silence or rejection with unacceptable rearrangement.

Table 17.2 presents the results of the analysis of the conceptual levels reached in the object sorting. By combining Levels I and II of the subjects' verbalized bases of sorting to form one category, and Level III another, and by further classifying subjects into two categories, those whose verbalized basis of sorting reached either Level I or Level II in three or more groups around the key objects and those whose verbalized bases did not, a 2 by 2 contingency table was constructed. Although all the results are in the expected direction, only at ages 11 to 12 is there a significant difference between the two groups in favour of the Ibusa group.

TABLE 17.2. *Conceptual levels of subjects' verbalization of their own sorting of objects*

	Ns		N reaching Level I or II in three or more groupings around key objects				
Age-groups	Ibusa	Glasgow	Ibusa	Glasgow	X_c^2	df	p
6–8	58	45	10	2	1·57	1	NS
9–10	32	30	14	7	2·04	1	NS
11–12	48	30	38	14	7·37	1	0·01

When the two groups were compared at all age-groups, no difference was found in the degree of accuracy of their sorting. Both the Glasgow and Ibusa subjects were equally able to match the 'intension' of their grouping operations in spite of the fact that Ibusa children were more familiar with the objects. This result did not confirm our expectation.

Table 17.3 shows the number of shifts made in the sorting of the animals.

TABLE 17.3. *Number of shifts made in the animal sorting*

Age-groups	Glasgow				Ibusa			
	N	Shifts	$\bar{X}$	SD	N	Shifts	$\bar{X}$	SD
6	15	18	1·2	0·66	20	15	0·75	0·46
7–8	30	36	1·2	0·94	38	38	1·00	0·62
9–10	30	63	2·1	1·58	32	46	1·44	0·66
11–12	30	80	2·7	2·22	48	174	3·63	3·01

No further statistical treatment of the above data was deemed necessary since by inspection it appears obvious that no significant difference exists between the two samples in their ability to shift their bases of classification as expected.

As expected, no differences were found in the use of abstract concepts between the groups in the animal sorting. The results showed clear age trends as can be seen from Tables 17.4 and 17.5.

DISCUSSION

The results presented earlier represent only a moderate support for our first hypothesis indicating that familiarity has only a moderate influence on classificatory behaviour. If, however, we take into account the fact that the degree of unfamiliarity of the task to the Glasgow group was not high the importance of the result increases. It seems, therefore, that the obtained level of significance constitutes quite a weighty evidence in support of the view that familiarity with objects to be classified does affect a child's efficiency in classification. The only statistically significant difference (in the 11 to 12 year age-group) may be explained, in part at least, in terms of the probability that it is at these ages that the influence of schooling begins to make a real impact on the Ibusa sample, while the start given the Glasgow sample by longer nursery or home reading and school experience begins to be closed. At the earlier ages the differential must have been so large that sheer moderate advantage in familiarity could not offset it.

It is interesting to note that while greater familiarity gave the Ibusa *S*s an edge over the Glasgow *S*s in the use of superordinate concepts

TABLE 17.4. *Trend analysis of conceptual levels reached in the verbalization of the object sorting test*

Ibusa

Age-groups	N reaching Levels I and II for three or more stimulus objects	Total
6–8	10	58
9–10	14	32
11–12	38	48
Total	62	138

Source of variation	df	X^2	$p <$
Due to linear regression	1	40·537	0·001
Departure from regression	1	0·192	NS
Overall value	2	40·729	0·001

Glasgow

Age-groups	N reaching Levels I and II for three or more stimulus objects	Total
6–8	2	45
9–10	7	30
11–12	14	30
Total	23	105

Source of variation	df	X^2	$p <$
Due to linear regression	1	22·606	0·001
Departure from regression	1	3·798	NS
Overall value	2	18·808	0·001

in the verbalization of the bases of their grouping, it did not give them any advantage in their coordination of the 'intension' of their groupings with their 'extension'. This is quite surprising; it was thought that being more familiar with the objects, the Ibusa children could more easily pick out all the objects that belonged to the groups formed. Perhaps all that familiarity does to aid classification is to facilitate in a given context the availability of appropriate verbal templates and provide some visual cues for defining classes.

Although the results confirm the second hypothesis, a few points arising from the animal sorting task need to be discussed. In comparison with Price-Williams's (1962) results in a study of classificatory behaviour among the Tiv, both the Glasgow and Ibusa Ss made relatively fewer 'shifts'. The highest average number of shifts among the present samples is about the same as the lowest average of shifts among the Tiv. Yet the author suggested on the basis of his data that the Tiv children seemed to lag a little behind their European counterparts in development. This difference between Price-Williams's results and the results reported here may be due partly to differences in the actual animals classified, differences in the scoring criteria adopted, and differences in other experimental conditions, especially the school atmosphere of the present study, in contrast to the more relaxed home atmosphere of the Tiv study. Poole (1968) has cautioned against 'assuming that because one test has been modelled on another, or inspired by it, the results of each may be validly compared' (p. 57). The writer is therefore constrained in comparing the present results with Price-Williams's, and by the same token it is thought that his comparison of his results with unspecified European results seems rather unwarranted, especially as his study represented an important departure from older approaches to that kind of investigation. Nonetheless, it must be pointed out that in some ways the results presented here are a direct confirmation (since the present investigator used the same materials under comparable conditions for testing a Western and a non-Western group of children) of the general conclusions both he and Kellaghan (1965) reached by extrapolation: that when tested on appropriate (i.e. familiar) materials, no differences may be found between a Western and a non-Western sample in classificatory attitude.

It is noteworthy that while about 25 per cent (most of whom are in the 6 to 8 years group) of the Ibusa sample classified the animals on the basis of colour, none did so among the Glasgow sample. Many reports of psychological studies in Africa have observed this relative dominance of colour in classificatory activities. It is not clear why

TABLE 17.5. *Trend analysis of conceptual level reached in the verbalization of subjects' own sorting of the animals*

Ibusa

Age-groups	N reaching Levels I and II	Total
6–8	5	58
9–10	13	32
11–12	34	48
Total	52	138

Source of variation	df	X^2	$p <$
Due to linear regression	1	40·300	0·001
Departure from regression	1	3·140	NS
Overall value	2	43·440	0·001

Glasgow

Age-groups	N reaching Levels I and II	Total
6–8	11	45
9–10	16	30
11–12	24	30
Total	51	105

Source of variation	df	X^2	$p <$
Due to linear regression	1	22·611	0·001
Departure from regression	1	1·453	NS
Overall value	2	24·064	0·001

colour concepts are so salient for Africans, even among adults, but cease to be so among Euro–Americans relatively early, probably before school age (Lee, 1965). It may be a case of 'systematic preference' for colour cues. This preference is obviously not innate since it dwindles not only with age but also with amount of schooling experience.

The results we have presented here are in no way conclusive because of the procedure adopted in administering the tests, for reasons stated earlier. Yet the study does indicate that this method of direct comparison of widely differing cultural groups which is rare in the literature can be very fruitfully employed in cross-cultural research.

PART THREE
Cognitive development: Piagetian approaches

Introduction

This third section concentrates on the cross-cultural study of cognitive development, and is restricted to aspects related to Piaget's theory and its derivations.

Piaget's work is concerned with basic mental functioning. His approach to intelligence is a complete departure from quantitative measures towards an attempt to uncover the nature of the structures of thought as they unfold in the development of the individual, and which enable man to understand his world. Intelligence is defined as adaptation to the environment, and its ontogenetic development is shown to occur in a hierarchical series of stages, according to general laws of equilibration.[1]

The nature of the structures and the stages through which they develop seem to be identical in all Western cultures, whereas the rate of progression is affected by environmental influences (e.g. socioeconomic status), sensory disabilities (e.g. deafness, blindness) or mental retardation. However, Western cultures are usually considered to be too homogeneous to allow of an adequate testing of the theory in respect of the universality of the nature of the structures and of the order of their unfolding. Thus many cross-cultural studies have recently attempted to assess the influence of culture on these aspects of cognitive development.

Piaget himself has recognized the importance of cross-cultural studies, and, in a theoretical paper (Chapter 18) has placed the discussion at a high level of generalization. Piaget hopes that cross-cultural research will help to unravel the old problem of the relative influence of maturation and environment on cognitive development and outlines the different possibilities. He draws his examples mainly from an unpublished French doctoral dissertation (Mohseni, 1966) on conservation concepts in Iran.

The subsequent chapters (19 to 24) are all concerned with studies of

[1] The reader with little knowledge of Piaget's theory may well find this section rather unrewarding. He may wish to consult an introduction; several competent texts may be suggested: Ginsburg and Opper, 1969; Beard, 1969; Phillips, 1969. Flavell (1963) provides a very complete introduction, and Furth (1968) a highly theoretical one. Droz and Rahmy (1972) have recently produced a very useful guide to reading Piaget's work in the original.

the development of concrete operations in various cultural groups. These structures of thought can be at least partly inferred from the subject's handling of the materials, and although verbal communication is an important part of Piaget's *clinical method*, its cross-cultural difficulties can be overcome in various ways (e.g. Chapter 20). The important fact is the uncovering of concepts and their structural organization, and, whereas their study seems to be difficult without the help of test materials and questions, these can be adapted to each particular situation.

The distinction which has been made throughout this book between *qualitative* and *quantitative* differences in cognitive processes among different cultural groups is also basic to the thinking within the Piagetian framework. Piaget has mainly been concerned with the qualitative aspects of intellectual development: basic structures of processes and their organization into a hierarchical succession of stages. Thus, the basic question is: Do these stages occur qualitatively in the same way and in the same *sequence* in various cultural groups? But the cross-cultural approach also enables us to ask a second question, dealing with the quantitative aspects of this development: Does the *rate* of cognitive growth change under the influence of culture?

Most authors deal with both questions, but put more or less emphasis on one or on the other. Bovet's original contribution (Chapter 19) provides a very detailed qualitative analysis of cognitive development in illiterate children and adults. Her work certainly comes closest to strictly Piagetian methodology, and interesting extensions of the basic tasks enable her to discover an interim stage of 'pseudoconservation', which represents a momentary departure from the course of development known in Western children; this is a unique finding so far, which would have been missed if a less qualitative approach had been used.

The development of conservation concepts has received by far the largest attention, and the inclusion of four articles on this topic (19–21 and 24) reflects this heavy emphasis. Other concepts, however, are just as important, if not more, to Piagetian theory. De Lacey's study (Chapter 22) deals with classification; his sociopsychological approach is interesting because he combines ethnic and socioeconomic comparisons. De Lemos's early work on spatial concepts, which was hitherto difficult to obtain, has been completely rewritten and updated for inclusion as Chapter 23. Dasen's original contribution (Chapter 24) combines the study of several areas of conceptual development, and provides a link with theoretical formulations presented earlier in this book (Chapter 7).

The final contribution (Chapter 25) tries to summarize the field and to catch some of the latest trends. It also attempts to structure some of the problems and to point out future research needs. However, it is not a critical summary, since it assumes comparability of results and makes no judgement of the value of the individual studies.

Our collection is designed to provide an overview of the field, including its achievements and difficulties; however, it is by no means complete, and several major contributions had to be left out. This is the case in particular of Jahoda's (1958a) summary of cross-cultural studies of Piaget's early work, of de Lemos's (1969b) study of conservation in Australian Aboriginal children, and of the much quoted study by Greenfield (1966) on the development of conservation concepts in Wolof children; this paper is, however, easily available and has been reprinted in Price-Williams's (1969) reader. Care has been taken to include several approaches and techniques, variation in the nationalities of the authors and in the cultural groups studied, and a selection of theoretical, experimental and review papers. It is hoped that this collection will help to stimulate further research, and we would like to conclude, very egocentrically, by agreeing with Goodnow (1969b) that 'time devoted to Piaget is one of the best investments a student of milieu effects can make'.

18

J. Piaget (1966)

Need and significance of cross-cultural studies in genetic psychology[1]

International Journal of Psychology, 1(1), pp. 3–13

Genetic psychology is the study of the ontogenesis of cognition. The study of child development may provide an explanation, or at least additional information as to the cognitive mechanisms in the adult. In other words, genetic psychology uses developmental psychology to solve general psychological problems.

It becomes more and more obvious that, from such a point of view, developmental psychology is an essential tool of psychological investigation. But it has been less often realized that its role could be almost as important in sociology. Auguste Comte maintained with good reason that the formative action of one generation upon the next is one of the most important phenomena of human societies, and Durkheim inferred from this that ethical feelings, judicial norms and logic itself must have a collective origin. But there is only one experimental method to verify such hypotheses: the study of the progressive socialization of the individual, that is to say the analysis of his development as a function of general or particular social influences.

Any comparative research, bearing on different cultures and social environments, leads one initially to consider the problem of the delineation of factors which are specific to the spontaneous and internal development of the individual, and of social and cultural factors which are specific to the society under study. But this delineation, which must be done initially, can produce unexpected results. In the field of psychoanalysis, for example, the first Freudian doctrines provided a model of endogenous individual development in which the various stages (in particular that of the so-called 'Oedipal' reactions) were seen as essentially due to the successive manifestations of a single 'instinct',

[1] Nécessité et signification des recherches comparatives en psychologie génétique. Translated by Catherine Dasen with the assistance of Dr H. Sinclair, J. W. Berry and P. R. Dasen.

that is to say of internal tendencies independent of society. On the other hand, we know that a large group of contemporary psychoanalysts, called 'cultural relativists' (e.g. Fromm, Horney, Kardiner, Glover, joined by some anthropologists, such as Benedict and Mead) maintains the hypothesis of a close interdependence between the various Freudian complexes, and notably the Oedipal tendencies, and the social environment.

DEVELOPMENTAL FACTORS

In the field of cognition, the main advantage of cross-cultural studies is to allow a dissociation of the sociocultural and individual factors in development. But it is essential to distinguish which factors are to be considered.

1. *Biological factors*

First of all there are biological factors linked to the *epigenetic system* (interactions between the genotype and the physical environment during growth), which appear especially in the maturation of the nervous system. These factors, which owe nothing to society, play an as yet little-known role. But their importance probably remains crucial in the development of cognitive functions, and it is thus important to consider their possible influence. In particular, the development of this 'epigenetic system' implies, from a biological point of view, the occurrence of *sequential stages*, the existence of *creodes*, and the intervention of a mechanism of *homeorhesis*. These stages are of a sequential nature, each one being necessary to the next in a constant order. The creodes are necessary channels or paths in the development of each particular area of the organism. Homeorhesis is a dynamic equilibration by which a deviation from the creodes is more or less compensated for by a return to the normal path.

We have considered it possible to recognize these characteristics in the development of the operations and the logico-mathematical structures of intelligence. If this is so, it would naturally mean a certain constancy or uniformity in development, whatever the social environments in which individuals live. On the other hand, inversions in the succession of stages, or major modifications of their characteristics, from one milieu to another would mean that these basic biological factors do not intervene in the cognitive development of individuals. This is the first fundamental problem, the solution of which requires extensive cross-cultural studies.

2. *Equilibration factors*

In numerous Western countries, where the study of our stages has been undertaken, the investigation of the development of intellectual operations shows that the psychobiological factors are, by far, not the only ones. Indeed, if there were a continuous action of the internal maturation of the organism and of the nervous system alone, the stages would not only be sequential but would also be bound to relatively constant chronological ages, as are, for example, the coordination of vision and prehension (around four to five months) and the appearance of puberty. One finds in children of the same town, depending on the individuals and on the social, family or school environments, advances or delays that are often considerable. These do not contradict the order of succession, which remains constant, but show that other factors are added to the epigenetic mechanisms.

A second group of factors must therefore be introduced: these are equilibration factors, seen as an autoregulation closer to homeostasis than to homeorhesis. In principle these still depend on activities specific to behaviour in general, in its psychobiological as well as sociocultural aspects. We must reserve judgement on the possible links of these factors with social life.

Individual development is indeed a function of multiple activities, exercising, experiencing or acting upon the environment. Among these actions there arise particular, followed by more and more general, coordinations. This *general coordination of actions* presupposes multiple systems of autoregulation or equilibration, which depend upon the environmental circumstances as well as on epigenetic potentialities. The operations of intelligence can be considered as the highest form of these regulations; this shows the importance of the factor of equilibration as well as its relative independence of biological givens.

But if the equilibration factors can be hypothesized to be very general and relatively independent of the social environment, this hypothesis requires cross-cultural verification. Equilibration processes can be observed in particular in the formation of the concepts of conservation, the stages of which show, in our society, not only a sequential order, but also systems of *compensations*. The intrinsic characteristics of the latter are typical of regulations according to successive levels. But are these particular stages found everywhere? If so, one would not yet have a confirmation of the hypothesis, but at least a more or less favourable indication. If not, it would be, on the contrary, the sign of particular cultural and educational influences.

3. *Social factors of interpersonal coordination*

In the psychobiological field we have made a basic distinction between the epigenetic potentialities and equilibration factors. With regard to the sociocultural factors, it is necessary to introduce a distinction, just as essential, between the general social or interpersonal interactions or coordinations, which are common to all cultures, and cultural and educational transmissions, which change from one culture to another, or from one specific social environment to another.

Whether one studies a child in Geneva, Paris, New York or Moscow, or in the mountains of Iran, the centre of Africa or a Pacific island, one finds social exchanges among children or between children and adults. These operate by themselves, independently of educational transmissions. In any environment individuals ask questions, exchange information, work together, argue, object, etc. This constant interpersonal exchange occurs during the whole of development, according to a socialization process which involves the social life of children among themselves, as well as their relations with elders.

Durkheim referred to general social mechanisms, and maintained that 'under civilizations is Civilization'. In the same way, it is indispensable, in order to discuss the relations between cognitive functions and social factors, to start with opposing the *general coordinations of collective actions* and particular cultural transmissions which have crystallized in a different way in each society. If one were to find, in all the societies studied, our stages and results, it still would not prove that these convergent developments are of a strictly individual nature. Just as it is obvious that, everywhere, a child has social contacts from a very early age, it would also show that certain common socialization processes exist which interact with the equilibration processes discussed in the previous section.

These interactions are so highly probable, and likely to be so close, that one may readily put forward the hypothesis (which should be confirmed or refuted by future cross-cultural studies) that, at least in the field of cognitive functions, the general coordination of actions affects interpersonal actions as well as individual ones. The progressive equilibration of this general coordination of actions seems to be the basis of the formation of logical or logico-mathematical operations. In other words, one should find the same laws of coordination and regulation in individual actions or in social interactions involving, for example, exchanges, cooperation and competition. These laws would result in the same final structures of operations or of cooperations, as 'co-operations'.

One could thus consider logic as a final form of equilibration, as being simultaneously individual and social: individual since it is general and common to all individuals, and social since it is general and common to all societies.

4. Factors of educational and cultural transmission

On the other hand, besides this functional and partly synchronistic (constant or universal) nucleus, one must naturally consider the mainly diachronic (divergent or culturally relative) factor constituted by traditions and the educational transmissions which vary from one culture to another. When one speaks of 'social factors', one in fact is usually referring to these differential cultural pressures. In so far as cognitive processes can vary from one culture to another, it is obvious that one ought to consider this group of factors which is distinct from the former. To start with, one could look at the various languages which are likely to have a more or less strong influence, if not on the operations themselves, at least on the detail of the conceptualizations (e.g. content of classifications, relations).

CROSS-CULTURAL STUDIES IN THE FIELD OF COGNITIVE PROCESSES

Once we have agreed on this classification into four groups of factors, according to the types of relations between the individual and the social environment, we must try to define the usefulness of cross-cultural studies for our understanding of cognitive processes. The main problem in this respect is that of the nature of intellectual operations, and particularly of logico-mathematical structures. Several hypotheses are possible which correspond, among other things, to the four factors distinguished previously, eventually with some additional subdivisions.

Biological factors and factors of coordination of actions

One could interpret these structures, if not as innate, at least as the exclusive result of biological factors of an epigenetic nature (e.g. maturation). Lorenz, one of the founders of contemporary ethology, tends towards this interpretation: he believes in the *a priori* nature of knowledge, and interprets it as instinctual.

From the point of view of cross-cultural data already collected, or still to be obtained, one should distinguish between two questions:

1. Shall we always find the same stages of development, considering of course the possibility of corrections and improvements to the theory?
2. Shall we always find them at the same average ages?

To answer these two questions, it is useful and almost necessary to have available a point of reference in comparing the development of the response to operational tasks (e.g. conservations, classification and inclusion, seriation, numerical correspondence) with the development of the response to tests of intellectual performance, such as those generally used to determine an IQ.

Cross-cultural studies are only beginning, and it would be very unwise to draw conclusions, given the available information, and the great difficulties, linguistic and others, which there are in multiplying these studies. An additional difficulty is the long training necessary to master the testing methods, which become more difficult to use as they get closer to operational functions. But the results of the first studies, assuming they can be generalized, indicate at least a possible line of interpretation.

In Iran, for example, Mohseni (1966) examined schooled children of Teheran and young rural illiterates on conservation tasks on the one hand, and on performance tests on the other (e.g. Porteus Maze, graphical tests). The three main results obtained with the children (aged 5 to 10 years) are as follows: (a) on the whole, the same stages are found in both city and country, in Iran, as in Geneva (succession of the conservations of substance, weight, volume); (b) one notes a systematic delay of two to three years for the operational tests between country and city children, but about the same ages in Teheran as in Europe; (c) the delay is greater, sometimes four but usually five years, for the performance tests, between country and city children, to the extent that the country children would appear mentally defective without the operational tests. For the performance tests, schooled children of Teheran are one to two years behind European and American children.

Assuming that such results are found elsewhere, one would be led to make the following hypotheses:

(a) A more general verification of the constancy in the order of the stages would tend to show their sequential characteristic. Until now, this constant order seems to have been confirmed in Aden by Hyde (1959), in Nigeria by Price-Williams (1961), in Hong Kong by Goodnow

(1962), and in the Martinique by Boisclair (personal communication). But it is obvious that we need to have much more data.

Now, if the sequential order were to be verified cross-culturally, one could see an analogy with the epigenetic development (according to Waddington), and consequently a certain probability of the intervention of biological factors (factor 1). But up to what point? In order to involve biological factors of maturation with certainty, one ought to be in a position to establish the existence not only of a sequential order of stages, but also of certain average ages of appearance. Mohseni's results, however, show a systematic delay of the country children compared to those of the city, which means, of course, that factors other than maturation intervene.

On the other hand, in the area of figurative thinking, one could possibly find everywhere the same age for the appearance of the *semiotic function* (e.g. symbolic play, mental images, and the development of language), which develops in our culture between 1 and 2 years of age. Apparently the main factor which makes this semiotic function possible is the interiorization of imitation: at the sensori-motor level, it already constitutes a sort of representation in action, a motor copy of a model, in such a way that its prolongations, firstly in delayed imitation, then in interiorized imitation, allow the formation of representation in images. But the existence of delayed reactions, and of interiorization, naturally implies certain neurological processes, such as the freezing, at a certain level of connections, of the actualization of action schematas. A cross-cultural study of the sensori-motor forms of imitation and of the ages of appearance of the semiotic function from delayed imitation could show some chronological regularities, not only in the sequential order of stages, but also in the more or less fixed ages of formation. In this case we would get closer to the factors of maturation, which are related to the epigenetic system (e.g. intervention of the language centres).

(b) The second clear result of Mohseni's study is the fairly general delay of country children, compared with those of Teheran, on the operational tasks (conservations) as well as on the performance tests. This delay proves the intervention of factors distinct from those of simple biological maturation. But here one hesitates to decide among the three groups of factors named above: (2) factors of equilibration of actions; (3) factors of general interpersonal interaction, and (4) factors of cultural and educational transmission. Indeed, each one of these could intervene. Concerning factor 2, Mohseni noticed the astounding lack of activity of the young country children who do not go to school and who have no toys, except stones or sticks, and who show a constant passivity and apathy. Thus one finds at the same time a poor development of the coordinations of individual actions (factor 2), of interpersonal actions (factor 3), and educational transmissions (factor 4), which are reduced since these children are illiterate. This implies a convergence of the three groups of factors. But how are they to be differentiated?

(c) In this respect, the third result obtained by Mohseni is interesting. In spite of the dismal situation of the country children, their responses to the operational tasks are superior to their results on the performance tests; whereas one should consider these children as moderately or even severely mentally defective on the basis of the intellectual performance tests alone, they have but two to three years of delay on the conservation tasks, compared with Teheran schoolchildren. Here again, it is obvious that we should not risk a generalization before collecting data from many more cultures. But, in order to show the interest of the problem, and the multiplicity of the various situations still to be studied, let us point out that Boisclair, with Laurendeau and Pinard, has examined schoolchildren in Martinique who are not at all illiterate, since they are attending primary schools with a French curriculum, but who show nevertheless a delay of about four years on the main operational tasks. In this case, the delay seems to be attributable to the general characteristics of social interactions (factor 3, in connection with 2), more than to a lack of educational transmissions (factor 4).

In the case of Iran, the better results on the conservation tasks (indicative of operational mechanisms), compared to the performance tests, seems to indicate a difference in nature between the fairly general coordinations necessary to the functioning of operational structures, and the more special acquisitions relative to performance on particular problems. In the case of a confirmation of such results, this could help to distinguish between factors 2 and 3 taken together (general coordinations of actions, whether individual or interpersonal) and factor 4 (educational transmission). In other words, operational tasks would yield better results because they are bound to the coordinations necessary to intelligence itself, which are the products of progressive equilibration and not of innate biological conditions. Performances would be influenced by special cultural factors, which, in this case, are particularly deficient.

Such are, on the whole, the possibilities of interpretation of cross-cultural studies, such as Mohseni's, provided that the number of these studies be increased. But these are only the broad outlines, and it is important now to examine in detail the role played by the sociocultural factors (factors 3 and 4).

Cultural factors of educational transmission

If the operational structures could not be explained by the laws of the general coordination of actions, according to our hypothesis, one would have to think of more specific factors. Two of the main ones would be (a) educational activities of adults, and (b) language itself, as a crystallization of syntax and semantics which, in their general forms, involve a logic.

(a) The hypothesis of a formative action of education by adults certainly contains a part of the answer. Indeed, even from the perspective of the general coordination of actions (either as overt behaviour or interiorized as operations), the adult, being more advanced than the child, can help him and speed up his development during educational processes in the family or in the school. But the question is whether this factor plays an exclusive part: this was Durkheim's idea, for whom logic emanates (as do ethics and law) from the total structure of society, and is imposed on the individual, through social and especially educational constraints. This is partly Bruner's (1964) idea too, who maintains that one can teach anything, at any age, if one goes about it adequately; but Bruner thought of educational processes less in terms of schooling and more in terms of the American models of learning. With regard to Durkheim's perspective, and not that of Bruner, which is dependent on laboratory experiments[1] more than on cross-cultural studies, facts like those observed in Martinique by the Canadian psychologists seem to indicate that an ordinary schooling, with a French curriculum that facilitates comparison, is not sufficient to ensure a normal development of operational structures, since there are, in this case, three or four years of delay in comparison with Western cultural environments. But here again one should not conclude hastily: one still should differentiate the influences of the family from those of the school. We can simply assert that the cross-cultural method is, on this point as on others, likely to provide the desired solutions.

(b) The important problem of the interactions between language and operational development has been clarified by the studies of Inhelder and Sinclair on the linguistic development of the child, and on the role of language in the learning of operational structures.

[1] These have been done in Geneva by Inhelder and Bovet (Inhelder *et al.*, 1966; Pascual-Leone and Bovet, 1966); actually they are far from verifying Bruner's hypotheses.

L

Without going into the details of the methods and results, which have been described elsewhere (Sinclair, 1967), we shall limit ourselves to emphasizing the perspectives opened by Sinclair's studies from a cross-cultural point of view. Let us recall, for example, the experiment with two groups of children: one group of older children definitely mastered conservation structures (giving explicit jutifications) and one group of younger children were unequivocally nonconserving. The subjects of these two groups are asked to describe some objects (e.g. a short and thick pencil, another one long and thin; several little marbles, a smaller number of bigger marbles). The language used in the two groups differs as to the comparatives used: whereas the nonconserving subjects make use largely of what the linguist Bull has called *scalaries* (e.g. 'big', 'small', 'a lot' or 'a little'), the subjects at the operational level use *vectors* ('more' or 'less', etc.). Furthermore, the structure of the expressions differs: the conservers use binary modes (e.g. 'this one is longer and thinner'), whereas the nonconservers use quaternary modes (e.g. 'this one is thick and the other one is thin; this one is long and the other one is short'). Thus there is a very close correlation between operativity and language, but in which direction? Learning experiments, with which we are not directly concerned here, show that, in conditioning the pre-operational subjects to use the expressions of their elders, one obtains only a slight improvement in operational thinking (one case out of ten). However, there remains to be established whether it is an action of language as such or an influence of the practice in analysis induced by learning, and if a certain progress would not have taken place without this learning through the development of schematas as a function of various activities. Thus it seems that operativity leads to the structuration of language (of course through a choice among pre-existing linguistic models), rather than the reverse.

One immediately sees the great interest there would be in multiplying experiments of this type with various languages. Sinclair found the same results in French and English, but one should turn to very different languages. In Turkish, for example, there is only one vector, which corresponds to our word 'still'; to say 'more', one says 'still much' and to say 'less', 'still little'.

Evidently one will find many other combinations in other languages. In this case it would be of great interest to examine the delay in the development of operational structures as a function of the language used by subjects, and one ought to repeat Sinclair's experiments with children of different levels. The development of the similar structures of thought, in spite of linguistic variations, would argue in favour of the factors of progressive and autonomous equilibration. On the contrary, supposing we should find modification of operations according to the linguistic environments, one ought to examine closely the meaning of these interactions according to Sinclair's experimental model.

CONCLUSION

Psychology elaborated in our environment, which is characterized by a certain culture and a certain language, remains essentially conjectural as long as the necessary cross-cultural material has not been gathered as a control. We would like to see cross-cultural studies of cognitive functions which do not concern the child only but development as a whole, including the final adult stages. When Lévy-Bruhl raised the problem of the 'pre-logic' of 'primitive mentality', he undoubtedly over-emphasized the opposition, in the same way as his posthumous recantation exaggerates perhaps in the other way the universality of structures. It seems to us that a series of questions remains unanswered by the excellent work of Lévi-Strauss: for example, what is the operational level of adults in a tribal organization, as far as the technical intelligence (completely neglected by Lévy-Bruhl), verbal intelligence, the solution of elementary logico-mathematical problems, are concerned? The developmental data relative to the lower age levels will attain full significance only when we know the situation of the adults themselves. In particular it is quite possible (and it is the impression given by the known ethnographic literature) that in numerous cultures adult thinking does not proceed beyond the level of *concrete operations*, and does not reach that of propositional operations, elaborated between 12 and 15 years of age in our culture. It would thus be of great importance to know whether the preceding stages develop more slowly in children of such cultures, or if the equilibrium level which will not be exceeded is reached around 7 to 8 years of age, as with our children, or only with a small delay.

19

M. C. Bovet

Cognitive processes among illiterate children and adults[1]

A great many studies currently deal with the problem of the effects of differing sociocultural environments on mental development. The findings of these studies vary considerably and at times come up with surprising results, the variations being partly due to the different theoretical frameworks of the research and the consequent types of interpretation.

Most cross-cultural studies tend to report differences in the average ages at which success is attained in the various tasks. This type of data, however, is essentially descriptive and does not reveal the nature of the reasoning processes underlying a successful or an unsuccessful performance. What is more, it provides no answer to the question of a possible causal relationship between certain aspects of culture on the one hand, and differences in cognitive development on the other. What is required, therefore, is a theoretical framework which can explain the data.

The present article reports the results of a cross-cultural study carried out along Piagetian lines. The basic epistemological and developmental concern of this theory is to understand the processes of acquiring knowledge, a concern which is relevant to cross-cultural research. A comparison is made between groups of subjects living in two distinct cultural environments (Algeria and Geneva) with regard to the acquisition of different concepts. The types of responses are analysed and a tentative explanation proposed. Reference is also made to the data of one of the rare studies dealing with the same problem, but with a different theoretical approach, and a discussion follows of the methods applied and interpretations given to the two studies.

Before presenting the data, it is important to explain why Piagetian-type problems were selected for a cross-cultural study, and to present

---

[1] Translated from French by Dr Sylvia Opper.

the basic elements of Piaget's theory which make it a fitting framework for cross-cultural work.

Cross-cultural research in cognitive development should attempt to study the acquisition of certain concepts which are fundamental for scientific knowledge, and it should try to answer questions of a general nature, such as the following: 'How universal are these basic concepts?' And more precisely:

1. Is the adult form of these concepts identical in different cultural environments?
2. Do these concepts develop in an identical fashion regardless of cultural environment?
3. If various modes are found in the construction of the concepts or in their final adult form, do these differences occur in all or most basic notions or only in some? Can such differences be related to the daily activities of the various cultural environments?

One difficulty in cross-cultural work is the selection of the most suitable tasks to answer the above questions. Clearly, these tasks must permit the study of the basic concepts that serve as the instruments and foundation of knowledge. Any problems that can be solved by specific techniques or skills are to be avoided, since such skills derive from culture-specific teaching situations. The tasks must therefore be related to basic concepts which are acquired in the course of general daily activities. For instance, IQ tests are not suitable instruments for cross-cultural work because they measure aptitudes or performances which rely too heavily on teacher-transmitted information. Problem-solving tasks are more appropriate, since they permit an analysis of the mental processes involved in their solution. However, the general approach of this method is to record the various strategies of problem-solving, with no reference to the modification of the strategies in the course of development. Since the aim of the present research is to study the influence of culture on both adult thought and on cognitive development, problem-solving situations are not altogether suitable.

Piaget and Inhelder's work on cognitive development, by contrast, consists of studies of basic concepts, such as number (Piaget, 1952), spatial and temporal measurement (Piaget, 1970a, 1970b; Piaget, Inhelder and Szeminska, 1960), quantification of continuous quantities (Piaget and Inhelder, *1941*), or logical concepts of classes and relations (Piaget, 1952). Moreover, Piaget has shown that various levels of reasoning occur in the development of these notions, and that these levels may be analysed and ordered according to their logical structure.

We believe that the three basic aspects of Piaget's theory, namely his biological leanings and his emphasis on the principles of interaction and construction, provide a fitting framework for cross-cultural research (Piaget, *1966*, 1970c). Such research would then attempt to investigate to what extent the cognitive processes are universal, to delineate the respective parts played by the individual and the environment in intellectual development, and to highlight the importance of regulatory mechanisms in the building-up of knowledge.

METHODOLOGICAL PRINCIPLES OF PIAGETIAN THEORY

Piaget's theory attempts to explain the final stage of the cognitive functions through the study of their origins and development, and consequently requires a special method of exploration. With such an approach, it is not enough to record wrong or correct responses to questions. A method must be adopted that can reveal the reasoning processes which lead to a given response. Variations must be introduced into the experimental situation, and a dialogue must be conducted between the experimenter and the subject with the purpose of discovering on what type of reasoning the latter has based his response. The experimenter must have a number of hypotheses on the significance of each response to a given problem and must try to verify these hypotheses in the course of the questioning. This type of approach is quite different from that which relies on standardized questionnaires, but its successful use requires an extensive theoretical and experimental training.

It is evident that the type of data collected by the Piagetian method cannot be analysed by statistical methods that are commonly used in psychology. A qualitative analysis showing the development of thought is called for.

ADAPTATIONS REQUIRED BY CROSS-CULTURAL WORK

When applying the Piagetian method of questioning to cross-cultural research, certain difficulties are encountered.

1. In the first place, the main characteristic of the Piagetian interview is that it consists of a dialogue between the experimenter and the subject, during which the latter is encouraged to express his reasoning processes verbally, by means of arguments which support his judgements. There are many people, however, both adults and children, who are not used to expressing their thoughts, or who have not been taught this in school. In such cases, the Piagetian

type of dialogue becomes extremely difficult, if not impossible. In the section describing the present research, it will be seen that part of the verbal dialogue was replaced by manipulations on the part of the subjects. In this way, it was possible to reveal certain reasoning processes which were not expressed, due to the absence of a dialogue.

2. When comparisons are made between environments with different levels of technology, it is difficult to know whether these differences are reflected in differences in cognitive abilities. An inadequate mental performance within a specific environment may lead the investigator to an incorrect evaluation of the intellectual potential. Cross-cultural studies must therefore attempt to activate any latent cognitive structures which might not be immediately evident. Learning situations in the form of 'exercises in operativity' might serve the purpose of activating such mental structures (Inhelder *et al.*, 1973).

RESEARCH

The concepts selected were amongst those studied by Piaget in Geneva. They included some concepts which are frequently used by our Algerian population in their daily occupations, as well as some which are hardly used at all. The former included the notions of conservation of physical properties (quantity and weight), and the latter certain spatial and temporal concepts such as length, speed and time.

Our hypothesis was that the logical structuring and the types of reasoning used by adults for concepts that are closely linked to everyday activities would reach a higher level than those of concepts which are not frequently used in regular daily activities. Moreover, even if the underlying structure of these activities is based on an intuitive approach rather than on rigorous processes, our belief is that the level of thinking of a given population might nevertheless reach the stages of concrete or formal operations as a result of regulatory coordinations of the various cognitive processes. By contrast, if a concept is not used extensively in everyday activities, it might be inadequately structured.

The present study investigated the development of the notions mentioned above in unschooled children from 6 to 13 years of age, and in illiterate adults between 35 and 50 years of age.

Sample

A number of the adult subjects and the children came from various areas located on the outskirts of Algiers. The inhabitants of these areas were not from the city itself, but had originated from rural areas some 100 to 200 kilometres away, and had emigrated to the capital. The remainder of the population came from two villages, one of which was situated 20 kilometres from Algiers, and the other some 50 kilometres from Orleansville. These villages were each composed of approximately ten houses.

The main characteristics of the daily activities of this population were the following:

(a) The women spent their time doing housework, and, for the most part, rarely left their homes, except for funerals or religious feasts. They never went to the market, since this was the area of the men.

(b) The men, on the other hand, spent the greater part of the day away from their homes, due to the fact that the men who lived on the outskirts of Algiers were usually occupied in selling or bartering in the different urban neighbourhoods. In the villages, the men cultivated small plots of land, or worked in collective agricultural communities. In all cases the men were used to walking several kilometres, either to reach the particular part of the city where they worked in the case of the city dwellers, or to visit neighbouring villages in the case of the rural subjects.

(c) As for the children, they generally remained in their own neighbourhoods, playing games with stones (resembling a game with marbles), or building houses with branches and planks. Boys and girls played together until 8 to 9 years of age, but from then on the girls had to take care of the younger children and to begin to help in the house.

Interviewing procedures and language problems

The interviews were held in Arabic, and were conducted by psychology students of Algiers University who had been trained to interview the subjects and were perfectly competent to do so. No questioning was done at home, since it was felt that this situation would provide too much distraction. The age of the subjects was taken from the family book, in which each family must register the dates of birth of its various members.

Throughout the interview a very flexible approach was adopted. If the experimenter had the impression that the subjects were having difficulty in understanding the instructions or the situation, these would be repeated, several times if necessary.

RESULTS

The results are presented in the same chronological order as they were obtained in the actual study so as to draw attention to the various difficulties encountered.

A. *Children*

1. *Conservation of quantities: liquids and plasticine*
Conservation of liquids and plasticine (clay) were the first tasks to be presented. In both cases, the situation consisted of two initially identical quantities, A and A'. For the liquids, one of these, A, was then poured into a container B of different dimensions, whereas for clay, one of the clay balls, A, was changed into a different shape B. In both cases the subject was then questioned as to whether quantities B and A' were equivalent or not.

Children of 5 to 6 years ($N = 8$) gave nonconservation responses for all changes in shape, and when asked to explain their judgements they referred to the action of pouring in the case of the liquid or of changing the shape in the case of clay, as well as to the difference in appearance between the initial and subsequent situations. This type of response is similar to the reactions of Genevan children.

Children of 7 to 8 years ($N = 12$), on the other hand, had quite different reactions and affirmed the conservation of quantity, despite the changes in shape. It seemed, however, that the subjects of this age paid surprisingly little attention to the dimensions of the objects; this was particularly clear when we tried to draw their attention to these features with the aim of obtaining a justification of their judgements of invariance (e.g. the compensation of the two dimensions which had been changed). It was not possible to elicit verbal comments since our questions had the effect of upsetting the children; they were evidently not used to this type of interrogation. Consequently, it was difficult to discover the reasoning processes underlying the judgements of invariance.

To get around the above difficulty we then presented the following additional situations relating to the same notions, but which instead of requiring verbal explanations, called for actions and manipulations by the subject.

(a) The child was asked to pour quantities of liquid as equal as possible into pairs of glasses which differ either in diameter (c, c'), or in height (b, b'), or in both dimensions (a, a') (Fig. 19.1a).

(b) One full and several empty glasses of different dimensions were shown and the children were asked to indicate how high the level of the liquid would be if it was poured into one of the empty glasses. After each prediction, the liquid was actually poured, and the children could observe how right or wrong they had been (Fig. 19.1b).

Fig. 19.1a

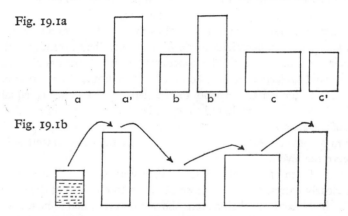

Fig. 19.1b

With Genevan subjects, a-problems are correctly solved at about the same time age as conservation problems, while b-problems are solved rather earlier.

The answers to these problems given by the 5 to 6 year old Algerian group were the same as those of Genevan subjects of the nonconservation stage for quantity.

To our surprise, the 7 to 8 year old group, who had given conservation judgements, gave incorrect responses.

(a) In the pouring problems, the children poured out 'a little here and a little there', and refused to say beforehand what level they wanted to reach, or they filled both glasses completely, without taking into account the differences in size.

(b) For the questions involving a prediction of the height of the level of the liquid, the answers of this group of children were quite inconsistent; they did not coordinate the diameter of the glasses and the level of the liquid. It was clear that the subjects had not learned from the previous situations where they had had the opportunity to observe levels after pouring.

These types of responses are totally different from the reactions of Genevan conserving subjects; the latter are always able to coordinate the two dimensions, since they compensate for a smaller diameter by making the level go up higher. This led us to doubt the validity of the statements of invariance of quantity and, as a result, to continue our research with older subjects.

An additional group of 8 to 9 year olds was consequently tested ($N = $ 10), and it was found that, contrary to the above 7 to 8 year olds, they gave nonconserving responses in the conservation tasks. Their judgements, however, were not identical to those of the 5 to 6 year old group, since their explanations made it clear that they carefully took the dimensions into account. The nonconservation judgements of these 8 to 9 year old subjects were based on the levels of liquid. Furthermore, these subjects tended to respond to the a-problems (pouring equal quantities) by pouring out liquid to equal levels, regardless of the diameters of the glasses. The responses to b-problems (prediction of levels) tended to become correct after a few trials, where the subjects were able to observe the levels.

A group of 9 to 11 year olds, intermediate stage ($N = $ 15), gave responses closely corresponding to those of Genevan children of the same stage. In the a-problems, their actions showed that they had some idea of compensating for a smaller diameter by a higher level of the liquid, and immediately found correct solutions for the prediction problems (b-problems).

Finally, 10 to 12 year old subjects ($N = $ 6) affirmed the invariance of quantity, justifying judgements by arguments of reversibility, identity, or compensation, which indicate the existence of a system of logical reasoning. For both the a- and b-problems, the subjects of this group gave correct solutions based on the understanding of the relation between diameter and height of the liquid.

The above findings have two unusual features. In the first place, we note the reappearance at 8 to 9 years of nonconservation judgements, although there appears to be conservation at 7 to 8 years. This nonconservation is then followed by a progressive development resulting in conservation at 12 years of age. Secondly, we note the correspondence from 8 to 9 years onwards in the types of responses to the conservation problems, and those of the pouring of liquids and predictions of levels, whereas this does not appear to be the case for the younger children.

These findings confirmed our doubts about the validity of the conservation responses of the 7 to 8 year old group, and our conclusion was that the responses of this group were not based on the same sort of reasoning as those of the 12 year old subjects. We therefore decided to present, once again, the conservation tasks. Our reasons were that the previous experiments on the pouring of equal quantity and level-prediction might have had some learning effects which would result in an improvement of the conservation judgements. It was also felt that this repetition would serve as a control for any possible misunderstanding that might have existed between children and experimenter.

The 5 to 6 year old group showed the same responses to the repeated task as during the initial situation. To our surprise, however, the results of the 7 to 8 year old group showed a regression when compared with their initial responses. Most judgements were now nonconserving, although some children showed fluctuations. Judgements were now based on the modified dimensions, a feature which had not appeared to influence their answers previously. No compensation was, however, made between the dimensions, and quantity was judged on the basis of the most noticeable feature, the level.

For the conservation problems, the pattern of acquisition is given in Table 19.1.

In the two older age-groups there was an improvement when compared with earlier responses. At 8 to 9 years dimensions were now compared, although not in a systematic fashion, and this resulted in a few conservation responses. The 10 to 11 year old group coordinated the dimensions and changes in form, and thus produced logical conservation judgements.

2. *Conservation of weight*

Thirty-nine subjects were given the conservation of weight task, thirty-one of whom had already been given the liquid and clay conservation tasks. The child was asked to produce two clay balls, A and A', of equal weight, as measured by hand. Ball A was then divided into four or six pieces, B was left untouched, and the child was asked whether the weights of A' and B were equal or not.

TABLE 19.1. *Type of response to conservation of quantity task*

		Global NC	Non-opera-tional C	Dimen-sional NC and inter-mediate	Inter-mediate	Opera-tional C	
							Total N
Initial presenta-tion	N	8	12	10	15	6	51
	Age-group (years)	5–6	7–8	8–9	9–11	10–12	
Final presenta-tion	N	8	3	14	11	15	51
	Age-group (years)	5–6	7–8	7–9	8–10	9–12	

NC = Nonconservation.   C = Conservation.

The results will not be presented at great length, since they are very similar to those of the conservation of liquid and plasticine described above. The following types of responses were observed:

1. Nonconservation responses based on an overall judgement of non-identity of form ('global' NC).
2. Conservation judgements which were not supported or explicitly justified, but were maintained even when the experimenter drew attention to the changed dimensions (non-operational C).
3. Nonconservation judgements based on detailed aspects of the dimensions (small pieces versus large ball; lots of pieces versus a single ball, etc.) (dimensional NC).
4. Fluctuating responses of an intermediate level with some fragile conservation responses (intermediate −), or a variety of responses ending up with conservation (intermediate +).
5. Explicit conservation responses supported by precise arguments which indicate a logical understanding of the problem (operational C).

The ages of the subjects producing these different types of responses overlap to a certain extent, but a developmental trend may be clearly seen (Table 19.2).

The above findings are very similar to those of the liquids and plasticine tasks, in that there are two levels of nonconservation judge-

TABLE 19.2. *Type of response to conservation of weight task*

	Global NC	Non-opera-tional C	Dimen-sional NC	Inter-mediate	Opera-tional C	
N	5	6	8	11	9	Total N 39
Age-group (years)	5–6	7–9	9–10	9–11	12–13	

NC = Nonconservation.   C = Conservation.

ments, and two levels of conservation. The first nonconservation results from a global apprehension of the change in appearance, whereas the latter nonconservation results from a detailed analysis of the changes in the dimensions. As for the two levels of conservation, the first is characterized by a lack of apprehension of the dimensions, and the second by a precise coordination of these various dimensions. The development of this notion shows the same trend from NC, through intermediate to operational C, interrupted by the appearance of fragile C responses at an early age.

3. *Spatial relations: conservation of length*

The concept of length was studied by means of two situations:

(1) A conservation problem: of two sticks, A and B, of different lengths, the longest, A, was broken into pieces and laid out so that both ends of both sticks A and B coincided. Later, the pieces of the long stick A were put down so that the right-hand end of the straight stick B extended byond the right end of A, while the left-hand ends of both A and B coincided (cf. Figs. 19.2a and 19.2b).

(2) A construction problem. The experimenter built two models with branches of irregular length, and asked the child to build two straight 'roads' of the same length as the models. The starting point of the child's construction was indicated to him and was situated beneath one end of a zig-zag model (Fig. 19.2c), or a little beyond one end of a straight model (Fig. 19.2d).

These problems were presented to thirty-three children from 6 to 12 years of age. The findings showed similarities in the responses to the two types of problems.

At 6 to 7 years the children produced nonconservation judgements for both situations of problem 1. When the child had to build a line of equal length (problem 2), his construction coincided with both ends of the model, without taking into account the zigzags in between. This

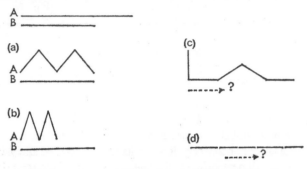

Fig. 19.2

type of response shows a lack of differentiation between the order of the ends and the length of the interval between the initial and the final ends.

At 7 to 9 years there were some cases of judgements of invariance for the conservation situation when the two ends coincided, but when one end extended beyond the other, the judgements were still based on the overlap. In the construction problem for the straight model, the children did make their 'road' go slightly beyond the right-hand end of the given model, so as to compensate for the difference in the starting points at the other end. For the zigzag model, however, the solution was to have the two ends of both sticks coincide. These responses were thus transitional and slightly superior to those of the 6 to 7 year old group.

The subjects of a 8 to 10 year old group gave clear judgements of invariance of length in the situation where the two ends coincided, but fluctuated between nonconservation and invariance for the situation where the shorter stick extended beyond the other. Responses to the construction situation with the straight model where the initial ends did not coincide were correct, but the subjects continued to produce solutions where the two ends coincided for the zigzag model, though sometimes they made their own construction extend slightly beyond the final end of the model.

Finally, at 10 to 12 years, judgements of invariance were given for both conservation problems, and correct constructions were made for both models.

The developmental trend for these two types of problems for the notion of length can be seen in Table 19.3.

TABLE 19.3. *Type of response to conservation of length tasks*

Conservation task	Nonconservation	Intermediate −	Intermediate +	Conservation
Construction task	Primitive solutions (correspondence of end points)	Intermediate solutions −	Intermediate solutions +	Correct solutions
N	8	10	10	5
Age-group (years)	6–7	7–9	8–10	10–12

Total *N* for the *N* row: 33

The following remarks need to be made:

1. Both the responses noted and the developmental trend correspond to Genevan results; no unexpected responses were observed.
2. The average age of acquisition of this notion was a little higher than in Geneva, since these problems are generally solved by 9 years of age by the Genevan subjects (Inhelder, 1968, and Inhelder *et al.*, 1973).

Comparison between response patterns to conservation of quantities and length tasks

For the concept of quantity, conservation responses were noted at 7 to 8 years, although these were not of the same type as the conservation responses at 12 years, or those elicited from the 10 to 11 year old group by various operational exercises.

For the notion of weight, the same phenomenon of conservation judgements, which are not based on a system of operations, was observed at a slightly different age than for the above concept, so that the explicitly logical judgements were only found around 12 to 13 years of age.

In both types of problems, therefore, there seems to be a sort of precocious conservation resulting in a temporary deflection from the developmental trend which is generally characterized by a gradual cognitive construction leading to logical conservation.

The notion of the conservation of length, on the other hand, shows an identical development in Algerian subjects as that observed in Geneva, with the exception of a slight difference in the age of acquisition.

These variations in the development of two distinct notions are more interesting than a simple difference in the age of acquisition between two cultural environments. They point to the existence of two types of notions, the one parallel to the trends noted in Geneva, the other showing a deviation. Data obtained from an adult population might help us to explain these differences in development.

One further point which might be made is that the relationship between the ages is not the same as in the Geneva data. The notions of conservation of quantities (liquid and plasticine) and length are all acquired at the same age by the Algerian subjects (approximately 10 to 11 years), whereas the conservation of weight is acquired later (at 12 to 13 years). In Geneva, on the other hand, the notions of weight and length are acquired at the same age (approximately 9 years), whereas the conservation of liquid and plasticine is reached earlier (7 to 8 years). The present cross-cultural comparison therefore shows up a difference in the order of acquisition.

B. *Adults*[1]

The same conservation tasks were also presented to an unschooled population of adults of the same cultural environment, aged from 35 to 50 years.

1. With regard to the *concepts of quantity*, the liquid conservation and pouring problems presented no difficulty. By contrast, two unusual types of responses were noted for the *weight* conservation problem:

   (a) Several female subjects refused to make a judgement after one of the clay balls had been broken into several pieces. These subjects said that it was impossible for them to judge without first weighing the clay in their hands, and refused to 'guess'.

   (b) Moreover, in several instances, the initial response was a conservation one. Then when the experimenter, in an attempt to obtain a justification for this response, pointed out the differences in appearance of the two objects, the subjects would

[1] For a more detailed description of the research see Bovet, 1971.

no longer give a conservation response. In the course of the dialogue, however, the subjects would return to a conservation judgement, and would be able to relate the various dimensions of the objects by means of a reasoning based on compensation. These adults' reactions seem to replicate in a condensed sequence the developmental trends noted in the children where an initial non-operational conservation finally becomes, at a later stage, an explicit conservation judgement.

For some of the nonconserving subjects, all that was required for them to grasp the notion of conservation was to weigh the two pieces of clay once on a pair of scales in front of them. They then accompanied their judgements by logical justifications and, what is more, generalized their conservation responses to various changes in shape.

It has been noted, however, that in the case of children a single demonstration is not sufficient to elicit a more advanced judgement (Smedslund, 1961). We conclude therefore that in these adult subjects an underlying logical way of apprehending the problem coexists with an intuitive approach.

2. Three types of problems dealing with *spatial-temporal relations* were also presented. A *length* problem was solved by most of the subjects, but often only after a period of trial and error which allowed them to correct their initially incorrect responses.

A problem dealing with various aspects of the concepts of *speed* was found to be more difficult: less than half the subjects were able to give correct solutions, and only after a number of repetitions of the problem.

Finally, it was found that the majority of our subjects did not have a stable grasp of the concept of *time* which we investigated by means of a variety of situations. On the one hand we had considerable difficulty in getting our subjects to understand the problem we were presenting, and on the other, the results which we were able to obtain corresponded to the non-operational level of responses of Genevan subjects.

It must be noted that for all three problems the responses seemed to correspond to certain typical characteristics of the developmental stages for these concepts in children. These results are therefore in striking contrast with those for the concept of weight where we discovered responses that have not been noted in research carried out in Geneva.

DISCUSSION OF OTHER FINDINGS AND INTERPRETATIONS

(a) Bruner and Greenfield (Greenfield, 1966) have also studied the problem of conservation of liquid, but with a population of unschooled Senegalese children. In their findings they were struck by the attitude of many of these children, who did not concentrate on the perceptual features of the situation, such as the dimensions of the diameter, or the level of the water, but focused their attention on the action of pouring. When schooled children of the same area were given the tasks, their responses indicated that they paid considerable attention to the perceptual features. This was also true of an American population. These authors conclude that 'the first effect of schooling is to increase their analytic attention to the perceptible features of situations such as our experiment' (Greenfield, 1966, p. 237).

Unschooled children of the two cultures studied, in Algeria and Senegal, seem to have a different approach from children with schooling. This differential approach would explain to a certain extent the precocious conservation observed in the Algerian children of 7 to 8 years. After a number of exercises, these same children regress to nonconservation judgements based in particular on the perceptual features which had previously been neglected. Furthermore, an older group of children of the same population also gave nonconservation judgements for the same reasons. From this stage onwards, the development of the notion is the same as for the Genevan children, that is, it is characterized by a gradual comparison of the dimensions which later results in their coordination by compensation, an indication of conservation based on a system of operations. At this point we should like to disagree with Bruner and Greenfield when they state that the increase in attention to perceptual features resulting from schooling '. . . is followed by a systematic and drastic reduction of the importance of such features' (Greenfield, 1966, p. 237). We believe that it is not so much a question of the reduction of the importance of these features, as their mastery by coordination, and it is this coordination which results in an understanding of the compensation in the changes of dimensions which occur through the act of pouring.

The same remarks apply to Bruner's learning experiments on conservation with a population of schooled children in the United States (Bruner, 1964).

Bruner and Greenfield also did some learning experiments with the unschooled Senegalese children which try to minimize the concentration on the act of pouring. They believe that the child attributes a 'magical' element to the pouring, due to the fact that it is done by the experimenter: '. . . the child . . . is willing to attribute "magical" powers to an authority figure like the experimenter . . .' (Greenfield, 1966, p. 245). Consequently, they alter their technique by asking the children to pour the water themselves, both in the initial situation of producing the two equal quantities in identical glasses and in the subsequent situation of pouring the liquid from one glass into containers of different shapes. This simple modification in technique, called the 'pouring procedure', results in several nonconservation judgements becoming conservation responses: at 6 to 7 years they find an increase from 25 per cent to 70 per cent of correct responses (Greenfield, 1966, p. 247). Bruner and Greenfield believe that in this way they have promoted the acquisition of conservation.

Our own feeling is that in both the pouring and the masking procedures, there is a shifting of attention, but that in the former case the attention is shifted from one aspect of the action to another, whereas in the latter it is shifted from one perceptual feature to others. Whenever the experimenter carries out the action of pouring the water, either in the initial situation when he makes the initial quantities equal, or in the later changes in containers, the young child responds to the most striking and recent action, that is to the actual pouring into a container of a different shape, and this leads to nonconservation responses. When the child himself carries out all the action, his attention is more concentrated on the initial action, making the quantities equal, since it is a difficult task to pour out exactly equal quantities in two glasses. Consequently, the subsequent act of pouring into a different glass is de-emphasized.

The result of this focus on the initial act of making the quantities equal leads to judgements of equality, rather than of nonconservation, that is to say to 'correct' responses. It is doubtful, however, whether these correct responses indicate a better understanding of the notion than the nonconservation responses. By contrast, we think that the nonconservation responses of the Algerian subjects of 7 to 8 years who were again given the conservation task after the exercises show a deeper understanding of the problem than in their initial conservation judgements.

One further criticism of Bruner and Greenfield's results might be that their table of correct responses (Greenfield, 1966, fig. 2, p. 233) shows a figure of 45 per cent for the 8 to 9 year old group, which seems somewhat high when compared with our own results. The 11 to 13 year old group, on the other hand, shows a figure of only 50 per cent correct responses, which seems very low and would suggest relatively

little progress between the two age-groups. It is possible that the responses of the two groups are not based on the same reasoning processes,
and that only the conservation responses of the 11 to 13 year olds are
similar to judgements based on systematic logical reasoning. It is also
possible that if a group of 9 to 10 year old subjects had been questioned,
they would have given nonconservation or fluctuating responses, typical
of the transitional stage. From our point of view, the responses of 9 to 10
year olds would have been interesting, since these might have shown the
existence of a significant stage in the overall development of this notion.

Before ending this 'critical' analysis, we should like to stress the
intrinsic value of Greenfield's (1966) study which seeks to provide an
explanation of certain unusual characteristics of the findings by means of
a more extensive investigation.

(b) We would like to comment briefly on an article (Furby, 1971)
where a theoretical framework is proposed for the interpretation of
cross-cultural data refering particularly to Greenfield's (1966) study of
the conservation of continuous quantities. Furby states that the conservation problem depends upon the acquisition of three types of reasoning: (1) conservation of identity; (2) transitivity or logical thinking; and
(3) a perceptual flexibility which, according to the author, consists of
conserving an equality judgement in spite of perceptual differences.

L. Furby proposes a classification based on the distinction between
Western and non-Western types of culture, and between manual
versus automated environment. Western cultures would be characterized by empirical reasoning whereas non-Western cultures would use
magical reasoning. Empirical reasoning is conducive towards the
acquisition of conservation of identity and transitivity, whereas magical
reasoning inhibits these acquisitions. Furthermore a manual environment results in a great deal of perceptual flexibility, while this skill is
barely developed in an automated environment.

Greenfield's sample characteristics are discussed within this particular framework. The unschooled Senegalese bush children reason
magically, and thus fail to conserve identity and to master transitivity,
but since they live in a manual environment, they have considerable
perceptual flexibility. To quote Furby: 'the bush child is more adept at
assessing perceptual cues as indicators of object properties' (p. 247).
The city Senegalese, or American children, are taught to reason empirically on the basis of their own observations, and thus are good at the
conservation of identity, and at transitivity, but have less perceptual
flexibility, since they live in an automated environment.

The distinction between magical and empiricial reasoning does not seem to us to be a valid one. On the contrary we have distinguished between an intuitive and a logical approach. Moreover, we have two main objections to Furby's interpretation of perceptual flexibility. First both Greenfield's data and our own observations with Algerian children refute the statement that bush children have great perceptual flexibility. Indeed, one notable characteristic of these subjects is that they are 'action centred' (Greenfield, 1966), and that they pay no attention to the perceptual features in the experimental situation. The Algerian findings also show clearly, in the prediction and pouring problems, that the younger children's analysis of the dimensions is inadequate and becomes systematic and coherent at a much later age than in Genevan children (or in any subjects from an automated environment). These findings seem to contradict Furby's notion of perceptual flexibility. Furthermore, and this is our second criticism, Furby believes that the greater the child's perceptual flexibility, the more is he able to *neglect* the perceptual features; or, in her own words: '... to teach the child to ignore irrelevant perceptual differences – in other words to increase his perceptual flexibility ...' (p. 251). In Piaget's view, however, conservation is not a result of the child's *ignoring* the perceptual differences, but of his coordinating them by means of a logical understanding of the transformation. This is the same criticism that we made of Bruner and Greenfield's method of masking the disturbing perceptual features in order to obtain correct conservation responses.

These remarks explain why we are somewhat reluctant to accept as such Furby's proposed framework for cross-cultural interpretations.

GENERAL DISCUSSION

(a) *Adults*

How do our findings relate to the hypothesis, which directed the choice of the two types of notions studied in the present research, based on the extent of usage in the everyday activities of the population under study?

With regard to the activities associated with the notions of conservation of quantity, the following remarks may be made. In the area of weight, the information collected on the household activities of the women showed that they often used weight measurement, particularly when baking bread. Scales were never used for this activity, although the women knew how to use such an instrument. The procedure was to estimate the required weight in their hands. It was obvious from the interviews that the women were extraordinarily skilful in equalizing the weight of the two clay balls used in the experiment, and that weighing in the hand was an effective measuring instrument for them.

The unusual response of a refusal to give a judgement before being able to hold the modified ball of clay in their hands, and the behaviour which consisted of an initial conservation judgement followed by a regression as soon as attention was drawn to the changed dimensions, were observed only in the women. The behaviour of the men consisted of either stable conservation responses, or truly nonconserving ones.

One explanation of these types of responses might be that the proprioceptive and intuitive method of weight measurement used by women in their daily activities is reflected in their method of apprehending the problem of the experimental situation. However, as stated above, they were quite capable of producing a logical justification of the equality of weight, once this equality had been shown up by measuring on the scales. It is interesting to observe therefore the existence of two concomitant ways of approaching the problem, with an intuitive approach characteristic of everyday practical use being the spontaneous response, and at the same time the logical approach being latent.

In the case of the spatial and temporal relations, one might ask what features of daily activities bear some relation to these notions? The women are very much tied to their homes, and rarely leave them to go out and walk. The men, on the contrary, spend a great deal of their time away from home, and walk considerable distances. As for the children, they run around in the neighbourhood of their homes. The general impression is that there is no feeling of having to get a certain activity accomplished within a specific time limit. This applies both to the travelling and the agricultural activities of the men, and the household chores of the women.

The findings indicate that the majority of the subjects have a good understanding of the notion of length, although correct responses are often only reached after a period of trial and error.

It is important to point out that the responses of all the men questioned were immediately correct, whereas the women gradually reached the correct responses by a process of trial and error. This differential approach between men and women might be due to their varying modes of existence, the women being bound to their homes, and the men being accustomed to travelling around, choosing short cuts, etc. The problems of speed and time, on the other hand, indicated no differences between women and men. The major difficulties noted in the experimental situations, therefore, seem to be a direct reflection of the general lack of use of these notions of daily activities.

(b) *Children*

Differences between the responses to the problems of conservation of quantities and those of the spatio-temporal situations were noted in both adults and children. In the case of quantity conservation, the responses were characterized by the presence of unusual reactions and a deviation in the developmental trend, whereas for the spatial-temporal relations, a certain amount of difficulty was noted as well as a simple delay in the age of acquisition.

Three characteristics of the cultural environment might provide explanations for the types of responses observed in the Algerian subjects of the present research. As mentioned above, one of the most striking aspects of the responses was the lack of attention paid by the younger subjects to the perceptual features, which is in distinct contrast to the types of behaviour noted in Geneva. Bruner and Greenfield (Greenfield, 1966) have also observed this feature amongst unschooled children in Senegal, and we entirely agree with their view that schooling plays a specific part in developing an analytic approach which results in a precise comparison of the dimensions of the objects involved.

A further point to be mentioned is that the eating and cooking utensils (bowls, glasses, plates) of the particular environment studied were of all shapes and sizes, which makes it somewhat difficult to make any comparisons of dimensions. Furthermore, the way of serving food at table was for each person to help from a communal dish, rather than for one person to share it out amongst those present; no comparison of the size of the portions takes place. Finally, the attitude of the mother who does not use any measuring instrument, but 'knows' how much to use by means of intuitive approximations and estimations, may have some influence on the child's attitude. Thus, adult modes of thought can influence the development of notions of conservation of quantity in the child by means of familiar types of activities, in which the child participates, even if only as spectator. It is important to note in this respect that during the interviews with the adults, the same sequence of reactions were observed as those noted during the development of the notions in children. Moreover, the adult responses indicated that for the notion of weight, a logical type of reasoning was concomitant with an intuitive use of the notion in the course of daily activities, and that the former type of reasoning could be activated by means of appropriate exercises. In the same way, in the acquisition of conservation of quantity, the deviation observed at 7 to 8 years is only temporary, and the logical understanding of these notions is acquired regularly at later ages, or can be activated by certain types of practice.

The concept of length was acquired by 11 to 12 years of age, which is slightly behind the Geneva norms. These problems are also solved with a certain amount of difficulty by the major portion of the adult population. The important factors for this concept appear to be schooling, and the influence of adult reasoning on the rate of development. (The problems of speed and time were not given to the children, owing to the difficulty of explaining the experimental situations.)

The above discussion may suggest some answers to the three problems set out at the beginning of this article.

1. Concepts of physical properties and the spatial relations of lengths seem to have a similar meaning for the adults in the two cultures compared. The results concerning the problems of speed and time, however, showed that the lack of environmental pressure towards the use of a particular type of concept could lead to unstable adult reasoning in this area.

2. With children, we have seen that certain characteristics of a given cultural environment can produce important variations in concept formation, such as the deviation in the acquisition of conservation of quantity. In the present case, this deviation was a temporary one, which reveals the strength of the mechanisms of cognitive development. It is quite possible, however, that other kinds of environmental features may result in more permanent types of deviations.

3. Finally, our suggestion was that a certain causal relationship existed between the everyday activities implying the application of particular notions, on the one hand, and certain forms of reasoning observed in the course of the experimental situations, on the other.

Notwithstanding the limitations of the present research, it would seem that the frequent use of a variety of activities related to basic scientific concepts is beneficial for the logical development of such concepts, even when the activities are intuitive rather than logical. By contrast, the infrequent use of such activities in everyday life seems to lead to certain shortcomings in logical reasoning.

Before ending, we should like to return to some *methodological aspects* of cross-cultural research. It is evident from the literature in this area that there is a need for general principles that would render the different data comparable, and permit valid analysis of the reasoning processes underlying the observed behaviour. In this respect, we feel that the basic principles of Piaget's developmental epistemology (e.g. Piaget, *1950*) provide a useful frame of reference.

In our investigation, instead of establishing a rigid plan, we proceeded in a gradual manner, deciding on additional experimentation whenever initial results led to a new hypothesis. This step-by-step procedure yielded some encouraging results.

(a) In the first place it showed how useful, and even necessary, it is to modify an essentially verbal procedure by which the subject is required to provide verbal judgements in an experimental situation, and to replace this type of interview with situations where the subject is required to manipulate the material, or construct certain models. These changes in procedure are especially necessary for children with whom it proves difficult to have a real dialogue, but they are also recommended with adults when discussing unfamiliar concepts. For instance, the pouring-of-equal-quantities problems made us wonder what kind of reasoning led the children to their correct judgements of conservation. When it appeared that these judgements were not based on a logical system of reasoning, we pursued the investigation until a later stage, when such reasoning was fully acquired.

Our own study of the notions of speed and time with adults, which involved only situations requiring judgements, remains thus inadequate, particularly since the problems proved to be difficult for our subjects.

(b) Secondly, the introduction of certain problems that resemble learning situations is in our opinion necessary in cross-cultural research. The findings of the present study have shown the effects of exercises which in this case consisted of prediction and construction situations for the notion of conservation of quantity, and their role in revealing the lack of logical basis of certain precocious conservation judgements. These exercises also served to show up the essential, constructive nature of the phase when the subject makes a detailed analysis of the various dimensions of the objects. The use of scales in the weight problems, although not actually an exercise in itself, did provide the opportunity for the adult subjects to express a logical type of reasoning which was not evident in their initial responses.

The use of learning situations therefore seems essential in any cross-cultural study, in order to try and reach the potential reasoning capacity of the subjects. A number of precautions must, however, be taken. If these learning techniques are related to the Piagetian type of concepts, they need to come within the framework of Piagetian theory, that is to say, they should consist of 'exercises in operativity'.

20

A. Heron and M. Simonsson (1969)

Weight conservation in Zambian children: a nonverbal approach

International Journal of Psychology, 4(4), pp. 281–92

The research literature on the application of Piaget's approach in countries where the cultural milieu of the child is markedly different from that to be expected in Europe or North America is not extensive. If the field is narrowed to consider only the stage of concrete operations and the appearance of conservation behaviour, the list becomes even shorter (Aden: Hyde, 1959; Nigeria: Price-Williams, 1961; Hong Kong: Goodnow, 1962; Senegal: Greenfield, 1966; Australian Aborigines: de Lemos, 1966; Papua-New Guinea: Prince, 1968b; Jamaica, Canadian Esquimaux and Indians: Vernon, 1969). There is also work by Boisclair in Martinique and by Mohseni in Iran, referred to by Piaget (*1966*). Although these investigators have varied in their precise use of the Genevan 'clinical method', all have depended on verbal communication with the child, whether direct or through an interpreter, and in either the mother tongue or a second language. The Zambian study now to be described is, so far as can be ascertained, the first in which conservation behaviour has been evaluated by a nonverbal method among children from a non-European cultural background.

METHOD

The samples

These were drawn from two urban schools in Kitwe, the largest town in the Copperbelt of Zambia, with a population of about 200,000. One school is non-fee-paying and all the children are Zambian Africans; the other school, formerly segregated for the use of non-African children during the years of the defunct Federation of Rhodesia and Nyasaland,

TABLE 20.1. *Distribution by grade and by age (African 'stated',*

Stated or ve[rified]

School grade		5 E	5 A	6 E	6 A	7 E	7 A	8 E	8 A	9 E	9 A	10 E	10 A	I
7	C													
	?													
	NC													
	Σ													
6	C										5	1		
	?													
	NC													
	Σ										5	1		
5	C									2	9	6		
	?										2	1		
	NC									1	2			
	Σ									3	13	7		
4	C						2	1	3	6	2	4		
	?						1	1	2			1		
	NC						3	2	4	2		1		
	Σ						6	4	9	8	2	6		
3	C					6	5	3	1	3	1			
	?						7		1	4	2			
	NC				1					2	5			
	Σ				1	6	12	3	2	9	8			
2	C		1		2	2		5	2	1				
	?			1	6	3		3						
	NC		2	1	2	2	1	3	2	1				
	Σ		3	2	10	7	1	11	4	2				
1	C		1	1		1		1						
	?		4	2		3		1						
	NC	1	4	6	1	4		5						
	Σ	1	9	9	1	8		7						
T	C		2	1	2	9	7	10	6	11	16	13		
	?		4	3	6	6	8	5	3	4	2	4		
	NC	1	6	7	4	6	4	10	5	6	2	7		
	Σ	1	12	11	12	21	19	25	14	21	20	24		
%	C	—	17	9	17	43	37	40	43	52	80	54		
	?	—	33	27	50	28	42	20	21	19	10	17		
	NC	100	50	64	33	29	21	40	36	29	10	29		

age

12 A	12 E	13 A	13 E	14 A	14 E	15 A	15 E	16 A	16 E	17 A	17 E	Total A	Total E	% A	% E
	9	1	1	4	1	8		2		2		17	11	59	85
	1	2		1		1				1		5	1	17	8
	1	2		1				4				7	1	24	7
	11	5	1	6	1	9		6		3		29	13		
8	4	1		2								12	14	39	82
5		1		3								9	1	29	6
3	1	4		1		2						10	2	32	12
16	5	6		6		2						31	17		
4		3		3								16	13	54	72
4		3		1		1						10	2	33	11
2		2										4	3	13	17
10		8		4		1						30	18		
6				3								20	7	69	41
1		1										4	3	14	18
												5	7	17	41
7		1		3								29	17		
2												15	6	50	40
1				1								8	8	27	53
												7	1	23	7
3				1								30	15		
												10	3	37	21
1												8	6	30	43
												9	5	33	36
1												27	14		
												3	1	13	9
												6	4	25	36
												15	6	62	55
												24	11		
0	13	5	1	12	1	8		2		2					
2	1	7		6		2				1					
5	2	8		2		2		4							
7	16	20	1	20	1	12		6		3		200	105		
4	81	25	100	60	100	67		33		67					
2	6	35	—	30	—	16		—		33					
4	13	40	—	10	—	17		67		—					

is fee-paying and, although open to children regardless of their ethnic group, at present contains only a small number of Zambian Africans. The premises, equipment and teaching methods of the fee-paying school at the time of this study were superior to those of the other school. This is not surprising in view of the fact that prior to the achievement of independence by Zambia, the amount spent on the education of African children was one-tenth that spent on those in the Federal segregated school system. The samples obtained from these two schools consist of 117 boys and 108 girls from the non-fee-paying school (all African) and 60 boys and 51 girls from the fee-paying school (all of European extraction and upbringing). As will be seen in Table 20.1 (pp. 336–7), these came from all seven grades of the primary system. For all but a few of the African children it was not possible to obtain a verified age: the range of 'stated' ages is from 7 to 17 years. For the other sample, the range of verified ages is from 5 to 14 years, all but three children falling within the range of 6 to 12 years.

Procedure

Each child was seen individually, an explanation having been given to him or her previously by the teacher that 'a game is to be played with this visiting teacher in which it is a rule of the game that neither of you is allowed to speak'. (During the training and practice periods, the question 'Do you see?' and the encouragement 'Good' were in fact used following pilot studies.) The nonverbal or miming method employed was that developed by Furth (1966) for use with deaf children.[1] In essence, this method involves three stages: the first consists of practice with actual scale-weights of one ounce and one ‚pound, followed in the present procedure by weights of two ounces and half-pound; the second with obviously equal and obviously unequal balls of plasticine; and the third stage is the test itself. The object of the two stages of practice is to ensure that the child has fully understood that 'same weight' is indicated by a horizontal movement of both hands simultaneously, and that a judgement of 'heavier' must be communicated by allowing the hand concerned to fall sharply to the table. A criterion of six consecutive correct trials (two equal, two left heavier, two right heavier) is required before passing from the first stage to the second, and again before starting the test proper.

---

[1] The author is grateful to Professor G. Jahoda for drawing his attention to this possibility.

The test

This, following Furth, consists of thirteen trials as follows:

1. two similar balls	8. one ball – one ring
2. one ball – one snake	9. one disc – one ring
3. half ball – one snake	10. half disc – half ring
4. two similar balls	11. half disc and half ring
5. one ball – two halves	in each hand
6. one ball – one half	12. one ball – half ring
7. two similar balls	13. two similar balls

Furth describes 1, 4, 7 and 13 as 'base' trials; 5, 10 and 11 as 'dividing'; 3, 6 and 12 as 'control'; and 2, 8 and 9 as 'critical'. He does not, however, make explicit his use of the first three groups in arriving at a criterion for conservation: a perfect performance on the 'critical' group is required. He employed a 'second attempt' procedure in respect of items where the child was hesitant or made an error and then corrected himself. This took place after the first full series had been completed.

For the present study, the following criteria were established: (a) 'second attempt' results obtained for all incorrect or hesitant responses in first series; (b) two of the three 'control' items required as evidence of test comprehension and absence of 'set' to respond identically to all thirteen items - failure to meet this criterion resulted in the rejection of the protocol as unreliable; (c) from Ss meeting (b), those with all three 'critical' items correct who also met the double criterion of three of four and two of three correct respectively in *both* the other groups ('base' and 'dividing') were classified as conservers; (d) those also meeting this double criterion who obtained only two of the three 'critical' items were classified as '?',[1] together with those with all three 'critical' items correct who failed on *either* part of the double criterion.

RESULTS

Of the 111 children of European extraction, 6 were discarded as presenting unreliable protocols as defined in (b) above: all were in Grades 1 and 2. The 225 African children yielded 25 unreliable protocols: of these 14 were in Grades 1 and 2, the remaining 11 being spread fairly evenly over the next five school grades. The distribution of reliably

---

[1] The ? classification is *not* regarded as corresponding to Piaget's 'transitional' classification.

M

classified results is set out in Table 20.1 (pp. 336–7), which combines school grade with age (stated or verified). Since no significant difference in conservation performance was found between boys and girls, the data have been combined in the interests of clarity and economy. The data by age-level are also shown graphically in Figs. 20.1 and 20.2, together with results from other studies.

Evaluation of nonverbal method

Using the children in Zambia of European extraction and upbringing as the means of comparing the nonverbal with the classical method, it is at once apparent from Fig. 20.1 that it can provide highly similar results. Although the 50 per cent level is reached about one year later than by the Genevan data, the 75 to 80 per cent age-level is identical at 10 years, going on to a firm 100 per cent at age 13. It would therefore seem reasonable to regard the application of the nonverbal method to the Zambian African children as likely to be at least as valid as the classical method, thus providing a sound basis for comparison with data obtained elsewhere.

Analysis of ? cases

It will be remembered that to be classified as a conserver, each child was required to respond correctly to all three critical terms (nos. 2, 8, 9). Among those failing only *one* of these items, no less than 80 per cent (African) and 88 per cent (European) were accounted for by failure on item 2. It may be noted that the numbers of those failing only one critical item, 48 Africans and 25 Europeans, are in both cases the same proportion (24 per cent) of the total sample. Only two children (both African) with perfect performance on the three critical items were relegated to the ? category for failure to meet the additional criterion.

Performance of Zambian children as compared with Aborigines

Examination of the comparative data on the Zambian children and two groups of Australian Aboriginal mission-school children (de Lemos, 1966) reveals a marked tendency for the percentage of age-group samples showing weight conservation to vary sharply from one year to the next after age 10 or 11 years. In the Aboriginal study, this might readily have been attributed to the very small age-samples (varying from five to twelve children, modally ten) but a similar explanation is somewhat harder to adduce for the Zambian material, where the samples – at least to age 14 – are considerably larger. In Fig. 20.2, the age trends are shown using grouped data (indicated by broken lines) to

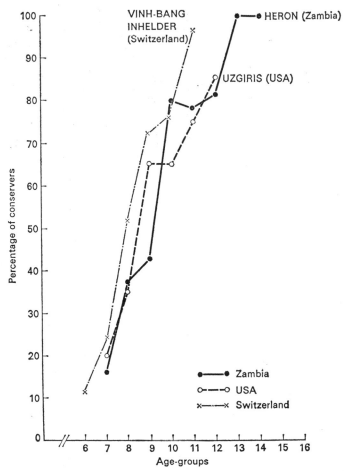

Fig. 20.1 Nonverbal method (Zambian European *S*s) compared with classical method.

deal with this problem for the purposes of discussion. The grouping is as follows: Elcho 12, 13, 14; Hermannsburg 11–15; Zambia 12, 13, 14 and 15, 16, 17. The most striking feature is the way in which the curve levels off at 10 years of age in the Zambian sample and in one of the two Aboriginal samples, the former at the 50 to 55 per cent level,

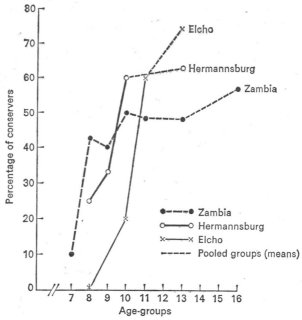

Fig. 20.2 Conservation of weight: Zambian and Australian data.

the latter somewhat higher. The other Aboriginal sample (Elcho) however, shows no such tendency.

DISCUSSION

The method

In general, the nonverbal method appears to function satisfactorily, but in view of the finding that over 80 per cent of the ? cases can be attributed to failure on the first critical item (no. 2), consideration should be given to the design of pilot experiments in which the number and order of items are varied. Such an investigation would lend itself to the inclusion of one model in which, by considerably increasing the number of critical items, a continuous score could be obtained instead of the present division into conservers, doubtfuls and nonconservers. It would then not be difficult, by employing the questioning procedure of the classical method, to establish satisfactory cutting-points for classification as conservers, transitionals and nonconservers. The principal disadvantage of the nonverbal method lies in the fact that, without the questioning characteristic of the clinical method, one is left without the evidence of the reasons given by the child for his response. In the circumstances for which the present study was designed, however, the difficulty of obtaining such verbal explanations reliably is very great, especially with the younger children. The modified procedure suggested above might provide a useful and relatively objective compromise solution.

The data on Aborigines

The relevance for comparative purposes of the results obtained by de Lemos with Aboriginal children must be limited to some unknown extent by the facts that:

(a) She gave not one, but a series of conservation tests, in which series that for weight came third (after quantity and length) for the Elcho sample and fourth (after number, quantity and length) for the Hermannsburg sample. It is possibly significant for our present purposes that of the seventy children of all ages from both her samples who achieved conservation of weight, twenty-seven had *not* achieved conservation of quantity. This is a substantial reversal of Piaget's 'Invariant Order', and is tentatively attributed by de Lemos (1966, p. 296) to the effects of experience with the quantity test upon performance (shortly afterwards) on the weight test.

(b) She employed tea leaf, poured into plastic bags of different sizes and shapes. (For the earlier test for conservation of quantity, she had used sugar, poured into glasses of different sizes and shapes.) Uzgiris (1964) compared results obtained using plasticine, plastic wire, wire coils and metal cubes; she found that with metal cubes (the only discontinuous material) higher proportions of conservers were obtained than with any of the three continuous materials. Although there were individual differences across materials, her analysis showed no systematic trends within these three.

The different patterns in Fig. 20.2 presented by the two samples of Aboriginal children are attributed by de Lemos (1966, pp. 304ff.) to a combination of differences in the educational milieu of the two samples according to age. The sample of older children at Elcho, which presents a superior weight conservation performance, was apparently highly selected due to the departure from the school of the 'less promising' children. At Hermannsburg, more adequate school staffing had permitted the retention of all children up to the age of 15 years. On the other hand, increases in equipment and teaching staff had permitted improvements which were probably already effective among the younger (8–10 years) children at Hermannsburg, but not yet at Elcho.

The Zambian data

With these various considerations in mind, let us turn to the Zambian results. The performance of the younger children (7, 8 and 9 years of age) is approximately level with that of the Zambian children of European extraction and upbringing; that of the two youngest groups is also comparable with the Illinois data of Uzgiris (1964) shown on Fig. 20.1. From 10 years of age onwards, however, the proportion of conservers among these Zambian urban schoolchildren fails to increase at the expected rate and – subject to the methodological reservations above – lags behind both the samples of rural mission-school Aborigines.

Implications

Without a longitudinal study of an age-cohort of children it is not possible to do more than speculate about precise causes of the inability to conserve weight even by the ages of 14 to 16 displayed by 40 to 50 per cent of these Zambian children. While it is true that they are urban dwellers – most but probably not all from birth – neither their domestic nor their school environments can be said to have approximated to the models we are coming to regard as appropriate for adequate intellectual stimulation. As Hooper (in Sigel and Hooper, 1968) puts it, ' . . . cognitive change is made possible by the active interaction of the child and his surrounding physical and social environment. . . . The student must be actively engaged if the learning process is to be effective. For the concrete operations, this entails an actual concrete manipulation of the objects or task materials in question. Regardless of content area, the child should perform the actions represented by the concepts' (p. 429).

At the time of this investigation (1968) less than four years had elapsed since Zambia obtained its independence: on the basis of a median age of entry into Grade 1 in 1964 of about 8 years – it was still 7·7 in 1968 – one can safely assume that all children aged 12 or more in 1968 had entered Grade 1 before any effects of post-independence educational improvements could have been felt. Allowing for some lag, one could probably lower this to 10 years. On this basis, it may be stated without fear of contradiction that the early educational experiences of the *older* children were probably as far from meeting the criteria set out by Hooper as can well be imagined. Many of these schoolchildren would have spent their days in crowded classrooms with absolutely bare walls and/or a total lack of manipulative materials and even of individual textbooks; due to inadequate education and training many of their teachers would rely mainly on rote-learning methods; and with some exceptions no regular questioning or discussion would form part of the child's school experience.

Finally, the language of instruction during their lower primary years for all the older Zambian children in this study had been the designated Zambian language for the region in which this school is located (Ci-Bemba). It is certainly not the case that this is the first language of both (or even one) of the parents for many of these children, nor even of all the teachers through whose hands they pass during their primary school years. Even under optimal conditions, where Ci-Bemba is in fact the language of child, parents, teacher and a majority of classmates, it cannot be assumed that the conceptual content of the language as found in the textbooks and as used in teaching is fully adequate to the task of facilitating Piaget's process of equilibration.

By contrast, the children now in Grades 1, 2 and 3 have been exposed to English-medium teaching, under the new policy being gradually introduced since 1966. The classrooms of these younger children are provided with posters, pictures, and other usual wall-materials, and a limited amount of manipulative material has recently been supplied for the first time. In this connection, it should be noted that the language of instruction from Grade 1 for the Aborigine children studied by de Lemos at Elcho and Hermannsburg missions is English. Concerning the educational environments, de Lemos reports for Hermannsburg (1966, p. 140) that 'a wide variety of activity materials are in use in the younger classes. There is a workshop containing tools for carpentry and craftwork classes, and regular art and craft classes are held where the children engage in constructive work.' At Elcho 'a preschool was established in 1963 under a trained pre-school teacher . . . in 1961 the Cuisenaire equipment was introduced in the (then parttime) pre-school class. . . . Compared with Hermannsburg the range of school equipment appeared to be more limited, and there were no special facilities for art or craftwork' (pp. 148–9). The other difference between Elcho and Hermannsburg is to be found in the degree of contact with the European-type culture, which is very much greater in the latter. Elcho is accessible only by air or sea and few of its population of nearly 600 people have ever been to Darwin, 350 air miles distant.

The domestic and social milieu of the Zambian children is clearly very much more in contact with a European-type industrial, commercial and technological culture than that of either of these two Aborigine groups. In accounting for the relatively better performance on the conservation task of the latter, one is therefore obliged to focus attention mainly on (a) the educational milieu, and (b) the possible significance of the languages used as the medium of instruction from Grade 1. On the former, one is reminded of the study by Goodnow (1962) in Hong Kong, in which she reported an actual *decline* in the proportion of age-groups conserving weight from age 10 to age 13 in samples drawn from three Chinese schools and clubs in low-income districts. This decline is from 62 per cent conservers at age 10 to 40 per cent at ages 12 and 13; she attributes it to the fact that this group 'encounters poor text-books along with the least-trained teachers and the most traditional methods' (p. 10). She also mentions the fact that a primary science course for Grades 5 and 6 had, in the Chinese schools, involved 'at least six textbooks none [of which] . . . call for demonstrations or laboratory work of any kind . . .' (p. 9). The hypothesis is that this course as taught 'leaves many boys with the general feeling that the obvious answer must be wrong in all tasks like these (conservation of weight, volume and space)' and she supports her hypothesis with the observation that even in one Anglo-Chinese school, the retention of this teaching approach continues to handicap 13 year olds on conservation of weight (p. 10). She suggests that the basic handicap – partly at least induced by the teaching methods and lack of suitable materials – may be in a lack of 'some kind of sophistication, maturity, assurance, or whatever it is that gives one confidence in one's own judgement' (p. 10). Her third suggestion, which may also be relevant to the Zambian situation, concerns the use made by Chinese boys of the terms 'same' and 'different'. She says 'when in doubt Chinese boys said "not the same", while European boys said "close enough" ' (p. 11). Although she notes that this difference does not stem from the lack of phrases like 'close enough' in the Chinese vocabulary or practice, one cannot help recalling the problems faced in other Zambian work when it was found that no word or phrase for 'the same' existed in certain Zambian languages (Heron, 1968).

It is, however, essential to emphasize the point that linguistic variables should not be evaluated in isolation from the total environmental situation of the child. The progress of any child through the Piagetian 'stages' to what he regards as the goal – the fully-developed ability to reason reflectively, to 'operate on operations' – is now generally recognized as being dependent on a fruitful interaction between genetically-determined potentialities and the products of experience. There is a widespread tendency to evaluate the child's 'experience' mainly in terms of overt and frequently intentional stimulation. But certain values with cognitive relevance are *implicit* in the total pattern of adult and older sibling behaviour which may be regarded as the 'ambience' within which development takes place: such values need not be overtly taught. To take but one example, the 'carpentered world' to which attention has been directed, most notably by Segall, Campbell and Herskovits (1966), involves an implicit rather than an explicit placing of value on (or attribution of importance to) the convention of rectangularity, parallels and plane surfaces, which has contributed to the intellectual development of most children in 'developed' countries during the whole of Piaget's 'pre-operational' period, i.e. between the ages of approximately 2 to 7 years. For most children in Zambia, this is *not* the case, and quite without regard to whether the child lives in a round hut or in a rectangular house. Similarly, questions of amount or quantity are not dealt with in the terms of precision and exactitude with which they are invested in other cultures; the probability of a Zambian preschool child becoming aware of any importance being attached by his elders to exact identity or equivalence is effectively zero.

The potential importance for cognitive development of the language employed in the school as the medium of education from first grade onwards is to be sought in its contribution to this 'ambience'. If the culture of which the indigenous language or languages form the main channel of social communication places value on concepts and behaviours important for full cognitive development, where 'full' implies the goal specified by Piaget, then, by and large, the language will be consistent with those values in its capacity for encoding them. In such a case, the indigenous language is clearly a satisfactory medium, at least to start with, for primary education. If, on the other hand, the opposite condition prevails, the case becomes strong for the employment as the educational medium of a language known to be favourable to full cognitive development, not solely or even mainly because it contains the appropriate concepts, but because its use will increase the probability of the child's exposure to the implicit 'cognitively-relevant values' of the culture with which that language is associated. The extent to which this occurs will of course be considerably affected by the cultural-linguistic 'integrity' of the teachers: clearly, an indigenous teacher whose own cognitively-relevant values are largely inconsistent with those implicit in the second language he is employing as a medium of education will not be an effective channel. In this connection it is highly relevant to note that the primary-school teachers of the Aborigine children at both Elcho and Hermannsburg, using English as the educational medium from Grade 1, are themselves of European extraction and upbringing, while those in the Zambian school, using Ci-Bemba as the medium, are without exception of African extraction and upbringing. The problem to which attention has just been drawn will arise as the new policy of using English as the medium of instruction is progressively implemented in Zambian primary schools.

A note on nutrition

Finally, one can at present only speculate on the possible implications for cognitive performance of malnutrition. The present study was partly supported by the National Food and Nutrition Commission in Zambia because such implications can at least no longer be ignored despite the lack of satisfactory evidence (cf. Heron, in Scrimshaw and Gordon, 1968). It is known that some of the Zambian schoolchildren included in this study had been hospitalized for marasmus or kwashiorkor during infancy, but lack of adequate clinical data precludes any further investigation of these cases. What is certain is that most of these children are currently malnourished, being dependent on a diet low in protein and consisting largely of a maize porridge (*nshima*). Most children come to school not having eaten anything since the early part of the previous evening and teachers regard drowsiness and lassitude as familiar symptoms. By contrast, school meals and other supplements are provided at Hermannsburg, and at Elcho Island the ready availability of fish considerably reduces the likelihood of protein deficiency.

SUMMARY AND CONCLUSIONS

The nonverbal method for evaluating conservation of weight behaviour suggested originally by Furth for use with deaf children has been employed successfully in a study of primary schoolchildren in Zambia. Data obtained from a control group of children of European extraction and upbringing are comparable to those reported from Switzerland and the USA in studies using the classical Genevan method. Although some improvements in the method are suggested, there appears to be a satisfactory basis for comparing the data on Zambian children with those reported elsewhere.

On the basis of these results, it seems clear that between 40 and 50 per cent of these urban Zambian primary schoolchildren cannot demonstrate the ability to conserve weight by the time they leave school at a median stated age of 15 years. This contrasts with the finding that the proportion of conservers among younger Zambian children is comparable with that found elsewhere: in other words, the question is raised as to whether those Zambian children who *will* be weight-conservers when they leave primary school had already achieved this several years earlier. An alternative hypothesis, suggested by the data of Goodnow in Hong Kong, is that the ability to demonstrate conservation is suppressed by unsatisfactory teaching methods and materials in the upper primary school grades. These results are compared with data reported by de Lemos in a study of Australian Aborigine children.

Attention has been drawn to the need for distinguishing between purely linguistic problems, whether narrowly conceived within the actual testing situation or more broadly in terms of the conceptual content of indigenous languages, and those concerned with the 'ambience', both at home and at school, within which cognitive development must take place. By 'ambience' is meant the total pattern of implicit cognitively-relevant cultural values, communicated through linguistic and other behaviour by adults and older children.

Given that for economic and political reasons those responsible for deciding on social objectives in developing countries such as Zambia are obliged to set educational objectives which permit the production of adults capable of dealing with European-type intellectual concepts in industry, commerce, agriculture and administration, it is evident from this study that the *major investment* should be in the early education of their children. Very high priority should be given to the support of carefully planned and executed controlled longitudinal studies of the consequences for the intellectual development of individual children of differing experiences during the primary-school period. Special attention should be given to the variables of language of instruction, nature and variety of demonstration and manipulative materials and the actual uses made of these, and of the extent to which discussion or rote-learning methods are employed by the teachers, and to which their own cognitively-relevant values are consistent with the language they are using as the educational medium.

Meanwhile, experimental studies are needed of *young adults* displaying clear signs of nonconservation in the various media employed by the Piaget school. Such studies can probably only be carried out in developing countries or among such groups as the Australian Aborigines, but this is where the need is greatest for ascertaining the implications for further education or training of these deficits which Piagetian theory predicates as evidence of basic intellectual handicaps. In such adult studies it would also be possible to obtain evidence concerning the tentative 'critical periods' hypothesis put forward by Hunt (1961) as a corollary to his 'matching' concept. The potential value, both for theoretical and practical purposes, of conservation training studies at this adult end of the developmental spectrum would appear to be considerably greater than at the other end, preschool or kindergarten, where all such studies (e.g. Sigel and Hooper, 1968) have so far been concentrated.

21

D. Price-Williams, W. Gordon and M. Ramirez III (1969)

Skill and conservation : a study of pottery-making children[1]

Developmental Psychology, 1(6), p. 769

A series of conservation tests of the Piaget type was given to Mexican children in two separate locations. The concepts investigated were those of number, liquid, substance, weight and volume. Application of the tests followed the classic procedure of previous investigations, but translated into Spanish. An experimental group was composed of children who had grown up in pottery-making families. A control group was composed of children of matching age, years of schooling, and socioeconomic class, but whose families engaged in skills other than pottery-making. The two locations were the town of Tlaquepaque, Jalisco, and the village of San Marcos, Jalisco. In the Tlaquepaque sample, there were twelve children in both the experimental and control group, all boys, composed of three children in each of the four age-groups with an age range of 6 to 9 years. In the San Marcos sample there were sixteen children in each of the two groups, four from each year group of 6 through 9.

The guiding principle behind the choice of selecting children versed in pottery-making was that of the role of experience and specifically manipulation in the attainment of conservation. It was predicted that experience in pottery-making should promote for these children earlier conservation in at least the concept of substance (in which clay is the experimental medium), while the question of transfer to other concepts of number, liquid, weight and volume was left open.

Conservation was judged present if all answers were correct on all

[1] The study was funded by the Advanced Research Projects Agency under ARPA Order No. 738, monitored by the Office of Naval Research, Group Psychology Branch, under Contract No. N00014–67–A–0145–0001, NR 177–909.

trials. In the Tlaquepaque sample, Fischer's exact probability test was used for each of the five conservation tests. Nonsignificant results were found on the four tasks of number, liquid, weight and volume, but were found to be significant for substance ($p < 0.05$), in the direction of the pottery group. On all five tasks the potters' sons conserved more frequently than the other group, but not significantly. Overall, there was a one-third more conservation in the pottery group. Analysis of reasons given by the children in both samples, in equality or inequality, supported the direction of the quantitative results. The results of the San Marcos sample were more dramatic. Out of a possible eighty total, composed of five tests for sixteen children, seventy-seven of the sample showed conservation in the pottery group, while there were ten only in the non-pottery group. The reasons given in either group supported the quantitative results.

This study suggests that the role of skills in cognitive growth may be a very important factor. Manipulation may be a prior and necessary prerequisite in the attainment of conservation, but a skill embodies a set of operations with a recognizable end – making cups from clay for example. The authors chose pottery-making as the variable to be investigated for the study of conservation, but the craft of weaving may be another skill by means of which a child's appreciation of coordinate systems and one-to-one relationships could be tested.

22

P. R. de Lacey (1970)

A cross-cultural study of classificatory ability in Australia[1]

Journal of Cross-Cultural Psychology, 1(4), pp. 293–304

In recent decades, the question of the influence of social and physical environmental upon human mental development has claimed the increasing attention of a growing number of psychologists. This emphasis, particularly in North America, has probably supplanted an alternative approach based on the assumption that certain identifiable groups of people transmit to their progeny different maximal cognitive capacities.

In Australia, too, we find some earlier studies in whole or part directed at this kind of comparison. Porteus and his colleagues, for example, after extensive investigations with his maze and other non-verbal tests of intelligence, found substantial differences between Aboriginal and European Australian intellectual performance in favour of the Europeans (Porteus, 1933). Porteus also tested samples from a number of other ethnic groups, and, on the basis of his results, constructed a hierarchy of ethnic groups in terms of the levels of their intellectual functioning (Porteus, 1966). More recently, a measure of support for Porteus's findings was provided by de Lemos (1969b), who reported that a small sample of part Aboriginals performed better on Piagetian conservation tests than a group of full-blood Aboriginals in the same environment in central Australia.

But in Queensland, Kearney (1966) found that Aboriginal children tend to score higher on a battery of nonverbal intelligence tests when they live in close association with Europeans than when they live in more isolated communities. Kearney's approach again emphasizes the relevance of environment to intellectual functioning.

The same switch in emphasis has been noted in studies of

[1] The research on which this report is based was sponsored by grants from the Australian Institute of Aboriginal Studies and the University of New England.

intellectual functioning within one ethnic group. Early in the present century, Spearman (1904) considered intelligence to be an inherited quality, and relatively impervious to environmental influences. More recently, low intelligence found among many children of Western culture has been considered to be often associated with – and even substantially attributed to – unstimulating environments (Hunt, 1969). Such children are often described as 'culturally deprived' or 'culturally disadvantaged'.

ABORIGINAL COGNITION

Although there is an absence of previous investigation of classificatory ability among Aboriginals, a number of studies have shown that they have not performed as well as Europeans on a variety of mental tests, including the Porteus Maze (Porteus, 1917, 1933), a battery of seven nonverbal tests (Piddington and Piddington, 1932), the Illinois Test of Psycholinguistic Abilities (Hart, 1965), and on Piagetian tests of conservation (de Lemos, 1969b). But Fowler (1940) has warned that standardized mental tests are not appropriate measures of Aboriginal mental functioning, while McElwain (1968) has suggested that Aboriginals' lower performances might be explained in terms of the nature and variety of their life experiences, which are less relevant than those of Europeans to satisfactory mental test performance.

Consequently, McElwain and others at the University of Queensland developed a battery of nonverbal tests (the Queensland Test) which employed simple materials and in which communication between examiner and subject was facilitated by such devices as miming and demonstrating the test tasks required before each individual administration. McElwain (1968) describes the Queensland Test thus:

> The Queensland Test is administered individually. The mean time of testing is forty to sixty minutes. The test has five item types, administered in a noncyclic, omnibus form similar to the Wechsler Test rather than to the Binet form:
>
> Knox Cube Imitation Test
> Beads Test
> Alexander's Passalong Test
> Form Assembly Test
> Pattern Matching Test
>
> Among the features common to these test types are
> (i) the material is completely nonverbal in both administration and response;

(ii) all the material is nonrepresentational; there are no pictures, and no object used in the test has a common use or meaning; (iii) in all the tests the goal of the test is clear. Generally, the tester invites the subject to imitate some manipulation of material towards an overt goal. The tasks are then made progressively more difficult. (pp. 13-14)

Although the Queensland Test was shown to be characterized by both predictive validity and substantial score variance, it could be argued that the range of abilities tapped tended to be somewhat narrow for it to be regarded as a test of intelligence.

Three cross-cultural studies of other ethnic groups are of interest at this point. Price-Williams (1962) found that Nigerian children lagged a year or so behind European children in classificatory ability, whether or not they had been to school, though Bruner, Olver and Greenfield (1966) subsequently found that schooling did make a difference to the performance of African children in tests based on stimulus equivalence. Goodnow (1962) found small differences between children from various European and Chinese milieus in Hong Kong on conservation and combination tests. These studies leave the question of the influence of race and milieu on classificatory performance rather inconclusively answered.

The question of a relationship between milieu and mental functioning has appeared under another guise in some reports of a possible association between the mental test scores of Aboriginals and the extent of their contact with Europeans. Gregor and McPherson (1963), for example, using the Porteus Maze Test, and Kearney (1966), using the Queensland Test, noted that performance of Aboriginals tended to vary directly with the extent of the contact they had experienced with Europeans and their technology. The result might be due to opportunities for high-contact Aboriginal children to learn to perform the specific tasks of these tests. Another possible explanation is that Aboriginal children in close contact with Europeans might enjoy a richer variety of experiences than remote Aboriginal children, and the cognitive growth rate of high-contact Aboriginal children might thereby be accelerated.

Milieu effects among Europeans

Consideration of milieu effects upon levels of cognitive functioning have not, of course, been confined to Aboriginals. European children encountering a greater-than-average variety of life experiences which match the mental schemata established at any given time in the course of their mental development (Hunt, 1961) are also likely to show faster cognitive growth than disadvantaged European children. Both the range and the ordering of the experiences of disadvantaged children are likely to be restricted (Deutsch, 1963), and such children tend to be characterized by low intelligence-test scores, especially on verbal tests (Eells *et al.*, 1959), by low school achievement (Choppin, 1967) and poorly-developed language and communication skills (Bernstein, 1960; Deutsch, 1963; Laton, 1968), and by a low socioeconomic level (Whiteman and Deutsch, 1968).

In a study in Italy, Peluffo (1967) administered conservation tests to city born-and-bred children, rural children, and children who had originally lived in the country but had since moved to a city. He concluded from his results that 'low cultural level' or an 'underdeveloped milieu' does not stimulate the development of operational thinking, though transfer to a more favourable milieu may do so.

As a result of these studies, an outstanding question is whether classificatory ability and milieu are associated in each of the major ethnic groups in Australia. It was the purpose of the present study to try to answer this question, and to attempt a comparison of performances of Aboriginal and white Australian children living in similar environments.

METHOD

The samples

To meet the aims of this study, a relatively advantaged sample and a relatively disadvantaged sample of children were drawn from both European and full-blood Aboriginal populations. The two European populations, which were drawn from Sydney, were described as high-socioeconomic and low-socioeconomic, in so far as they occupied extreme positions on the occupational prestige scale of Congalton (1963). Thus the fathers of the high-socioeconomic European children were professionals or executives, while the fathers of the low-socioeconomic European children were semi-skilled or unskilled manual workers. The two Aboriginal populations were designated high- or low-contact, according to an index of contact (de Lacey, 1970c) calculated for each population. From each population about ten children were randomly sampled at each age range from 6 to 10, though some younger European and some older Aboriginal children were also included.

The index of contact was designed to express compositely the effect of seventeen variables considered to contribute to contact with Europeans. These variables were the proportion of the school population that was European, whether English was the mother tongue, whether English was used by the adult community, whether English was used by peer groups, the proportion of the school teachers who were European, and the degree of access the children had to the mass media of communication. These six variables were considered to be essentially language variables. The remaining variables were the proportion of the community population that was European, the frequency of visits to European houses, shopping experiences of the children, travel to centres of European population, access to European artifacts, European-style school physical environment, persistence of the indigenous culture, European games and hobbies, European food, home physical environment and European-type community organization.

The reason for identifying the first six as language variables was that Smith (1966) in Queensland has shown that an inverse relationship obtains between the amount of English verbal content in mental tests and Aboriginal children's scores on them. Consequently, in calculating the indices, a double weighting was arbitrarily assigned to the language variables. Scores of 0 to 2 were allotted for each variable (0 to 4 in the case of the language variables), and each total score was expressed as a decimal fraction of the total possible score. The indices calculated for the low- and high-contact samples were respectively 0·13 and 0·83. The low-contact Aboriginal children lived at Aurukun ($N = 63$) and at Weipa ($N = 23$), on the west coast of Cape York peninsula of northern Queensland, and the indices of contact for these locations were respectively 0·07 and 0·30. The high-contact children lived at Palm Island ($N = 45$) and Townsville ($N = 34$) on the north-eastern Queensland coast, and their indices of contact were respectively 0·71 and 0·98.

The nature of classification

The measures of classificatory ability, it has been noted, were four tests based on the classification tests of Inhelder and Piaget (1964). The term 'classification' in the present context refers neither to simple sorting procedures nor to stimulus equivalence. Rather, in its technical sense, classification implies an understanding of the relationship between extension and intension. Extension is defined as the variety of species in which a common character is shown, while intension is the common character to be seen in this variety (Joseph, 1916). Extension is thus the list of class members (if the class is finite), while intension is the defining attribute, or criterion, of the class.

In their Geneva studies, Inhelder and Piaget (1964) describe a number of different kinds of classificatory skills. Of these, we are concerned with two which are indicators of the transition from pre-operational to operational stages of cognitive development. These two kinds of classification are additive (involving the use of quantifiers of hierarchical classification) and multiplicative (requiring the application of two or more attributes simultaneously). Inhelder and Piaget found that additive and multiplicative classification develop in parallel or simultaneously.

The test battery

The battery consisted of four tests. The first test examined the children's ability to use the quantifiers 'some' and 'all' appropriately, implying an understanding of the relationship between a part and the whole of which it is a part. The materials, which were identical with those of Inhelder and Piaget (1964, p. 60), were small blocks of wood, $\frac{3}{4}$ by $\frac{3}{8}$ in, and in the form of red or blue squares or circles, arranged in a line and attached to a piece of cardboard. The original four questions of Inhelder and Piaget were used: 'Are all the circles blue?' 'Are all the red ones square?' 'Are all the blue ones circles?' 'Are all the square ones red?' In the manner of the clinical method, additional questions or prompts (such as 'Show me which ones', 'Point to them') were put after each principal question, until the experimenter was satisfied that the child understood the question, and that, in turn, the experimenter understood the intention of the child's response. To ensure that the younger children understood the terms 'red', 'blue', 'circles', 'squares', and 'round', they were shown and invited to handle replicas of the wooden squares and circles from the test, and were asked to indicate examples of the terms.

The second test consisted of five questions on hierarchical classification. The materials used constituted a four-tier hierarchy: all objects in a basket, food and other objects, fruit and other food, and bananas and oranges. The five questions posed in this test were modelled on questions of Inhelder and Piaget (1964, p. 101). They were:

   1. If we put all the fruit in another basket, will this one (indicating an orange) go in?

2. Is a basket of all the bananas more or less than a basket of all the fruit?
3. Is there more fruit or more food?
4. If we eat all the oranges, will there be any fruit left?
5. If we eat all the fruit, will there be any oranges left?

The third test was a multiple-classification test similar in design to Raven's Progressive Matrices. 'Operational' solutions (in Piaget's terms) to each of the eight multiple-choice items required selection of the correct option according to two or three simultaneous criteria, which the child had to nominate. The criteria were various combinations of shape, colour and orientation. In addition, subjects had to show some resistance to the experimenter's suggestion that another option would solve each item as well as the one chosen. The materials were again based on those of Inhelder and Piaget (1964, pp. 160–1), though some of the content was changed to elements more familiar to Australian children (e.g. Swiss flowers were replaced by hands and feet). There were four 2-criteria items and four 3-criteria items.

The fourth test was Nixon's reclassification test (Nixon, n.d.), which required subjects to perform six reclassifications according to new criteria defined each time by two exemplars. The materials consisted of twenty wooden rods about 2 inches long, varying in three attributes: height, diameter and colour. The following is an example of a reclassification task from this test. The set of four red rods and the set of four white rods are grouped before the subject to be reclassified. If the tall red fat rod and the tall red thin rod are selected and are moved to new and separated positions as exemplars, the only possible solution of the reclassification will be a grouping according to the criterion of diameter. A response was considered to be operational when the reclassification was correctly executed, and also when the new distinguishing criteria were indicated (e.g. 'These are all fat, and those are all skinny'). Since the administration procedure for this test is standardized, the clinical method was not used.

RESULTS

Two analyses were made of the results. The significance of any differences was tested by means of nonparametric statistics (χ^2 for pooled ages, and the Mann-Whitney U test for those individual age-groups where there were sufficient scores). The statistical analysis, which is given in detail elsewhere (de Lacey, 1970a), showed that significant differences in test performance ($p < 0.01$) were revealed by either one or both of the statistical tests between low- and high-contact Aboriginals, and between low- and high-socioeconomic Europeans. On the other hand, no such differences were found between high-contact Aboriginals and low-socioeconomic Europeans, though the x^2 test

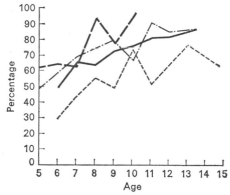

Fig. 22.1 Operational-item percentages: Test No. 1 (questions on use of 'all').

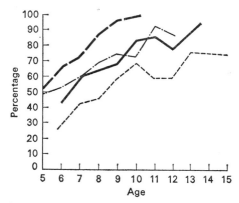

Fig. 22.2 Operational-item percentages: Test No. 2 (hierarchical classification).

applied to our Tests No. 3 and No. 4 showed differences where $0.05 > p > 0.01$.

The second analysis was carried out by inspecting tables of mean scores for each age range in each sample and for each test (de Lacey, 1970a). There was general agreement in inferring trends by both methods.

The results consistently showed a relationship between the milieus and the classificatory performance of the children (Figs. 22.1–22.4). In all four tests, the order of performance among the four samples

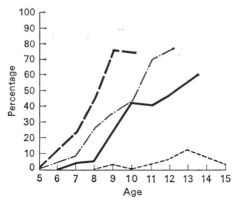

Fig. 22.3 Operational-item percentages: Test No. 3 (multiplicative classification).

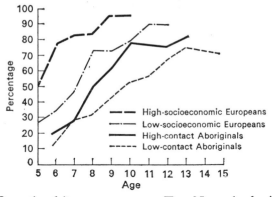

Fig. 22.4 Operational-item percentages: Test No. 4 (reclassification).

was: high-socioeconomic Europeans highest, low-socioeconomic Europeans second, high-contact Aboriginals third and low-contact Aboriginals lowest. This order obtained whether the criterion applied was the proportion of total items answered correctly (expressed as operational-item percentages), or the proportion of the total sample judged to respond operationally (i.e. percentage of subjects giving consistently right answers at each age level).

When the high-contact Aboriginal sample was considered as very high-contact (Townsville) and medium-contact (Palm Island) sub-samples, the Palm Island children performed at a level between the total high-contact sample and the low-contact Aboriginal sample. The

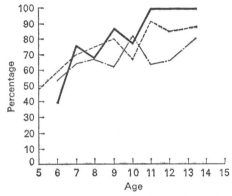

Fig. 22.5 Operational-item percentages: Test No. 1 (questions on use of 'all').

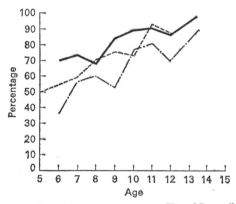

Fig. 22.6 Operational-item percentages: Test No. 2 (hierarchical classification).

performance of the Townsville children, on the other hand, was generally indistinguishable from the performance of the low-socioeconomic Europeans (Figs. 22.5 to 22.8). The Palm Island and Townsville sub-samples were too small to compare at all, meaningfully, with any other group.

While all four tests discriminated between the four milieus, the test most sensitive to milieu differences was the matrix test. The low-socio-economic Europeans and both Aboriginal samples scored lower on this multiple-classification test than on the two additive classification tests (Tests 1 and 2). However, like the other three tests, the matrix test did not reveal any differences between the very-high-contact Aboriginal subsample and the low-socioeconomic Europeans.

Among the Aboriginals, there was a consistent and strong direct

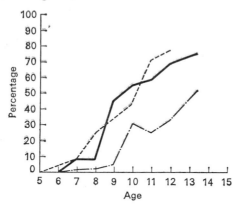

Fig. 22.7 Operational-item percentages: Test No. 3 (multiplicative classification).

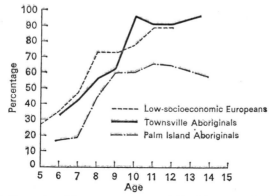

Fig. 22.8 Operational-item percentages: Test No. 4 (reclassification).

relationship between classificatory performance and the degree of contact with Europeans and their technology. Similarly, there was a consistent and direct association between socioeconomic level and test performance among the European children.

Inferences regarding the high performance of the very-high-contact Aboriginals might properly be made with some caution, for they numbered only thirty-four. There is, however, no reason to suppose that

Townsville Aboriginal children are substantially different from any other urban full-blood children. Indeed, they probably constitute a substantial part of the population of urban full-blood Aboriginal children, who are not particularly numerous in the few towns they inhabit, for generally the higher the contact the Aboriginals have with Europeans the less they tend to be full-bloods.

It was possible to make a meaningful comparison of performances of Aboriginal and European children only at the low-socioeconomic urban level, for there are almost no middle-class Aboriginal children; neither are there to be found any groups of European children living in huts in remote reserves or missions. The environment of the high-contact Aboriginals was generally considered not to be quite as stimulating as the low-socioeconomic Europeans. It has been noted that the differences in the test performance of these two samples are not as decisive as the differences between the other pairs of samples.

CONCLUSION

A marked relationship has been demonstrated between the degree of enrichment in children's environments and the particular area of mental growth manifested in the ability to classify. Further, this relationship is to be found in both Aboriginal and European children. It seems to be sufficient to explain the differences found in classificatory performance in terms of environmental differences. Particularly in the case of the low-contact Aboriginals, these environmental differences might include malnutrition in foetal and early post-natal life, resulting in an attenuated braincell population and shown to occur among Aboriginals in the Northern Territory of Australia (Nurcombe, 1970a). Although this influence cannot be ruled out of the present study, the Aurukun Aboriginals generally have access to adequate protein food, and, under the supervision of a qualified nursing sister, the infants are fed regularly with daily issues of milk.

The results of this study also imply that the parallel development between additive and multiple classificatory ability reported by Inhelder and Piaget (1964, p. 289) might occur only where the child's environment provides a favourable opportunity for cognitive growth, as in the case of our high-socioeconomic European sample.

That the relationship between milieu and classificatory ability was found to obtain so unequivocally throughout the test battery points to possible important implications for Aboriginal welfare policy. If the present findings are shown to replicate, it could be argued that the interests of the optimal cognitive development of Aboriginal children would best be served by ensuring that they should in the future be reared near or even integrated with substantial European settlements. Selective migration is unlikely to be a major contributory factor, since the greater part of the Townsville and Palm Island Aboriginals are the descendants of an Aboriginal settlement which was completely evacuated after a hurricane destroyed their homes in a more remote region further north some fifty years ago. In more general terms, the findings of this study lend a measure of support to the notion that the variety and nature of a child's life experiences are crucial determinants of his level of cognitive functioning.

23

M. M. de Lemos

The development of spatial concepts in Zulu children[1]

An increasing number of studies on the application of Piaget's tasks to children from different cultural groups are now being undertaken. The importance of these studies lies in the light they throw on developmental processes and the environmental factors affecting these processes. The studies undertaken have been mainly in the areas of conservation, classification and number concepts. Relatively few studies have been undertaken in other areas of development.

In the study summarized here a number of Piaget's tests on the development of spatial concepts were applied to Zulu and white children in South Africa. These spatial tests have not been applied in other cross-cultural studies, and the results of this study may therefore contribute to our knowledge of the development of these concepts under different cultural conditions.

The study was based on Piaget and Inhelder's (1956) investigation of the development of topological, projective and Euclidean concepts of space. On the basis of their results on a number of different tests, they concluded that topological relationships are constructed before projective and Euclidean relationships. This development at the conceptual or representational level follows the same pattern that Piaget (1955) had previously found at the sensori-motor level.

Topological space involves only the internal relationships of a particular figure viewed in isolation; for example, relationships of proximity, separation, order and enclosure. These remain constant in any

---

[1] The research reported in this paper was carried out by the author in 1957 for an M.Sc. research thesis at the University of Natal, Pietermaritzburg. The study is reported in full in the thesis (Murray, 1961). A report on the study was also published in the *Journal for Social Research* (Cowley and Murray, 1962). The present report is a summary of the main findings of this study. In this case, the results have been presented in a slightly different form from the previous reports, i.e. in terms of the achievement of Piaget's stage of concrete operations rather than in terms of mean scores.

spatial transformation, and are independent of changes in the shape or size of the figure.

Projective and Euclidean space involves the relating of a number of figures into a common spatial structure. Projective space arises when the single figures or objects of topological space are related to one another according to a point of view, while Euclidean space arises when these objects are located in relation to a coordinate system on a vertical-horizontal axis. Piaget and Inhelder maintain that projective and Euclidean concepts of space develop concurrently, and are both derived, though independently, from topological concepts of space. Their development is later because they depend on a general system of organization, and are therefore more complex.

The purpose of the investigation reported here was to examine the development of spatial concepts in Zulu and white children in South Africa. We were particularly interested to determine whether the same stages and the same order in the development of spatial concepts would be found in these children as in Swiss children, and whether any differences either in the qualitative aspects of development or in the rate of progress would be found between the Zulu and the white children which could be related to the differences in culture and environment between these two groups.

METHOD

Subjects

Forty Zulu children and forty white children were tested. Their ages ranged from 5 to 12 years, with equal numbers at each of these ages. An equal number of boys and girls in each group were tested.

The white children were selected from a local kindergarten and a local primary school in the town of Pietermaritzburg. The children attending these schools were drawn from a wide range of economic levels, including wage-earning, salaried and professional classes.

The Zulu children were selected from two schools in a Zulu township on the outskirts of Pietermaritzburg. The social and economic conditions of this township were better than in many other such townships, and the parents of the children were therefore considered as coming mainly from the higher wage-earning Zulu group. The sample is therefore not representative of the urban Zulu population as a whole.

Tests and testing procedure

The children were tested individually at the schools. Each child was tested in three separate sessions, each session lasting thirty to forty-five minutes. In the case of the Zulu children, an interpreter was used. The interpreter was a trained school teacher, and was instructed in the administration of the tests and required to translate any comments or questions the child made.

Three main tests, each comprising a series of subtests, were used in the investigation. The first test dealt with the development of topological space concepts, the second with the development of projective space concepts, and the third with the development of Euclidean space concepts. The subtests were selected in each case from Piaget and Inhelder's sections on topological, projective and Euclidean space.

The tests and procedures followed as closely as possible those described by Piaget and Inhelder, but were standardized to the extent that the same problem and materials were used for each child, and the same basic questions were asked.

Following is a brief statement of the tests used. The details of the procedures and materials are given elsewhere (Murray, 1961).

Test 1. Topological space

Subtest 1: Copying of geometrical figures (e.g. circle, square, triangle, ellipse with small circle inside, outside, and touching the boundary, composite figures of circle and triangle with triangle inside, touching or intersecting the circle, circles touching and intersecting, etc.).

Subtest 2: Haptic perception – identification. Identification from a duplicate set of a series of cardboard shapes handled through an opaque screen, but not seen. The shapes include a square, a circle, a triangle, a cross, a star, open and closed rings, and a number of other simple shapes and purely topological forms.

Subtest 3: Haptic perception – drawing. As above, but in this case the figures handled were drawn instead of being identified from the duplicate set.

Test 2. Projective space

Subtest 1: The construction of a straight line, parallel and oblique to the edge of the table.

Subtests 2 and 3: The drawing of perspective views of a pencil and a penny from the child's own viewpoint and from that of an observer sitting at right angles to the child.

Subtests 4 and 5: As above, but in this case the child was asked to identify the correct perspective views from a set of drawings including correct and incorrect perspectives.

Subtests 6 to 8: The coordination of perspectives. The child was asked to identify the correct perspective view of a model of three different coloured mountains seen from different positions.

This was done by asking the child to construct the correct view using cardboard cut-outs of the mountains (Subtest 6), by asking the child to choose the correct perspective view for various positions from a series of pictures showing different perspective views of the model (Subtest 7), and finally by showing the child a series of pictures of different views and in each case asking the child to place a doll in a position around the model where it would see the particular view represented (Subtest 8).

Test 3. Euclidean space

Subtest 1: Similarity of rhombi. The child was asked to sort into similar pairs a series of small and large rhombi cut out of cardboard, and varying in angle.

Subtest 2: Similarity of triangles. The child was asked to sort a set of cardboard triangles of different shapes and sizes into groups according to their similarity.

Subtest 3: Judgement of similarity of inscribed triangles. The child was asked to judge the similarity of a series of pairs of inscribed triangles, some of which were similar and others not similar.

Subtest 4: Drawing of similar triangles. The child was asked to draw a triangle similar to and inscribing a given model, the base line of which was extended to form the base line of the required triangle.

Subtest 5: Judgement of similar rectangles. The child was asked to judge the similarity of a series of rectangles to a smaller, standard model.

Subtest 6: Judgement of similarity of inscribed rectangles. The child was asked to judge the similarity of two rectangles, the smaller one inscribed in the lower left-hand corner of the larger one.

Subtest 7: Drawing of similar rectangles. The child was asked to draw a rectangle similar to and inscribing a given model, the base line of which was extended to form the base line of the required rectangle.

Scoring of the tests

The children's responses were classified into five stages of development, corresponding as far as possible to the stages of development described by Piaget (details of the scoring and classification are given by Murray, 1961).

RESULTS

The number of Zulu and white children achieving the stage of development corresponding to Piaget's Stage III, i.e. the level of concrete operations, is shown in Table 23.1. On each test more white children than Zulu children achieved the level of concrete operations. Applying chi-square tests of significance, it was found that the differences were significant on all the tests.

Test 1. Topological space

Subtest 1 (copying of geometrical figures). In the copying of geometrical figures, Piaget and Inhelder found that the first distinctions made were between open and closed forms, and that in the early stages topological relationships only were indicated (from 3·5 to 4 years). There was then a crude differentiation between curved and straight-sided figures, but without the latter being differentiated among themselves (4 to 4·5 years). The children only gradually mastered the copying of Euclidean figures, the shapes being distinguished according to the number of sides, angles and dimensions.

Piaget and Inhelder give the age of 6·5 to 7 years for the achievement of Stage III, the level of concrete operations, when the children were able to copy all the figures correctly.

In our group, Piaget's Stage III was found in the majority of white children from 6 years and the majority of Zulu children from 9 years.

Our results confirmed the stages of development described by Piaget, and the age of achievement for the white children, but the development of the Zulu children lagged some three years behind that of the white children, although following the same pattern of development.

Subtests 2 and 3 (haptic perception). In their test on haptic perception, Piaget and Inhelder find that the first forms distinguished with any accuracy are the topological forms (open and closed rings, shapes with one or two holes, etc.). A distinction is also made between indented and

N

TABLE 23.1. *Number of Zulu and white children classified at stages corresponding to Piaget's Stage IIIa and above*

	Younger age-group (5–8 years)		Older age-group (9–12 years)		Total		X^2	Significance level
	Zulu N = 20	White N = 20	Zulu N = 20	White N = 20	Zulu N = 40	White N = 40		
Test 1 Subtest 1	6	13	13	20	19	33	10·77	$p > 0·001$
Subtest 2	2	6	2	16	4	22	18·46	$p > 0·001$
Subtest 3	0	5	2	17	2	22	25·63	$p > 0·001$
Test 2 Subtest 1	5	14	17	20	22	34	8·57	$p > 0·01$
Subtest 2	0	8	6	19	6	27	22·74	$p > 0·001$
Subtest 3	0	8	7	19	7	27	20·46	$p > 0·001$
Subtest 4	0	9	4	19	4	28	30·00	$p > 0·001$
Subtest 5	0	11	7	19	7	30	26·59	$p > 0·001$
Subtest 6	0	2	0	9	0	11	11·62	$p > 0·001$
Subtest 7	0	2	2	16	2	18	16·01	$p > 0·001$
Subtest 8	0	4	4	15	4	19	13·73	$p > 0·001$
Test 3 Subtest 1	0	0	0	5	0	5	4·32	$p > 0·05$
Subtest 2	0	3	0	9	0	12	12·96	$p > 0·001$
Subtest 3	0	2	0	5	0	7	6·61	$p > 0·02$
Subtest 4	0	2	3	10	3	12	5·92	$p > 0·02$
Subtest 5	0	4	3	12	3	16	10·78	$p > 0·01$
Subtest 6	0	3	1	8	1	11	8·85	$p > 0·01$
Subtest 7	0	0	0	7	0	7	6·61	$p > 0·02$

non-indented forms. This is followed by a differentiation first between curved and straight-sided figures, then between the simpler straight-sided figures (square triangle, etc.) and finally between the more complex straight-sided figures (hexagon, octagon, etc.). This is achieved at Stage III, at 6·5 to 7 years.

This order of development was confirmed in our groups. Our 5 year olds were generally at Piaget's earliest stage of development, distinguishing only the topological and indented figures with any accuracy. A differentiation between curved and straight-sided figures was found from about 5 years in the white group and 6 years in the Zulu group.

The distinction between the simple straight-sided figures was found at about 6 years in the white group and 9 years in the Zulu group, while the more complex straight-sided figures were distinguished by the white children at about 8 years. The Zulu children continued to show difficulty in distinguishing the various straight-sided figures even up to 12 years.

Thus while the order of development was confirmed, the Zulu children again lagged some three to four years behind the white children, who in turn lagged a year or so behind the Swiss children on this particular test.

Test 2. Projective space

Subtest 1 (construction of straight line). Piaget's criterion for the achievement of concrete operations in this test is the ability to construct straight lines both parallel and oblique to the edge of the table.

This level was achieved by virtually all of the white children from 6 years. Some of the Zulu children from 7 to 9 years and all the Zulu children over 9 years achieved this level. Again a lag of some three years was found between the white and the Zulu children, although a number of the younger Zulu children were able to succeed on this test.

We did not find any evidence of the pre-operational stage described by Piaget where the child is completely unable to construct a straight line oblique to the table edge.

Piaget states that this stage is found up to 7 years, and his explanation is that the perceptual background of the table edge acts as an 'intellectual obstacle' to the child. The child is able to construct the line where the background contains examples ready to hand, as for example the table edge, but when he must construct a line without the help of such examples, he is unable to do so, making instead two straight lines parallel to the edge of the table. He also states that when the line is made for the child oblique to the table edge, he is able to recognize this line as straight although he is unable to construct the line himself. Our results do not support this finding. In both Zulu and white groups it was found that children from 5 years were able to construct approximately straight lines oblique to the table edge.

Subtests 2 to 5 (perspective views of pencil and penny). There were marked differences between the Zulu and white children in their ability to represent and to recognize perspective views. The majority of the Zulu children up to 9 years were unable to recognize changes in shape with changes in perspective. From 10 to 12 years most of the children were able to recognize or to represent some change in shape with changes in perspective, but only a few children were able to distinguish between their own point of view and that of an observer, and so to reach the criterion for Piaget's stage of concrete operations.

The white children, on the other hand, were able to recognize that changes in shape occur with changes in perspective from 5 years, and to distinguish between their own view and that of an observer at 7 years, thus achieving Piaget's Stage III at the same age as Swiss children.

Thus the recognition of perspective changes develops much later in Zulu children than in white children, and few of the Zulu children even up to 12 years were able to represent perspective changes correctly.

Subtests 6 to 8 (coordination of perspectives). In the coordination of perspectives, Piaget finds that a comprehensive coordination of viewpoints is not achieved until Stage IIIb, at 9 to 10 years. Stage IIIa, from 7 to 9 years, marks the beginning of the ability to coordinate perspectives, with the child succeeding in recognizing some relationships, particularly the before-behind positions. Prior to this, Piaget finds an egocentric stage, at 4 to 5.5 years, when the child is able to build only his own view of the mountains, or to choose only his own view or any view showing all three of the mountains (Stage IIa). This is followed by a transitional stage (IIb) in which the child attempts to differentiate the different viewpoints, but is unable to relate them correctly and usually relapses into the egocentric reactions of the previous stage.

The correct coordination of perspectives was found in the white children from about 10 years. However, very few of the Zulu children succeeded in this task. From 7 or 8 years the children usually showed some awareness of perspective, recognizing that the view of the mountains seen from different positions would change. However, they were generally unable to construct the correct view of the mountains from different positions, or to relate the views to the pictures representing them.

These results therefore confirm those of the previous subtests, indicating a failure on the part of the Zulu children to deal operationally with problems of perspective.

Test 3. Euclidean space

Subtests 1 to 4 (similarity of rhombi and triangles). Piaget's criterion for the Stage III level in the understanding of geometrical similarity of forms is an explicit and consistent reference to the parallelism of sides and the direct comparison of angles by superimposition. According to Piaget, this level is achieved between 7·5 and 9 years. However, he finds that complete understanding of dimensional proportion is achieved only at Stage IIIb, at 9 to 10 years.

Very few of the Zulu children and relatively few of the white children in this study achieved the Stage III level.

The Zulu children relied almost exclusively on perceptual estimates in their judgements of similarity. The white children showed some awareness of the criterion of parallelism of sides from about 7 or 8 years, but this criterion and the direct comparison of angles was not consistently applied to judgements of similarity until about 11 or 12 years.

The children's responses were not necessarily consistent across the subtests. It appeared that the method of presentation of the tests affected the method the child applied to the problem, so that the classification of responses in terms of stages of development was not very reliable.

Subtests 5 to 7 (similarity of rectangles). Piaget's criterion for the achievement of Stage III in the judgement of similar rectangles was the appearance of spontaneous attempts at measurement, found from 7·5 to 9 years. However, he found that the concept of proportion was not fully understood until Stage IV, from 10 to 12 years.

We found very few children who made any attempt to judge proportion by measurement or who were able to give a correct explanation of proportion. Both the white and the Zulu children relied on perceptual estimates in judging the similarity of rectangles.

The tendency in the Zulu children was to choose a rectangle that was too short as similar to the model. It is possible that this response was determined by a consideration of size rather than proportion, the shorter rectangles being closer in size to the smaller standard rectangle. This suggests that these children did not have a concept of rectangularity.

The tendency among the white children was to choose a rectangle that was too long as similar to the model. This is the response which Piaget described as typical of the pre-operational Stage II child, and is due to a general transposition of overall shape. The longer the rectangle, relative to its height, the more rectangular it is judged to be. And since the child is unable to take into account the relative dimensions of the rectangle, he bases his judgement on rectangularity as such, thus judging the longer rectangles as 'more like' the model. This tendency was found even up to 12 years in our group of white children.

Our groups were therefore less successful than Piaget's in their judgement of similarity of rectangles, and few of the Zulu children appeared to have developed a concept of rectangularity. However, the responses of both samples on this test were generally inconsistent, and some revision of the test would appear to be necessary to obtain a more reliable assessment of the development of concepts of proportion and similarity as applied to rectangles.

DISCUSSION

The development of spatial concepts in the Zulu and white children studied were similar to the findings reported by Piaget. The same sequence and types of response reported by Piaget were generally found, although in some cases our findings were at variance with those reported by Piaget and Inhelder. Among the white children the stages of development described by Piaget were found at approximately the same ages as given by Piaget, except in the case of the recognition of geometrical similarity and proportion, where our white group appeared to be inferior to Piaget's group. Among the Zulu children these stages were found at a later age, and very few of the Zulu children achieved the stage corresponding to Piaget's stage of concrete operations. Only in the tests on the copying of geometrical figures (Test 1, Subtest 1) and the construction of the projective straight line (Test 2, Subtest 1) did approximately half the Zulu children achieve the level of concrete operations (see Table 23.1).

Our results support Piaget and Inhelder's view that topological relationships are constructed before projective and Euclidean relationships. In the first test it was found that the children were able to represent topological relationships before they were able to copy correctly the Euclidean properties of figures. In the test of haptic perception we found that the identification of topological forms and the distinction between open and closed and indented and non-indented forms was found before the correct identification of Euclidean forms as a whole. We did not find that curved Euclidean forms were identified as easily as topological forms as stated by Lovell (1959). While we would agree with Lovell that the presence of gaps, holes, curves and points appears to make identification of figures easier, we do not see this as necessarily refuting Piaget's position that topological properties are recognized before Euclidean properties, and would agree with Laurendeau and Pinard's (1966) argument that the reason why such forms are more easily identified is because these properties are assimilated to the qualitative properties of the object, such as its continuity, proximity, order and enclosure, which are fundamental to topological space as opposed to the metric properties of Euclidean space.

The study of Kidd and Rivoire (1965) gives further support for the order of development from topological to projective and Euclidean concepts of space postulated by Piaget. This study also supports our finding of cultural differences in the development of projective and Euclidean concepts of space. In their study, Kidd and Rivoire made an analysis of the spatial items in a number of studies using so-called 'culture-free' tests, and found that those items which were 'culturally weighted' contained projective and Euclidean properties in addition to topological properties, whereas those items that were 'culturally fair' contained only topological properties.

On the basis of their findings Kidd and Rivoire suggest that in comparing the abilities of children from different cultural groups, test items based on topological properties only should be used. They apparently fail to recognize that the failure to develop projective and Euclidean concepts of space may relate to important differences in intellectual development that could affect other intellectual abilities, and that a 'culture-free' test devised by the process of excluding any items which discriminate between ethnic groups, regardless of whether these items are measuring important intellectual capacities or not, would be quite meaningless.

We found some differences between our results and Piaget's in the development of projective space. Like Lovell (1959), we found that the children's ability to construct a straight line both parallel and oblique to the edge of the table is far better than Piaget and Inhelder state.

We also did not find clear evidence of Piaget's 'egocentric' stage in the development of the coordination of perspectives. While we found that few of the Zulu children and few of the white children up to 10 years were able to coordinate perspectives correctly, we did not find any marked tendency for the children to believe that their own view was the only possible view of the mountains. They appeared to be aware of changes in perspective, and were sometimes able to state what the correct perspective view would be, although they were unable to construct it or select the correct representation.

We found marked differences between the Zulu and the white children in their ability to differentiate correctly the different perspective views of the pencil and the penny, to differentiate between their own view and that of an observer, and to coordinate perspectives.

Since few of the Zulu children even up to 12 years were able to succeed on these tests, the question as to whether these concepts are developed at the adult level in the Zulu culture is raised.

Differences between white and Bantu groups in the perception of pictorial depth have been reported by Hudson (1960, 1962). Such differences are likely to be related to the differences in the development of spatial concepts of perspectives found in this study. In analysing his results Hudson concludes that intellectual, educational and cultural factors are involved in the development of pictorial depth perception. He refers to the educational implications of his findings, pointing out that educational methods developed for one cultural group may not necessarily be appropriate for a different culture, and that adaptation and modification of such methods may be required.

In the tests of Euclidean space involving the recognition of geometrical concepts of similarity and proportion as applied to rhombi, triangles and rectangles, we found that our groups appeared to be inferior to Piaget's, and we did not find a systematic or consistent recognition of similarity or proportion even up to the age of 12 years in the white group. Recognition of similarity and proportion was even poorer in the Zulu group. We found difficulties in applying Piaget's method of classifying the responses on these tests, and a lack of consistency in the children's responses across the subtests.

It would therefore seem that there were weaknesses both in the tests and in the method of classification. It seems likely that children's notions of similarity and proportion are directly affected by their schooling, so that the tests chosen were not suitable for investigating the development of intuitive notions of Euclidean space.

CONCLUSION

It is clear that there are marked differences between the white and Zulu groups in the development of spatial concepts. Topological, projective and Euclidean relationships emerge at a later age level in the Zulu children than they do in the white children, and in the Zulu group relatively few children appear to understand the representation and coordination of perspectives or the principles of geometrical similarity and proportion.

Differences in intellectual development between different cultural groups are usually attributed to differences in the cultural and physical environments of the groups concerned. In this case it could be argued that the Zulu children were handicapped by a poorer home environment, lack of familiarity with the test media and situations, poorer quality of schooling, poorer physical health, and so on. Biesheuvel (1943, 1952b) has discussed at length the differences between the environments of African and European children in South Africa, and the extent to which such differences may influence the test performance of Africans.

However, regardless of the environmental factors that may affect the development of Zulu children, the differences found in this study between the white and the Zulu children are important in that they indicate a basic difference in the extent to which spatial concepts are developed in their respective cultures. The development of such concepts would be determined by a complex interaction of both cultural and biological factors. But since the development of a society is dependent on the individuals within that society, a close relationship must be expected to exist between the development of the society and the development of individuals within that society. According to Piaget, the development of spatial concepts is related to the development of the basic intellectual structures that determine the level of logical thought and abstract reasoning ability. A retardation in the development of spatial concepts may therefore indicate a retardation in other areas of mental functioning.

A general retardation in the development of the concrete operational structures defined by Piaget could have important implications for education and training. The spatial concepts studied in this investigation are likely to affect the child's understanding of basic mathematical concepts, and his ability to understand and to follow pictorial and diagrammatic representations. Delays in the development of other basic concepts could similarly affect the child's verbal reasoning ability, abstract thinking and understanding of basic scientific concepts. In view of the importance of these abilities in our present technological society it would seem important to undertake further studies to investigate the development of other basic concepts in African children, and particularly the environmental factors and experiences that may affect the development of these concepts. The aim of such studies would be to investigate the causal relationships involved, so that modifications could be introduced in the physical, social or educational environment of these children which would help them to achieve the same level of conceptual development as is found in children from Western technological societies.

24

P. R. Dasen

The influence of ecology, culture and European contact on cognitive development in Australian Aborigines[1]

Piaget's theory has been studied extensively in non-Western cultures during the past ten years; these data are extremely rich but heterogeneous and have been summarized elsewhere (Dasen, 1972a). Whenever Piagetian tests are applied in non-Western cultures, the same stages as those originally described by Piaget are found, but the rate of development is usually affected by environmental influences. The present trend of cross-cultural research in this area is to go beyond a simple replication of Piaget's theory, using specific cultural differences in a quasi-experimental situation in order to assess these environmental influences more closely.

The present paper describes a study of cognitive development in two groups of Australian Aborigines differing in amount of European contact, and attempts to relate the rate of development of different areas of cognitive development to cultural-ecological characteristics.

Two previous studies are directly relevant to this project. De Lemos (1966, 1969b) studied the development of the concepts of conservation of quantity, weight, volume, length, area and number in two groups of Australian Aboriginal children living on remote mission stations. De Lemos found that those children who did acquire the concepts of conservation did so qualitatively in exactly the same way as described

[1] This research was supported by a research scholarship at the Australian National University (Canberra, A.C.T.); the preparation of this report was made possible through a grant of the Fonds National Suisse de la Recherche Scientifique to Professor Bärbel Inhelder (Grant No. I. 133–69). Grateful acknowledgement is also made to Professor G. N. Seagrim for his guidance, to Catherine Dasen for her collaboration in the collection of the data and their analysis, and to the Finke River Mission, to the Welfare Branch of the Northern Territory Administration and to the Department of Education of New South Wales for granting admission to the schools.

by Piaget (i.e. going through the same substages on these tests, and giving the same explanations of their answers as European children). The rate of development, however, was much slower than in European children and the developmental curves were asymptotic (i.e. some children did not acquire the concepts at all).

De Lacey (1970a, b) applied four Piagetian tests of classification to four samples of Australian children. Two of these were samples of Australian Aboriginal children, one group living in isolated, rural, mainly Aboriginal communities, and the other living in much closer contact with Europeans. The two samples of European children were identified as high- and low-socioeconomic status. The rate of development of classificatory concepts was extremely slow in the low-contact group, yielding developmental curves similar to those reported by de Lemos. A subsample of high-contact Aboriginals, on the other hand, performed as well as, or better than, white Australian children of a low-socioeconomic background.

THE EUROPEAN CONTACT VARIABLE

In de Lacey's study, the difference in European contact between the two Aboriginal samples was extreme. The two groups lived in widely different areas of Australia, the low-contact group having retained much of its traditions and language, whereas the high-contact group had become completely acculturated, shedding all aspects of Aboriginal values and culture, speaking the English language only, attending the same schools as their European peers, and living largely the life of poor Europeans.

In the present study, the two groups of Aboriginal children differ also on the variable of European contact, but are more comparable on many other aspects: both groups live in semi-desert country west of Alice Springs, in central Australia, in isolated, mainly Aboriginal communities; both groups have retained some or most of their Aboriginal values and traditions, speak the vernacular as their language, with English being used only at school; both groups live on social welfare or, even if employed, have no direct intercourse with the European economy.

The low-contact group consists of Pitjantjara (Pitjantjajara) Aborigines living at the *Areyonga* Government Settlement, which was established as a ration depot in 1944 and which has included a school since 1950 and a medical dispensary since 1952. Some contact between the Western Desert tribes and European missionaries had existed since 1920, but even when Areyonga was established, contact with European culture was only sporadic, and mainly limited to the distribution of goods, the Aboriginal population remaining mainly nomadic. In later years, some Aborigines became more sedentary, but traditions and customs were constantly revived by the arrival of new groups from the desert (up until about 1965). In 1969, when this study was carried out, the Aboriginal population at Areyonga had become sedentary for part of the year, although most families did not use the houses provided by the settlement, but lived in tin shacks resembling the traditional shelters and which could be moved from time to time. For about four months each year, however, most of the population still leaves on 'walkabout', visiting their ancestral sacred grounds and performing ceremonies, travelling over wide distances in the Western Desert, and living mainly from hunting and gathering. During the sedentary months, the children attend school more or less regularly and most adults have some form of employment, although these jobs tend to be rather artificial because there is no real economic reason for them, except welfare. Access to the settlement, which is situated on Reserve 1028, is restricted and is subject to a permit issued by the welfare administration; access is further hindered by distance (approximately 140 miles from Alice Springs) and poor road conditions.

The medium-contact group consists of Aranda (Arunta) Aborigines living at *Hermannsburg* Mission, which was established in 1877, with school activities dating back to 1880. Schooling was initially conducted in Aranda, but from the 1930s onward English became more important, and finally the sole language of instruction; the curriculum and facilities were extremely basic until the 1950s. In 1969, the schooling conditions in Areyonga and Hermannsburg tended to be quite similar, although Hermannsburg had slightly better equipment and a more stable staff. The Aboriginal population at Hermannsburg still uses the vernacular almost exclusively, but Aboriginal values and traditions have been abandoned to some extent, without being necessarily replaced by their European equivalents. Housing tends to be of a better standard than at Areyonga, although this is a recent achievement and a few families are moving back into tin shacks. The population is more stable than at Areyonga; there is no annual 'walkabout', although many Aborigines tend to travel frequently to other settlements. Adults are employed on the same type of jobs as at Areyonga, but the mission also has a productive cattle industry and a tannery, and a cash economy is promoted by a well-equipped store. Access to Hermannsburg is free, and tourist buses pay regular visits to the mission; the station is linked to the nearest European centre by 70 miles of a relatively good road.

Applying de Lacey's 'index of contact' (de Lacey, 1970c) to the two samples, Areyonga has an index of 0·13 and Hermannsburg an index of 0·39 (maximum 1·00). This compares with 0·13 for de Lacey's low-contact group, and 0·83 for his high-contact group (de Lacey, 1970b).

Most previous studies in cross-cultural Piagetian psychology dealing with the variable of European contact have attempted to maximize the difference between the samples to be compared; further, they have either used the urban/rural difference (Greenfield, 1966; Pcluffo, 1967; Poole, 1968; Vernon, 1969; de Lacey, 1970b) or the literate/illiterate difference (Greenfield, 1966; Hendrikz, 1966) or both (Mohseni, 1966). In the present study, on the other hand, the children of both samples live in rural communities and receive the same type of schooling; the main difference lies in the length of European contact and in the extent to which traditional values and activities have persisted. It is hypothesized that, in spite of the relatively small difference which exists between the two groups, a significant difference in the rate of cognitive development will be found.

THE CULTURAL/ECOLOGICAL VARIABLE

It has been argued by Berry (1966b, 1971) that ecological demands placed on a group of people, plus their cultural adaptation to this ecology ('cultural aids') would lead to the development of certain perceptual and spatial skills. 'Cultural and psychological development are congruent; cultural characteristics allow people to develop and maintain those skills which they have to' (Berry, 1966b, p. 228). Specifically 'hunting peoples are expected to possess good visual discrimination and spatial skill, and their cultures are expected to be supportive of the development of these skills through the presence of a high number of "geometrical spatial" concepts, a highly developed and generally shared arts and crafts production, and socialization practices whose content emphasizes independence and self reliance, and whose techniques are supportive and encouraging of separate development' (Berry, 1971, p. 133).

Berry (1966b) was able to demonstrate that on four tests seen as measuring spatial ability (Kohs Blocks, Witkin Embedded Figures Test, Morrisby Shapes and Raven Matrices), the performance of Eskimos (hunting economy; language rich in spatial terms; highly developed arts and crafts; lenient socialization practices) not only exceeded that of the Temne (agricultural economy; language poor in spatial terms; poorly developed arts and crafts skills; harsh socialization practices) but very nearly matched Scottish (the European reference group) performance.

Later (Berry, 1971) other samples which were ecologically intermediate were also included (one of which was an Arunta sample), and the pattern of the data displayed only a single error in the rank ordering of the dependent variables.

Extending Berry's ecological functionalism to the Piagetian framework, we may expect that people with a hunting economy should develop the concepts of space (Piaget and Inhelder, 1956) in preference to concepts in other cognitive areas on which there are no or fewer ecological demands.

The Australian Aborigines depend traditionally on hunting and food gathering, travelling for long distances in a relatively barren environment (Hellbusch, 1941; Elkin, 1964; Strehlow, 1965; and many others). Water is a rare commodity, and the journeys are usually organized to lead from one waterhole to the next; the Aborigine knows the location of these waterholes, and indeed of every other feature in the environment over a wide area, of which he seems to have a detailed 'cognitive map', which enables him to find his way and to give directions to others. Aborigines do not use transportable maps, but draw symbolic maps on the ground or as rock paintings. These maps simply represent locations by circles, connected by lines which represent the journey between them, and which seem to be accurate as to direction but not distance. (Analysed into Piagetian terms, these maps contain topological and projective, but not Euclidean spatial relationships.)

Related 'cultural aids' are also present: Aboriginal artistic traditions are well-known (bark paintings, and more recently the Namatjira water-colour style developed at Hermannsburg mission) and child-rearing practices are generally described as very permissive (Kaberry, 1939; Malinowski, 1963; Nurcombe and Cawte, 1967; Dawson, 1969).

On the other hand, the concepts of number and measurement seem to be absent in Aboriginal culture.

Aborigines know their food-gathering and water places and have some idea of clan and tribal boundaries. . . . But they do not measure and have no terms for expressing size or distance. . . . Of course, the craftsman knows the length he wants to make his spear, but not in feet and inches. He works by sight, weight and balance.

This matter of measurement is related to the problem of numbers – a real problem for Aborigines. Their languages have words for one and two, and indicate three and four by saying two-one and two-

two respectively. Sometimes five is indicated by the open hand. . . .
But this is not counting; it is only a concrete method of indicating
individual persons or places. After five they usually say many, or a
'mob' or a 'big mob'. And this is quite understandable. Individual
persons are known by names and their tracks. A hunter only hunts
and spears one kangaroo at a time. . . . Likewise he is lucky if he
spears more than one wallaby, though he might see 'plenty' or 'big
mob' wallaby. . . . Consequently, though children in school learn by
rote to count up to a given number and to recite various tables, these
numbers have no relevance to their parents' and grandparents' life
– i.e. to hunting and food-gathering. (Elkin, 1964, pp. 236–7)

This same explanation for the absence of a number system was put
forward by Strehlow (1944), and while it may well be found to be
unsatisfactory (one would certainly wish to have more anthropological
evidence concerning the use of basic concepts), the fact that the Aborigine is not concerned with number, measurement or exact quantities
is well established.

We might thus expect that Australian Aborigines would develop
spatial concepts more readily than concepts related to number or measurement (what we will call 'logico-mathematical' concepts) because
the former are ecologically and culturally more relevant than the latter.

In European children this is not so; the two areas of conceptual
development may be seen to develop conjointly during the period of
concrete operations, or logico-mathematical concepts may even be
acquired relatively earlier than spatial concepts:

At the age of seven years on the average the child is able to carry
out logico-arithmetical operations (classifications, arrangements in
series and one-to-one correspondence) but it is a year later that the
time-space operations are achieved (including co-ordinates, projective concepts and simultaneity). (Inhelder, 1956, p. 83)

In more general terms, our hypothesis is that the rate of cognitive development may vary from one area of conceptual development to another,
under the influence of ecological and cultural demands.

SUMMARY OF HYPOTHESES

1. On the basis of the findings of most previous studies dealing with
the development of concrete operations in non-Western cultures (cf.
Dasen, 1972a) and in particular of the previous study of conservation

concepts in Australian Aborigines (de Lemos, 1966, 1969b), we propose the following general hypothesis:

> HYPOTHESIS 1: The qualitative aspects of operational development (i.e. the stages) are identical in Australian Aborigines and in Europeans, but the rate of development is slower in Aborigines.

2. On the basis of previous findings that European contact, broadly defined, favoured the development of concrete operations in non-Western cultures (Greenfield, 1966; Mohseni, 1966; Poole, 1968; Lloyd, 1971a, b) and in particular on the basis of the previous study of the influence of European contact in Australian Aborigines (de Lacey, 1970b), the following hypothesis is to be tested:

> HYPOTHESIS 2: The rate of operational development is faster in the medium-contact group (Hermannsburg) than in the low-contact group (Areyonga).

3. Following Berry's ecological and cultural functionalism (Berry, 1966b, 1971), an analysis of the ecology and culture of Australian Aborigines gives rise to the following hypothesis:

> HYPOTHESIS 3: Aborigines, because of their ecological and cultural background, will develop spatial concepts more readily than 'logico-mathematical' concepts.

METHOD

Samples

One hundred and forty-five Australian Aboriginal children, aged 6 to 16 years, and twenty adults, were tested in two different locations in central Australia, both west of Alice Springs. The low-contact group consisted of the total school population at *Areyonga* Settlement ($N =$ 55); the medium-contact group ($N = 90$) was sampled from the 148 children attending the *Hermannsburg* Mission school, so as to include at each age level five children of each sex. In both groups, children whose age could not be firmly established, who had obvious deficiencies in vision or hearing, or who were recognized by teachers as mentally retarded were excluded from the samples. The adults, ten in each sample, volunteered because they were interested and/or because of the additional incentive of cigarettes, oranges or cool drinks. The mean age of the adult samples was 23;3 years at Areyonga and 25;0 years at Hermannsburg; they tend to represent the younger, better educated and more acculturated portion of the adult population.

In addition, a reference group of eighty Europeans (white Australians, excluding those children of migrant origin, who were not completely fluent in English) was selected from a state primary school in a lower middle-class suburb in Canberra, Australian Capital Territory.

The age-groups were defined as $(n-1);7$ to $(n);6$ years, e.g. for 12 year olds, 11 years 7 months to 12 years 6 months.

Details of sampling procedures and sample characteristics are given elsewhere (Dasen, 1970)

Testing conditions

The children were tested individually, during normal school hours. At Hermannsburg and Areyonga, two subjects were tested at one time in the same room by separate experimenters, but facing away from each other. This helped to overcome initial shyness.

Total testing time varied with age and among subjects, and occupied (including five perceptual tests which are not discussed in this paper) from one to three hours, with an average of approximately two hours for Aboriginal subjects and seventy-five minutes for Europeans. This total time was subdivided into several sessions (from two to six) of varying length (fifteen to forty-five minutes) depending on the subject's attention and the school's timetable. The sessions were usually separated by one or two days.

At Areyonga and Hermannsburg, a great deal of time had to be spent on establishing *rapport* with the children. This was accomplished as follows:

(1) At first, the experimenters attended school activities, showed slides, and made it clear that they were interested in what the children were doing and thinking; they also spent a great deal of time with the children outside school hours.

(2) In a second stage, the subjects came to the experimental room and were allowed to play games, to look at photographic books dealing with Aboriginal children, to draw, and, if possible, to take a first test.

In most cases, no reinforcement had to be given; it was considered a reward in itself to 'play the games'. Subjects were encouraged by words such as 'good' irrespective of their actual performance, and no feedback was given, except to some older subjects and adults after the testing was completed.

Procedure

The tasks were based on those described by Piaget and his colleagues, and standardized by Vinh-Bang (in preparation). The procedure was standardized in so far as the same basic problems and questions were put to each child, but the flexibility of Piaget's clinical method was retained in that individual children were questioned further according to their particular response. Suggestions and counter-suggestions, which are usually made to test the stability of the answers,[1] were not used for the following reason: the Aboriginal child is not used to expressing and maintaining his own opinion. Any counter-suggestion is likely to be taken as criticism, and the subject will change his answer. Whether the child actually changes his mind or not is difficult to say: he could well give an answer which he knows to be wrong, but which he thinks will please the European authority figure.

All actions were performed by the subject and not by the experimenter; this was designed to avoid the occurrence of what Greenfield (1966, pp. 245–63) has called 'action-magic', i.e. the attribution of 'magical' powers to an authority figure such as the experimenter. For example, in the conservation tests nonconservation could be rationalized as having been produced by adult magical power in addition to the physical transformation.

A time limit was never set and the subjects were never led to believe that they had to answer or work quickly. The testing procedures were devised to be suitable for the low-contact group; the same procedures were then used for the two other samples, except that, for the European sample, a more sophisticated English was used. The tests were selected and the questioning procedures were adopted after a pilot study conducted at Amoonguna Settlement near Alice Springs. Some changes were made in the materials and procedures following this testing. In particular it was found that the materials used by de Lemos (1966) for the conservation of quantity (namely sugar) and weight (namely tea in plastic bags of various sizes) were not practical and did not seem to be more familiar to the children than the usual water (or cordial) and plasticine; the standard test materials were therefore retained. For the test of seriation, it proved necessary to show a model with the instructions to the first part. Each test was preceded by a training sequence and by check items to ensure adequate communication. The vocabulary of the

---

[1] For a discussion of the requirements used by the Genevan school in the assessment of an operational task, see Goodnow, 1969b, pp. 440–52.

child was assessed, and the same words were subsequently used for the critical items.

The testing was carried out in English. It would have been impossible to learn the Pitjantjara and the Aranda languages to any sufficient degree of fluency in the time available for this study. However the experimenters were familiar with a few key words of the vernaculars, and used these to establish contact or to trigger a response. Translations into Aranda were kindly supplied by Dr de Lemos, and translations into Pitjantjara were cross-checked with several Aboriginal and European informants. As English is the only language of instruction, most subjects understood simple instructions and questions and could speak sufficiently for the tasks. It was felt that communication had always been adequate; the few cases in which this was not the case were classified separately. It proved impracticable to use an interpreter because Europeans speaking Aboriginal languages are extremely rare, and would not have been able to spend a sufficient time on this project. Nor were suitable Aboriginal interpreters available. A short attempt was made to secure the help of a native teaching assistant, but the experimenter felt that he had no real control over the communication. (The interpreter proved later to be a nonconserver herself, and might have influenced the subjects against a conserving response.) The same observations had been made by de Lemos (1966, pp. 372–3). As has also been mentioned by de Lemos (1969b, p. 257), it was not possible to use questions containing more than one alternative, since the children frequently answered simply 'yes' or 'no', presumably to the last alternative mentioned in the question. Each alternative was therefore put as a separate question, or the question was formulated as 'What about now?' (Almy *et al.*, 1966, p. 51).

Tasks

A summary of the tasks used is given below. The detailed procedures are reported fully elsewhere (Dasen, 1970).

1. *Conservation of quantity.* After having been successful on five consecutive check-items, involving equal and unequal quantities, the subject was asked to pour the same amount of cordial into two standard beakers (A and A'). The subject was then asked to pour A' into B, a long thin measuring cylinder. After the equality between A and A' had been re-established, the subject was invited to pour A' into C, a wide culture dish. In each case the child was asked whether the quantities of cordial were still the same, or if there was more to drink in one of the

glasses. The child was asked which one he preferred to drink and was allowed to do so.

2. *Conservation of weight.* The subject's understanding of the balance was assessed. After having been successful on five consecutive check-items involving equal and unequal weights, the subject was asked to choose two balls of plasticine (A and A') which were of the same weight. He was then asked to roll A' out into B, a long, thin 'sausage'. After the equality between A and A' had been re-established by a check with the balance, the subject was requested to flatten A' into C, a flat 'pancake'. In each case the child was asked whether the weight was still the same, or whether one was heavier. The questions were also put in terms of the balance remaining 'level' or 'going down' on one side.

3. *Conservation of volume.* Two glasses about two-thirds filled with water were placed in front of the child, and the levels were marked off by rubber bands. The subject was asked to predict the rise in water level when equal- and unequal-sized balls of plasticine were placed inside the glasses. After having been successful on five successive check-items, the subject was asked to perform the same transformations as with the conservation of weight test, and the usual questions were asked.

4. *Conservation of length.* The task started with a series of vocabulary test-items. *Part 1*: Two sticks of equal length (16 cm) were placed in front of the child, parallel and with ends coinciding. One stick was then displaced from left to right so as to overlap the other by about 5 cm. *Part 2*: The subject was given one of the sticks of 16 cm (A) and four small sticks of 4 cm (a's) and he was asked to align the latter with the former. It was made sure that he understood that the four short lengths added up to the length of A. The four a's were then displaced to form a 'W' shape. *Part 3*: Two unequal-length pipe cleaners, a straight one and one curved in a zigzag shape, were placed in front of the child in such a way that the ends coincided. In each case the child was asked if the two sticks were the same length, if it would be the same distance to walk from one end to the other on the two sticks. The question as to whether it would take the same time to walk (de Lemos, 1966) was not used, since it would have introduced a different concept.

On all items of all the conservation tasks, the child was asked for an explanation of his judgement.

5. *Seriation. Part 1*: The subject was given a set of ten loose sticks,

increasing from 10·6 to 16·0 cm by steps of 0·6 cm, displayed randomly on the table, and he was shown a model of the seriation, which he was asked to copy. The model was removed once the subject had started working, but was presented again any number of times if necessary. *Part 2*: The subject was given the model, and was asked to place the ten loose sticks 'in the right place'. (The lengths of the sticks were so designed that an exact insertion was possible.)

6. *Orders. Part 1*: Linear order. The subject was asked to copy a linear display of nine miniature clothes (cut out of coloured cardboard so as to form an inverted 'V' shape which enabled them to be hung on a string). *Part 2*: Reverse order. The child was asked to choose exactly the same clothes as those on the model (as in Part 1), but to reverse their order. This rather difficult instruction was formulated in different ways, until the experimenter was sure that the child had understood the problem. *Part 3*: Circular order. The experimenter put nine items into a circle on the table and asked the subject to copy the display in the same order, but in a straight line.

7. *Rotation.* Two identical landscape models, adapted to the central Australian landscape, but including the same spatial features as described by Piaget and Inhelder (1956, p. 421), were placed side by side on a desk, in the same orientation. The child was asked to name the elements on one of the models and to show the corresponding elements on the other; the fact that the two models were identical was pointed out. The experimenter then placed a toy sheep in several locations on one of the models, asking the child to place his toy sheep in exactly the same position (checking the location and the direction 'into which it looked'). After the child understood the problem, one of the models was turned around by 180°, and the same check-items were repeated. Finally a screen was placed between the two models to prevent the possibility of a purely perceptual solution. For the test items, the sheep were placed successively in seven standard positions on one of the models, the child being asked to find the same position and direction on the rotated model. The child was not asked to verbalize his reasoning.

8. *Horizontality.* A round bottle, half filled with blue coloured water, was placed in the vertical position on a stand. The subject was presented with a corresponding outline drawing, and was asked to draw the water in the bottle. The bottle was then hidden in a bag, so that the shape was

still apparent but the water no longer visible, and a second check-item in the vertical position was performed. *Part 1*: Anticipation. The bottle, still hidden in the bag, was placed successively in five different positions (from the subject's point of view: 1. tilted to the right; 2. on its side, cork to the right; 3. upside down; 4. tilted so that the cork touched the stand on the right; 5. tilted to the left). Each time the child was given the corresponding outline drawing, the record sheet being folded so that only one picture was visible at any one time. The subject was asked where the water was, and to draw it. *Part 2*: Copy. The bag was removed, and the same procedure was repeated for the positions on which the child was not successful on Part 1. *Part 3*: Anticipation after copy. The same procedure was repeated once more, the bottle being again hidden in the bag; however, this was done only for the positions on which the subject, in Part 2, improved on his performance in Part 1. It should be noted that this was the only task in which pictorial material was used; this, however, was so simple that it should not have caused any difficulties.

Task sequence

The order in which the tasks were administered was randomized. The order of the tasks of conservation of quantity, weight and volume, however, was counterbalanced, so that in the overall sample as well as in each age-group, the number of subjects taking each task first, second or third was approximately equal.

All tasks were not administered to all age-groups. In Areyonga, the conservation tasks were not administered to the 6 and 7 year olds; in the European sample, conservation of volume was not administered to the 5 year olds, and testing was discontinued for each task if 100 per cent Stage III behaviour had been attained in the previous age-group. The task of orders was presented to the following age-groups: 5 to 8 in Canberra, 6 to 10 in Hermannsburg, and 6 to 11 in Areyonga.

Adults in the Aboriginal samples were presented with the following tasks: conservation of quantity, weight and volume, and horizontality. The number of subjects in the Areyonga sample varies somewhat with the tasks because some subjects left on 'walkabout' before testing was completed.

Grouping of tasks for data analysis

The tasks were grouped in the following way:

Conservation and logico-mathematical tasks: conservation of quantity, weight, volume, and length; seriation.

Spatial tasks: orders, rotation and horizontality.

The conservation and logico-mathematical tasks were considered to be theoretically related to the concept of number (Piaget, *1941*) whereas the spatial tasks were selected so as to include topological, projective and Euclidean spatial relationships (Piaget and Inhelder, 1956). The task of conservation of length, although referring to a spatial content, was grouped with the 'logico-mathematical' tests because of the structural similarity with the other conservation tasks, and because anthropological evidence showed that Aborigines did not traditionally compare and measure lengths.

The two groups of tasks could also be called, respectively: ecologically and culturally irrelevant, and ecologically and culturally relevant.

Scoring and classification

The responses of the children were recorded on specially devised score sheets, and the interviews for the conservation tasks were tape-recorded. The responses were then classified into Piaget's stages of development. These stages, and the operational procedures used for scoring and classifying the responses into stages, have been described in full elsewhere (Dasen, 1970). For the conservation tasks, the same conventions as described by de Lemos (1969b, p. 260) were applied, except that children appearing to answer randomly, or failing the check-items, were classified separately into a category F (for 'failure to communicate').

Each type of response was also attributed a number of points; if a task comprised several subtests, these were added to form a score for each task. The scores of the conservation and logico-mathematical tasks were added to form the 'logico-mathematical score' and the scores of the spatial tasks were added to form the 'spatial score'. This scoring system is, of course, quite arbitrary, but provides the possibility of adding the performance of different tasks. The details of the scoring in points, and the results for each task and group of tasks are reported in full elsewhere (Dasen, 1970).

RESULTS

Qualitative analysis

A detailed qualitative analysis of the results revealed an exact correspondence between the answers and explanations given by Aboriginal children and by European children in Canberra. The Aboriginal child may use only a word or two, or a gesture, instead of a long verbal explanation, but the reasoning he expresses is precisely the same.

This general conclusion needs one qualification: by about age 10 years and thereafter, European children begin to give more complex statements, which seem to reflect a new way of thinking about the problems; the children start to use formal concepts, sometimes without fully comprehending them. They also tend to formulate their explanations into general laws (for example: 'It is always the same weight, whatever you do to it, unless you add some or you take some off').

No such generalizations or complex explanations were given by Aboriginal subjects. This may be due partly to the lack of verbal fluency in English. However, even the older subjects and the adults who had acquired a very good command of the English language did not make any of these involved statements. The formal properties of thought, which are evidenced by some of the formulations the European children use, are absent from the explanations the Aborigines give.

It was found that the responses and explanations given by the Aboriginal children could be classified without difficulty into the stages described by Piaget.

TABLE 24.1. *Conservation of quantity (liquids): percentage of subjects classified at each stage*

Age	5	6	7	8	9	10	11	12	13	14	15	16	Ad.
Canberra[a]													
C	0	30	70	90	100	100	—	—					
T	10	10	20	0	0	0							
NC	90	60	10	10	0	0							
Hermannsburg[a]													
C			0	10	20	40	30	10	50	70		70	40
T			10	10	40	10	0	30	10	10		20	20
NC			60	80	30	50	70	60	40	20		10	40
F			30	10	0	0	0	0	0	0		0	0
Areyonga[b]													
C				17		0		20		30			30
T				0		0		27		10			20
NC				75		89		40		60			50
F				8		11		13		0			0

C = Conservation.   T = Transitional.   NC = Nonconservation.
F = Failure to communicate.

[a] N = 10 Ss per age.
[b] N = 12, 9, 15, 10, 10 Ss respectively.

Quantitative analysis

For each test, the percentage of children at each age level classified at the various stages of development are presented in Tables 24.1 to 24.8. In each case, Stage III (or C for conservation) represents the attainment of the concrete operational stage.

TABLE 24.2. *Conservation of weight: percentage of subjects classified at each stage*

Age	5	6	7	8	9	10	11	12	13	14	15	16	Ad.
Canberra[a]													
C	0	0	20	60	80	20	50	80					
T	0	30	40	30	0	20	20	20					
NC	100	70	40	10	20	60	30	0					
Hermannsburg[a]													
C		0	0	10	10	10	10	20	20		50		20
T		10	20	0	20	0	20	10	40		40		0
NC		70	50	60	70	90	70	70	40		10		80
F		10	40	20	0	0	0	0	0		0		0
Areyonga[b]													
C					8		11		13		9		10
T					25		22		20		37		10
NC					42		56		60		27		80
F					25		11		7		27		0

[a] N = 10 Ss per age.
[b] N = 12, 9, 15, 10, 10 Ss respectively.

TABLE 24.3. *Conservation of volume: percentage of subjects classified at each stage*

Age	5	6	7	8	9	10	11	12	13	14	15	16	Ad.
Canberra[a]													
C		10	10	10	50	10	60	50					
T		20	40	50	30	10	10	40					
NC		70	50	40	20	80	30	10					
Hermannsburg[a]													
C		10	10	0	30	30	10	20	20		60		30
T		10	20	40	30	60	20	30	30		30		0
NC		40	40	20	40	10	70	50	50		10		70
F		40	30	30	0	0	0	0	0		0		0
Areyonga[b]													
C					25		22		13		30		0
T					42		56		13		20		0
NC					17		22		53		50		100
F					17		0		20		0		0

[a] N = 10 Ss per age.
[b] N = 12, 9, 15, 11, 10 Ss respectively.

TABLE 24.4. *Conservation of length: percentage of subjects classified at each stage*

Age		5	6	7	8	9	10	11	12	13	14	15	16
Canberra[a]													
Part 1	C	0	10	60	70	80	90						
	T	10	0	30	10	0	0						
	NC	90	90	10	20	20	10						
Part 2	C	0	10	40	70	100							
	T	0	30	30	20	0							
	NC	100	60	30	10	0							
Part 3	C	10	50	40	100	100							
	T	10	0	30	0	0							
	NC	80	50	30	0	0							
Hermannsburg[a]													
Part 1	C		20	50	40	30	50	50	60	20		70	
	T		0	0	0	10	10	20	10	10		0	
	NC		70	40	50	60	40	30	30	70		30	
	F		10	10	10	0	0	0	0	0		0	
Part 2	C		0	10	10	10	40	40	50	20		40	
	T		0	0	0	0	10	0	0	0		0	
	NC		80	80	80	90	50	60	50	80		60	
	F		20	10	10	0	0	0	0	0		0	
Part 3	C		0	10	20	30	30	0	10	10		20	
	T		10	10	0	0	0	0	10	20		0	
	NC		70	70	70	70	70	100	80	70		80	
	F		20	10	10	0	0	0	0	0		0	

Age		8	9	10	11	12	13	14	15
Areyonga[b]									
Part 1	C	17		25·0		27		37·5	
	T	25		12·5		0		12·5	
	NC	58		62·5		67		37·5	
	F	0		0		7		12·5	
Part 2	C	8		0		20		25·0	
	T	17		0		0		12·5	
	NC	75		87·5		73		50·0	
	F	0		12·5		7		12·5	
Part 3	C	17		12·5		13		50·0	
	T	0		12·5		27		0	
	NC	83		75·0		53		37·5	
	F	0		0		7		12·5	

[a] $N = 10$ Ss per age.
[b] $N = 12, 8, 15, 8$ Ss respectively.

Culture and Cognition

TABLE 24.5. *Seriation: percentage of subjects classified at each stage*

Age	5	6	7	8	9	10	11	12	13	14	15	16
Canberra[a]												
Stage III	0	30	60	100								
„ II	40	60	40	0								
„ I	60	10	0	0								
Hermannsburg[a]												
Stage III		0	0	10	10	40	60	80	100			100
„ II		30	70	70	90	60	40	20	0			0
„ I		70	30	20	0	0	0	0	0			0
Areyonga[b]												
Stage III		0		17			33·3		27		75	
„ II		62·5		66			55·5		60		25	
„ I		37·5		17			11·1		13		0	

[a] $N = 10$ Ss per age.
[b] $N = 8, 12, 9, 15, 8$ Ss respectively.

TABLE 24.6. *Orders: percentage of subjects classified at each stage*

Age	5	6	7	8	9	10	11
Canberra[a]							
Stage III	20	80	80	100	100	—	
„ Int.	0	0	20	0	0		
„ IIb	50	20	0	0	0		
„ IIa	30	0	0	0	0		
Hermannsburg[b]							
Stage III	—	50	70	80	100	100	—
„ Int.		10	20	20	0	0	
„ IIb		30	10	0	0	0	
„ IIa		10	0	0	0	0	
Areyonga[a]							
Stage III		0	40	100	88	100	100
„ Int		33·3	40	0	0	0	0
„ IIb		66·6	10	0	12	0	0
„ IIa		0	0	0	0	0	0

[a] $N = 10$ Ss per age.
[b] $N = 3, 5, 4, 8, 6, 2$ Ss respectively.

TABLE 24.7. *Rotation: percentage of subjects classified at each stage*

Age	5	6	7	8	9	10	11	12	13	14	15	16
Canberra[a]												
Stage III	0	10	0	30	70	100	80	100				
„ IIb	40	50	70	70	30	0	20	0				
„ IIa	40	30	30	0	0	0	0	0				
„ I	20	10	0	0	0	0	0	0				
Hermannsburg[a]												
Stage III		0	10	0	20	40	50	30		80		80
„ IIb		50	40	70	80	60	50	70		20		20
„ IIa		40	40	30	0	0	0	0		0		0
„ I		10	10	0	0	0	0	0		0		0
Areyonga[b]												
Stage III		0			25		0			36		37·5
„ IIb		75			58		67			64		62·5
„ IIa		0			17		33			0		0
„ I		25			0		0			0		0

[a] $N = 10$ Ss per age.
[b] $N = 8, 12, 9, 14, 8$ Ss respectively.

TABLE 24.8. *Horizontality: percentage of subjects classified at each stage*

Age	5	6	7	8	9	10	11	12	13	14	15	16	Ad.
Canberra[a]													
Part 1													
Stage IIIb	0	0	0	30	10	20	70	50					
„ Int.	10	20	30	40	70	70	30	50					
„ IIb	30	10	50	30	20	10	0	0					
„ IIa	60	50	20	0	0	0	0	0					
„ I	0	20	0	0	0	0	0	0					
Parts 1–3													
IIIa and IIIb	0	10	20	60	50	70	100	90					
Hermannsburg[a]													
Part 1													
Stage IIIb		0	0	20	0	20	10	0		30		30	40
„ Int.		0	10	10	50	30	60	70		40		50	50
„ IIb		60	20	30	30	50	20	30		30		10	10
„ IIa		30	70	30	20	0	10	0		0		10	0
„ I		10	0	10	0	0	0	0		0		0	0
Parts 1–3													
IIIa and IIIb		0	10	30	0	40	50	30		50		50	60

Table continued on page 400

Table continued from page 399

Age		5	6	7	8	9	10	11	12	13	14	15	16	Ad.
Areyonga[b]														
Stage	IIIb	0			17		0		7		30			20
"	Int.	25			25		56		33		30			70
"	IIb	0			17		11		40		40			10
"	IIa	75			33		33		20		0			0
"	I	0			8		0		0		0			0
Parts 1–3														
IIIa and														
IIIb		0			33		22		13		70			90

[a] $N = 10$ Ss per age.
[b] $N = 8, 12, 9, 15, 10, 10$ Ss respectively.

The logico-mathematical scores of the three samples were pooled, and transformed into z' scores with a mean of 50 and a standard deviation of 10. The same computation was performed for the spatial scores. The means and standard deviations of logico-mathematical and spatial z' scores for each sample and each age level are presented in Table 24.9.

DISCUSSION

Hypothesis 1

Whenever the comparison can be made, the results obtained in Canberra are similar to those reported from Geneva (Piaget and Inhelder, 1969; Inhelder, 1968); this is also true of comparisons with unpublished data (Vinh–Bang, in preparation). The surprising drop in the conservation of weight (and to a lesser degree volume) which is noticeable at ages 10 and 11 in the Canberra sample was attributed, after a careful analysis of the protocols and the retesting of the same and other samples, to the interference of quasi-formal concepts such as pressure and gravity (Dasen and Christie, 1972). Similar findings were reported by Goodnow (1962, p. 9) and Pinard *et al.* (1969, p12).

The rate of development of all the concepts studied is much lower in both Aboriginal samples. When considering the achievement of the concrete operational stage, the 100 per cent level is reached only on the tests of seriation and orders. In most cases, the developmental curves are asymptotic at the higher ages. This means that a more or less large proportion (depending on the particular concept and sample) of Aborigines do not develop these concrete operational concepts at all. In fact,

TABLE 24.9. *Logico-mathematical and spatial tests: z' scores*

Age		5	6	7	8	9	10	11	12	13	14	15	16	Total sample
Canberra														
Logico-mathematical	$\bar{x}$	36·1	45·6	54·5	59·7	63·8	59·1	63·9	64·4					56·0
	SD	2·8	6·2	5·5	5·0	5·0	4·0	4·4	3·2					10·6
Spatial	$\bar{x}$	32·2	42·1	45·5	54·6	57·2	59·3	61·0	60·9					51·6
	SD	4·9	6·4	4·8	4·3	3·4	1·7	2·4	3·0					10·7
Hermannsburg														
Logico-mathematical	$\bar{x}$		37·1	41·1	43·8	48·7	49·6	47·1	51·6	52·6			58·8	47·7
	SD		3·8	4·6	4·9	8·2	7·2	5·0	6·6	4·2			5·6	8·3
Spatial	$\bar{x}$		36·0	42·3	44·1	49·0	51·9	53·3	54·4	58·5			58·4	49·7
	SD		4·8	7·9	9·0	6·3	6·9	8·5	2·8	2·6			3·5	9·9
Areyonga														
Logico-mathematical	$\bar{x}$			36·8		45·6		44·9		45·5	50·5			44·7
	SD			2·4		5·1		4·9		6·1	5·2			6·4
Spatial	$\bar{x}$			36·6		47·9		48·0		50·9	55·4			47·9
	SD			9·1		8·4		6·8		5·7	6·8			9·0

the incidence of operational thinking is found to be less in adults than in the older schoolchildren. Since, theoretically, once a concept has been acquired, it is not likely to be lost, we may suppose that these adults had not reached the concrete operational stage at ages 14 to 16 years. The superior performance of the older schoolchildren can be interpreted as either being due to improved education or to the possibility that the generally larger amount of European contact is more influential in children than in adults. Perhaps education and/or European contact are only effective during a 'critical period' in childhood, and we may assume that European contact is greater for the children of today than it was for their parents. A longitudinal study which is presently under way at Hermannsburg should be able to provide further information.

One feature of the results on the conservation of quantity (Table 24.1) which requires some comment is the drop in the number of conservation responses at ages 10 and 11 in both Aboriginal samples. A similar discontinuity is present in de Lemos's data at age 11; the relatively better performance of the younger children was interpreted as being due to new teaching methods which had been introduced recently (de Lemos, 1969b, p. 267). If this interpretation had been correct, we would have expected that, in the five years separating the two studies, this advantage would have been maintained by all children up to 14 to 15 years of age. Since the drop still occurs at the same age, it seems to be an age-specific occurrence. One possible explanation (de Lemos, Bovet, personal communications) would be that the relatively good performance at the early ages did not represent true conservation behaviour, but was due to pseudo-conservation, such as found by Bovet (1973) in Algerian children. To answer this question, additional procedures such as learning tasks (Bovet, 1973) should have been used.

The rates of development of conservation and logico-mathematical concepts reported in this study and by de Lemos (1966, 1969b) and de Lacey (1970b) for low-contact Aborigines, are extremely slow. On the conservation tasks, for which a lot of cross-cultural data exist, the rates are comparable only to those reported by Kelly (1970) and slightly below those obtained by Waddell (1968) and Prince (1969a) in New Guinea Highland children. Many Aboriginal children fail to reach the concrete operational level, and formal logical thought (as assessed by the task of conservation of volume, which is considered to be intermediate between the concrete operational and the formal levels) is almost absent. Although these facts result from the quantitative analysis of the results, they represent a limitation of the cross-cultural generality of Piaget's stages.

Although the correlation between the attainment of conservation concepts and school performance has recently been questioned in a cross-cultural situation (Heron, 1971), it is likely that the low educational achievement of Aboriginal children is linked to the failure to develop these thought structures which are so basic to the European school system that they have been assumed, until recently, to be present without an attempt to test them or to teach them.

In summary, considering the qualitative analysis of the results and the rates of development presented in Tables 24.1 to 24.9, Hypothesis 1 is confirmed.

Hypothesis 2

Chi-square tests were calculated on the number of subjects, in each Aboriginal sample, attaining Stage III on each test (Table 24.10).

For the logico-mathematical tests, all chi-square values, except one, are statistically significant, or are approaching significance. For the spatial tests, on the other hand, only one chi-square value is approaching significance.

This analysis is confirmed by treatments-by-levels analyses of variance on the logico-mathematical and spatial z' scores, where the treatments F value (European contact) is statistically significant ($F = 8,727$, $df = 1$, $p < 0.01$) for the logico-mathematical scores only.

Although the interaction F values (European contact by age) are not statistically significant, an inspection of the z' values (Table 24.9) as well as of the results on the individual tests (Tables 24.1 to 24.8) reveals that the difference between the two Aboriginal samples increases with age for both the logico-mathematical and the spatial scores, a finding which corroborates the results obtained by de Lacey with classification tasks (de Lacey, 1970a).

Thus, Hypothesis 2 is supported. It should be noted that the influence of European contact is more marked where concepts are concerned which are less relevant to the Aboriginal culture.

Hypothesis 3

In the European sample, the mean scores for the spatial tests are consistently lower than the mean scores for the logico-mathematical tests (Table 24.9), whereas in both Aboriginal samples, this is reversed: the mean scores for spatial tests are consistently higher than the mean scores for the logico-mathematical ones. Treatments-by-levels analyses

o

TABLE 24.10. *Comparison of the number of subjects classified at Stage III in the Hermannsburg and Areyonga samples*

Test	N^b Hermannsburg	N^b Areyonga	Stage III Hermannsburg	Stage III Areyonga	Chi-square	p
Logico-mathematical tests						
Quantity	80	56	33	11	7·0176	0·001
Weight	80	57	15	6	1·7262[a]	NS(0·10)
Volume	70	56	20	10	1·9656	NS(0·10)
Seriation	90	52	40	15	3·3654	0·05
Length 1	70	43	32	11	4·5765	0·025
Length 2	70	43	21	6	3·7629[a]	0·05
Length 3	70	43	12	9	0·2486	NS
Spatial tests						
Orders	50	26	40	19	0·1520[a]	NS
Rotation	90	51	31	11	2·5662	NS(0·10)
Horizontality	100	64	32	24	0·5084	NS

[a] Yates correction for continuity applied.
[b] The number of subjects varies with the age range at which the tests were applied; at Areyonga some subjects left before testing was completed.

TABLE 24.II. *Analyses of variance: logico-mathematical and spatial z' scores*

Source of variation	Canberra			Hermannsburg			Areyonga		
	df	F	p	df	F	p	df	F	p
Inter	15	50·542	0·01	17	12·464	0·01	9	6·152	0·01
Treatments (logico-mathematical/spatial)	1	36·701	0·01	1	4·877	0·05	1	5·582	0·05
Levels (age)	7	101·333	0·01	8	25·015	0·01	4	11·940	0·01
Interaction	7	1·729	NS	8	0·863	NS	4	0·505	NS

of variance (Table 24.11) confirm that the differences observed are statistically significant. Although the interaction F values are not statistically significant, an inspection of the z' values (Table 24.9) indicates that the relative differences between the development of logico-mathematical and spatial concepts increases with age.

In other words, the Aborigines in our samples, on the average, acquire the particular set of spatial operations we are testing before they acquire the particular set of logico-mathematical operations, whereas the Europeans in our sample find the logico-mathematical tests relatively easier. Hypothesis 3 is thus supported.

However, from the fact that the spatial skills needed by people of a nomadic hunting and gathering economy are nowadays (and in fact, traditionally) more relevant to the Pitjantjara people of Areyonga than to the more acculturated Aranda of Hermannsburg, one might have expected the operational development of the Areyonga sample, in regard to spatial tasks, to be superior to that of the Hermannsburg sample. This is not the case, although the difference between the two samples is statistically significant for the logico-mathematical, but not for the spatial tasks (see preceding discussion).

Similar results were obtained by Berry (1966b): the more acculturated Eskimos scored higher on spatial (performance) tests than did traditional Eskimos. This is possibly due to the fact that the spatial concepts (respectively spatial skills, in Berry's study) we are studying are only partly equivalent to those needed for survival by Aborigines (respectively Eskimos), whereas they are the spatial concepts typically relevant to the European culture. It would be interesting to analyse, in less general terms than we have done here, the spatial skills and concepts actually required by nomadic people, and to construct tests accordingly.

The relationship we have thus established between ecology, culture and operational development is correlational only. Additional research is needed, varying the ecological/cultural variable, possibly by using a type of design similar to Berry's (1971).

Furthermore, alternative explanations are possible and need to be ruled out by further experimentation. One of these objections concerns the type of tasks used: the spatial tasks all involved some kind of manipulation by the subject and a mainly nonverbal expression of behaviour; the so-called logico-mathematical tasks, on the other hand, imply a verbal judgement (conservation), except for the task of seriation, which is the only logico-mathematical task on which 100 per cent success is reached in one of the Aboriginal samples. The difference between the two types of tasks could therefore be simply explained away by the interference of some verbal factor. That this is unlikely to be so is attested by the results of a mainly nonverbal logico-mathematical test, the Nixon reclassification test (following de Lacey, 1970a), which was administered to the Hermannsburg sample in the first phase of a longitudinal follow-up study. This test involves six successive reclassifications of objects according to three dimensions: height, width and colour. The percentage of subjects reaching Stage III are presented in Table 24.12. The developmental curve is asymptotic, just as those obtained with conservation tasks.

TABLE 24.12. *Percentage of subjects reaching Stage III on Nixon reclassification test (Hermannsburg longitudinal study)*

Age	6	7	8	10	12	14
Stage III (%)	9	31	25	64	40	50
N	11	13	12	11	10	10

CONCLUSION

Piaget (*1966*) has suggested that cross-cultural research would provide the possibility of distinguishing the relative influence of four factors in the development of cognitive functions:

1. Biological factors (maturation of nervous system);
2. Equilibration or autoregulation factors, corresponding 'to the sequential forms in general coordination of the actions of individuals as interacting with their physical environment';
3. General social factors: interactions among children or between adults and children;
4. Educational and cultural transmission.

The present study, however, does not enable us to assess the relative importance of any one of these factors. On the one hand, the fact that the concepts develop through the same substages in both cultures suggests that biological and equilibration factors are universal to some extent. On the other hand, the extremely slow rate of development found in Aboriginal subjects in the present and other studies (de Lemos, 1966, 1969b; de Lacey, 1970a, 1970b) points to the fact that social and cultural factors are more important for cognitive development than Piaget had hypothesized. The present research, centring on the influence of European contact and of general ecological and cultural variables, stresses the importance of Piaget's fourth factor. The slow rate of development, however, may also be due partly to malnutrition (Maxwell and Elliott, 1969; Jose and Welch, 1970; Tatz, 1970) which could possibly affect factor 1.

Personal observation of Aboriginal child-rearing behaviour as well as informal evidence (Hamilton, personal communication) suggests that the Aboriginal infant's interaction with his environment (factor 2) and with adults (factor 3) is severely restricted through traditional custom. According to Hamilton, babies are allowed to explore the environment within the boundaries of an area of approximately the size of the circle of light shed by the camp fire; if they crawl beyond, even during day time, they are immediately pulled back. This behaviour was probably adaptive in the traditional setting, but is likely to hinder sensori-motor development. In any case, the physical environment of the Aboriginal child is extremely poor and monotonous compared to the environment of a middle-class European child. Also, as Zempleni (1970) has shown for the Wolof (Senegal), objects do not seem to have a role as mediators between the child and his mother or other adults; this function is performed by body contact.

Subsequently, verbal exploration also seems to be discouraged, and Aboriginal children do not, apparently, go through the period – well known to European parents – of asking 'why'. This is probably due to the cultural norm of accepting the laws of nature, the social customs and the decisions of the elders without question. Furthermore, any form of competition is discouraged in Aboriginal culture (Sommerlad and Bellingham, 1972).

In other words, the implicit values with cognitive relevance or cognitive 'ambiance' (Heron and Simonsson, 1969) are not favourable to the development of operational thinking; European contact provides some of this 'ambiance', and ecological/cultural factors favour the development of certain concept areas over others. Further research is needed to describe these factors with greater precision and to assess their relative influence on cognitive development.

25

P. R. Dasen (*1972*)

Cross-cultural Piagetian research : a summary[1]

Journal of Cross-Cultural Psychology, 3(1), pp. 23–39

Following the disappointing results of the 'culture-free' and 'culture-fair' movements, the attention of many cross-cultural cognitive psychologists has turned to the developmental psychology of Jean Piaget (often called 'genetic psychology'). The Piagetian psychologist is not concerned with the score on a test, but attempts to describe the basic structures and functioning of higher mental processes. He studies how the child gets to know about his world, how he develops basic scientific concepts, and how reasoning obeys certain structural properties which can be described by models drawn from logic and mathematics. It is thus interesting for the cross-cultural psychologist to determine whether these properties of thought, which are described by Piaget as basic to any knowledge, are universal or whether they are influenced by cultural factors.

Piaget's methodology is also attractive to cross-cultural research, since the development of reasoning is not studied through standardized tests, but through a 'clinical method' (see Ginsburg and Opper, 1969) which may be adapted to each cultural situation.

Publications in this area have greatly increased in the last few years, and it seems important to attempt to summarize the extremely heterogeneous data collected so far, thus providing for more concerted research.

Piaget (*1966*) has discussed the relevance of cross-cultural research in genetic psychology at a time when only a few references were available.

[1] This summary was written while the author was a research scholar at the Australian National University. The final preparation of the manuscript was assisted by a grant of the Fonds National Suisse de la Recherche Scientifique to Professor Bärbel Inhelder (No.I. 133. 69). Thanks are due to Professor G. N. Seagrim, Professor J. W. Berry and to the editors of *JCCP* for critical comments. A great deal of material for this review was collected through the assistance of the correspondents of the newsletter, *Inventory of Cross-Cultural Piagetian Research*, edited by Professor G. N. Seagrim and the author.

Subsequently, de Lemos (1969b), Goodnow (1969a), Vernon (1969), Hyde (1970), Jahoda (1970a), Zempleni and Zempleni (1972) and Le Vine (1970) have provided some discussion and general comments on the cross-cultural implications of Piaget's work, but without providing a detailed summary. The present paper is designed to fill this gap. It is assumed that the reader has a basic knowledge of Piaget's theory; good introductions have recently been provided by Ginsburg and Opper (1969) and Furth (1969).

This summary will not deal with Piaget's early work on animism, causality, and moral judgement (Piaget, 1929, 1930), which has been extensively applied to various cultures (Mead, 1932; Dennis and Russell, 1940; Dennis, 1943; Huang, 1943; Huang and Lee, 1945; Jones and Arrington, 1945; Havighurst and Neugarten, 1955; Jahoda, 1958b, 1958c, 1969b; Dubreuil and Boisclair, 1960, 1966; Peluffo, 1962, 1967; Boehm, 1966; Nurcombe, 1970b; Prince, 1969b). A good summary of the studies prior to 1958 has been provided by Jahoda (1958a).

Furthermore we shall restrict ourselves mainly to research dealing with non-Western cultural groups. A third limitation of a different kind should also be mentioned: although we are dealing with a relatively restricted area, there is no guarantee that the results are strictly comparable. The techniques, scoring methods, age ranges, the extent to which verbalization is taken into account, and indeed the whole conceptualization of Piaget's framework, vary a great deal from one investigation to the next. This question of comparability of results has been expertly discussed by Goodnow (1969b), who points out some major differences between the Genevan and Anglo-Saxon approaches.

Piaget is very cautious in his interpretation of the first cross-cultural results (Piaget, *1966*, p. 304). Elsewhere (Piaget, *1971*) he warns himself:

> Cross-cultural studies are difficult to carry out because they pre-suppose a good psychological training in the techniques of operational testing, namely with free conversation and not standardization in the manner of tests, and all psychologists do not have this training; a sufficient ethnological sophistication, and a complete knowledge of the language are also prerequisites. We know only a few attempts of this quality. (Present author's translation.)

On the other hand, this lack of comparability is not restricted to comparative genetic psychology. In fact, as Goodnow (1969b, pp. 247–8) points out:

> The biggest difficulty with cross-cultural studies has been the lack

of overlap between pieces: each study a new culture and very often, a new task.

A noteworthy exception is a

group of people who have come to overlap through no deliberate intent on their part, but through a shared interest in tasks developed by Piaget and his colleagues. . . . It offers some nice overlaps in several respects: in the sample of tasks, the sample of subjects, the environmental variable, and happiest of all, in some of the results.

Let us thus leave aside, for the purpose of this summary, a further discussion of the methods and techniques used in the various studies, and assume that a comparison of the results has some value, be it only to focus on new problems.

THE CROSS-CULTURAL VERIFICATION OF PIAGET'S STAGES

Descriptive studies

Implicitly or explicitly, most cross-cultural studies in genetic psychology ask whether cognitive development in non-Western cultures follows the same sequential succession of stages as described by Piaget and by many other investigators in middle-class Western children. And, if so, do these stages appear at approximately the same age levels?

This issue has been obscured by an unfortunate failure to distinguish three different interpretations of Piaget's 'stages':

(1) The succession of the three global stages: sensori-motor (pre-operational), concrete operational and formal.

(2) The successive acquisition of operations that bear on different contents, but obey identical structural laws: the so-called 'horizontal décalages' such as the sequence of the conservations of Q (S), W and V.[1]

(3) The sequence of substages on any particular task.

These three interpretations should be discussed separately.

1. *The three global stages*

A verification of the succession of the three global stages would require longitudinal studies, or at least the examination of all three stages in the same ethnic group. As far as we know, this has not been done in any

[1] The following abbreviations will be used throughout the review for conservation tests: Q = quantity (S = substance, e.g. plasticine; Liq. = liquids); W = Weight; V = volume; A = area; L = length; N = number.

non-Western culture. We shall therefore be restricted to discussing the presence and nature of each stage independently from the others.

(a) *The sensori-motor (s.s.m.) stage.* The development of s.s.m. intelligence has received little cross-cultural attention, although a few investigations are currently under way, for example, a study conducted in Athens (Paraskevopoulos and Hunt, 1971), Teheran and Israel under the direction of J. McV. Hunt (personal communication) with a scale of infant development devised by Uzgiris and Hunt (1966). One completed study is that of Golden and Birns (1968), using a Piaget (Permanent) Object Scale and the Cattell Infant Intelligence Scale, in which no social class differences in intellectual performance were found during the first two years of life in American Negroes.

(b) *The formal stage.* A few studies have been conducted on formal thought. Goodnow (1962) and Peluffo (1967) used tasks of 'combinations' and 'permutations' based on those of Piaget and Inhelder (*1951*). Goodnow, in Hong Kong, found that Chinese children with English schooling performed as well as or better than Europeans, whereas the results of her two other groups (low income and semi- or full-Chinese schooling) were somewhat depressed. Peluffo found that sons of workers, born and educated in Genova, and sons of clerks and professionals, born and living in Sardinia, attained a 50 to 60 per cent success level at age 11, while those living in an underdeveloped agricultural milieu in Sardinia and illiterate Sardinian adults performed less well (25 per cent at age 11, and 20 per cent respectively).

Were (1968) administered verbal-logical and empirical formal tests to 14 to 16 year old subjects in New Guinea. He failed to find any trace of formal thought in those age-groups. His negative findings have been confirmed with different tests and samples in New Guinea (Kelly, 1970).

Clearly, there is not nearly enough evidence on which to draw firm conclusions. However, it seems that Piaget's 'prediction' (*1966*, p. 309; 1971) that the reasoning of many individuals in so-called 'primitive' societies would not develop beyond the stage of concrete operations, may one day be verified.

(c) *The concrete operational stage.* By far the largest number of studies deal with the passage from the pre-operational to the concrete operational stage, and all report that some subjects at least attain the latter. The question is, to what extent, and at what age.

If we look at the proportion (or percentage) of children attaining the concrete operational stage as a function of age, on any given and appropriate task, we obtain some sort of ogive (Fig. 25.1). Let us assume that curve x has been obtained with European children: all eventually acquire the given concept, but the age at which this occurs varies with the difficulty of the concept, or with the test-materials used.

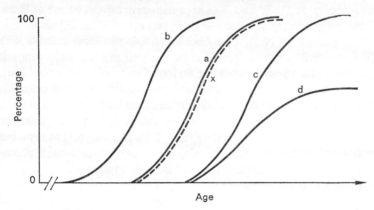

Fig. 25.1 Percentage of subjects attaining the concrete operational stage as a function of age.

If the same task is applied to a different cultural group, several possibilities exist:

(a) The concept develops at the same time as in European children.
(b) The concept develops earlier, or more quickly.
(c) The concept develops later, or more slowly; there is a 'time-lag', or retarded development; all children, however, eventually reaching concrete operational thinking.
(d) The concept starts to develop at the same time or later, but the curve is asymptotic – it flattens out at the higher ages: some children, and even adults, do not reach the concrete operational stage.

Fig. 25.1 shows one possible example of each of these curves. We shall now discuss them individually.

(a) *Curve a.* Three authors have reported results corresponding to curve a. Price-Williams (1961) finds no difference between Tiv (Central Nigeria) and European children: by age 7–6 to 8–16, all subjects of the sample had acquired the conservations of continuous Q (earth), discontinuous Q (nuts) and N.

In Goodnow's studies (1962; Goodnow and Bethon, 1966) three cultural subgroups (Europeans in Hong Kong, 'average' Americans and the Chinese with low [sic] socioeconomic status and almost no schooling) were almost indistinguishable for conservation of A, W and V.

However, the performance of the Chinese who had full English or Chinese schooling was much poorer, yielding a c- or d-type curve.

Thirdly, schoolchildren in Teheran (Mohseni, 1966) developed conservation of Q, W and V at approximately the same time as Europeans, whereas they were one or two years retarded on IQ tests.

A subsample of Australian Aborigines living in close contact with European civilization performed at least as well as a low socioeconomic group of white Australian children on four classification tasks (de Lacey, 1970b). Okonji (1971b) showed that 'when tested on appropriate (i.e. familiar) materials, no differences may be found between a Western and a non-Western sample in classificatory attitude'. Similarly, Zambian children do not differ significantly from Scots on re-sorting of toys, but do less well than Scots when resorting colour or black-and-white photographs of these toys (Deregowski and Serpell, 1971).

(b) *Curve b.* Tuddenham (1968, 1969), when applying a battery of fifteen concrete operational tests to European, Negro and Oriental children in California, found that the Oriental children were superior to the whites on at least half of the items (possibly curve b).

Intermediate (a and c) curves. An interesting example of an apparently intermediate case between curves a and c has recently been reported by Bovet (1968, 1971, 1973). When testing conservation of Q (Liq. and S). in unschooled Algerian children, she found that the 7 to 8 year olds, in contrast to the younger children, seemed to have a solid concept of conservation; at 8 to 10 years, however, there was a 'regression', and only in the 9 to 11 year old group was conservation established again. Bovet argues that the initial conservation found at 7 to 8 years of age was not completely operational; if so, this case can be assimilated into the next group of findings (curve c).

Kohlberg's (1968) results are also difficult to classify: Atayal children, a Malaysian Aboriginal group in Formosa (Taiwan), acquired conservation of Q at the usual age (7 to 8 years) but partially 'lost' it between 11 and 15 years. However:

> . . . the loss did not seem to be a genuine regression but an uncertainty about trusting their own judgement, that is, there was an increase in 'don't know' responses. Apparently, adolescent confrontation with adult magical beliefs led them to be uncertain of their natural physical beliefs, whether or not they were in direct conflict with the adult ideology. (p. 1029)

Voyat (personal communication) applied a large series of Piagetian tasks to Oglala Sioux (South Dakota). He reported little or no difference in the developmental curves between Sioux and Swiss performance until the age of about 10 years, but a levelling-off after that age.

(c) *Curve c.* A typical curve c of 'retarded' development has been reported many times. The extent of the time-lag, however, has not always been precisely established in these studies, either because a European standardization was not available, or because, in many cases, the age of the subjects could not be established with precision; it seems to vary from about 1 to 6 years.

The Tiv children tested by Price-Williams (1962) lagged slightly behind on classification. Schooled Wolof children (Senegal) all eventually achieved conservation of Q by age 11 to 13 years (Greenfield, 1966). A systematic time-lag of two to three years is reported in illiterate rural children in Iran (Mohseni, 1966); in Lebanese schoolchildren on conservation of Liq. and N (Za'rour, 1971a), and a similar difference in the rhythm of development was obtained by Bovet (1968; 1971; 1973, pp. 321-4) on conservation of L in illiterate Algerian subjects, whereas the time-lag was found to be much greater for speed/time concepts (1973, p. 325).

A number of studies show that both non-Western and low-socio-economic class Western children lag behind in their concept development when compared to middle-class Western children. Because of the restricted age range used in these studies, however, it is not clear whether all subjects would have developed these concepts at some later age (curve c) or not (curve d). This ambiguity is evident in a study of Arab, Indian and Somali children, aged 6 to 8 years, tested in Aden with a battery of thirteen tests (conservations, seriation, classification) by Hyde (1959, 1970), and similarly in a study of urban Shona (Rhodesia) aged 5 and 6, tested with a similar series of tests by Hendrikz (1966), and in a study of young Baganda children of Kampala, Uganda (Almy, 1970).

Vernon included a variety of Piaget items in a large battery of tests; his subjects were 11 to 12 year old boys of several ethnic groups. He confirmed (Vernon, 1967a, 1967b, 1969) that Kampala boys scored lower than English ones. The worst deficiencies were found in all the conservation tasks – over 50 per cent of the subjects being nonconservers on every item. Their performance was also very low on number concepts.

The median West Indian performance (Vernon, 1965a, 1965b, 1969) was 86 on English norms, the greatest deficiencies occurring in number concepts, in conservation of Q, L and A, and in a mental imagery test. The differences were negligible on conservation of S and on logical inclusion, and quite small on time concepts and on the concept of horizontality.

In Eskimo and Canadian Indians (Vernon, 1966, 1969), all subgroups were weak relative to the English norms on conservation of Q, L and A as well as on time concepts, on knowledge of left and right and on number concepts, but only slightly inferior on logical inclusions. Eskimos were similar to whites on tasks involving spatial concepts. Indians were poorer on these tests, but were better on a test of mental imagery.

Exactly what these differential patterns mean, and how they are related to cultural characteristics, is not clear at first glance; one partial interpretation has been made by Goodnow (1969a), who has tentatively identified the vulnerable tasks as those involving 'imaged transformations' or 'mental shuffling'.

A lower performance on Piagetian tasks for low-socioeconomic class European children is reported by Peluffo (1962, 1967), Wei (1966), Vernon (1969) and de Lacey (1970a, 1970b). In the last study ,10 to 20 per cent of low socioeconomic Australian Europeans had not reached concrete operational thinking (classification) at age 12.

(d) *Curve d.* In the fourth group of investigation, on the other hand, there is clear evidence that some subjects, even of the higher ages (12 to 18), do not reach the concrete operational stage.

Boonsong's (1968) results on conservation in Thai children seem to be an intermediate case: at age 13, about 80 per cent of the subjects had attained conservation of Q and W and 50 per cent of V; most of those who were not conserving were at the transitional stage.

Similarly, Prince (1968c, 1969a) found that about 80 per cent of New Guinea pupils sampled by him acquired conservation of Q and W by Form III of high school (age 16 to 18), while the percentage was considerably less for conservation of V, L and A.

At age 12, many Zulu children (Pietermaritzburg, Natal) had not fully developed topological, projective and Euclidean concepts of space (Murray, 1961; Cowley and Murray, 1962; de Lemos, 1973). This is also true of Australian Aboriginal adolescents and adults, although their performance on spatial tests was significantly better than on conservation and seriation (Dasen, 1970, 1973a). In the same area of spatial relations, Nepalese subjects apparently of even older ages drew a sequence of actions rather than a set of relationships when asked for a route-map from their home to school; the authors (Dart and Pradhan, 1967) suggest that the reactions of adults would most likely have been the same.

In two subsamples of Chinese children tested by Goodnow (1962), only some of those aged 13 had developed conservation of A, W and V.

Similarly, only a small percentage (25 to 67 per cent) of 14 to 15 year old Australian Aborigines attained the concrete operational stage on conservation tasks (de Lemos, 1966, 1969a, 1969b; Dasen, 1970, 1973a). Nor do all Australian Aborigines develop the concept of classification, except those who live in a European community, speak English at home, and generally live in the same way as Europeans of a low-socioeconomic status. In this latter group, classification is attained by most children at age 14 years, whereas only some subjects of a 'low-contact' group have reached the concrete operational stage at age 15 (de Lacey, 1970b).

In New Guinea, some children of 12 to 15 years still lacked conservation of Q, L and A (Waddell, 1968), and these findings have been replicated by Prince (1968a, 1968b, 1968c, 1969a) and Kelly (1971) on various tasks and samples in New Guinea.

Only about half of the unschooled rural Wolof children (Senegal) tested by Greenfield (1966) attained conservation of Q at 11 to 13 years, and the proportion of Zambian children of African extraction, tested with a nonverbal method of conservation of W (Heron and Simonsson, 1969), reached a near-asymptote of 55 to 60 per cent after the age of about 11 years.

There is no proof in these studies that the subjects who had not attained the concrete operational level at the higher ages would not do so some time later. On the other hand, a series of studies have included adult samples. Ponzo, as reported by Peluffo (1967), found that conservation was uncertain in Kohorosciwetari and Tukano adults (Amazon). Waddell (1968) and Kelly (1971) found relatively little conservation in illiterate adults in the Highlands of New Guinea, and Prince (1968a) reports that many trainees of two teachers' colleges in New Guinea did not display conservations of Q (S and Liq.), W, V, A and L.

In adult Australian Aborigines, de Lemos (1969b) found 50 per cent conservation of Q and 75 per cent conservation of L, whereas Dasen (1973a, pp. 395–400) found only 30 to 40 per cent conservation of Q (low- and medium-contact respectively), 10 to 20 per cent conservation of W and 0 to 30 per cent of V, whereas 60 to 90 per cent had acquired the spatial concept of horizontality.

Most illiterate adults in Algeria (Bovet, 1973, pp. 324–5) were found to conserve L and W, although they often started the session with non-conserving answers, proceeding through the stages during the experiment, in a sort of *Aktualgenese*. The same adults, however, found it difficult to differentiate the concepts of speed and time (duration). Similarly, illiterate Gueree and Mossi adults from Ivory Coast (Piller,

1971) conserved Q, L and W to some extent, but failed to conserve V and had extreme difficulties with the speed and time concepts. Illiterate adults in Sicily (Bovet and Baranzini, personal communication), on the other hand, had no problems differentiating speed and time, but many failed to conserve V.

Peluffo (1967) found only 20 per cent conservation of V in adults of Sardinia (although it seems that practically all subjects had the conservation of Q).

According to this evidence, it can no longer be assumed that adults of all societies reach the concrete operational stage. However, the cross-cultural differences summarized above are *quantitative* ones only. It is the rate of development which is in question, not the structure of thinking. As such, the generality of Piaget's system is not threatened. The results simply point to the fact that, among the factors influencing cognitive development, cultural ones might be more important than had previously been hypothesized, a possibility which Piaget (*1966*) himself has stressed.

On the other hand, it may be considered surprising, and a limitation of the universality of Piaget's stages, to find more and more evidence accumulating to show that concrete operational thought is not necessarily attained. Furthermore, considerable individual differences have been reported within ethnic groups where the physical and social environments, child-rearing practices, health conditions, etc. seem to be relatively homogeneous.

Evidence on this particular problem is scanty and negative. In a study of Zambian primary schoolchildren (Heron, 1971), there was no correlation between conservation of W and measures of nonverbal 'reasoning' ability ('induction' and 'matrices'), or objective measures of school performance.

Whether or not it is of any practical importance to be at the concrete operational stage can thus be questioned, and this topic urgently needs further research.

2. 'Horizontal décalages'

A second conception of the succession of stages refers to the sequential application of the same structure of thought to different contents. The best known example of this is the usual succession of difficulty in the conservation of Q, W and V. Strictly speaking, the usage of the word 'stage' in this case is wrong, although Piaget has not always been consistent on this point (e.g. *1966*, p. 304); 'horizontal décalage' should be used instead to describe this event (Pinard and Laurendeau, 1969).

Here again, comparative experimental evidence collected to date is not consistent. Mohseni (1966) has verified the sequence of difficulty of Q, W and V in Iran; Peluffo (1967) seems to find this sequence as well, and Goodnow (1962) found W to be easier than V in all her subsamples.

There is some indication in Boonsong's work (1968) that V is more difficult for Thai children than Q and W, which seem to be about equally difficult. Much the same conclusion can be drawn from Prince's work in New Guinea (1968c; 1969a, p. 60), although Q seems to be slightly easier than W.

De Lemos (1966, 1969b), on the other hand, found conservation of W to be considerably easier than Q in Australian Aborigines, whereas the later development of V was confirmed. Dasen (1972b) failed to replicate this Q/W reversal, but found that W and V developed more or less simultaneously.

Other studies have found variations in the sequence of acquisition of Piagetian concepts. Bovet (1973, p. 324) found the conservation of L to develop at the same time as Q in illiterate Algerians, whereas it is usually contemporary with W in European children. Otaala (1971) found that the parallel development of conservation, seriation and classification was supported only partially in Iteso children of Uganda.

It should be noted, however, that Piaget's theory does not (yet) predict or explain particular horizontal décalages. Cross-cultural variations thus cannot be seen as contradicting the theory, but have to be interpreted as being due to the influence of familiarity with the test-contents (e.g. Waddell, 1968), to the influence of particular day-to-day activities (Price-Williams, Gordon and Ramirez, 1969; Bovet, 1971) or to general ecological demands and cultural characteristics (Dasen, 1973a), such as described by Berry (1966b) for perceptual and spatial skills.

A point of confusion may be noted: the results for or against a constant order hypothesis are always reported in broad statistical terms, usually in terms of the frequency of conserving responses over age; it is in the total sample or subsample that one test appears to be or not to be more difficult than another. If the concept of hierarchical development has any qualitative value, however, a constant order of development should be found in each individual.

In Hyde's (1959) study, for example, there is some indication that Q (S and Liq.) is easier than W and V, 'but the results of individual subjects suggest that the sequence is not invariable. . . . There was no support for the theory that the concepts of S, W and V are invariably acquired in that order.' A similar conclusion was drawn by Dasen (1970).

The question cannot be decided until more data on 'horizontal décalages' in individuals is obtained, both in the usual middle-class European child and in children of other cultures. However, some further light might be shed on this problem by a re-analysis of existing data.

3. *Stages on individual tests*

A third conception of Piaget's stages concerns the responses or reactions to individual tests; these are said to be hierarchically organized into a succession of stages for each particular concept, the number of stages varying with each problem.

Only Hyde (1959), de Lemos (1973, p. 378), and Waddell (1968) have reported any difficulty in classifying the children's reactions into readily identifiable stages.

Most authors of cross-cultural research have found the same stages as those described by Piaget (e.g. Noro, 1961; Price-Williams, 1961; Mohseni, 1966; de Lemos, 1966, 1969a, 1969b; Almy, 1970; Boonsong, 1968; de Lacey, 1970a; Dasen, 1970; Otaala, 1971; Za'rour, 1971a; Voyat, personal communication). There could be several reasons for this consensus of opinion. First, the concepts described by Piaget, if and when they develop, could well do so *qualitatively* in exactly the same way in every culture; they would thus constitute *universals*.

Second, as our approach is *etic*, rather than *emic*, the consistency in the findings may be due to a failure to allow alternatives to be detected. According to Berry (1969a), our existing descriptive categories and concepts (imposed etic) should be modified to the extent that they become a more adequate description from within the culture under study (emic); new categories valid for both systems (derived etic) could then be developed, and possibly expanded until they constitute a *derived universal*. Some thinking in this direction has started within the Piagetian area (Le Vine and Price-Williams, 1970; Jacopin, Wald, personal communications).

Third, the absence of discrepancies could be due to the scale used in our investigations: we would be more likely to find differences if we identified a larger number of substages, as has recently been done by Pinard *et al.* (1969) for the conservation tasks.

Furthermore, two authors (Greenfield, 1966; Bovet, 1971, 1973) have added training techniques to the classical test of conservation of Q. Both report, although in partially conflicting ways, that 'different modes of thought can lead to the same results' (in Greenfield's words, 1966, p. 255).

In conclusion it is obvious that there is now much more experimental evidence available than when Piaget made his first review of cross-cultural studies in genetic psychology (Piaget, *1966*). However, it is still very tentatively that we summarize the present state of affairs: in all cultures studied so far, some or all individuals reach the stage of concrete operations, although usually at a later age than middle-class Europeans. The fact, however, that some individuals, even of adult age, continue to show a pre-operational type of reasoning, and that some qualitative differences are being reported, indicates that environmental factors may be more important than Piaget seemed to hypothesize in his earlier writings.

THE IMBROGLIO OF FACTORS AFFECTING OPERATIONAL DEVELOPMENT

Quasi-experimental studies

Cross-cultural research in genetic psychology has not been restricted to verifying Piaget's stages, qualitatively or quantitatively. In studying ethnic groups or subgroups which differ in some specific ways, it is possible to assess the respective importance of factors influencing cognitive development, a task which is impossible or more difficult when research is restricted to relatively homogeneous Western cultures.

According to Piaget (e.g. *1966*, *1968*), four main factors are interacting in enabling the child to acquire progressively more complex structures of thought: 1) maturation; 2) equilibration, or autoregulation; 3) general socialization; and 4) educational and cultural transmission.

Piaget himself, contrary to the opinion of some, does not believe in a complete determination of cognitive development by biological factors (maturation).[1] Piaget claims that 'logic becomes *a priori*' (Piaget, *1950*, p. 256), but only through a continuous process of equilibration.

It is because of their constant interaction that it is difficult to examine these factors directly. In most studies concerned with the various influences on operational development, more than one of Piaget's four factors could be involved at any one time. Thus, cross-cultural Piagetian

[1] This seems to be a common misconception, which has apparently penetrated as far as China: Cheng and Lee (1960) conclude that the conception of number depends on educational circumstances, 'contrary to the results by the bourgeois scholar Piaget that children's conception of numbers is completely determined by age'!

research has concentrated so far on assessing two kinds of influences of cognitive development: schooling and European contact.

Schooling. On the basis of studies by Goodnow (1962), Goodnow and Bethon (1966), Mermelstein and Shulman (1967), Waddell (1968), Kelly (1971), and Heron (1971), among others, it is generally believed that there is no direct relationship between the development of concrete operations and Western-type schooling.

On the other hand, Greenfield (1966), Hendrikz (1966), Prince (1968a), and Pinard et al. (1969), found that schooling was one of the principal cultural influences on operational development.

Waddell (1968) and, independently, de Lemos (1969b) proposed a partial resolution of the apparent contradiction between these results: schooling would be influential in New Guinea or Senegal because it brings with it the cultural stimulation that children in Hong Kong obtain without schooling. Furby (1971) proposes a matrix of interaction between schooling, urbanization and Westernization, the various combinations of which would produce predictable results.[1]

European contact. Thus, more important than schooling itself seems to be the contact with Western cognitive values and stimulation which schooling brings with it. European contact, however, is difficult to define precisely (de Lacey, 1970c); it is usually linked to the urban/rural difference (Mohseni, 1966; Greenfield, 1966; Peluffo, 1967; Poole, 1968; Vernon, 1969; de Lacey, 1970b), to linguistic difference, either in the richness of the vernacular (Greenfield, 1966), or in the fluency of the acquired European language (Vernon, 1969; de Lacey, 1970b), or to social class (Lloyd, 1971a).

All authors report significant differences in the rate of operational development in favour of the high-contact groups, even if schooling, urbanization, language and social class are held constant, the difference being then due to the length of contact and to the extent to which traditional values and activities have subsisted (Dasen, 1973a). The only exception is the study by Greenfield (1966), in which city-schooled Wolof children performed less well than bush-schooled children until the age of 11 to 13 years.

Other factors. Other factors influencing operational development in the cross-cultural situation are often mentioned: malnutrition, early physical and social stimulation, linguistic structures, etc., but these have never been investigated in relation to Piaget's theory. Three studies have dealt with the genetic factor (de Lemos, 1969a, 1969b; Dasen, 1972b)

---

[1] The difficulty of Furby's analysis is that it relies almost exclusively on Greenfield's results, which are at variance with most other findings in this area.

but with conflicting results, and one study has related operational development to ecological and cultural characteristics (Dasen, 1973a).

CONCLUSION

Whereas a large number of descriptive studies have recently clarified the cross-cultural validity of Piaget's theory, a great deal of further, quasi-experimental research is needed in order to link the qualitative and quantitative aspects of operational development to specific cultural factors. It should then be possible to apply this knowledge to the educational problems in developing countries.

Epilogue

The basic achievements, remaining problems and future directions of the cross-cultural study of cognition require some final drawing together. This collection has totally ignored the conventional psychological studies of the 1930s and 1940s in which IQ test scores were compared between two or more groups, usually one non-Western and an implied Western norm. We have assumed that this stage has largely passed, and that its passing is a real achievement for cross-cultural cognitive psychology. For a science of behaviour which is so firmly rooted in a technologically dominant culture to recognize its ethnocentrism is indeed an achievement. However, as we have cast away these simplistic acts of comparison, we have laid bare once again the basic problems which were so clearly articulated early in the century: do, indeed, cognitive processes differ, and do levels of competence differ from culture to culture?

Although no clear answers have emerged from the studies collected in this volume, some clear lines of approach to the questions have been demonstrated. Firstly, analyses from within each cultural system, attempting to grasp the qualitative variety of cognitive operations as they are manifested in different cultures (*emic* approach) have clearly demonstrated their value. Secondly, a reorientation toward continuities and universal similarities in cognition have replaced an earlier emphasis on anecdotal differences. Note, however, that this latter approach no longer *assumes* a single cognitive dimension, but attempts to establish it on the basis of cultural and biological considerations. It is precisely when this assumption of a unitary cognitive dimension is no longer maintained that variation discovered within the framework of the *emic* approach is no longer threatening; differences need no longer be interpreted as deficiencies or superiorities. Thus, a major achievement of these studies has been the liberation of cross-cultural cognitive psychology from a distressing concern with *intelligence*, and its impossible attempts to make it 'culturally-neutral' through culturally-independent ('culture-free', 'culture-fair', or 'culture-reduced') measures.

While pursuing the basic issues once again, researchers in the area of culture-and-cognition might wish to heed the following assessment of what is needed and what might be avoided.

Firstly, we believe that there have been enough anecdotal or merely descriptive studies. It is no longer of great interest that two cultural groups produce different means or patterns of scores on a set of tests or tasks. What would be of interest is the *prediction* of such differences based upon prior analysis of crucial cultural variables. Of greater interest would be the detailed consideration of the *mechanisms* involved in such cultural-behavioural relations. A clear understanding of these mechanisms might very profitably be sought in developmental studies in which both non-Piagetian studies are made with children, and Piagetian approaches are extended to adults. Until we are able to tie down relations between sets of variables with some predictive power, and plausibly explain them by some psychological, ecological, cultural or biological mechanism, then we are mere travelling salesmen, peddling our wares while knowing them to be of poor quality.

Secondly, we believe that 'one-shot' studies are no longer of great interest. These hurried research efforts preclude an *emic* approach even with the assistance of a psychologist from the host culture. They also preclude serious developmental or longitudinal studies, and the possibility of any culturally-relevant interpretation of the findings that do emerge. If carried out without an overall research objective, they frequently result in inadequate sampling from the available cultural variation. In sum, they display the worst characteristics of the hurried academic on his way around the world, and should be avoided. We imply from these negative comments that carefully-planned, long-term, culturally-based and adequately sampled researched projects are clearly required if a degree of coherence is to emerge in the literature of cross-cultural cognitive psychology.

Finally, the practical implications of our studies should be kept clearly in view. Although some applications are highly controversial (for example, use in industrial, military or 'development' planning), there is a fairly universal acceptance of education as a goal by most peoples in the world. However, the studies collected in this volume should be sufficient to show that basic questions of what people can do, and what they want to be able to do (their values, their goals) may vary widely across cultural contexts. Thus, if education be defined as the process of building upon what people can do until they are able to reach their particular goals, then education must also vary widely across cultural contexts. A very practical role for the cognitive psychologist cross-culturally, then, is to help chart what people are able to do, listen carefully to their articulated cultural goals, and then to assist in the design of an educational system which will help them to reach those goals.

The future of cross-cultural cognitive psychology thus lies in the careful design of culturally-relative studies, and in the contribution of our results to the people who have permitted us to extend the boundaries of our discipline.

References

ADAMS, R. N. (1962) *The formal analysis of behavioral segments: a progress report.* MS read at the 61st Annual Meeting of the Anthropological Association, Chicago.

AL-ISSA, I. and DENNIS, W. (1970) *Cross Cultural Studies of Behaviour.* New York: Holt, Rinehart & Winston.

ALLPORT, G. W. (1924) Eidetic imagery. *Brit. J. Psychol.*, **15**, 19–120.

ALLPORT, G. W. (1937) *Personality: A Psychological Interpretation.* New York: Holt, Rinehart & Winston.

ALMY, M. (1970) The usefulness of Piagetian methods for studying primary school children in Uganda. In ALMY, M., DURITZ, J. L. and WHITE, M. A. *Studying School Children in Uganda.* New York: Teachers College Press.

ALMY, M., CHITTENDEN, E. and MILLER, P. (1966) *Young Children's Thinking: Studies of Some Aspects of Piaget's Theory.* New York: Teachers College Press.

BALFET, H. (1952) La Vannerie: Essai de classification. *L'Anthropologie*, **56** (3–4), 259–80.

BARBICHON, G. (1968) La diffusion des connaissances scientifique et techniques dans le public. *See* Conditions dans les pays en voie de développement. *J. Soc. Issues*, **24**, 135–56.

BARCLAY, A. and CUSUMANO, D. R. (1967) Father absence, cross-sex identity and field dependent behavior in male adolescents. *Child Develop.*, **38**, 243–50.

BARKER, R. G. (1963) *The Stream of Behavior: Explorations of its Structure and Content.* New York: Appleton-Century-Crofts.

BARKER, R. G. (1965) Explorations in ecological psychology. *Amer. Psychol.*, **20**, 1–14.

BARKER, R. G. (1968) *Ecological Psychology.* Stanford: Stanford University Press.

BARKER, R. G. and BARKER, L. S. (1961) Behavior units for the comparative study of cultures. In KAPLAN, B. (ed.) *Studying Personality Cross-culturally.* Evanston, Ill. and New York: Row, Peterson. pp. 457–76.

BARKER, R. G. and WRIGHT, H. F. (1955) *Midwest and Its Children: The Psychological Ecology of an American Town.* Evanston, Ill.: Row, Peterson.

BARNETT, H. G. (1961) The innovation process. *Kroeber Anthropological Society Papers*, No. 25. Berkeley. pp. 25–42.

BARRY, H. (1969) Cross-cultural research with matched pairs of societies. *J. Soc. Psychol.*, **79**, 25–33.

BARRY, H., BACON, M. and CHILD, I. (1957) A class-cultural survey of sex differences and socialization. *J. Abnorm. Soc. Psychol.*, **3**, 55.

BARRY, H., CHILD, I. and BACON, M. (1959) Relation of child training to subsistence economy. *Amer. Anthrop.*, **61**, 51–63.

BARTLETT, F. C. (1932) *Remembering: A Study in Experimental and Social Psychology*. Cambridge: Cambridge University Press.

BATESON, G. (1936) *Naven* (2nd ed., 1958). Cambridge: Cambridge University Press.

BATESON, G. (1942) Social planning and the concept of 'deutero-learning'. *Conference on Science, Philosophy and Religion, Second Symposium*. New York: Harper & Row.

BEARD, R. M. (1969) *An Outline of Piaget's Developmental Psychology for Students and Teachers*. London: Routledge & Kegan Paul.

BEATTIE, J. (1964) *Other Cultures*. London: Cohen & West.

BEE, H. L., VAN EGEREN, L. F., STREISSGUTH, A. P., NYMAN, B. A. and LECKIE, M. S. (1969) Social class differences in maternal teaching strategies and speech patterns, *Develop. Psychol.*, **1**, 726–34.

BEFU, H. and NORBECK, E. (1958) Japanese usages of terms of relationship. *S. W. J. Anthrop.*, **14**(1), 66–86.

BENEDICT, R. (1934) *Patterns of Culture*. Boston: Houghton Mifflin.

BEREITER, C. and ENGLEMANN, S. (1966) *Teaching Disadvantaged Children in the Preschool*. Englewood Cliffs, N. J.: Prentice-Hall.

BERLIN, B. and ROMNEY, A. K. (1964) Descriptive semantics of Tzeltal numeral classifiers. In ROMNEY, A. K. and D'ANDRADE, R. G. (eds.) Transcultural Studies in Cognition, *Amer. Anthrop.*, **66**(3), Part 2, 79–98.

BERNSTEIN, B. (1960) Language and Social Class. *Brit. J. Sociol.*, II, 217–76.

BERNSTEIN, B. (1961a) Social class and linguistic development: a theory of social learning. In HALSEY, A. H., FLOUD, J. and ANDERSON, C. A. (eds.) *Education, Economy and Society*, New York: Free Press. pp. 288–314.

BERNSTEIN, B. (1961b) Social structure, language and learning. *Educ. Res.*, **3**(3).

BERNSTEIN, B. (1970) A sociolinguistic approach to socialization: with some references to educability. In WILLIAMS, F. (ed.) *Language and Poverty*. Chicago: Markham Press. pp. 25–61.

BERRY, J. W. (1965) *A Study of Temne and Eskimo visual perception.* Preliminary Report, No. 28. Psychological Laboratory, University of Edinburgh.

BERRY, J. W. (1966a) *Cultural determinants of perception.* Unpublished Ph.D. thesis, University of Edinburgh.

BERRY, J. W. (1966b) Temne and Eskimo perceptual skills. *Int. J. Psychol.*, **1**, 207–29.

BERRY, J. W. (1967) Independence and conformity in subsistence-level societies. *J. Personal. Soc. Psychol.*, **7**, 415–18.

BERRY, J. W. (1968) Ecology, perceptual development and the Muller-Lyer illusion. *Brit. J. Psychol.*, **59**, 205–10.

BERRY, J. W. (1969a) On cross-cultural comparability. *Int. J. Psychol.*, **4**, 119–28.

BERRY, J. W. (1969b) Ecology and socialization as factors in figural assimilation and the resolution of binocular rivalry. *Int. J. Psychol.*, **4**, 271–80.

BERRY, J. W. (1971) Ecological and cultural factors in spatial perceptual development. See Chapter 7 in this volume.

BERRY, J. W. (n.d.) *Ecology, Cultural Adaptation and Psychological Differentiation* (monograph in preparation).

BEVERIDGE, W. M. (1939) Some racial differences in perception. *Brit. J. Psychol.*, **30**, 57–64.

BIESHEUVEL, S. (1943) *African Intelligence.* Johannesburg: South African Institute of Race Relations.

BIESHEUVEL, S. (1952a) Personnel selection tests for Africans. *S. A. J. Sci.*, **49**, 3.

BIESHEUVEL, S. (1952b) The study of African ability. *African Studies*, **11** (2), 45–57.

BIESHEUVEL, S. (1954) The measurement of occupational aptitudes in a multiracial society. *Occup. Psychol.*, **28**, 4.

BIESHEUVEL, S. (1969) *Methods for the Measurement of Psychological Performance.* IBP Handbook, No. 10. Oxford and Edinburgh: Blackwell.

BIRDWHISTELL, R. L. (n.d.; preface dated 1952) *Introduction to Kinesics: An Annotation System for Analysis of Body Motion and Gesture.* Louisville: University of Louisville.

BISILLIAT, J., LAYA, D., PIERRE, E. and PIDOUX, C. (1967) La notion de lakkal dans la culture Djerma-Songhai. *Psychopathologie Africaine*, **3**, 207–64.

BITTERMAN, M. E. (1965) The evolution of intelligence. *Scient. Amer.*, **212**, 92–100.

BLANK, M. and SOLOMON, F. (1969) A tutorial language program to develop abstract thinking in socially disadvantaged preschool children. *Child Develop.*, **40**, 47–61.

BLOOM B. S. (1964) *Stability and Change in Human Characteristics.* New York: Wiley.

BOAS, F. (1911a) Introduction. In BOAS, F. (ed.) *Handbook of North American Indian Languages*, Part 1. Bureau of American Ethnology Bulletin, No. 40. Washington: Government Printing Office.

BOAS, F. (1911b) *The Mind of Primitive Man.* New York: Macmillan.

BOAS, F. (1938) Language. In BOAS, F. (ed.) *General Anthropology.* Boston: Heath.

BODDE, D. (1939) Types of Chinese categorical thinking. *J. Amer. Orient. Soc.*, **59**,(2), 200–19.

BOEHM, L. (1966) Moral judgement: a cultural and sub-cultural comparison with some of Piaget's research conclusions. *Int. J. Psychol.*, **1**, 143–50.

BOONSONG, S. (1968) *The Development of Conservation of Mass, Weight and Volume in Thai Children.* Unpublished M.Ed. thesis, Bangkok College of Education.

BOVET, M. C. (1968) Etudes interculturelles de développement intellectuel et processus d'apprentissage. *Revue Suisse de Psychologie Pure et Appliquée*, **27**, 190–9.

BOVET, M. C. (1971) *Etude interculturelle des processus du raisonnement. Notions de quantités physiques et relations spatio-temporelles chez des enfants et des adultes non-scolarisés.* Ph.D. thesis, University of Geneva.

BOVET, M. C. (1973) Cognitive processes among illiterate children and adults. See Chapter 19 in this volume.

BRIGHT, W. (1963) Language and music: areas for cooperation. *Ethnomus.*, 7(1), 26–32.

BRISLIN, R. (1970) Back-translation for cross-cultural research. *J. Cross–Cult. Psychol.*, **1**, 185–216.

BROWN, R. W. and LENNEBERG, E. H. (1954) A study in language and cognition. *J. Abnorm. Soc. Psychol.*, **49**, 454–62.

BRUNER, J. S. (1964) The course of cognitive growth. *Amer. Psychol.*, **19**, 1–15.

BRUNER, J. S. (1970) *Poverty and Childhood.* Merrill–Palmer Institute Monographs.

BRUNER, J. S. and OLVER, R. R. (1963) Development of equivalence transformations in children. *Monogr. Soc. Res. Child Develop.*, **28** (2), 125–43.

BRUNER, J. S., GOODNOW, J. J. and AUSTIN, G. A. (1956) *A Study of Thinking*. New York: Wiley.

BRUNER, J. S., OLVER, R. R. and GREENFIELD, P. M. (1966) *Studies in Cognitive Growth*. New York: Wiley.

BRUNER, J. S., SHAPIRO, D. and TAGIURI, R. (1958) The meaning of traits in isolation and in combination. In TAGIURI, R. and PETRULLO, L. (eds.) *Person Perception and Interpersonal Behaviour*. Stanford: Stanford University Press.

BRUNSWIK, E. (1958) *Representative Design in the Planning of Psychological Research*. Berkeley: University of California Press.

BURLING, R. (1963) Garo kinship terms and the analysis of meaning. *Ethnology*, 2(1), 70–85.

BURLING, R. (1964) Cognition and componential analysis: God's truth or hocus-pocus. *Amer. Anthrop.*, 66(1), 20–8.

BURT, C. (1968) Mental capacity and its critics. *Bull. Brit. Psychol. Soc.*, 70(21), 11–18.

BURT, C. (1969) The concept of intelligence. *J. Assoc. Educ. Psychol.*, 16–38.

CALDWELL, B. M. *et al.* (1970) Infant day care and attachment. *Amer. J. Orthopsychiat.*, 40, 397–412.

CAMPBELL, D. T. (1957) Factors relevant to the validity of experiments in social settings. *Psychol. Bull.*, 54, 297–312.

CAMPBELL, D. T. (1961) The mutual methodological relevance of anthropology and psychology. In HSU, F. L. K. (ed.) *Psychological Anthropology*. Homewood, Ill.: Dorsey Press. pp. 333–352.

CAMPBELL D. T. (1964) Distinguishing differences in perception from failures of communication in cross-cultural studies. In NORTHROP, F. S. C. (ed.) *Cross-Cultural Understanding: Epistemology in Anthropology*. New York: Harper & Row. pp. 308–36.

CAMPBELL, D. T. and LEVINE, R. A. (1970) Field manual anthropology. In NAROLL, R. and COHEN, R. (eds.) *Handbook of Method in Cultural Anthropology*. Garden City: Natural History Press. pp. 366–87.

CAMPBELL, D. T. and STANLEY, J. C. (1966) *Experimental and Quasi-Experimental Designs for Research*. Chicago: Rand McNally.

CANCIAN, F. (1963) Informant error and native prestige ranking in Zinacantan. *Amer. Anthrop.*, 65(5), 1068–75.

CARDEN, J. A. (1958) *Field dependence, anxiety, and sociometric status in children*. Unpublished master's thesis, University of Texas.

CARMICHAEL, L., HOGAN, H. P. and WALTER, A. A. (1932) An

experimental study of the effect of language on the reproduction of visually perceived form. *J. Exp. Psychol.*, **15**, 73–86.

CARROLL, J. B. (1956) *Language, Thought and Reality: Selected Writings of Benjamin Lee Whorf*. New York: Wiley.

CARROLL, J. B. and CASAGRANDE, J. B. (1958) The function of language classifications in behaviour. In MACCOBY, E. E., NEWCOMB, T. M. and HARTLEY, E. L. (eds.) *Readings in Social Psychology*. New York: Holt, Rinehart & Winston.

CASSIRER, E. (1953) *The Philosophy of Symbolic Forms*, Vol. I. *Languages*. New Haven: Yale University Press.

CAZDEN, C. (1970) The neglected situation in child language research and education. In WILLIAMS, F. (ed.) *Language and Poverty*. Chicago: Markham Press. pp. 81–101.

CHAFE, W. L. (1962) Phonetics, semantics and language. *Language*, **38**(4), 335–44.

CHAO, Y. R. (1956) Chinese terms of address. *Language*, **32**(1), 217–41.

CHENG, TSU-HSIN and LEE, MEI-KE (1960) An investigation into the scope of the conception of numbers among 6–7 year old children. *Acta Psychologica Sinica*, **1**, 28–35.

CHOMSKY, N. (1966) *Cartesian Linguistics*. New York: Harper & Row.

CHOPPIN, B. (1967) Social class and educational achievement. *Educ. Res.*, **10**, 213–17.

CLARK, K. B. (1940) Some factors influencing the remembering of prose material. *Archives Psychol.*, **35**(253).

COLE, M., GAY, J. and GLICK, J. (1968) Reversal and nonreversal shifts among a West African tribal people. *J. Exp. Psychol.*, **76**, 323–4.

COLE, M., GAY, J., GLICK, J. and SHARP, D. W. (1971) *The Cultural Context of Learning and Thinking*. New York: Basic Books.

COLLINS, P. (1965) Functional analyses. In LEEDS, A. and VAYDA, P. (eds.) *Man, Culture and Animals*. Washington: American Association for the Advancement of Science.

COLSON, E. (1962) *The Plateau Tonga*. Manchester: Manchester University Press.

CONGALTON, A. A. (1963) *Occupational status in Australia*. Studies in Sociology, No. 3. Kensington, N.S.W.: University of New South Wales.

CONKLIN, H. C. (1951) *Co-existing sets of relationship terms among the Tanay Tagalog*. Unpublished MS read at the 50th Annual Meeting of the American Anthropological Association, Chicago.

CONKLIN, H. C. (1955) Hanunóo color categories. *S.W.J. Anthrop.*, **11**(4), 339–44.

CONKLIN, H. C. (1962a) Lexicographical treatment of folk taxonomies. In HOUSEHOLDER, F. W. and SAPORTA, S. (eds.) *Problems in Lexicography*. Indiana University Research Center in Anthropology, Folklore and Linguistics, Publication No. 21. Also in *Int. J. Amer. Ling.*, **28**(2), Part 4, 119–41.

CONKLIN, H. C. (1962b) Comment [on Frake 1962]. In GLADWIN, T. and STURTEVANT, W. C. (eds.) *Anthropology and Human Behaviour*. Washington: Anthropological Society of Washington. pp. 86–91.

CONKLIN, H. C. (1964) Ethnogenealogical method. In GOODENOUGH, W. H. (ed.) *Explorations in Cultural Anthropology: Essays in Honor of George Peter Murdock*. New York: McGraw-Hill. pp. 25–55.

CORAH, N. L. (1965) Differentiation in children and their parents. *J. Personal.*, **33**, 300–8.

COWLEY, J. J. and MURRAY, M. M. (1962) Some aspects of the development of spatial concepts in Zulu children. *J. Soc. Res.*, **13**, 1–18.

CRAVIOTO, J. (1968) Nutritional deficiencies and mental performance in childhood. In GLASS, D. C. (ed.) *Environmental Influences*. New York: Russell Sage. pp. 3–51.

CRAWFORD, J. R. (1967) *Witchcraft and Sorcery in Rhodesia*. London: Oxford University Press.

CRONBACH, L. J. (1961) *Essentials of Psychological Testing*. New York: Harper & Row.

CROPLEY, A. J. (1964) Differentiation of abilities, socioeconomic status, and the WISC. *J. Consult. Psychol.*, **28**, 512–17.

CRUDDEN, C. H. (1941) Form abstraction by children. *J. Genet. Psychol.*, **58**, 113–29.

CRUTCHFIELD, R. S. (1955) Conformity and character. *Amer. Psychol.*, **10**, 191–8.

CRUTCHFIELD, R. S., WOODWORTH, D. G. and ALBRECHT, R. E. (1958) *Perceptual Performance and the Effective Person*. USAF, WADC Technical Note, No. 58–60. Lackland AFB, Texas.

CRYNS, A. G. J. (1962) African intelligence: a critical survey of cross cultural intelligence research in Africa south of the Sahara. *J. Soc. Psychol.*, **57**, 283–301.

DART, F. E. and PRADHAN, P. L. (1967) Cross-cultural teaching of science. *Science*, **155**, 649–56.

DASEN, P. R. (1970) *Cognitive development in Aborigines of Central*

P

Australia: concrete operations and perceptual activities. Unpublished Ph.D. thesis, Australian National University, Canberra.

DASEN, P. R. (1972a) Cross-cultural Piagetian research: a summary. See Chapter 25 in this volume.

DASEN, P. R. (1972b) The development of conservation in Aboriginal children: a replication study. *Int. J. Psychol.*, 7(2), 75–85.

DASEN, P. R. (1973a) The influence of ecology, culture and European contact on cognitive development in Australian Aborigines. See Chapter 24 in this volume.

DASEN, P. R. (1973b) Piagetian research in Central Australia. In KEARNEY, G. E., DE LACEY, P. R. and DAVIDSON, G. (eds.) *The Psychology of Aboriginal Australians.* Sydney: Wiley.

DASEN, P. R. and CHRISTIE, R. D. (1972) A regression phenomenon in the conservation of weight. *Archives de Psychologie*, 41(162), 145–52.

DASEN, P. R., DE LACEY, P. R. and SEAGRIM, G. N. (1973) An investigation of reasoning ability in adopted and fostered Aboriginal children. In KEARNEY, G. E., DE LACEY, P. R. and DAVIDSON, G. (eds.) *The Psychology of Aboriginal Australians.* Sydney: Wiley.

DAVIES, A. D. M. (1965) The perceptual maze in a normal population. *Percept. Mot. Skills*, 20, 287–93.

DAVILA, F. DE LA LUZ, DIAZ-GUERRERO, R. and TAPIA, L. L. (1966) *Primera fase en la investigacion de la prueba de figuras ocultas de Witkin en escolares Mexicanos.* Paper presented at 10th Inter-American Congress of Psychology, Lima, Peru.

DAWSON, J. L. M. (1963) *Psychological effects of social change in a West African community.* Unpublished D.Phil. thesis, University of Oxford.

DAWSON, J. L. M. (1966) Kwashiorkor, gynaecomastia and femininization processes. *J. Trop. Med. Hygiene*, 69, 175–9.

DAWSON, J. L. M. (1967a) Cutural and physiological influences upon spatial–perceptual processes in West Africa. Parts I and II. *Int. J. Psychol.*, 2, 115–28 and 171–85.

DAWSON, J. L. M. (1967b) Traditional versus western attitudes in West Africa: the construction, validation and application of a measuring device. *Brit. J. Soc. Clin. Psychol.*, 6, 81–96.

DAWSON, J. L. M. (1969) Attitude change and conflict among Australian Aborigines. *Austral. J. Psychol.*, 21(2), 101–16.

DE LACEY, P. R. (1970a) *Classificatory performance among Aboriginal and white Australian children.* Report to the Australian Institute of Aboriginal Studies, Canberra. Cyclostyled.

DE LACEY, P. R. (1970b) A cross-cultural study of classificatory ability in Australia. See Chapter 22 in this volume.

DE LACEY, P. R. (1970c) An index of contact for Aboriginal communities. *Austral. J. Soc. Issues,* 5(3), 219–23.

DE LACEY, P. R. (1971a) Classificatory ability and verbal intelligence among high-contact Aboriginal and low-socioeconomic white Australian children. *J. Cross-Cult. Psychol.,* 2(4), 393–6.

DE LACEY, P. R. (1971b) Verbal intelligence, operational thinking and environment in part-Aboriginal children. *Austral. J. Psychol.,* 23(2), 145–9.

DE LEMOS, M. M. (1966) *The Development of the Concept of Conversation in Australian Aboriginal Children.* Unpublished Ph.D. thesis, Australian National University.

DE LEMOS, M. M. (1969a) Conceptual development in Aboriginal children: implications for Aboriginal education. In DUNN, S. S. and TATZ, C. M. (eds.) *Aborigines and Education.* Melbourne: Sun Books. pp. 244–63.

DE LEMOS, M. M. (1969b) The development of conservation in Aboriginal children. *Int. J. Psychol.,* 4(4), 255–69.

DE LEMOS, M. M. (1973) The development of spatial concepts in Zulu children. See Chapter 23 in this volume.

DEMPSEY, A. D. (1971) Time conservation across cultures. *Int. J. Psychol.,* 6, 115–20.

DENNIS, W. (1943) Animism and related tendencies in Hopi children. *J. Abnorm. Soc. Psychol.,* 38, 21–36.

DENNIS, W. and RUSSELL, R. W. (1940) Piaget's questions applied to Zuni children. *Child Develop.,* 11, 181–7.

DENNY, P. and BENJAFIELD, J. (1969) Concept identification strategies used for positive and negative instances. *Psychon. Sci.,* 14, 277–80.

DEREGOWSKI, J. B. and SERPELL, R. (1971) Performance on a sorting task with various modes of representation: a cross-cultural experiment. *Int. J. Psychol.,* 6(4), 273–81.

DEUTSCH, M. (1963) The disadvantaged in the learning process. In PASSOW, A. H. (ed.) *Education in Depressed Areas.* New York: Teachers College Press.

DEUTSCH, M. (1967) *The Disadvantaged Child.* New York: Basic Books.

DOOB, L. W. (1960) *Becoming More Civilized: A Psychological Exploration.* New Haven: Yale University Press.

DOOB, L. W. (1961) *Communication in Africa. A Search for Boundaries.* New Haven: Yale University Press.

DOOB, L. W. (1966) Eidetic imagery: a cross-cultural will-o-the-wisp? *J. Psychol.*, **63**, 13–34.

DROZ, R. and RAHMY, M. (1972) *Lire Piaget*. Brussels: Dessart.

DUBREUIL, G. and BOISCLAIR, C. (1960) Le réalisme enfantin à la Martinique et au Canada Français. Etude génétique et expérimentale. In *Thought from the Learned Societies of Canada*. Toronto: Gage. pp. 83–95.

DUBREUIL, G. and BOISCLAIR, C. (1966) Quelques aspects de la pensée enfantine à la Martinique. In BENOIST, J. (ed.) *Les sociétés antillaises: études anthropologiques*. Department of Anthropology, University of Montreal. pp. 79–99.

DUIJKER, H. C. J. and FRIJDA, N. H. (1960) *National Character and National Stereotypes*. Amsterdam: North Holland.

DUNDES, A. (1962) From etic to emic units in the structural study of folk-tales. *J. Amer. Folklore*, **75**(296), 95–105.

DURKHEIM, E. and MAUSS, M. (1903) De quelques formes primitives de classification; contribution à l'étude des représentations collectives. *L'Année Sociologique*, **6**, 1–72.

DYK, R. B. and WITKIN, H. A. (1965) Family experiences related to the development of differentiation in children. *Child Develop.*, **30**, 21–55.

EBBINGHAUS, H. (1897) Über eine neue Methode in Prüfunt geistiger Rühigkeiten und ihre Awendung bei Schulkindern. *Z. Psychol.*, **13**, 401–57.

EDWARDS. A. L. (1950) *Experimental Design in Psychological Research*. New York: Holt, Rinehart & Winston.

EDWARDS, A. L. and ENGLISH, H. B. (1939) The effect of the immediate test on verbatim and summary retention. *Amer. J. Psychol.*, **52**, 372–5.

EELLS, K. W., DAVIS, A., HAVIGHURST, R. J., TYLER, R. W. and HERRICK, V. E. (1959) *Intelligence and Cultural Differences*. Chicago: University of Chicago Press.

EIDENS, H. (1929) Experimentelle Untersuchungen über den Denkuerlauf bei unmittel barren Folgerungen. *Arch. ges. Psychol.*, **71**, 1–66.

EIFERMANN, R. (1968) *School Children's Games*. Washington: Department of Health, Education and Welfare.

ELKIN, A. P. (1964). *The Australian Aborigines: How to Understand Them* (4th ed.). Sydney: Angus & Robertson.

ENGLISH, H. B., WELBORN, E. L. and KILLIAN, C. D. (1934) Studies in substance memorization. *J. Gen. Psychol.*, **11**, 233–59.

ETUK, E. (1967) *The development of number concepts: an examination of Piaget's theory with Yoruba-speaking Nigerian children.* Unpublished Ed.D. dissertation, Teachers' College, Columbia University.

EVANS-PRITCHARD, E. E. (1936) *Witchcraft, Oracles and Magic among the Azande.* Oxford: Clarendon Press.

FEINBERG, I. R. (1951) *Sex differences in resistance to group pressure.* Unpublished master's thesis, Swarthmore College, Pennsylvania.

FERGUSON, G. A. (1954) On learning and human ability. *Cdn. J. Psychol.*, 8, 95–112.

FERGUSON, G. A. (1956) On transfer and the abilities of man. *Cdn. J. Psychol.*, 10, 121.

FINK, D. M. (1959) *Sex differences in perceptual tasks in relation to selected personality variables.* Unpublished doctoral dissertation, Rutgers University, N.J.

FISCHER, J. L. (1958) The classification of residence in censuses. *Amer. Anthrop.*, 60(3), 508–17.

FISHMAN, J. A. (1956) An examination of the process and function of social stereotyping. *J. Soc. Psychol.*, 43, 27–64.

FISHMAN, J. A. (1957) Some current research needs in the psychology of testimony. *J. Soc. Issues.*, 13, 60–7.

FISK, M. L. (1939) *The Educability of the South African Native.* Research Series No. 8. Pretoria: South African Council for Education and Social Research.

FITZGERALD, L. (1970) *Cognitive development among Ga children: environmental correlates of cognitive growth within the Ga tribe.* Unpublished Ph.D. thesis, University of California.

FLAVELL, J. H. (1963) *The Developmental Psychology of Jean Piaget.* Princeton, N.J.: Van Nostrand.

FLAVELL, J. H. and WOHLWILL, J. F. (1969) Formal and functional aspects of cognitive development. In ELKIND, D. and FLAVELL, J. H. (eds.) *Studies in Cognitive Development.* New York: Oxford University Press. pp. 67–120.

FORDE, D. (1954) *African Worlds.* London: Oxford University Press.

FOWLER, H. L. (1940) Report on psychological tests on natives in the north-west of Western Australia. *Austral. J. Sci.*, 2, 124–7.

FRAKE, C. O. (1960) The Eastern Subanun of Mindanao. In MURDOCK, G. P. (ed.) *Social Structure in Southeast Asia.* Viking Fund Publications in Anthropology, No. 29. pp. 51–64.

FRAKE, C. O. (1961) The diagnosis of disease among the Subanun of Mindanao. *Amer. Anthrop.*, 63(1), 113–32.

FRAKE, C. O. (1962) The ethnographic study of cognitive systems. In

GLADWIN, T. and STURTEVANT, W. C. (eds.) *Anthropology and Human Behavior*. Washington: Anthropological Society of Washington. pp. 72–85, 91–3.

FRAKE, C. O. (1964) Notes on queries in ethnography. *Amer. Anthrop.*, 66(3), Part 2, pp. 132–45.

FRENCH, D. (1963) The relationship of anthropology to studies in perception and cognition. In KOCH, S. (ed.) *Psychology: A Study of a Science*, Vol. 6. New York: McGraw-Hill. pp. 388–428.

FRENCH, J. W., EKSTROM, R. B. and PRICE, L. A. (1963) *Kit of Reference Tests for Cognitive Factors* (new ed.). Princeton, N.J.: Educational Testing Service.

FRIJDA, N. and JAHODA, G. (1966) On the scope and methods of cross-cultural research. *Int. J. Psychol.*, 1, 109–27.

FURBY, L. (1971) A theoretical analysis of cross-cultural research in cognitive development: Piaget's conservation tasks. *J. Cross-Cult. Psychol.*, 2(3), 241–55.

FURTH, H. G. (1966) *Thinking without Language: Psychological Implications of Deafness*. New York: Free Press.

FURTH, H. G. (1969) *Piaget and Knowledge. Theoretical Foundations*. Englewood Cliffs, N.J.: Prentice-Hall.

GALTON, F. (1879) Psychometric experiments. *Brain*, 2, 149–62.

GARFINKLE, H. (1967) *Studies in Ethnomethodology*. Englewood Cliffs, N.J.: Prentice-Hall.

GASTIL, R. D. (1959) Relative linguistic determinism. *Anthrop. Ling.*, 1(9), 24–38.

GATES, A. I. (1917) Recitation as a factor in memorizing. *Arch. Psychol.*, 6(40).

GAY, J. and COLE, M. (1967) *The New Mathematics and an Old Culture*. New York: Holt, Rinehart & Winston.

GELFAND, M. (1967) *The African Witch*. Edinburgh: Livingstone.

GINSBURG, H. and OPPER, S. (1969) *Piaget's Theory of Intellectual Development: An Introduction*. Englewood Cliffs, N. J.: Prentice-Hall.

GLADWIN, T. (1970) *East is a Big Bird*. Cambridge, Mass.: Harvard University Press.

GLADWIN, T. and SARASON, S. B. (1953) *Truk: Man in Paradise*. Viking Fund Publications in Anthropology, No. 20. New York: Wenner-Gren Foundation for Anthropological Research, Inc.

GLADWIN, T. and STURTEVANT, W. C. (1962) *Anthropology and Human Behaviour*. Washington: Anthropological Society of Washington.

GLENN, E. S. (1959) Paper presented at the American Psychological Association meeting, Cincinnati.

GLUCKMAN, M. (1944) The logic of African science and witchcraft. *Rhodes-Livingstone J.*, **1**, 61.

GOFFMAN, E. (1964) The neglected situation. In GUMPERZ, J. and HYMES, D. (eds.) The ethnology of communication. *Amer. Anthrop.*, **66**(6), Part 2, 133.

GOLDEN, M. and BIRNS, B. (1968) Social class and cognitive development in infancy. *Merrill-Palmer Quart.*, **14**, 139–49.

GOLDSCHMIDT, W. (1966) *Comparative Functionalism*. Berkeley: University of California Press.

GOLSON, J. (1963) *Polynesian Navigation: A Symposium on Andrew Sharp's Theory of Accidental Voyages*. Memoir 34. Wellington: Polynesian Society.

GOODENOUGH, D. R. and EAGLE, C. J. (1963) A modification of the embedded-figures test for use with young children. *J. Genet. Psychol.*, **103**, 67–74.

GOODENOUGH, F. (1936) The measurement of mental functions in primitive groups. *Amer. Anthrop.*, **38**, 1–11.

GOODENOUGH, W. H. (1956a) Componential analysis and the study of meaning. *Language*, **32**(2), 195–216.

GOODENOUGH, W. H. (1956b) Residence rules. *S. W. J. Anthrop.*, **12**(1), 22–37.

GOODENOUGH, W. H. (1957) Cultural anthropology and linguistics. In GARVIN, P. L. (ed.) *Report of the 7th Annual Round Table Meeting on Linguistics and Language Study*. Monograph Series on Languages and Linguistics No. 9. Washington: Institute of Languages and Linguistics, Georgetown University. pp. 167–73. Also published 1956, in *Bull. Phil. Anthrop. Soc.*, **9**(3), 3–7.

GOODNOW, J. J. (1962) A test of milieu effects with some of Piaget's tasks. *Psychol. Monogr.*, **76**(36), Whole No. 555.

GOODNOW, J. J. (1969a) Cultural variations in cognitive skills. In PRICE-WILLIAMS, D. R. (ed.) *Cross-cultural Studies*. Harmondsworth: Penguin Books. pp. 246–64.

GOODNOW, J. J. (1969b) Problems in research on culture and thought. In ELKIND, D. and FLAVELL, J. H. (eds.) *Studies in Cognitive Development: Essays in Honor of Jean Piaget*. New York: Oxford University Press. pp. 439–62.

GOODNOW, J. J. and BETHON, G. (1966) Piaget's tasks: the effects of schooling and intelligence. *Child Develop.*, **37**, 573–82.

GREENBERG, J. (1963) *Universals of Language*. Cambridge, Mass.: MIT Press.

GREENFIELD, P. M. (1966) On culture and conservation. In BRUNER,

J. S., OLVER, R. R. and GREENFIELD. P. M. (eds.) *Studies in Cognitive Growth.* New York: Wiley. pp. 225–56. Reprinted in PRICE-WILLIAMS, 1969.

GREENFIELD, P.M. and BRUNER, J. S. (1966) Culture and cognitive growth. *Int. J. Psychol.*, **1**, 89–107.

GREGOR, A. J. and MCPHERSON, D. A. (1963) The correlation of the Porteus Maze and the Gestalt Continuation as personnel selection tests of peripheral peoples. *J. Psychol.*, **56**, 137–42.

GRIAULE, M. and DIETERLEN, G. (1954) The Dogon. In FORDE, D. (ed.) *African Worlds: Studies in the Cosmological Ideas and Social Values of African Peoples.* London: Oxford University Press for the International African Institute. pp. 83–110.

GUETZKOW, H. (1951) An analysis of the operation of set in problem-solving behaviour. *J. Gen. Psychol.*, **45**, 219–44.

GUTHRIE, G. M. (1963) Structure of abilities in a non-western culture. *J. Educ. Psychol.*, **2**, 94.

HABER, R. H. and HABER, R. B. (1964) Eidetic imagery. I: Frequency. *Percept. Mot. Skills*, **19**, 131–8.

HALL, E. T. (1959) *The Silent Language.* New York: Doubleday.

HALL, E. T. (1963a) *Field methodology in proxemics.* Unpublished lecture before the Anthropological Society of Washington, 19 March.

HALL, E. T. (1963b) Proxemics: one study of man's spatial relations. In GALDSTON, I. (ed.) *Man's Image in Medicine and Anthropology.* Monograph IV, Institute of Social and Historical Medicine, The New York Academy of Medicine. New York: International Universities Press. pp. 422–45.

HALLOWELL, A. I. (1951) Cultural factors in the structuralization of perception. In ROHRER, J. H. and SHERIF, M. (eds.) *Social Psychology at the Crossroads.* New York: Harper & Row.

HALLOWELL, A. I. (1955) *Culture and Experience.* Philadelphia: University of Pennsylvania Press.

HAMMOND, K. R. (1966) *The Psychology of Egon Brunswik.* New York: Holt, Rinehart & Winston.

HANFMANN, E. and KASANIN, J. (1936) A method for the study of concept formation. *J. Psychol.*, **3**, 521–54.

HANNAN, M. J. (1959) *Standard Shona Dictionary.* London: Macmillan.

HARRIS, D. B. (1963) *Children's Drawings as Measures of Intellectual Maturity.* New York: Harcourt, Brace & World.

HARRIS, Z. S. (1944) Simultaneous components in phonology. *Language*, **20**(4), 181–205.

HART, J. A. (1965) *A study of the cognitive capacity of a group of Australian Aboriginal children.* Unpublished M.A. qualifying examination thesis, University of Queensland.

HAVIGHURST, R. G. and NEUGARTEN, B. L. (1955) *American Indian and White Children.* Chicago: University of Chicago Press.

HAYGOOD, R. C. and BOURNE, L. (1965) Attribute and rule learning aspects of conceptual behavior. *Psychol. Rev.*, **72**, 175–95.

HEBB, D. O. (1949) *The Organisation of Behavior.* New York: Wiley.

HELLBUSCH, S. (1941) *Einfluss der Jagd auf die Lebensformen der Australier.* Berlin: Ebering.

HELM, J. (1962) The ecological approach in anthropology. *Amer. J. Sociol.*, **67**, 630–9.

HENDRIKZ, E. (1966) *A cross-cultural investigation of the number concepts and level of number development in five-year-old urban Shona and European children in southern Rhodesia.* Unpublished M.A. thesis, University of London.

HERON, A. (1966) Experimental studies of mental development in conditions of rapid cultural change. *Proc. XVIII Int. Congr. Psychol. Symp.* (Moscow), **36**, 119.

HERON, A. (1968) Studies of perception and reasoning in Zambian children. *Int. J. Psychol.*, **3**, 23–9.

HERON, A. (1971) Concrete operations, 'g' and achievement in Zambian children. *J. Cross-Cult. Psychol.*, **2**(4), 325–36.

HERON, A. and SIMONSSON, M. (1969) Weight conservation in Zambian children: a nonverbal approach. See Chapter 20 in this volume.

HERTZIG, M. E., BIRCH, H. G., THOMAS, A. and MENDEZ, O. A. (1968) Class and ethnic differences in the responsiveness of preschool children to cognitive demands. *Monogr. Soc. Res. Child. Develop.*, **33**(1), Serial No. 117.

HESS, R. D. and SHIPMAN, V. (1965) Early experience and socialization of cognitive modes in children. *Child Develop.*, **36**, 869–86.

HIRSCH, J. (1963) Behavior genetics and individuality understood. *Science*, **142**, 1436–42.

HOCKETT, C. F. (1954) Chinese versus English: an exploration of the Whorfian theses. In HOIJER, H. (ed.) *Language in Culture.* American Anthropological Association Memoir, No. 79. Chicago: University of Chicago Press. pp. 106–23.

HOIJER, H. (1945) Classificatory verb stems in the Apachean languages. *Int. J. Amer. Ling.*, **11**, 13.

HOIJER, H. (1951) Cultural implications of some Navaho linguistic categories. *Languages*, **27**, 11–120.

HOIJER, H. (1954) *Language in Culture*. American Anthropological Association Memoir, No. 79. Chicago: University of Chicago Press.

HONIGMANN, J. (1967) *Personality in Culture*. New York: Harper & Row.

HOPKINS, N. S. (1963) Dogon classificatory systems. *Anthrop. Tomorrow*, 9(1), 48–54.

HORNER, F. A., STREAMER, C. W., LOURDES, L., ALEJANDRINO, M. D., REED, L. H. and IBBOTT, F. (1962) Termination of dietary treatment of phenylketonuria. *New Engl. J. Med.*, 266, 79–81.

HORTON, R. (1967) African traditional thought and western science: part one, from tradition to science. *Africa*, 37(1), 50–71.

HOUTSMA, M. T., ARNOLD, T. W., BASSETT, R. and HARTMANN, R. (1913) *Encyclopaedia of Islam*. London: Luzac.

HSU, F. L. K. (1961) *Psychological Anthropology*. Homewood, Ill.: Dorsey Press.

HUANG, I. (1943) Children's conception of physical causality: a critical summary. *J. Genet. Psychol.*, 63, 71–121.

HUANG, I. and LEE, H. W. (1945) Experimental analysis of child animism. *J. Genet. Psychol.*, 66, 69–74.

HUDSON, W. (1960) Pictorial depth perception in sub-cultural groups in Africa. *J. Soc. Psychol.*, 52(2), 183–208.

HUDSON, W. (1962) Pictorial perception and educational adaptation in Africa. *Psychologia Africana*, 9, 226–39.

HUNT, J. MCV. (1961) *Intelligence and Experience*. New York: Ronald Press.

HUNT, J. MCV. (1969) Has compensatory education failed? Has it been attempted? *Harvard Educ. Rev.*, 39, 278–300.

HUNTER, G. (1962) *The New Societies of Tropical Africa*. London: Oxford University Press.

HUNTER, W. S. and SIGLER, M. (1940) The span of visual discrimination as a function of time and intensity of stimulation. *J. Exp. Psychol.*, 26, 160–79.

HUSÉN T. (1945) Studier Rörande de Eidetiska Fenomenen. *Lunds Universitets Arsskrift*, 41, vii, 1–128.

HYDE, D. M. G. (1959) *An investigation of Piaget's theories of the development of the concept of number*. Unpublished Ph.D. thesis, University of London.

HYDE, D. M. G. (1970) *Piaget and Conceptual Development*. London: Holt, Rinehart & Winston.

HYMES, D. H. (1964) Directions in (ethno-) linguistic theory. *Amer. Anthrop.*, 66(3), Part 2, 6–56.

HYMES, D. H. (1966) *On Communicative Competence*. Report of a conference on research planning on language development among disadvantaged children. New York: Yeshiva University Press.

INHELDER, B. (1956) Criteria of the stages of mental development. In TANNER, J. M. and INHELDER, B. (eds.) *Discussions on Child Development.* London: Tavistock. pp. 75–107.

INHELDER, B. (1968) *The Diagnosis of Reasoning in the Mentally Retarded.* New York: John Day. (*Le diagnostic du raisonnement chez les débiles mentaux,* originally published Neuchâtel, *1943*; 2nd ed., *1963.*).

INHELDER, B. and PIAGET, J. (1964) *The Early Growth of Logic in the Child* (trans. E. A. Lunzer and D. Papert). London: Routledge & Kegan Paul; New York: Harper & Row.

INHELDER, B., BOVET, M., SINCLAIR, H. and SMOCK, C. D. (1966) Comments on Bruner's course of cognitive development: letter published in *Amer. Psychol.,* 21, 160–4.

INHELDER, B., SINCLAIR, H. and BOVET, M. (1973) *Les structures de la connaissance: apprentissage et développement.* Paris: PUF.

IRVINE, S. H. (1963) Ability testing in English-speaking Africa – an overview of comparative and predictive studies. *Rhodes-Livingstone J.,* 34, 44.

IRVINE, S. H. (1964) Selection of Africans for post-primary education: pilot survey June–July 1962. *Bull. Inter-Africa Lab. Inst.,* 11, 69.

IRVINE, S. H. (1966) Towards a rationale for testing attainments and abilities in Africa. *Brit. J. Educ. Psychol.,* 36, 24–32.

IRVINE, S. H. (1967) How fair is culture? Factorial studies of Raven's Progressive Matrices in Africa. *Int. Workshop on Educational Testing.* Berlin: Padagogisches Zentrum.

IRVINE, S. H. (1969a) Contributions of ability and attainment testing in Africa to a general theory of intellect. See Chapter 15 in this volume.

IRVINE, S. H. (1969b) Culture and mental ability. *New Scientist,* 42, 230–1.

IRVINE, S. H. (1969c) The factor analysis of African abilities and attainments: constructs across cultures. *Psychol. Bull.,* 71, 20–32.

IRVINE, S. H. (1970) Affect and construct – a cross-cultural check on theories of intelligence. *J. Soc. Psychol.,* 80, 23–30.

ISCOE, I. and CARDEN, J. A. (1961) Field dependence, manifest anxiety and sociometric status in children. *J. Consult. Psychol.,* 25, 184.

JAENSCH, E. R. (1923) Die Völkerkunde und der eidetische Tatsachenkreis. *Zeitschrift für Psychologie und Physiologie der Sinnesorgane,* 91, 88–111.

JAHN, J. (1961) *Muntu, An Outline of Neo-African Culture.* London: Faber.

JAHODA, G. (1958a) Child animism: I. A critical survey of cross-cultural research. *J. Soc. Psychol.,* 47, 197–212.

JAHODA, G. (1958b) Child animism: II. A study in West Africa. *J. Soc. Psychol.,* 47, 213–22.

JAHODA, G. (1958c) Immanent justice among West African children. *J. Soc. Psychol.,* 47, 241–8.

JAHODA, G. (1961a) Aspects of westernization: I. *Brit. J. Soc.,* 12, 375–86.

JAHODA, G. (1961b) Traditional healers and other institutions concerned with mental illness in Ghana. *Int. J. Soc. Psychiat.,* 7, 245–68.

JAHODA, G. (1961c) Magie, sorcellerie et developpement culturel. *Lumen Vitae,* 2, 334–42.

JAHODA, G. (1962) Aspects of westernization: II. *Brit. J. Sociol.,* 13, 43–56.

JAHODA, G. (1966) Social aspirations, magic and witchcraft in Ghana. In LLOYD, P. (ed.) *The New Elites of Tropical Africa.* London: Oxford University Press. pp. 199–215.

JAHODA, G. (1968) Scientific training and the persistence of traditional beliefs amongst West African university students. *Nature,* 220, 1356.

JAHODA, G. (1969a) Cross-cultural use of the perceptual maze test. *Brit. J. Educ. Psychol.,* 39, 82–6.

JAHODA, G. (1969b) Understanding the mechanism of bicycles. *Int. J. Psychol.,* 4, 103–8.

JAHODA, G. (1970a) A cross-cultural perspective in psychology. *The Advancement of Science,* 27, 1–14.

JAHODA, G. (1970b) Supernatural beliefs and changing cognitive structures among Ghanaian university students. See Chapter 8 in this volume.

JENSEN, A. R. (1969) How much can we boost IQ and scholastic achievement? *Harvard Educ. Rev.,* 39, 1–123.

JOHN, V. P. and GOLDSTEIN, L. S. (1964) The social context of language acquisition. *Merrill-Palmer Quart.,* 10, 265–75.

JONES, E. E. (1966) Conceptual generality and experimental strategy in social psychology (symposium). In *Methodological Problems of Social Psychology: Proceedings 18th Int. Congress Psychol.,* 34.

JONES, F. L. and ARRINGTON, M. (1945) The explanation of physical phenomena given by white and Negro children. *Comp. Psychol. Monogr.,* 18, 5.

JOSE, D. G. and WELCH, J. S. (1970) Growth retardation, anaemia and infection, with malabsorption and infestation of the bowel: the syndrome of protein-calorie malnutrition in Australian Aboriginal children. *Med. J. Austr.* (57th year), **1**(8), 349–55.

JOSEPH, H. W. B. (1916) *Introduction to Logic.* Oxford: Clarendon Press.

KABERRY, P. M. (1939) *Aboriginal Woman, Sacred and Profane.* London: Routledge & Kegan Paul.

KAGAN, J. (1969) Inadequate evidence and illogical conclusions. *Harvard Educ. Rev.*, **39**, 274–7.

KAGAN, J. and KOGAN, N. (1970) Individuality and cognitive performance. In MUSSEN, P. H. (ed.) *Carmichael's Manual of Child Psychology*, Vol. I. New York: Wiley. pp. 1273–365.

KATO, N. (1965) The validity and reliability of new rod frame test. *Jap. Psychol. Res.*, **4**, 120–5.

KAUFMAN, E. L., LORD, M. W. REESE, T. W. and VOLKMAN, J. (1949) The discrimination of visual number. *Amer. J. Psychol.*, **62**, 498–525.

KAVADIAS, G. (1966) The assimilation of the scientific and technological 'message'. *Int. Soc. Sci. J.*, **18**, 362–75.

KEARNEY, G. (1966) *Some aspects of the general cognitive ability of various groups of Aboriginal Australians as assessed by the Queensland Test.* Unpublished PhD. thesis, University of Queensland.

KELLAGHAN, T. P. (1965) *The study of cognition in a non-Western society with special reference to the Yoruba of South Nigeria.* Unpublished doctorial thesis, University of Belfast.

KELLY, M. R. (1971) Some aspects of conservation of quantity and length in Papua and New Guinea in relation to language, sex and years at school. *Territory of Papua and New Guinea J. Educ.*, **7**,(1), 55–60.

KIBUUKA, P. M. T. (1966) *Traditional education of the Baganda tribe.* Unpublished MS, National Institute of Education, Makerere University.

KIDD, A. H. and RIVOIRE, J. L. (1965) The culture-fair aspects of the development of spatial perception. *J. Genet. Psychol.*, **106**, 101–III.

KILPATRICK, F.P. (1955) Perception theory and general semantics. *Etc.*, **12**, 257–64.

KING, W. L. (1966) Learning and utilization of conjunctive and disjunctive classification rules: a developmental study. *J. Exp. Child Psychol.*, **4**, 217–31.

KLAUS, R. and GRAY, S. (1968) The early training project for disadvantaged children: a report after five years. *Monogr. Soc. Res. Child Develop.*, **33**(4).

KLINGELHOFER, E. L. (1967) Performance of Tanzania secondary school pupils on the Raven Standard Progressive Matrices Test. *J. Soc. Psychol.*, **72**, 205.

KLINGELHOFER, E. L. (1971) What Tanzanian secondary school students plan to teach their children. *J. Cross-Cult. Psychol.*, **2**, 189–96.

KLUCKHOHN, C. K. M. (1953) Universal categories of culture. In KROEBER, A. L. (ed.) *Anthropology Today: An Encyclopedic Inventory.* Chicago: University of Chicago Press. pp. 507–23.

KLUCKHOHN, C. K. M. (1956) Toward a comparison of value-emphases in different cultures. In WHITE, L. D. (ed.) *The State of the Social Sciences.* Chicago: University of Chicago Press. pp. 116–32.

KLUCKHOHN, C. K. M. (1958) The scientific study of values. In FRYE, N., KLUCKHOHN, C. K. M. and WIGGLESWORTH, V. B. *University of Toronto Installation Lectures: Three Lectures.* Toronto: University of Toronto Press. pp. 26–54.

KLUCKHOHN, C. K. M. (1962) *Culture and Behavior.* New York: Free Press.

KOHL, H. (1967) *36 Children.* New York: New American Library.

KOHLBERG, L. (1968) Early education: a cognitive developmental view. *Child Develop.*, **39**, 1013–62.

KROEBER, A. L. (1909) Classificatory systems of relationship. *J. Royal Anthrop. Inst.*, **39**, 77–84. Reprinted in KROEBER, 1952, pp. 175–81.

KROEBER, A. L. (1948) *Anthropology.* New York: Harcourt, Brace & World.

KROEBER, A. L. (1952) *The Nature of Culture.* Chicago: University of Chicago Press.

LABOV, W. (1970) The logical non-standard English. In WILLIAMS, F. (ed.) *Language and Poverty.* Chicago: Markham Press. pp. 153–89.

LAMB, S. M. (1964) The sememic approach to structural semantics. *Amer. Anthrop.*, **66**(3), Part 2, 57–78.

LAMBERT, R. and ZALESKA, M. (1966) Choix d'une strategie en fonction du mode de presentation d'une série aléatoire imaginaire de fréquence connue et determinants du comportement rationnel. *Bulletin du CERP*, **15**, 17–38.

LAMBO, T. A. (1955) The role of cultural factors in paranoid psychosis among the Yoruba tribe. *J. Ment. Sci.*, **101**, 239–66.

LATON, D. (1968) *Social Class, Language and Education.* London: Routledge & Kegan Paul.

LAURENDEAU, M. and PINARD, A. (1966) Le caractère topologique des premières représentations spatiales de l'enfant: examen des hypothèses de Piaget. *Int. J. Psychol.*, **1**(3), 243–55.

LEACH, E. R. (1961a) *Pul Eliya, a Village in Ceylon.* Cambridge: Cambridge University Press.

LEACH, E. R. (1961b) *Rethinking Anthropology.* Monograph on Social Anthropology, No. 22. London: London School of Economics.

LEACH, E. R. (1961c) Lévi-Strauss in the Garden of Eden: an examination of some recent developments in the analysis of myth. *Trans. N. Y. Acad. Sci.*, Series 2, **23**(4), 386–96.

LEE, C. L. (1965) Concept utilization in pre-school children. *Child Develop.*, **36**(1), 57–63.

LEE, D. D. (1944) Linguistic reflection of Wintu thought. *Int. J. Amer. Ling.*, **10**, 181–7.

LEHMANN, A. (1889) Über Wiedererkennen. *Philos. Stud.* (Wundt), **5**, 96–156.

LENNEBERG, E. H. (1953) Cognition in ethnolinguistics. *Language*, **29**, 463–71.

LENNEBERG, E. H. (1957) A probabilistic approach to language learning. *Behav. Sci.*, **2**, 1–12.

LESSER, G. S., FIFER, G. and CLARK, D. H. (1965) Mental abilities of children from different social class and cultural groups. *Child Develop. Monogr.*, **30**(4).

LEVINE, B. B. (1963) Nyansongo. In WHITING, B. B. (ed.) *Six Cultures: Studies of Child Rearing.* New York: Wiley.

LE VINE, R. A. (1970) Cross-cultural study in child psychology. In MUSSEN, P. H. (ed.) *Carmichael's Manual of Child Psychology*, Vol. 2. New York: Wiley. pp. 559–612.

LE VINE, R. A. and PRICE-WILLIAMS, D. R. (1970) *Children's Kinship Concepts: Preliminary Report on a Nigerian Study.* Paper presented at the American Anthropological Association, San Diego.

LÉVI-STRAUSS, C. (1955) The structural study of myth. *J. Amer. Folklore*, **68**(270), 428–44.

LÉVI-STRAUSS, C. (1962) *Le Totémisme aujourd'hui.* Paris: PUF.

LÉVI-STRAUSS, C. (1963) *Structural Anthropology.* New York: Basic Books (*Anthropologie structurale*, originally published Paris, 1958).

LÉVI-STRAUSS, C. (1966) *The Savage Mind.* Chicago: University of Chicago Press (*La Pensée savage*, originally published Paris, 1962).

LÉVY-BRUHL, L. (1923) *Primitive Mentality.* London: Allen & Unwin.

LÉVY-BRUHL, L. (1926) *How Natives Think* (trans. L. A. Clare).

London: Allen & Unwin (*Les Fonctions Mentales dans les Societes Inferieurs*, originally published 1910).

LEWIS, L. S. (1963) Kinship terminology for the American parent. *Amer. Anthrop.*, **65**(3), 649–52.

LINDEMAN, R. (1938) *Der Begriff der Conscience im Französichen Denken.* Leipzig: Jena.

LINTON, H. B. (1955) Dependence on external influence: correlates in perception, attitudes and judgment. *J. Abnorm. Soc. Psychol.*, **51**, 502–7.

LLOYD, B. B. (1971a) The intellectual development of Yoruba children: a re-examination. *J. Cross-Cult. Psychol.*, **2**(1), 29–38.

LLOYD, B. B. (1971b) Studies of conservation with Yoruba children of differing ages and experience. *Child Develop.*, **42**, 415–28.

LLOYD, B. B. (1972) *Perception and Cognition: A Cross-cultural Perspective.* Harmondsworth: Penguin Books.

LORAM, C. T. (1917) *The Education of the South African Native.* London: Longmans Green.

LOUNSBURY, F. G. (1956) A semantic analysis of the Pawnee kinship usage. *Language*, **32**(1), 158–94.

LOUNSBURY, F. G. (1960) Similarity and contiguity relations in language and culture. In HARRELL, R. S. (ed.) *Report on the 10th Annual Round Table Meeting on Linguistics and Language Studies.* Monograph Series on Languages and Linguistics, No. 12. Washington: Institute of Languages and Linguistics, Georgetown University. pp. 123–8.

LOUNSBURY, F. G. (1963) Linguistics and psychology. In KOCH, S. (ed.) *Psychology: A Study of a Science*, Vol. 6. New York: McGraw-Hill. pp. 552–82.

LOVELL, K. (1959) A follow-up study of some aspects of the work of Piaget and Inhelder on the child's conception of space. *Brit. J. Educ. Psychol.*, **29**.

LURIA, A. R. (1959) The directive function of speech development and dissolution. Part 1: Development of the directive function of speech in early childhood. *Word*, **15**, 341–52.

LYON, D. O. (1914) The relation of length of material to time taken for learning and the optimum distribution of time. *J. Educ. Psychol.*, **5**, 1–9, 85–91, 155–63.

MacARTHUR, R. S. (1967) Sex differences in field-dependence for the Eskimo: replication of Berry's findings. *Int. J. Psychol.*, **2**, 139–140.

MacARTHUR, R. S., IRVINE, S. H. and BRIMBLE, A. R. (1964) *The*

Northern Rhodesia Mental Ability Survey 1963. Lusaka, Zambia: Institute for Social Research.

MACDONALD, A. (1944–5) *Selection of African Personnel*. Reports on the work of the Selection of Personnel Technical and Research Unit, Middle East Force. London: Ministry of Defence Archives.

MCELWAIN, D. W. (1968) *Intellectual development in Aboriginal children*. Paper read to the Australian Medical Congress, Sydney.

MCFIE, J. (1961) The effect of education of African performance on a group of intellectual tests. *Brit. J. Educ. Psychol.*, **31**, 232–9.

MCLUHAN, M. (1962) *The Gutenberg Galaxy*. London: Routledge & Kegan Paul.

MAIER, N. R. F. (1930) Reasoning in humans: 1. On direction. *J. Comp. Psychol.*, **10**, 115–43.

MALINOWSKI, B. (1922) *Argonauts of the Western Pacific*. London: George Routledge & Sons.

MALINOWSKI, B. (1923) The problem of meaning in primitive languages. In OGDEN, C. K. and RICHARDS, I. A. *The Meaning of Meaning*. New York: Harcourt Brace.

MALINOWSKI, B. (1963) *The Family among the Australian Aborigines*. New York: Schochen Books.

MALKIEL, Y. (1962) A typological classification of dictionaries on the basis of distinctive features. In HOUSEHOLDER, F. W. and SAPORTA, S. (eds.) Problems in Lexicography, *Int. J. Amer. Ling.*, **28** (2), Part 4, 3–24.

MANDELBAUM, D. G. (1949) *Selected Writings of Edward Sapir*. Berkeley: University of California Press.

MARWICK, M. G. (1965) *Sorcery in its Social Setting*. Manchester: Manchester University Press.

MASLAND, R. L., SARASON, S. B. and GLADWIN, T. (1958) *Mental Subnormality: Biological, Psychological and Cultural Factors*. New York: Basic Books.

MASON, P. (1967) The revolt against Western values. *Daedalus*, **96**, 328–52.

MAXWELL, G. M. and ELLIOTT, R. B. (1969) Nutritional state of Australian Aboriginal children. *Amer. J. Clin. Nutr.*, **22**(6), 716–24.

MEAD, M. (1932) An investigation of the thought of primitive children, with special reference to animism. *J. Roy. Anthrop. Inst.*, **62**, 173–90.

MEGGARS, B. J. (1954) Environmental limitations on the development of culture. *Amer. Anthrop.*, **56**, 801–24.

MEHLER, J. and BEVER, T. (1968) The study of competence in cognitive psychology. *Int. J. Psychol.*, **3**, 273–80.

MERMELSTEIN, E. and SHULMAN, L. S. (1967) Lack of formal schooling and the acquisition of conservation. *Child Develop.*, **38**, 39–51.

METZGER, D. (1963) *Some ethnographic procedures.* MS read at Annual Meeting of Southwestern Anthropological Association, Riverside, California, 11–13 April.

METZGER, D. and WILLIAMS, G. (1962) *Tenejapa medicine II: Sources of illness.* Unpublished paper, Anthropology Research Projects, Preliminary Report, Stanford.

METZGER, D. and WILLIAMS, G. (1963a) Tenejapa medicine I: the curer. *S. W. J. Anthrop.*, **19**(2), 216–34.

METZGER, D. and WILLIAMS, G. (1963b) A formal ethnographic analysis of Tenejapa Ladino weddings. *Amer. Anthrop.*, **65**(5), 1076–101.

METZGER, D. and WILLIAMS, G. (1966) Some procedures and results in the study of native categories: Tzeltal firewood. *Amer. Anthrop.*, **68**(2), 389–407.

METZGER and WILLIAMS, G. (1967) Patterns of primary personal reference in a Tzeltal community. *Estudios de Cultura Maya*, **6**, 337–420.

MIDDLETON, J. and WINTER, E. H. (1963) *Witchcraft and Sorcery in East Africa.* London: Routledge & Kegan Paul.

MILLER, A. S. (1953) *An Investigation of Some Hypothetical Relationships of Rigidity and Strength and Speed of Perceptual Closure.* Unpublished doctoral dissertation, University of California.

MILLER, G. A. (1962) *Psychology: The Science of Mental Life.* New York: Harper & Row.

MILLER, G. A.. and SELFRIDGE, J. A. (1950) Verbal context and the recall of meaningful material. *Amer. J. Psychol.*, **63**, 176–85.

MILLER, G. A., BRUNER, J. S. and POSTMAN, L. (1951) Familiarity of letter sequences and tachistoscopic identification. In MILLER, G. A. (ed.) *Language and Communication.* New York: McGraw-Hill.

MILLER, G. A., GALANTER, E. and PRIBRAM, K. H. (1960) *Plans and the Structure of Behavior.* New York: Holt, Rinehart & Winston.

MILTON, G. A. (1957) The effects of sex-role identification upon problem solving skill. *J. Abnorm. Soc. Psychol.*, **55**, 208–12.

MISCHEL, W. (1966) Theory and research on the antecedents of self-imposed delay of reward. In MAHER, B. A. (ed.) *Progress in Experimental Personality Research*, Vol. 3. New York: Academic Press.

MOHSENI, N. (1966) *La comparaison des réactions aux épreuves d'intelligence en Iran et en Europe.* Unpublished thesis, University of Paris.

MURDOCK, G. P. (1945) The common denominator of cultures. In

LINTON, R. (ed.) *The Science of Man in the World Crisis.* New York: Columbia University Press. pp. 123–42.

MURDOCK, G. P. (1953) The processing of anthropological materials. In KROEBER, A. L. (ed.) *Anthropology Today.* Chicago: University of Chicago Press. pp. 476–87.

MURDOCK, G. P. (1954) *Outline of World Cultures.* New Haven: Yale University Press.

MURDOCK, G. P. (1957) World ethnographic sample. *Amer. Anthrop.,* **59,** 664–87.

MURPHY, G. (1947) *Personality.* New York: Harper & Row.

MURRAY, M. M. (1961) *The development of spatial concepts in African and European children.* Unpublished M.Sc. thesis, University of Natal.

MUSGROVE, F. (1952) Uganda Secondary School as a field of culture change. *Africa,* **22,** 234–49.

NAKAMURA, C. Y. (1955) *The Relation between Conformity and Problem Solving.* Technical Report No. 11, Stanford University.

NASR, S. H. (1966) *Ideals and Realities of Islam.* London: Allen & Unwin.

NDUKA, O. (1964) *Western Education and the Nigerian Cultural Background.* Ibadan: Oxford University Press.

NEEDHAM, R. (1962) Notes on comparative method and prescriptive alliance. *Bijdragen tot de Taal-, Land- en Volkenkunde,* 118(1), Anthropologica 3, 160–82.

NEWMAN, S. (1954) Semantic problems in grammatical systems and lexemes: a search for method. In HOIJER, H. (ed.) *Language in Culture.* Chicago: University of Chicago Press. pp. 82–91.

NISSEN, H. W., MACHOVER, S. and KINDER, E. F. (1935) A study of performance tests given to a group of native African Negro children. *Brit. J. Psychol.,* **25,** 308–55.

NIXON, M. C. (n.d.) *Children's Ability to Cross-Classify.* Report to ACER, Melbourne.

NORBECK, E. (1963) Lewis Henry Morgan and Japanese terms of relationship: profit through error. *S. W. J. Anthrop.,* **19**(2), 208–15.

NORO, S. (1961) Development of the child's conception of number. *Jap. J. Educ. Psychol.,* **9,** 230–9.

NORTHROP, F. S. C. (1947) *The Logic of the Sciences and the Humanities.* New York: Macmillan.

NURCOMBE, B. (1970a) Deprivation: an essay in deprivation with special reference to Australian Aborigines. *Med. J. Austr.,* **2,** 87–92.

NURCOMBE, B. (1970b) Precausal and paracausal thinking. Concepts of causality in Aboriginal children. *Austr. & N. Z. J. Psychiat.*, 4, 70–81.

NURCOMBE, B. and CAWTE, J. E. (1967) Pattern of behaviour disorder amongst the children of an Aboriginal population. *Austr. & N. Z. J. Psychiat.*, 1(3), 119–33.

ODHIAMBO, T. R. (1967) East Africa: science for development. *Science*, 158, 876–81.

ÖHMAN, S. (1953) Theories of the 'linguistic field'. *Word*, 9(2), 123–34.

OKONJI, O. M. (1969) The differential effects of rural and urban upbringing on the development of cognitive style. *Int. J. Psychol.*, 4, 293–305.

OKONJI, O. M. (1971a) A cross-cultural study of the effects of familiarity on classificatory behavior. See Chapter 17 in this volume.

OKONJI, O. M. (1971b) Culture and children's understanding of geometry. *Int. J. Psychol.*, 6, 121–8.

OPPER, S. (1971) *Intellectual development in Thai children*. Unpublished Ph.D. thesis, Cornell University.

ORD, I. G. (1971) *Mental Tests for Pre-literates*. London: Ginn.

OSGOOD, C. E. (1952) The nature and measurement of meaning. *Psychol. Bull.*, 49, 192–237.

OSGOOD, C. E. (1960) The cross-cultural generality of visual-verbal synthetic tendencies. *Behav. Sci.*, 5, 146–69.

OSGOOD, C. E., SUCI, G. J. and TANNENBAUM, P. H. (1957) *The Measurement of Meaning*. Urbana, Ill.: University of Illinois Press.

OTAALA, B. (1971) *The development of operational thinking in primary school children: an examination of some aspects of Piaget's theory among the Iteso children of Uganda*. Unpublished Ph.D. thesis, Teachers College, Columbia University.

PALAU MARTI, M. (1957) *Les Dogon*. Ethnographic Survey of Africa, Western Africa, French Series, No. 4. Paris: PUF for the Institut International Africain.

PARASKEVOPOULOS, J. and HUNT, J. MCV. (1971) Object construction and imitation under differring conditions of rearing. *J. Genet. Psychol.*, 119, 301–21.

PASCUAL-LEONE, J. and BOVET, M. (1966) Apprentissage de la quantification de l'inclusion et la théorie opératoire. *Acta Psychol.*, 25, 334–56.

PATEL, A. S. and GORDON, J. E. (1961) Some personal and situational determinants of yielding to influence. *J. Abnorm. Soc. Psychol.*, 61, 411–18.

PAUL, I. H. (1959) Studies in remembering: the reproduction of connected and extended verbal material. *Psychol. Issues*, 1(2).

PECK, L. and HODGES, A. B. (1937) Study of racial differences in eidetic imagery of preschool children. *J. Genet. Psychol.*, 51, 141–161.

PELUFFO, N. (1962) Les notions de conservation et de causalité chez les enfants provenant de différents milieux physiques et socioculturels. *Archives de Psychologie*, 38, 275–91.

PELUFFO, N. (1967) Culture and cognitive problems. *Int. J. Psychol.*, 2(3), 187–98.

PHILLIPS, J. jr. (1969) *The Origins of Intellect: Piaget's Theory*. San Francisco: W. H. Freeman.

PIAGET, J. (1926) *The Language and Thought of the Child* (trans. M. Gabain). London: Routledge & Kegan Paul; New York: Harcourt, Brace. (*Le langage et la pensée chez l'enfant*, originally published Neuchâtel and Paris, Delachaux & Niestlé, *1923*.)

PIAGET, J. (1929) *The Child's Conception of the World* (trans. J. and A. Tomlinson). London: Routledge & Kegan Paul; New York: Harcourt, Brace. (*La représentation du monde chez l'enfant*, originally published Paris, Alcan, *1926*.)

PIAGET, J. (1930) *The Child's Conception of Physical Causality* (trans. M. Gabain). London: Routledge & Kegan Paul. (*La causalité physique chez l'enfant*, originally published Paris, Alcan, *1927*.)

PIAGET, J. (*1950*) *Introduction à l'épistémologie génétique*, Tome III. *La pensée biologique, psychologique et sociologique*. Paris: PUF.

PIAGET, J. (1951) *Play, Drama and Imitation in Childhood* (trans. C. Gattegno and F. Hodgson). London: Heinemann; New York: Norton. (*La formation du symbole chez l'enfant*, originally published Neuchâtel, Delachaux & Niestlé, *1945*.)

PIAGET, J. (1952) *The Child's Conception of Number* (trans. C. Gattegno and F. Hodgson). London: Routledge & Kegan Paul. (*La genèse du nombre chez l'enfant*, originally published Neuchâtel, Delachaux & Niestlé, *1941*.)

PIAGET, J. (1955) *The Child's Construction of Reality* (trans. M. Cook). London: Routledge & Kegan Paul. (*La construction du réel chez l'enfant*, originally published Neuchâtel, Delachaux & Niestlé, *1937*.)

PIAGET, J. (*1966*) Nécessité et signification des recherches comparatives en psychologie génétique. See Chapter 18 in this volume.

PIAGET, J. (*1968*) Le point de vue de Piaget. *Int. J. Psychol.*, 3(4), 281–99.

PIAGET, J. (1970a) *The Child's Conception of Movement and Speed* (trans. G. E. T. Holloway and M. J. Mackenzie). London: Routledge & Kegan Paul. (*Les notions de mouvement et de vitesse chez l'enfant*, originally published Neuchâtel, Delachaux & Niestlé, *1946a*.)

PIAGET, J. (1970b) *The Child's Conception of Time* (trans. A. J. Pomerans). London: Routledge & Kegan Paul. (*Le développement de la notion de temps chez l'enfant*, originally published Neuchâtel, Delachaux & Niestlé, *1946b*.)

PIAGET, J. (1970c) *Genetic Epistémology* (trans. E. Duckworth). London and New York: Columbia University Press. (*L'épistémologie génétique*, originally published Paris, PUF, *1970c*.)

PIAGET, J. (1971) *Structuralism* (trans. C. Maschler). London: Routledge & Kegan Paul. (*Le structuralisme*, originally published Paris, PUF, *1968*.)

PIAGET, J. and INHELDER, B. (*1941*) *Le développement des quantités physiques chez l'enfant*. Neuchâtel: Delachaux & Niestlé.

PIAGET, J. and INHELDER, B. (*1951*) *La genèse de l'idée de hasard chez l'enfant*. Paris: PUF.

PIAGET, J. and INHELDER, B. (1956) *The Child's Conception of Space* (trans. F. J. Langdon and J. L. Lunzer). London: Routledge & Kegan Paul. (*La représentation de l'espace chez l'enfant*, originally published Paris, PUF, *1948*.)

PIAGET, J. and INHELDER, B. (1969) Intellectual operations and their development. In FRAISSE, P. and PIAGET, J. (eds.) *Experimental Psychology: Its Scope and Method*, Vol. 7. *Intelligence*. London: Routledge & Kegan Paul. (Les opérations intellectuelles et leur développement, in *Traité de psychologie expérimentale*, Vol. 7. *L'intelligence*, originally published Paris, PUF, *1963*.)

PIAGET, J., INHELDER, B. and SZEMINSKA, A. (1960) *The Child's Conception of Geometry* (trans. E. A. Lunzer). London: Routledge & Kegan Paul. (*La géométrie spontanée de l'enfant*, originally published Paris, PUF, *1948*.)

PIDDINGTON, M. and PIDDINGTON, L. R. (1932) Report of fieldwork in North-Western Australia. *Oceania*, **2**, 342–58.

PIKE, K. L. (1943) *Phonetics: A Critical Analysis of Phonetic Theory and a Technic for the Practical Description of Sounds*. Language and Literature Vol. 21. Michigan: University of Michigan Press.

PIKE, K. L. (1954) Emic and etic standpoints for the description of behavior. In PIKE, K. L. *Language in Relation to a Unified Theory of the Structure of Human Behavior*, Part I (Preliminary Edition). Glendale: Summer Institute of Linguistics. pp. 8–28.

PIKE, K. L. (1966) *Language in Relation to a Unified Theory of the Structure of Human Behaviour*. The Hague: Mouton.

PILLER, M. (1971) *Recherche de psychologie sur une population d'adultes analphabètes de la Côte d'Ivoire*. Unpublished report, University of Geneva.

PINARD, A. and LAURENDEAU, M. (1969) 'Stage' in Piaget's cognitive developmental theory: exegesis of a concept. In ELKIND, D. and FLAVELL, J. H. (eds.) *Studies in Cognitive Development*. New York: Oxford University Press. pp. 121–70.

PINARD, A., LAURENDEAU, M., BOISCLAIR, C., DAGENAIS, Y. and MORIN, C. (1969) *Compte rendu d'une étude préliminaire sur le développement intellectuel de l'enfant rwandais*. Unpublished report, Institute of Psychology, University of Montreal.

POOLE, H. E. (1968) The effect of urbanization upon scientific concept attainment among Hausa children of northern Nigeria. *Brit. J. Educ. Psychol.*, **38**, 57–63.

PORTEUS, S. D. (1917) Mental tests with delinquents and Australian Aboriginal children. *Psychol. Rev.*, **14**, 32–41.

PORTEUS, S. D. (1933) The Mentality of Australian Aborigines. *Oceania*, **4**, 30–6.

PORTEUS, S. D. (1937) *Intelligence and Environment*. New York: Macmillan.

PORTEUS, S. D. (1966) Mental capacity. In COTTON, B. C. (ed.) *Aboriginal Man in South and Central Australia*. Adelaide: Government Printer.

POSTMAN, L. and CONGER, B. (1954) Verbal habits and the visual recognition of words. *Science*, **119**, 671–3.

POSTMAN, L. and ROSENZWEIG, M. P. (1957) Perceptual recognition of words. *J. Speech and Hearing Disorders*, **22**, 245–53.

PRICE-WILLIAMS, D. R. (1961) A study concerning concepts of conservation of quantities among primitive children. *Acta Psychol.*, **18**(4), 297–305. Reprinted in PRICE-WILLIAMS, 1969.

PRICE-WILLIAMS, D. R. (1962) Abstract and concrete modes of classification in a primitive society. *Brit. J. Educ. Psychol.*, **32**, 50–61. Reprinted in PRICE-WILLIAMS, 1969.

PRICE-WILLIAMS, D. R. (1969) *Cross-cultural Studies*. Harmondsworth: Penguin Books.

PRICE-WILLIAMS, D. R., GORDON, W. and RAMIREZ, M. (1969) Skill and conservation: a study of pottery-making children. See Chapter 21 in this volume.

PRINCE, J. R. (1968a) The effect of Western education on science conceptualization in New Guinea. *Brit. J. Educ. Psychol.*, **68**, 64–74.

PRINCE, J. R. (1968b) Science concepts in New Guinean and European children. *Austral. J. Educ.*, **12**, 81–9.

PRINCE, J. R. (1968c) Science concepts among school children. *S. Pacific Bull.*, **18**(4), 21–8.

PRINCE, J. R. (1969a) *Science Concepts in a Pacific Culture*. Sydney: Angus & Robertson.

PRINCE, J. R. (1969b) *Views on physical causality in New Guinea students*. Paper presented at 41st ANZAAS Congress, Adelaide.

PRINCE, R. (1960) The 'brainfag' syndrome in Nigerian students. *J. Ment. Sci.*, **106**, 559–70.

PROSHANSKY, H. and SEIDENBERG, B. (1965) *Basic Studies in Social Psychology*. London: Holt, Rinehart & Winston.

RAPPAPORT, R. A. (1967) *Pigs for the Ancestors*. New Haven: Yale University Press.

RAVEN, J. C. (1956) *Coloured Progressive Matrices Sets A, Ab, B*. London: H. K. Lewis.

READ, M. (1959) *Children of their Fathers*. London: Methuen.

REED, H. B. (1924) Repetition and association in learning. *Ped. Sem.*, **31**, 147–55.

RICHARDS, A. I. (1956) *Chisungu: A Girl's Ceremony among the Bemba of Northern Rhodesia*. New York: Grove Press.

RIVERS, W. H. R. (1901) Introduction and vision. In HADDON, A. C. (ed.) *Report of the Cambridge Anthropological Expedition to the Torres Straits*, Vol. II. Cambridge: Cambridge University Press.

RIVERS, W. H. R. (1905) Observations on the sense of the Todas. *Brit. J. Psychol.*, **1**, 321–96.

ROBERTS, J. and SUTTON SMITH, B. (1962) Child training and game involvement. *Ethnology*, **1**, 166–85.

ROMNEY, A. K. and D'ANDRADE, R. G. (1964) Cognitive aspects of English kin terms. In Transcultural Studies in Cognition, *Amer. Anthrop.*, **66**(3), Part 2.

ROSENTHAL, R. (1965) The volunteer subject. *Human Relations*, **18**, 389–406.

ROSENTHAL, R. and JACOBSON, L. (1968) *Pygmalion in the Classroom*. New York: Holt, Rinehart & Winston.

ROSNER, S. (1956) *Studies of group pressure*. Unpublished doctoral dissertation, New School for Social Research.

ROTH, W. E. (1897) *Ethnological Studies among the North-West-Central*

Queensland Aborigines. Brisbane: Edmund Gregory; London: Queensland Agent-General's Office.

ROTTER, J. B. (1966) Generalized expectancies for internal versus external control of enforcement. *Psychol. Monogr.*, 80(1), Whole No. 609.

SAPIR, E. (1912) Language and environment. *Amer. Anthrop.*, n. s., 14, 226–42.

SAPIR, E. (1929) The status of linguistics as a science. *Language*, 5, 207–14.

SAPIR, E. (1933) Language. *Encycl. Soc. Sci.*, 9, 155–69.

SARLES, H. B. (1963) *The Question-Response System in Language.* MS.

SCHEGLOFF, E. A. (1968) Sequencing in conversational openings. *Amer. Anthrop.*, 70, 1075–95.

SCHNEIDER, D. M. and HOMANS, G. C. (1955) Kinship terminology and the American kinship system. *Amer. Anthrop.*, 57(6), 1194–1208.

SCHOGGEN, M. (1969) *An Ecological Study of Three-year-olds at Home.* Nashville, Tenn.: George Peabody College for Teachers.

SCHWARTZ, D. and KARP, S. A. (1967) Field dependence in a geriatric population. *Percept. Mot. Skills*, 24, 495–504.

SCRIMSHAW, N. S. and GORDON, E. (1968) *Malnutrition, Learning and Behavior.* Cambridge, Mass.: MIT Press.

SEARS, R. R. (1961) Transcultural variables and conceptual equivalence. In KAPLAN, B. (ed.) *Studying Personality Cross-culturally.* Evanston, Ill. and New York: Row, Peterson. pp. 445–55.

SEBEOK, T. A. (1946) Finnish and Hungarian case systems: their form and function. *Acta Instituti Hungaricic Universitatis Holmiensis*, Series B, Linguistica 3 (Stockholm).

SECORD, P. F. and BACKMAN, C. W. (1964) *Social Psychology.* New York: Holt, Rinehart & Winston.

SEDER, J. A. (1957) *The origin of differences in extent of independence in children: developmental factors in perceptual field dependence.* Unpublished bachelor's thesis, Radcliffe College.

SEGALL, M. H., CAMPBELL, D. T. and HERSKOVITS, M. J. (1966) *The Influence of Culture on Visual Perception.* New York: Bobbs-Merrill.

SELLS, S. B. (1936) The atmosphere effect. *Arch. Psychol.*, 29 (200).

SHARP, A. (1957) *Ancient Voyagers in the Pacific.* Pelican 404. Baltimore: Penguin Books.

SIGEL, I. E. (1953) Developmental trends in the abstraction ability of children. *Child Develop.*, 24(2), 131–44.

Q

SIGEL, I. E. and HOOPER, F. E. (1968) *Logical Thinking in Children.* New York: Holt, Rinehart & Winston.

SIMPSON, G. G. (1961) *Principles of Animal Taxonomy.* New York: Columbia University Press.

SINCLAIR, H. (1967) *Acquisition du langage et développement de la pensée.* Paris: Dunod.

SINGER, M. (1961) A survey of culture and personality theory and research. In KAPLAN, B. (ed.) *Studying Personality Cross-culturally.* Evanston, Ill. and New York: Row, Peterson. pp. 9–90.

SMEDSLUND, J. (1961) The acquisition of conservation of substance and weight in children: II. External reinforcement of conservation of weight and of the operations of additions and subtractions. *Scand. J. Psychol.,* 2, 71–84.

SMILANSKY, S. (1968) The effect of certain learning conditions on the progress of disadvantaged children of kindergarten age. *J. Sch. Psychol.,* 4(3), 68–81.

SMITH, D. H. and INKELES, A. (1966) The OM scale: a comparative sociopsychological measure of individual modernity. *Sociometry,* 29, 353–77.

SMITH, J. M. (1964) *Spatial Ability.* London: University of London Press.

SMITH, K. K. (1966) *A validation study of the Queensland Test.* Unpublished B.A. (Hons.) thesis, University of Queensland.

SOLOMON, R. L. and HOWES, D. H. (1951) Word frequency, personal values and visual duration thresholds. *Psychol. Rev.,* 58, 256–70.

SOMMERLAD, E. A. and BELLINGHAM, W. P. (1972) Cooperation-competition: a comparison of Australian European and Aboriginal schoolchildren. *J. Cross-Cult. Psychol.,* 3(2), 149–57.

SPAULDING, A. C. (1963) *The course of anthropological research as viewed from the National Science Foundation.* Unpublished paper read before the Annual Meeting of the Central States Anthropological Society, Detroit, Michigan, 17 May.

SPEARMAN, C. (1904) 'General intelligence' objectively determined. *Amer. J. Psychol.,* 15, 201–93.

SPUHLER, J. N. (1963) Review of *Mankind Evolving* by Th. Dobzhansky. *Amer. Anthrop.,* 65(3), 683–4.

STEWARD, J. H. (1955) *Theory of Culture Change.* Urbana, Ill.: University of Illinois Press.

STEWART, W. A. (1970) Toward a history of American Negro dialect. In WILLIAMS, F. (ed.) *Language and Poverty.* Chicago: Markham Press. pp. 351–79.

STODOLSKY, S. S. and LESSER, G. S. (1968) Learning patterns in the disadvantaged. *Harvard Educ. Rev.*, **38**, 546.

STREHLOW, T. G. H. (1944) Aranda phonetics and grammar. *Oceania Monogr.*, No. 7.

STREHLOW, T. G. H. (1965) Culture, social structure and environment in Aboriginal Central Australia. In BERNDT, R. M. and BERNDT, C. H. (eds.) *Aboriginal Man in Australia*. Sydney: Angus & Robertson. pp. 121–45.

STRODBECK, F. (1964) Considerations of meta-method in cross-cultural studies. In ROMNEY, A. K. and D'ANDRADE, R. G. (eds.) Transcultural Studies in Cognition, *Amer. Anthrop.*, **66**(3), Part 2, 223–9.

STURTEVANT, W. C. (1964) Studies in ethnoscience. See Chapter 2 in this volume.

SWARTZ, M. J. (1960) Situational determinants of kinship terminology. *S. W. J. Anthrop.*, **16**(4), 393–7.

SWEENEY, E. J. (1953) Sex differences in problem solving. *Technical Report*, No. 1, Stanford University.

TANNER, J. M. and INHELDER, B. (1960) *Proceedings of the Fourth Meeting of the World Health Organization Study Group on the Psychobiological Development of the Child, Geneva, 1956*, Vol. 4. New York: International Universities Press.

TATJE, T. A. (1970) Problems of concept definition for comparative studies. In NAROLL, R. and COHEN, R. (eds.) *Handbook of Method in Cultural Anthropology*. Garden City: Natural History Press. pp. 689–96.

TATZ, C. M. (1970) The health status of the Australian Aborigines: the need for an interdisciplinary approach. *Med. J. Austral.*, 57th year, **2**(4), 191–6.

THOMPSON, J. (1941) The ability of children of different grade levels to generalize on sorting tests. *J. Psychol.*, **11**, 119–26.

TITCHENER, E. B. (1916) On ethnological tests of sensation and perception. *Proc. Amer. Phil. Soc.*, **55**, 204–36.

TRAGER, G. L. (1958) Paralanguage: a first approximation. *Studies in Linguistics*, **13**(1–2), 1–12.

TRAGER, G. L. (1959) The systematization of the Whorf hypothesis. *Anthrop. Ling.*, **1**(1), 31–5.

TRIANDIS, H. C. (1964) Cultural influences on cognitive processes. In BERKOWITZ, L. (ed.) *Advances in Experimental Social Psychology*, Vol. 1. New York: Academic Press.

TSAO, J. C. (1948) Studies in spaced and massed learning: II.

Meaningfulness of material and distribution of practice. *Quart. J. Exp. Psychol.*, **1**, 79–84.

TUDDENHAM, R. D. (1951) Studies in reputation: III. Correlates of popularity among elementary school children. *J. Educ. Psychol.*, **42**, 257–76.

TUDDENHAM, R. D. (1952) Studies in reputation: I. Sex and grade differences in school children's evaluations of their peers. *Psychol. Monogr.*, **66**(1), 1–39, Whole No. 333.

TUDDENHAM, R. D. (1968) *Psychometricizing Piaget's méthode clinique*. Paper presented at the American Educational Research Association Convention, Chicago.

TUDDENHAM, R. D. (1969) *A 'Piagetian' Test of Cognitive Development*. Paper presented at the Symposium on Intelligence, Ontario Institute for Studies in Education, Toronto.

TYLER, L. E. (1965) *The Psychology of Human Differences* (3rd ed.). New York: Appleton-Century-Crofts.

TYLER, S. (1969) *Cognitive Anthropology*. New York: Holt, Rinehart & Winston.

TYLOR, E. B. (1881) *Anthropology, an Introduction to the Study of Man and Civilization*. New York: D. Appleton & Co.

UZGIRIS, I. C. (1964) Situational generality of conservation. *Child Develop.*, **35**, 831–41.

UZGIRIS, I. C. and HUNT, J. MCV. (1966) *An Instrument for Assessing Infant Psychological Development*. Revised provisional form, Dept of Psychology, University of Illinois.

VANDENBERG, S. G. (1959) The primary mental abilities of Chinese students. *Ann. N.Y. Acad. Sci.*, **79**, 257.

VANDENBERG, S. G. (1967) The primary mental abilities of South American students. *Multiv. Behav. Res.*, **2**, 175.

VAYDA, P. (1969) *Environment and Cultural Behavior*. Garden City: Natural History Press.

VAYDA, P. and RAPPAPORT, R. A. (1968) Ecology, cultural and non-cultural. In CLIFTON, J. (ed.) *Introduction to Cultural Anthropology*. Boston: Houghton Mifflin.

VERNON, P. E. (1955) The assessment of children. *Studies in Educ.*, **7**, 189–215.

VERNON, P. E. (1965a) Ability factors and environmental influences. *Amer. Psychol.*, **20**, 723–33.

VERNON, P. E. (1965b) Environmental handicaps and intellectual development. Parts I and II. *Brit. J. Educ. Psychol.*, **35**, 9–20 and 117–26.

VERNON, P. E. (1966) Educational and intellectual development among Canadian Indians and Eskimos. *Educ. Rev.*, **18**, 79–91 and 186–195.

VERNON, P. E. (1967a) Administration of group intelligence tests to East African pupils. *Brit. J. Educ. Psychol.*, **37**, 282–91.

VERNON, P. E. (1967b) Abilities and educational attainments in an East African environment. *J. Spec. Educ.*, **4**, 335–45. Reprinted in PRICE-WILLIAMS, 1969.

VERNON, P. E. (1967c) *Working papers on cross-cultural applications of factor analysis.* Mimeographed report, Institute of Education, University of London.

VERNON, P. E. (1969) *Intelligence and Cultural Environment.* London: Methuen.

VINACKE, W. E. (1954) Concept formation in children of school ages. *Education,* **75**, 527–34.

VINH-BANG (in preparation) *Standardisation des épreuves opératoires.* School of Psychology, University of Geneva.

VINH-BANG and INHELDER, B. (1963) Unpublished standardization material quoted by PIAGET, J. and INHELDER, B. (1969).

VOEGELIN, C. F. and VOEGELIN, F. M. (1957) *Hopi Domains: A Lexical Approach to the Problem of Selection.* Indiana University Publications in Anthropology and Linguistics, No. 14; also *Int. J. Amer. Ling.*, Memoir 14.

VOORHOEVE, J. (1961) Linguistic experiments in syntactic analysis. In LE PAGE, R. B. (ed.) *Proceedings of the Conference on Creole Language Studies.* Creole Language Studies, No. 11. London: Macmillan. pp. 37–60.

VYGOTSKI, L. S. (1939) Thought and speech. *Psychiatry,* **2**, 29–54.

VYGOTSKI, L. S. (1962) *Thought and Speech.* Cambridge, Mass.: MIT Press.

WADDELL, V. (1968) *Some cultural considerations on the development of the concept of conservation.* Unpublished paper presented to a genetic epistemology seminar, Australian National University.

WALKER, C., TORRANCE, E. P. and WALKER, T. S. (1971) A cross-cultural study of the perception of situational causality. *J. Cross-Cult. Psychol.*, **2**, 401–4.

WALLACE, A. F. C. (1961a) *Culture and Personality* (2nd ed., 1970). New York: Random House.

WALLACE, A. F. C. (1961b) The psychic unity of human groups. In KAPLAN, B. (ed.) *Studying Personality Cross-culturally.* Evanston, Ill. and New York: Row, Peterson. pp. 129–64.

WALLACE, A. F. C. (1962) Culture and cognition. *Science*, **135**(3501), 351–7.

WALLACE, A. F. C. and ATKINS, J. (1960) The meaning of kinship terms. *Amer. Anthrop.*, **62**(1), 58–80.

WEI, T. T. D. (1966) *Piaget's Concept of Classification: A Comparative Study of Advantaged and Disadvantaged Young Children.* Unpublished Ph.D. thesis, University of Illinois.

WEINREICH, U. (1963) On the semantic structure of language. In GREENBERG, J. H. (ed.) *Universals of Language.* Cambridge, Mass.: MIT Press. pp. 114–71.

WEIZMANN, F. (1971) Correlational statistics and the nature-nurture problem. *Science*, **171**, 589.

WELLS, H. (1963) Effects of transfer and problem structure in disjunctive concept formation. *J. Exp. Psychol.*, **65**(1), 63–9.

WELLS, R. (1963) Some neglected opportunities in descriptive linguistics. *Anthrop. Ling.*, **5**(1), 38–49.

WELMERS, W. E. (1948) *Spoken Kpelle.* Lutheran Church of Liberia.

WERE, K. (1968) *A Survey of the Thought Processes of New Guinean Secondary Students.* Unpublished M.Ed. thesis, University of Adelaide.

WERNER, H. (1940) *Comparative Psychology of Mental Development.* New York: Follett.

WERNER, O. and CAMPBELL, D. T. (1970) Translating, working through interpreters and the problem of decentering. In NAROLL, R. and COHEN, R. (eds.) *Handbook of Method in Cultural Anthropology.* Garden City: Natural History Press. pp. 398–420.

WHITEMAN, M. and DEUTSCH, M. (1968) Social disadvantage as related to intellective and language development. In DEUTSCH, M., KATZ, I. and JENSEN, A. R. (eds.) *Social Class, Race and Psychological Development.* New York: Holt, Rinehart & Winston.

WHITING, J. W. M. (1968) Methods and problems in cross-cultural research. In LINDZEY, G. and ARONSON, E. (eds.) *Handbook of Social Psychology.* (2nd ed.), Vol. 2. Reading, Mass.: Addison-Wesley. pp. 693–728.

WHORF, B. L. (1940) Science and linguistics. *Technol. Rev.*, **44**, 229–231, 247, 248.

WHORF, B. L. (1941) The relation of habitual thought and behavior to language. In SPIER, L. *et al.* (ed.) *Language, Culture and Personality.* Menasha, Wisc.: Sapir Memorial Publication Fund. pp. 75–93.

WILKINS, M. C. (1928) The effect of changed material on the ability to do formal syllogistic reasoning. *Arch. Psychol.*, **16**(102).

WITKIN, H. A. (1950) Individual differences in ease of perception of embedded figures. *J. Personal.*, **19**, 1–15.

WITKIN, H. A. (1967) A cognitive-style approach to cross-cultural research. See Chapter 5 in this volume.

WITKIN, H. A., BIRNBAUM, J., LOMONACO, S., LEHR, S. and HERMAN, J. L. (1968) Cognitive patterning in congenitally totally blind children. *Child Develop.*, **39**, 767–84.

WITKIN, H. A., DYK, R. B., FATERSON, H. F., GOODENOUGH, D. R. and KARP, S. A. (1962) *Psychological Differentiation*. New York: Wiley.

WITKIN, H. A., FATERSON, H. F., GOODENOUGH, D. R. and BIRNBAUM, J. (1966) Cognitive patterning in mildly retarded boys. *Child Develop.*, **37**, 301–16.

WITKIN, H. A., GOODENOUGH, D. R. and KARP, S. A. (1967) Stability of cognitive style from childhood to young adulthood. *J. Personal. Soc. Psychol.*, **7**, 291–300.

WITKIN, H. A., LEWIS, H. B., HERTZMAN, M., MACHOVER, K., MEISSNER, P. B. and WAPNER, S. (1954) *Personality through Perception*. New York: Harper & Row.

WOBER, J. M. (1966a) *Psychological factors in the adjustment to industrial life among employees of a firm in South Nigeria*. Unpublished doctoral dissertation, University of Edinburgh.

WOBER, M. (1966b) Sensotypes. See Chapter 6 in this volume.

WOBER, M. (1969) Distinguishing centri-cultural from cross-cultural tests and research. *Percept. Mot. Skills*, **28**, 488.

WOBER, M. (1973) Towards an understanding of the Kiganda concept of intelligence. See Chapter 16 in this volume.

WOHLWILL, J. F. (1957) The abstraction and conceptualization of form, colour and number. *J. Exp. Psychol.*, **9**(4), 253–62.

WOHLWILL, J. F. (1966) The physical environment: a problem for a psychology of stimulation. *J. Soc. Issues*, **22**, 29–38.

WOHLWILL, J. F. (1970) The emerging discipline of environmental psychology. *Amer. Psychol.*, **25**, 303–12.

WOODWORTH, R. S. and SELLS, S. B. (1935) An atmosphere effect in formal syllogistic reasoning. *J. Exp. Psychol.*, **18**, 451–60.

WUNDT, W. (1916) *Elements of Folk Psychology*. London: Allen & Unwin.

ZA'ROUR, G. I. (1971a) The conservation of number and liquid by Lebanese school children in Beirut. *J. Cross-Cult. Psychol.*, **2**, 165–72.

ZA'ROUR, G. I. (1971b) The conservation of weight across different materials by Lebanese school children in Beirut. *Science Education*, **55**(3), 387–94.

ZEMPLENI, A. and ZEMPLENI, J. (1972) Milieu africain et développement. In DUYCKAERTS, F., HINDLEY, C. B., LÉZINE, I., REUCHLIN M. and ZEMPLENI, A. *Milieu et Développement*. Paris: PUF. pp. 151–213.

ZEMPLENI, J. (1970) L'enfant Wolof de 2 à 5 ans (Senegal). Échanges corporels et échanges médiatisés par les objets. *Revue de Neuropsychiatrie infantile*, 18(10–11), 785–98.

ZIGLER, E. and BUTTERFIELD, E. (1968) Motivational aspects of changes in IQ test performance of culturally deprived nursery school children. *Child Develop.*, 39, 1–14.

Name Index

Adams, R. N., 58
Albrecht, R. E., 111
Al-Issa, I., xiv
Allport, G. W., 1, 203
Almy, M., 390, 415, 420
Arrington, M., 410
Atkins, J., 52
Austin, G. A., 165

Backman, C. W., 276
Bacon, M., 112, 120, 130, 132
Balfet, H., 54
Baranzini, C., 418
Barbichon, G., 157
Barclay, A., 107
Barker, R. G., 49, 129
Barnett, H. G., 57
Barry, H., 112, 120, 130, 132
Bartlett, F. C., 2, 25, 36, 68, 205, 207, 209, 214–16
Bateson, G., 1, 2, 27, 28, 29
Beard, R. M., 295
Beattie, J., 143
Bee, H. L., 231
Befu, H., 47
Bellingham, W. P., 408
Benedict, R., 194, 300
Bereiter, C., 234
Berlin, B., 45
Bernstein, B., 126, 231, 239, 257–8, 356
Berry, J. W., 14–17 *passim*, 19, 24, 108–10, 111, 113, 114, 116, 120, 126, 131–2, 135, 136, 139, 143, 145, 219, 225, 227–8, 248, 252, 261, 384–5, 387, 406, 419, 420
Bethon, G., 413, 422
Bever, T., 242
Beveridge, W. M., 116, 124
Biesheuvel, S., 159, 219, 248, 250, 261, 379
Birch, H. G., 237

Birdwhistell, R. L., 50
Birnbaum, J., 110, 117
Birns, B., 412
Bisilliat, J., 274
Bitterman, M. E., 195
Blank, M., 232
Bloom, B. S., 232
Boas, F., 3, 6–8, 41, 64, 76, 159, 226
Bodde, D., 57
Boehm, L., 410
Boisclair, C., 305, 306, 335, 410
Boonsong, S., 416, 419, 420
Bourne, L., 165
Bovet, M. C., 296, 307, 324, 402, 414, 415, 417–20 *passim*
Bright, W., 57
Brimble, A. R., 250
Brislin, R., 18
Brown, R. W., 71–2
Bruner, J. S., 36, 62, 159, 165, 219, 239, 276–9, 285, 307, 326–9, 331, 355, 415, 417
Brunswik, E., 129, 234, 243
Bull, W., 308
Burling, R., 51, 52
Burt, C., 221, 226, 247, 257, 258
Butterfield, E., 232

Caldwell, B. M., 232
Campbell, D. T., 1, 14–15, 18–20 *passim*, 167, 193, 195, 238, 248, 347
Cancian, F., 53
Carden, J. A., 112
Carmichael, L., 72
Carroll, J. B., 65, 70, 73, 77, 79, 80, 87
Casagrande, J. B., 70, 73, 77, 79, 80
Cassirer, E., 159
Cawte, J. E., 385
Cazden, C., 234
Chafe, W. L., 51, 52

Subject Index